D0083499

RADIOSITY AND GLOBAL ILLUMINATION

RADIOSITY AND GLOBAL ILLUMINATION

FRANÇOIS X. SILLION
CLAUDE PUECH

MORGAN KAUFMANN PUBLISHERS, INC.
SAN FRANCISCO, CALIFORNIA

Sponsoring Editor: Michael B. Morgan
Production Manager: Yonie Overton
Assistant Editor: Douglas Sery
Assistant Production Editor: Vicki Van Ausdall
Production Coordinator: Julie Pabst
Text Design: Peter Vacek
Composition: SuperScript Typography
Cover Design: Carron Design
Color Insert Design & Production: Carron Design
Copyeditor: Judith Brown
Proofreader: Gary Morris
Printer: Courier Companies, Inc.

About the cover: The images on the front cover depict a design by Mark Mack Architects for a proposed theater near Candlestick Park in San Francisco, California. The images were rendered using automatic database preprocessing and radiosity solution software developed by Daniel R. Baum, Steve Mann, Kevin P. Smith, and James W. Winget at Silicon Graphics Computer Systems. The database was modeled by Charles Ehrlich from the Department of Architecture at the University of California at Berkeley. For further information on the techniques used, refer to "Making Radiosity Usable: Automatic Preprocessing and Meshing Techniques for the Generation of Accurate Radiosity Solutions," by Daniel R. Baum, Steve Mann, Kevin P. Smith, and James W. Winget in *Computer Graphics* (SIGGRAPH '91 Proceedings), vol. 25, no. 4, July 1991, pp. 51–60.

The images on the back cover represent *(top)* a simulation of a scene with directional-diffuse reflectors (Courtesy of F. Sillion, J. Arvo, S. Westin, and D. Greenberg, Program of Computer Graphics, Cornell University) and *(bottom)* the Ontario legislature building, side view (Courtesy of Stuart Feldman, Lightscape Graphics Software Ltd. Design by A.J. Diamond, Donald Schmitt & Company. Rendered using the Lightscape Visualization System on a Silicon Graphics Computer.)

Editorial Offices:
Morgan Kaufmann Publishers, Inc.
340 Pine Street, Sixth Floor
San Francisco, CA 94104

Printed in the United States of America

98 97 96 95 94   5 4 3 2 1

Library of Congress Cataloging-in-Publication Data is available for this book.
ISBN 1-55860-277-1

Contents

Preface

Computer graphics technology is quickly becoming part of everyday experience. Special effects for the movie industry, as well as popular video games, rely more and more on sophisticated techniques for synthetic imaging, and *photorealistic* images can now be computed and mixed with photographs. Specialized applications of computer graphics, such as computer-aided lighting design, visualization of architectural spaces, medical imaging, and driving simulation are also blooming.

The production of realistic images requires in particular a precise treatment of lighting effects that can be achieved by *simulating* the underlying physical phenomena of light emission, propagation, and reflection. The purpose of this book is to provide a comprehensive description of the most advanced algorithms for such simulations of radiative light transfer, namely the *radiosity method* and *Monte Carlo* techniques. The distinguishing property of both these approaches is that they solve the *global illumination* problem; that is, they model the interreflection of light between all objects in a scene.

The radiosity method was first developed for the study of radiant heat transfer in simple configurations, and Monte Carlo methods were first applied to solve neutron transport problems in nuclear engineering. With the advent of more powerful computing resources, a vast body of research has been devoted to the improvement of these techniques for application to image synthesis, and the original methods have been continuously refined over the past ten years. The improved techniques are now being applied to many different fields, such as thermal radiation studies, lighting design, and remote sensing.

Since the most advanced techniques for photorealistic image synthesis all rely on the simulation of global illumination effects, the material covered in this book represents an essential area of modern computer graphics. Graduate courses can be built around it, and it can be used as a reference on advanced rendering techniques. Another major goal of this book is to reformulate some of the most recent research results into a consistent framework, thus allowing nonspecialists to quickly acquire a comprehensive view of the technique and its derivatives. In addition to a complete theoretical presentation of the various radiosity algorithms, practical implementation issues are reviewed and recommendations are offered. Thus we hope that the book will be useful for engineers and researchers interested in the simulation of radiant energy transfer on a computer. It should also provide a useful background to users and designers who want to better understand the techniques used in their application software. The practical guide in the Appendix should be helpful to those who need to implement some of the simulation techniques described.

Throughout the book we assume that the reader has some knowledge of basic computer graphics techniques, such as the z-buffer or ray casting algorithms. Familiarity with basic computer science, calculus, and linear algebra is also assumed, although we provide background information where necessary.

We believe that the state of the art in global illumination techniques has reached the point where many engineering situations can benefit from them. While this will probably remain an active area of research for years to come, the underlying principles and some of the practical algorithms are now well established. We hope that this book will help to disseminate these ideas to a new audience.

Organization of the book

The book presents and explains the most advanced techniques for the simulation of global illumination. These include the radiosity method and its recent evolution, and Monte Carlo techniques. A strong emphasis is given to the radiosity method and its many algorithmic variations, with a shorter portion devoted to Monte Carlo algorithms. This choice reflects the fact that the radiosity method is not as well documented as Monte Carlo techniques (for which there exists a wealth of excellent books [75, 159, 97]), as well as the greater conceptual and practical difficulty of using radiosity algorithms.

Some fundamental definitions are introduced in Chapter 2, to familiarize the reader with the physical processes involved in the simulation of global illumination. In particular, the *global illumination equation* is presented to express the balance of energy at a surface.

A general presentation of the radiosity algorithm for *ideal diffuse* surfaces is made in Chapter 3, showing how a computational algorithm can be derived from the equations of energy balance. Specific problems encountered in radiosity simulations are addressed in the following chapters, which provide a comprehensive review of possible solutions.

In Chapter 4 the computational cost of computing a useful image with the radiosity algorithm is reduced: the *progressive refinement* radiosity algorithm produces meaningful results in a very short time and allows a continuous display of the simulation results. A hierarchical formulation of radiosity always computes energy exchanges at the appropriate level of detail. Another approach to simplifying the calculation is to restrict the computation to energy exchanges that have a sizable impact on the final result. This is done by defining the notion of *importance* with respect to the desired results.

The issue of improving the accuracy of the simulation is addressed in Chapter 5, where improved numerical algorithms are proposed for the computation of form factors. In particular, meshing and reconstruction techniques are discussed, in the general framework of finite-elements methods.

Chapter 6 focuses on control of the simulation. Interactive applications of global illuminations require that the algorithms be reformulated to allow user intervention and steering.

Extensions of radiosity to more realistic materials are presented in Chapter 7. These are motivated by the wealth of physical behaviors encountered in the real world. The restriction of classic radiosity algorithms to diffuse reflectors is removed, and the simulation of volume scattering is incorporated in the algorithm.

Chapter 8 is devoted to the presentation of Monte Carlo methods. These probabilistic techniques can be used to simulate light propagation, as an alternative to the radiosity computation. They are also useful for the computation of integrals, and their application for solving the global illumination equation represents a generalization of the basic ray tracing approach. Monte Carlo methods can also be used to compute some numerical integrals used in the radiosity algorithm.

Finally, a practical guide is presented in the appendix. The goal here is to aid those interested in designing simulation software for global illumination. Alternatives are suggested based on the features most desired, and implementation details frequently omitted in published research papers are discussed.

Acknowledgements

We want to thank the many friends and colleagues who supported the effort of writing this book.

A special acknowledgement is owed to those who contributed a lot of their time to reading preliminary versions of this work. Greg Ward, Paul Heckbert, and David Sturman reviewed early versions of some chapters, and their comments helped us to shape the final structure of the book. Kevin Novins reviewed the entire manuscript under a very tight schedule and suggested many significant improvements.

We thank Holly Rushmeier and Greg Ward for their efforts in promoting open discussions of research issues in global illumination, and for their patience in explaining some of the terminology as well as discussing the practical issues faced in designing lighting simulation systems.

We are indebted to the following colleagues for discussions that helped us refine some of the material presented in the book: Dan Baum and Rod Recker for meshing and other practical issues; Michael Cohen and Nicolas Holzschuch for hierarchical algorithms; David George for developing the incremental radiosity algorithm presented in Chapter 6; Eric Haines for providing much of the bibliographic information.

Images and illustrations were kindly contributed by Dan Baum, Eric Chen, Michael Cohen, Julie O'Brien Dorsey, Stuart Feldman, David George, Pat Hanrahan, Paul Heckbert,

John Kawai, Campbell McKellar, Dani Lischinski, John Mardaljevic, Tomoyuki Nishita, Holly Rushmeier, Peter Schröder, Peter Shirley, Brian Smits, Jack Tumblin, John Wallace, and Greg Ward.

The first author wishes to thank Professor Donald P. Greenberg of Cornell University for the two very stimulating years spent at his Program of Computer Graphics. The many individuals who worked in the program at that time contributed, either directly or indirectly, to the maturation of this book. In particular Professor Kenneth Torrance and Jim Arvo provided examples of scientific excellence that remain a constant source of motivation.

We thank our colleagues and students at Ecole Normale Supérieure in Paris, and in the iMAGIS project in Grenoble, for helping us to maintain a creative work environment.

Clearly the whole enterprise would never have succeeded without the constant support of our wives Cécile Brisset-Sillion and Annie Raoult. We want to thank them for their continued patience.

Finally we thank our production manager Yonie Overton, our series editor Brian Barsky, and our publisher Michael Morgan for guiding us through the process of creating a book.

François X. Sillion
Claude Puech

CHAPTER 1

Introduction

The last three decades have seen a tremendous progression in the use of computers, and the emergence of entirely new concepts such as personal computers or interactive computer graphics has opened new applications fields for machine computing. The algorithms reviewed in this book can be used in many different engineering fields, but have recently received a lot of attention in the context of computer graphics. Therefore the presentation will stress their application to the production of images, although they are in fact much more general.

The brief presentation of classic computer graphics techniques offered in this chapter shows that the simulation of *global illumination* effects is required to obtain realistic images. Possible applications of such simulations are then reviewed that go far beyond the generation of "pretty" pictures.

1.1 Illumination in computer graphics

Early computer graphics users visualized the result of their calculations as black-and-white line drawings on CRT (*cathode ray tube*) displays. More elaborate rendering methods were invented with the advent of *raster graphics*. A raster picture is described as an array of color values, one for each point of the image. The color at each point can be computed based on the actual *illumination* of the visible surface.

Illumination models for computer graphics thus proceed by defining a set of light sources in the model of the scene, as well as illumination rules for the computation of the color of each visible point [74]. In the 1970s, as the processing power of computers steadily increased, illumination models were continuously improved in an exciting "quest for realism." In particular, elaborate models were proposed to describe the reflection properties of a surface. However, the production of photorealistic images remained an elusive goal as long as ad hoc models with no physical basis were employed.

To ensure a high level of realism, the actual physical mechanisms of light exchanges within a scene must be *simulated*. In particular, this requires a realistic model of light reflection at a surface, determination of visibility information to simulate cast shadows, and a computational model to evaluate the effect of multiple reflections.

Local and global illumination

The simulation of lighting effects begins with a *local* illumination model at each surface, describing the distribution of reflected light as a function of the incoming energy from a number of designated light sources. The term *local* here means that the illumination of the surface depends solely on its own characteristics and that of the light sources. Elaborate reflection models have been proposed to incorporate the effects of surface roughness and material properties on the appearance of the surfaces [178, 42, 94, 78, 188]. Surface detail can be added to improve the illusion of realism by means of *texture maps* and *bump maps* [17]. Almost all computer manufacturers today offer graphics software and hardware to represent, or *render*, objects illuminated by light sources using local illumination models. Rendering options include diffuse and specular materials and flat or interpolated shading.

Still, a local illumination model cannot produce accurate simulations of reality. The resulting images are easily recognized as computer-generated, and cannot be considered "realistic" renderings. In real scenes, every surface receives light both *directly* from the light sources, and *indirectly* from reflection off neighboring surfaces. In local models, the only attempt to represent the interreflection of light is the inclusion of a constant "ambient term." This falls short of capturing the subtle variations of indirect lighting across the surfaces.

Consider, for example, the images shown in Figure 1.1. The top image shows the result of the computation of *direct* illumination only. That is, only light received from the designated light sources is used to compute the color of each surface. Note that areas without a direct view of a light source appear very dark. The bottom image shows a view of the same room where *indirect* lighting has been added: the reflection of light on the surfaces is modeled, allowing light to reach all areas in the scene after one or several reflections. This image was computed in 1985 using one of the first radiosity algorithms for computer graphics.

As demonstrated by the images in Figure 1.1, the interreflection of light can account for a significant portion of the total illumination. This is especially true for indoor environments where light cannot escape the scene but instead is always reflected by some surface. In order to simulate the effects of interreflection, all objects must be considered as potential sources of illumination for all other objects in a *global* illumination model.

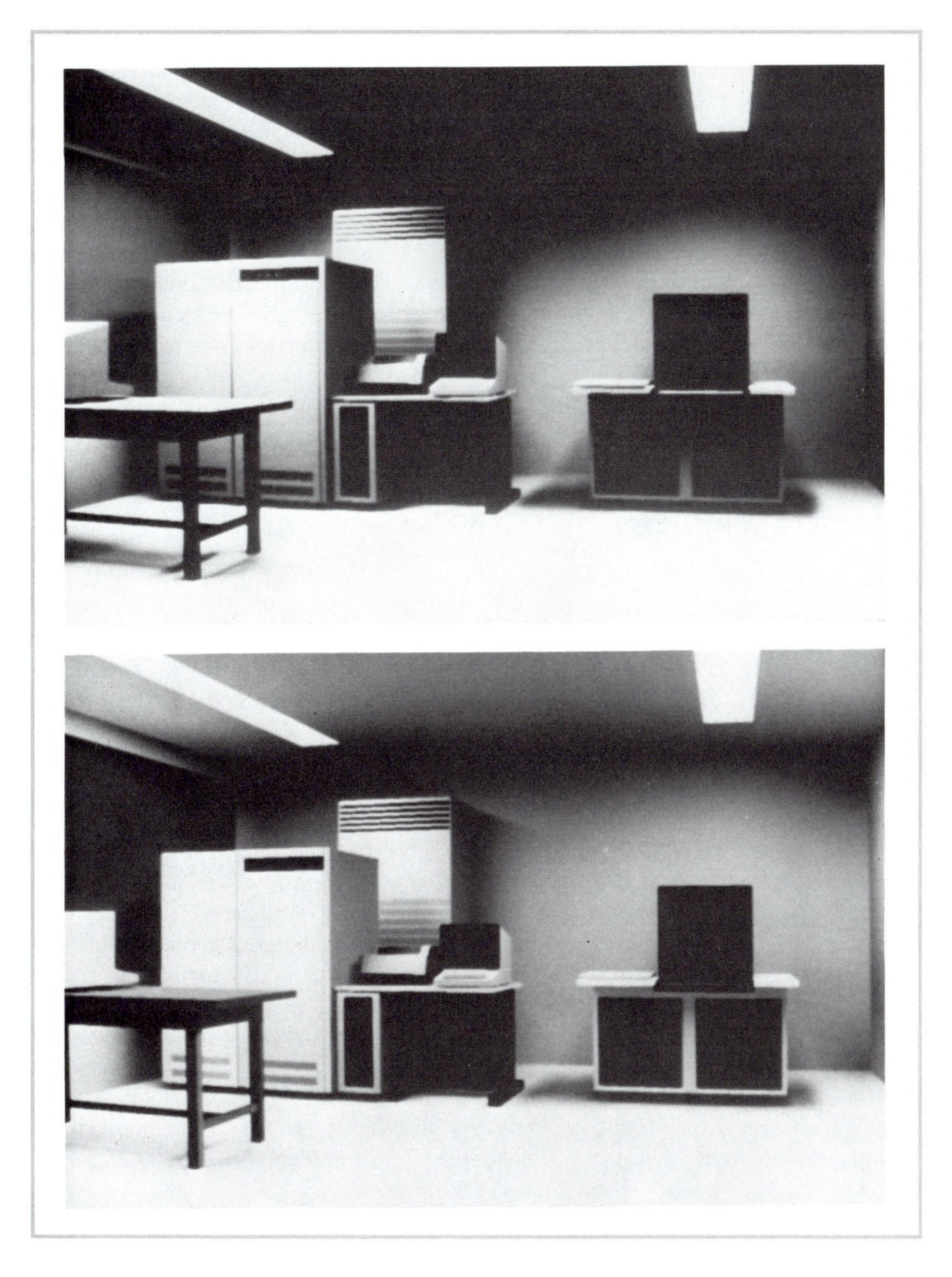

FIGURE 1.1 Two views of a computer room: (top) direct lighting only; (bottom) complete illumination, including indirect lighting. (*Courtesy of T. Nishita, Fukuyama University, and E. Nakamae, Hiroshima University.*)

The first global illumination algorithm was proposed in 1980 [200] and extends the notion of *ray tracing* [4] by recursively computing the illumination of surfaces: the color of a visible surface is determined by applying a local illumination model and adding a *reflected* contribution that is computed by spawning a new ray in the appropriate direction. Ray tracing has been extensively covered in the literature [67] and is only present in this book in the form of the more elaborate *Monte Carlo* methods, discussed in Chapter 8.

Radiosity techniques, invented by thermal engineers in the 1950s, were simultaneously applied to the problem of global illumination in computer graphics in the mid-1980s by researchers at Fukuyama and Hiroshima universities in Japan, and at Cornell University in the United States [123, 68]. These methods explicitly create a global system of equations to describe the interreflection of light in a scene, and automatically take into account the effect of multiple reflections.

1.2 Applications for global illumination algorithms

As the computational algorithms became more precise, the main thrust of research in computer graphics has moved from *image synthesis*, or the computation of a picture, to *simulation*, where the actual underlying physical phenomena are modeled and reproduced in a virtual setting. This trend is by no means limited to the rendering aspects of image synthesis, since it is also, for example, an essential ingredient of modern developments in computer animation and control. It is particularly apparent in the adoption of the radiosity method, which is based on physical principles and simulates the balance of energy between radiating surfaces for illumination computations.

The use of simulation for rendering images is considered a necessity for a number of applications. A first example is the domain of *prototyping*, where a representation of a project is obtained in machine-readable format and is used to evaluate and judge different design options. Obvious applications include architectural design, lighting design, and industrial design. Since important decisions are based on the computed picture, it is crucial that the representation be as faithful as possible.

Another domain requiring a true simulation of light exchanges is the mixture of synthetic images and "real" images, for example, images acquired using a video camera. Such manipulations are used to conduct site simulations for proposed buildings, or to integrate real actors in a virtual scene. In this case the synthetic part of the images should be indistinguishable from the real part, which means that its illumination must be accurately simulated.

Outside the domain of computer graphics, global illumination methods can be used in all simulations involving radiant energy exchanges. Current applications include heat transfer analysis, infrared and radar imagery, and the study of radio wave propagation.

CHAPTER 2

Principles of global illumination

Most of the concepts presented in this book have been used in different engineering fields, each with its own set of conventions and nomenclature. Three main fields that have been concerned with radiant energy transfer are heat transfer, illumination engineering, and computer graphics.

The terminology introduced in this section is consistent with the ANSI standard used in illumination engineering [90] and with the reflectance nomenclature suggested by the former National Bureau of Standards in the United States[1] [122]. Although all terms and units in the text comply with these standards, some symbols are different as they reflect their use in computer graphics.

This presentation of global illumination is aimed at the application to computer graphics and includes several simplifications of the general problem. For instance, the transfers of light take place between surfaces only, which are enclosed in a transparent, nonparticipating medium (for all practical purposes, a vacuum). The removal of this restriction will be considered in Chapter 7.

Energy can be transported in space using three different processes: *conduction* describes the flow of energy through the structure of a material or medium, *convection* refers to the energy transported by the movement of the medium itself, and *radiation* represents the energy transported by electromagnetic fields. Of these three processes, radiation is the only one that can occur in a vacuum, since the other two rely on a

[1]Now called National Institute of Standards and Technology (NIST).

supporting medium. In this chapter the theory of radiant energy transfer is presented along with all the quantities used to characterize the exchange of radiant energy between two surfaces.

2.1 Physical definitions useful for the study of global illumination

The primary goal of this section is to establish a precise terminology to be used later in the text. As you will see, the radiosity method is more than a rendering tool for computer graphics. It is also, and importantly, a powerful simulation technique, and as such must be carefully presented in a physically consistent manner. This section introduces several physical quantities relevant to the exposition of the radiosity method.

2.1.1 Solid angle

The precise description of radiant energy exchanges in space requires the notion of a *solid angle*, which is the three-dimensional (3D) extension of the angle between two lines. A solid angle is used to measure the portion of space occupied by an object as seen from a point. A more precise definition is the following:

> The solid angle subtended by an object from a point P is the area of the projection of the object onto the unit sphere centered at P.

Note that this definition extends a similar definition for the angle in two dimensions, whereby the angle subtended by an object is the arc length of the central projection of the object onto a unit circle.

Figure 2.1 illustrates these definitions of angle and solid angle. Solid angle is expressed in *steradians* (sr). The solid angle subtended by the whole sphere is 4π sr, that is, the entire area of a unit sphere; and naturally the solid angle subtended by a hemisphere is 2π sr. The hemisphere of directions "above" the tangent plane of a surface will often be denoted by Ω in this text.

Solid angle for a small area

Consider a small surface patch S with area ΔA, viewed from the origin (Figure 2.2). The projection of S onto the sphere centered at the origin and touching the center of S can be approximated by replacing the sphere locally by its tangent plane. Then the projection of S onto the plane perpendicular to the direction of the origin can be used in place of patch S, and has a surface area of $\Delta A \cos\theta$.

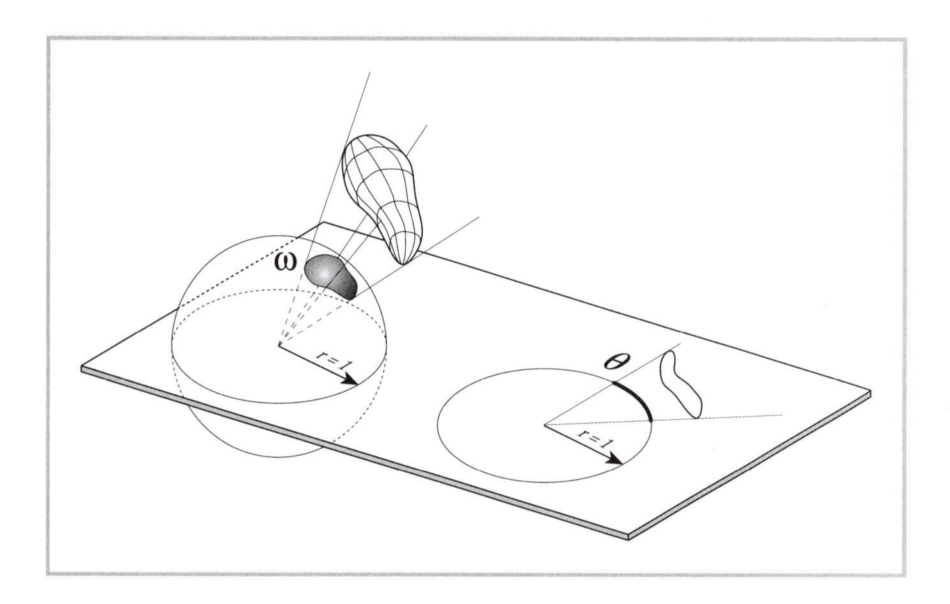

FIGURE 2.1 Definitions of angle and solid angle. θ, the angle subtended by a curve in the plane, is the length of the corresponding arc on the unit circle. ω, the solid angle subtended by an object, is the surface area of its projection onto the unit sphere.

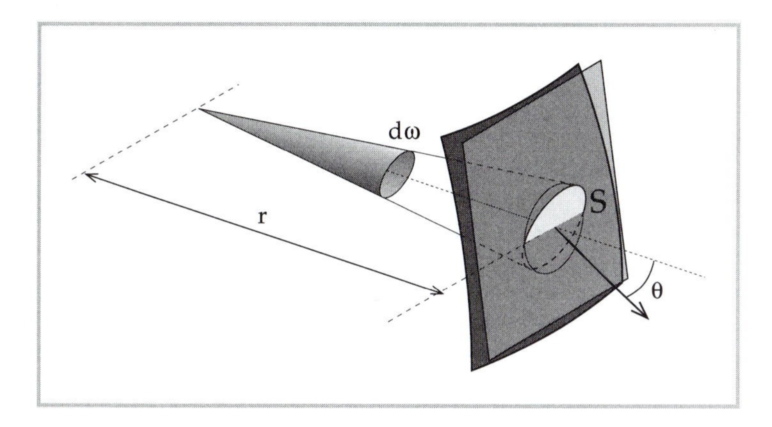

FIGURE 2.2 Solid angle subtended by a small area.

The solid angle subtended by S is obtained after dividing the area of this projection by the square of the distance to the origin, to account for the projection onto the unit sphere:

$$\Delta\omega \approx \frac{\Delta A \cos\theta}{r^2}. \tag{2.1}$$

Solid angle in spherical coordinates

Spherical coordinates are often used in illumination problems since a hemisphere of directions is considered above the surfaces, for light leaving the surface and light impinging on the surface. A direction is identified by the two angles (θ, ϕ), as shown in Figure 2.3, and a point is identified by the direction of the line connecting it to the origin and its distance r from the origin. θ is often called the *polar angle*, while ϕ is referred to as the *azimuth*.

A differential solid angle around direction (θ, ϕ) is expressed by considering the differential area on the unit sphere

$$d\omega = \sin\theta d\theta d\phi . \tag{2.2}$$

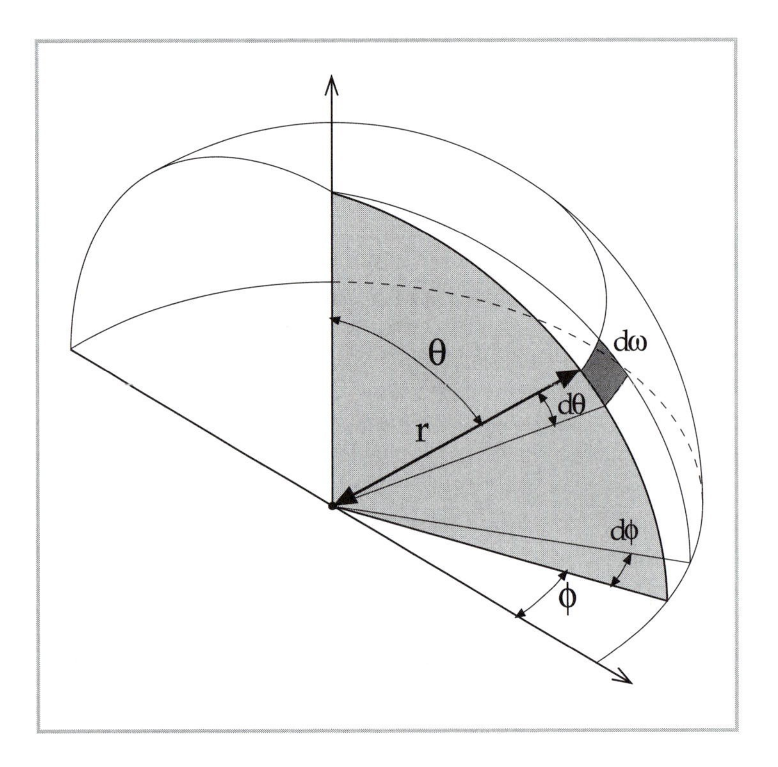

FIGURE 2.3 Spherical coordinates.

2.1.2 Radiometry

Radiometry is the science of measuring radiant energy transfers. Such transfers can be characterized using a set of physical quantities, which are defined below. These radiometric variables form a set of objective quantities, which can be measured using proper equipment such as spectral photometers. Note that for applications in computer graphics a corresponding set of *photometric* variables is often used. These include some elements

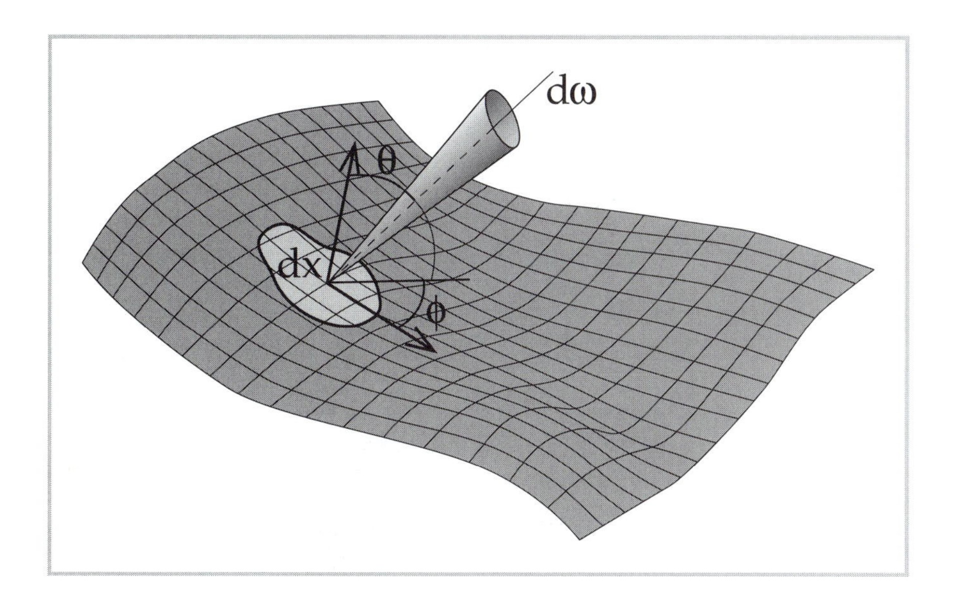

FIGURE 2.4 Definition of radiance.

from perceptual psychology to predict subjective impressions caused by the illumination [90], and are described in the next section.

Radiance

The relevant quantity used to describe radiant energy transfer is *radiance*, denoted by L. Radiance is defined as the amount of energy traveling at some point in a specified direction, per unit time, per unit area perpendicular to the direction of travel, per unit solid angle. Therefore in the situation depicted in Figure 2.4, the energy radiated in the small solid angle $d\omega$, from differential area dx,[2] during time interval dt is

$$L(x,\theta,\phi)\ \underbrace{dx\cos\theta}_{\text{projected area}}\ d\omega dt$$

and the power (energy per unit time) radiated in the same conditions is

$$d^2P = L(x,\theta,\phi)dx\cos\theta d\omega\,. \quad \textbf{(2.3)}$$

The following important property of radiance is worth noting: For any two mutually visible points x and y in space, the radiance leaving point x in the direction of point y is

[2]In most of this text all points considered in space will rest on the surface of an object. For simplicity the notation dx will be used to denote a differential area around point x on the relevant surface. Although questionable from a strict mathematical point of view, this notation is particularly convenient.

the same as the radiance impinging on point y from the direction of point x. To see why this is the case, let us consider dx and dy, two differential areas around x and y.

According to the preceding definition of radiance, the power transferred from dx to dy is

$$d^2P = L(x, \theta_x, \phi_x)dx \cos\theta_x d\omega_{xy} \tag{2.4}$$

where $d\omega_{xy}$ is the solid angle subtended by dy as seen from x. Thus from Equation 2.1

$$d\omega_{xy} = \frac{dy \cos\theta_y}{r^2}.$$

Rearranging the terms shows that

$$d^2P = L(x, \theta_x, \phi_x)dx \cos\theta_x \frac{dy \cos\theta_y}{r^2} \tag{2.5}$$

$$= L(x, \theta_x, \phi_x)dy \cos\theta_y \frac{dx \cos\theta_x}{r^2} \tag{2.6}$$

$$= L(x, \theta_x, \phi_x)dy \cos\theta_y d\omega_{yx}. \tag{2.7}$$

By definition of the radiance received at point y, we have

$$d^2P = L(y, \theta_y, \phi_y)dy \cos\theta_y d\omega_{yx},$$

and comparison to Equation 2.7 shows that radiance is conserved along the path from x to y:

$$L(x, \theta_x, \phi_x) = L(y, \theta_y, \phi_y). \tag{2.8}$$

Because of its "per unit solid angle" definition, radiance does not attenuate with distance. Since most light receivers, including the human eye and photographic cameras, are sensitive to radiance, the above property explains that a given surface produces the same visual impression due to its emitted radiance at all viewing distances. It also means that the knowledge of the radiances leaving all surfaces in a scene is sufficient to render a picture: when a visible surface is identified, its emitted radiance in the direction of the viewer is all that is needed to evaluate the effect produced on the receiver.

Spectral quantities

Since light is composed of electromagnetic waves of different frequencies and wavelengths, it is important to clarify the variation of energy transfer variables over the spectrum. Usually energy transfer occurs at different magnitudes for different wavelengths, which is the physical basis of the sensation of color. Most variables of the energy transfer problem are therefore defined as *spectra*, that is, continuous functions of wavelength λ.

Spectral quantities, defined at a specified wavelength and expressed per unit wavelength, are usually identified by the superscript λ. For instance, spectral radiance L^λ

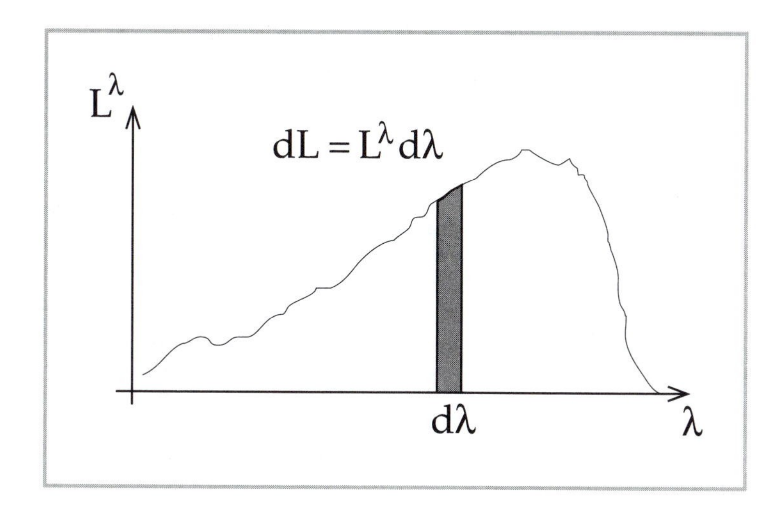

FIGURE 2.5 Spectral radiance represented over the spectrum.

is defined by the property that the radiance emitted in the range $[\lambda, \lambda + d\lambda]$ is $L^\lambda d\lambda$ (Figure 2.5).

Total radiance is then expressed as the integral of spectral radiance over the spectrum

$$L(x, \theta, \phi) = \int_0^\infty L^\lambda(x, \theta, \phi) d\lambda\,. \tag{2.9}$$

Radiosity

Radiosity is defined as the total power leaving a point on a surface, per unit area on the surface. Radiosity is usually denoted by B and is a function of position on the surfaces only (and of wavelength in the case of spectral radiosity). Recall that the power radiated through an infinitesimal solid angle $d\omega$ from an infinitesimal surface area dx is given by Equation 2.4. To obtain the total power radiated from dx above the surface, Equation 2.4 is integrated over the upper hemisphere Ω:

$$dP = \int_\Omega d^2 P \tag{2.10}$$

$$= dx \int_\Omega L(x, \theta, \phi) \cos\theta d\omega\,. \tag{2.11}$$

Since radiosity is defined per unit area, the radiosity at point x is

$$B(x) = \frac{dP}{dx} \tag{2.12}$$

$$= \int_\Omega L(x, \theta, \phi) \cos\theta d\omega\,. \tag{2.13}$$

Radiosity is a useful quantity since it characterizes the total radiation leaving a surface locally around a given point. A corresponding quantity, called *irradiance* and expressed in the same units, represents the total *incident* flux density at a point.

Emission of light

Light sources obviously play an important role in the illumination of a scene, and their characteristics must be known precisely if a computation is to be relied upon.

The standard property used to describe light sources is *exitance*, or radiant emitted flux density, defined as the energy radiated per unit time and per unit area on the surface. Having no directional dependence, it is fairly easy to measure with actual physical luminaires since only one measurement of the emitted power is required.

When a more precise directional description is needed, directional emission diagrams are used together with the exitance to obtain the emitted radiance, denoted by L_e, in a particular direction. The Illumination Engineering Society (IES) in the United States has defined a standard file format for the specification of directional information. Machine-readable files are available from most luminaire manufacturers and provide accurate far-field directional distributions for common fixtures. Since all real light sources have a nontrivial directionality, an accurate treatment of their directional properties is required for any meaningful simulation. The inclusion of directional light sources in a radiosity algorithm is discussed in Section A.1.4 in the Appendix.

Exitance is similar to radiosity in that it can be expressed as the integral of the emitted radiance—that is, the portion of radiance due to internal emission—over the hemisphere (note the similarity to Equation 2.13):

$$E(x) = \int_{\Omega} L_e(x, \theta, \phi) \cos\theta d\omega \, . \qquad \textbf{(2.14)}$$

2.1.3 Photometry

The human eye is only sensitive to a limited range of radiation. So-called visible light is composed of electromagnetic radiation with wavelengths ranging from 380 nm [3] to 770 nm. Furthermore, the response of our visual system is not the same for all wavelengths; for instance, the perceived brightness of a monochromatic radiation at 550 nm is much greater than that of radiation at 690 nm, even if the radiances are the same. A standard spectral response function $V(\lambda)$, or *luminous efficiency function*, has been adopted to characterize the average human response (for daytime vision) and is shown in Figure 2.6.

A set of photometric quantities can be derived from the radiometric quantities by integrating them against the luminous efficiency function $V(\lambda)$. These quantities are very useful in that they correspond to the visual experience of a human being. For instance, *luminous power*, expressed in units of *lumens* (lm), is the photometric equivalent of power (expressed in watts). The luminous efficiency function $V(\lambda)$ is therefore expressed in units of lumens

[3] A *nanometer* is a measure of length such that 1 nm $= 10^{-9}$ m.

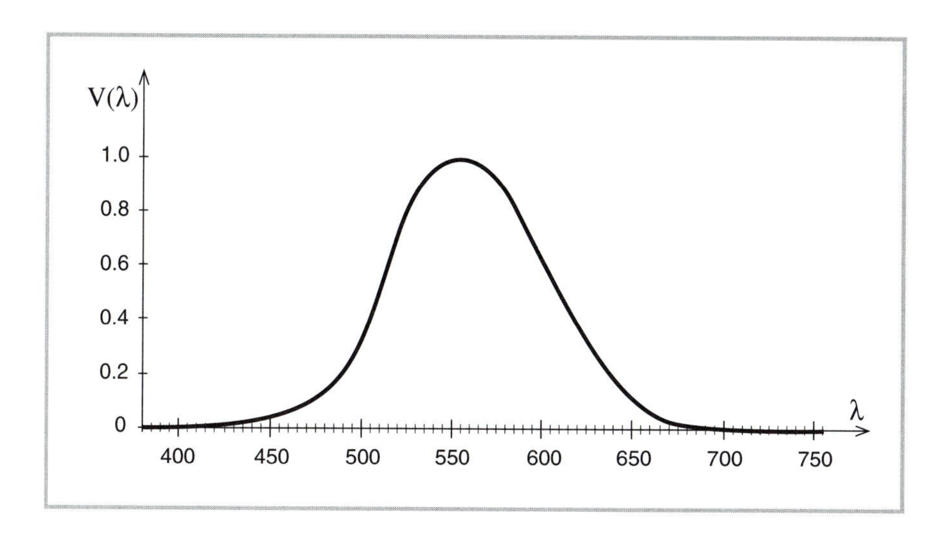

FIGURE 2.6 Luminous efficiency function $V(\lambda)$.

per watt (lm/W). Note that it reaches its maximum of 680 lm/W at $\lambda = 550$ nm.[4] Photometric units are derived from the lumen in the same way radiometric units are derived from watts.

Radiosity, representing flux density (W/m^2), has a photometric counterpart called *luminosity*. The corresponding unit of lm/m^2 is also called *Lux*. Radiance transforms to *luminance*, an important quantity since it is what the eye is ultimately sensing. Luminance is often expressed in *candelas* (cd) per square meters, the candela being another derived unit equivalent to lumens per steradian (1 cd = 1 lm/sr). The following table summarizes the photometric and radiometric quantities with the corresponding units.

Radiometry		→	Photometry	
W	Radiant power	→	Luminous power	Lumens (lm)
W/m^2	Radiosity Irradiance	→	Luminosity Illuminance	Lux (lm/m^2)
W/m^2/sr	Radiance	→	Luminance	cd/m^2 (lm/m^2/sr)

For the purpose of global illumination simulation, the calculation is generally performed on radiometric units, but most applications in visible light require that the results be expressed in photometric units (a discussion of some practical issues for the display of the results can be found in Section A.1.6 of the Appendix).

[4] A normalized curve is often used that has a maximum value of 1, as shown in Figure 2.6 It must then be multiplied by 680 to yield results in lumens.

2.1.4 Reflection of light

Various materials in nature reflect light in very different ways, which explains why their appearance can be dramatically different. The reflecting properties of a given material are described by the concept of *reflectance*, specifying the characteristics of the reflected light from a given sample of material. In this presentation materials are assumed to be opaque, and reflection is therefore treated purely as a surface phenomenon.[5] The various reflectances defined below are considered to be characteristics of the sample's surface.

Bidirectional reflectance

The most general expression of the reflectance is the *bidirectional reflectance distribution function*, in short BRDF, describing the directional distribution of reflected light. The BRDF is defined as the ratio of the radiance in the outgoing direction and the radiant flux density (irradiance) in the incident direction. It is a function of both the incident and outgoing directions[6] and is usually denoted by ρ_{bd}.

The incident radiant flux density (power per unit area) coming from a differential solid angle $d\omega$ around direction (θ, ϕ), as shown in Figure 2.7, is

$$d\Phi_i = L_i(x, \theta, \phi) \cos\theta d\omega\,, \tag{2.15}$$

and the preceding definition of the BRDF translates into

$$\rho_{bd}(\theta_0, \phi_0, \theta, \phi) = \frac{L(x, \theta_0, \phi_0)}{d\Phi_i} \tag{2.16}$$

$$= \frac{L(x, \theta_0, \phi_0)}{L_i(x, \theta, \phi) \cos\theta d\omega}\,. \tag{2.17}$$

Note that the BRDF is not necessarily a number in [0, 1]: it has units of inverse steradians (sr^{-1}) and can vary from 0 to infinity. A somewhat more intuitive measure of the reflective properties of a surface is the *directional-hemispherical reflectance* ρ_{dh}: the fraction of the incident radiant flux density in a given direction that is reflected by the surface (in all possible directions). This particular reflectance is a dimensionless number between 0 and 1 that is easily interpreted. The formal definition of the directional-hemispherical reflectance is the following integral of the BRDF over the hemisphere of reflected directions

$$\rho_{dh}(\theta, \phi) = \frac{d\Phi_r}{d\Phi_i} \tag{2.18}$$

[5]For many real-world materials, a significant portion of light is in fact transmitted across the surface and experiences some sort of scattering in the material before exiting again through the surface. While this effect is important when attempting to predict the actual reflectance functions of such materials, it is not relevant to this discussion. It is assumed that appropriate surface reflectance properties are available, either from a numerical model or from measurements.

[6]The standard notation is to specify the reflected direction first in the arguments of the BRDF.

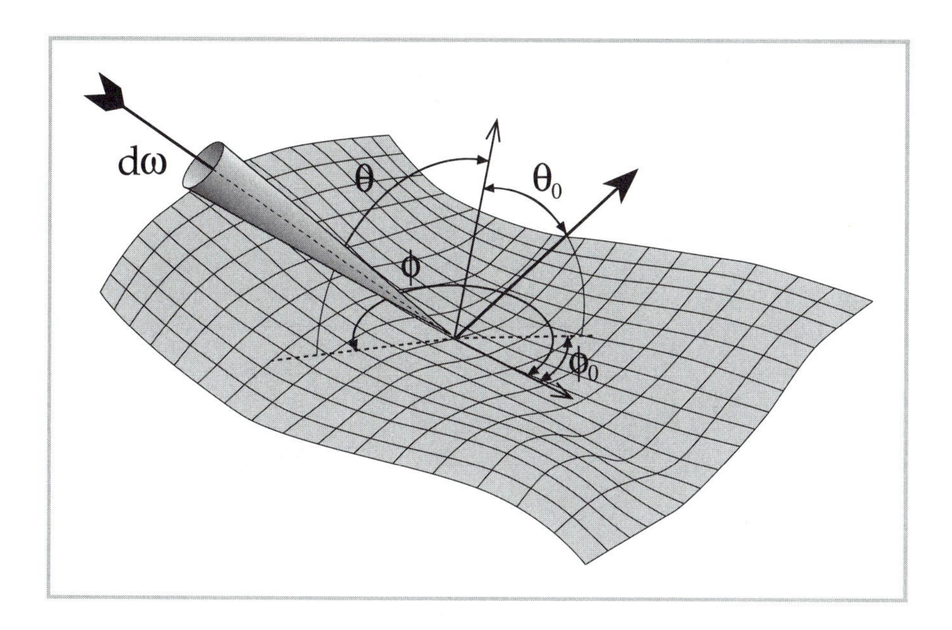

FIGURE 2.7 Notation for the definition of the BRDF.

$$= \frac{\int_\Omega L(x, \theta_0, \phi_0) \cos\theta_0 d\omega_0}{d\Phi_i} \quad \textbf{(2.19)}$$

$$= \int_\Omega \rho_{bd}(\theta_0, \phi_0, \theta, \phi) \cos\theta_0 d\omega_0 \quad \textbf{(2.20)}$$

where the defining equation of the BRDF, Equation 2.16, was used to obtain Equation 2.20. Two ideal cases are worth mentioning, and have been used extensively in computer graphics and elsewhere to simplify the models: diffuse and specular reflectors.

Ideal diffuse reflectors

An ideal diffuse reflector is characterized by a uniform BRDF, one that does not depend on the outgoing direction. As a consequence the reflected radiance is the same in all directions, and the appearance of the surface does not change with the viewing angle.

Because of basic thermodynamics principles, the law of reciprocity [160] states that the BRDF must obey a reciprocity condition:

$$\rho_{bd}(\theta_0, \phi_0, \theta, \phi) = \rho_{bd}(\theta, \phi, \theta_0, \phi_0) .$$

Therefore in the ideal diffuse case the BRDF is independent of both the incoming and outgoing directions, and reduces to a constant.

$$\rho_{bd}(\theta_0, \phi_0, \theta, \phi) \equiv \rho .$$

When light is reflected in such a uniform manner, the surface is easily characterized by its directional-hemispherical reflectance, which also becomes independent of direction. This dimensionless constant, which corresponds to the intuitive meaning of reflectance, is then called the *diffuse reflectance* ρ_d. From Equation 2.20 we see that

$$\rho_d = \rho \int_\Omega \cos\theta_0 d\omega_0 \tag{2.21}$$

$$= \rho \int_0^\pi \int_0^{2\pi} \cos\theta_0 \sin\theta_0 d\theta_0 d\phi_0 \tag{2.22}$$

$$= \pi\rho \,. \tag{2.23}$$

Ideal specular reflectors

An ideal specular reflector reflects light only in the mirror direction given by Snell's Law:[7] The outgoing direction is contained in the plane of incidence, and the outgoing polar angle is equal to the incident polar angle. The BRDF in that case is not a well-behaved function but a Dirac distribution

$$\rho_{bd}(\theta_0, \phi_0, \theta, \phi) = \rho_s(\theta) \cdot 2\delta(\sin^2\theta_0 - \sin^2\theta) \cdot \delta(\phi_0 - \phi \pm \pi)\,, \tag{2.24}$$

where δ denotes the normalized Dirac distribution, which is zero everywhere except where its argument is zero, and has a unit integral. More precisely, for any interval I containing zero,

$$\int_I \delta(u)du = 1\,.$$

Note that the form $2\delta(\sin^2\theta_0 - \sin^2\theta)$ is used instead of the simpler $\delta(\theta_0 - \theta)$ for proper normalization, so that the first multiplier term $\rho_s(\theta)$ has a simple physical meaning. If we carry the integration to compute the reflected radiance in a given direction (θ_0, ϕ_0), we see that

$$L(x, \theta_0, \phi_0) = \int_\Omega \rho_{bd}(\theta_0, \phi_0, \theta, \phi) L_i(x, \theta, \phi) \cos\theta d\omega \tag{2.25}$$

$$= \int_0^\pi \rho_s(\theta)\, 2\, \delta(\sin^2\theta_0 - \sin^2\theta) \cos\theta \sin\theta \int_0^{2\pi} L_i(x, \theta, \phi)\, \delta(\phi_0 - \phi \pm \pi) d\phi d\theta \tag{2.26}$$

$$= \int_0^\pi \rho_s(\theta) L_i(x, \theta, \phi_0 \pm \pi) \delta(\sin^2\theta_0 - \sin^2\theta) d\left(\sin^2\theta\right) \tag{2.27}$$

$$= \rho_s(\theta_0) L_i(x, \theta_0, \phi_0 \pm \pi)\,. \tag{2.28}$$

[7] Interestingly the same laws of light reflection are known in France as Descartes' laws. Maybe just another example of the long-standing French-British rivalry. . .

ρ_s is thus the ratio of the reflected radiance in the specular direction and the incoming radiance. It is a dimensionless quantity between 0 and 1 called the *specular reflectance*.

Spectral variation

Just like other radiometric quantities, reflectance is a function of wavelength. Spectral reflectances are obtained simply by using spectral radiance and irradiance in the definition of the BRDF and all the derived quantities. For example, the spectral BRDF is defined by modifying Equation 2.17:

$$\rho_{bd}^{\lambda}(\theta_0, \phi_0, \theta, \phi) = \frac{L^{\lambda}(x, \theta_0, \phi_0)}{L_i^{\lambda}(x, \theta, \phi)\cos\theta d\omega}. \quad \textbf{(2.29)}$$

Note that although spectral radiances have different units than usual radiances (as mentioned above they are defined per unit wavelength), spectral reflectances retain their usual dimensions since they are defined as a ratio of spectral quantities.

A simple additive color model explains how the reflectance spectrum relates to the color of an object. Consider a diffuse object, characterized by its spectral diffuse reflectance $\rho_d{}^{\lambda}$. At each wavelength λ, the reflected spectral radiance (in any direction) is proportional to the product of the spectral reflectance value and the spectral irradiance:

$$L^{\lambda} = \frac{\rho_d{}^{\lambda}}{\pi}\Phi^{\lambda}.$$

The spectrum of the reflected light is thus obtained by performing this product at each wavelength (Figure 2.8). Note that the same object can produce very different impressions when viewed under different spectral conditions. The measured color of an object is not an intrinsic property of the object but instead depends on the illumination conditions at that particular moment.

The ability of colored surfaces to modify the spectrum of light upon reflection is the cause of the phenomenon called *color bleeding*, whereby the appearance of some surfaces is influenced by the light coming from a colored reflector. We shall see in Section 3.2.2 that the radiosity method automatically simulates this effect, in contrast to other rendering techniques.

Reflectance models

The two ideal cases just presented (ideal diffuse and ideal specular reflectors) are very restrictive, and are crude approximations to real reflectors. The BRDF can assume nonuniform shapes, and a precise knowledge of these functions is essential to the production of physically accurate images.

The reflection of light by a surface is a complex phenomenon, and elaborate physical models are needed to describe it. A variety of parameters have a direct influence on the reflective behavior of a given material, such as its electrical properties—index of refraction—and the geometrical characteristics of its surface (for example, its roughness).

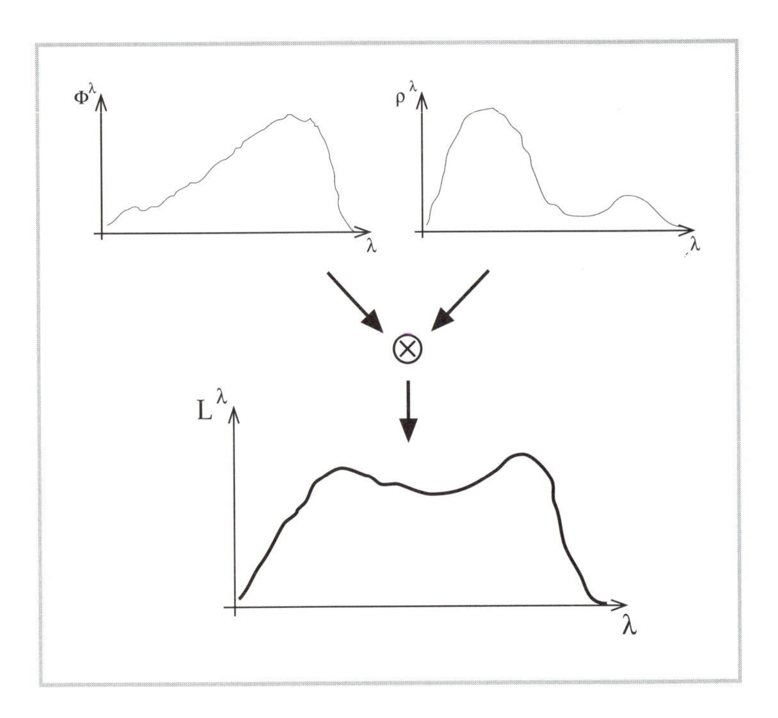

FIGURE 2.8 Combination of the incident irradiance spectrum and the reflectance spectrum.

Roughness (irregularities on the surface at a scale comparable to the wavelength) plays a key role in the variation of the BRDF. For example, an ideally smooth surface will reflect light according to Snell's law and act as an "ideal specular" reflector. On the other hand, a very rough surface will appear to scatter light more or less uniformly in all directions, being closer to an "ideal diffuse" reflector.

This has been explained in *geometrical optics* terms, where light is viewed as composed of light rays, by the fact that rays are reflected by *microfacets* of varying orientation [178, 17].

However, for a full and accurate description when the scale of the surface irregularities is comparable to the wavelength, a *physical optics* model is needed. Physical optics considers the wave effects—such as interference—that occur in the reflection from a rough surface, and yields a continuous description of the reflected light valid for a wide range of physical parameters.

Figure 2.9 shows the different components of a BRDF as predicted by a general physical optics model [78]. The *directional diffuse* component has a complicated directional dependence, which varies with the surface roughness and other physical characteristics. Predictive models for this component are both difficult to establish and complex, as they must take into account wave effects as well as self-shadowing effects. This term is sometimes called *rough specular* in computer graphics, in contrast to the *ideal specular* component, which accounts for mirrorlike reflection. The *ideal diffuse* component is a constant representing the combined effects of subsurface reflection and multiple reflections on the surface.

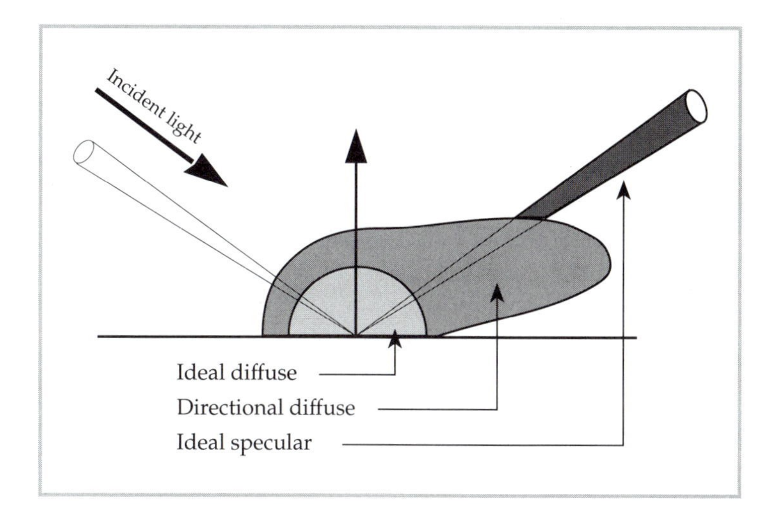

FIGURE 2.9 Different components of a general BRDF, as predicted by physical optics.

Before a solution of the problem of global illumination can be computed, a precise description of the local reflection characteristics of all surfaces must be obtained. Empirical measurements are difficult to conduct over the entire domain of directions, but analytical reflection models, once validated by a comparison with experimental measurements, allow the precomputation of BRDFs for a variety of material and surface finishes.

It is therefore possible to envision that collections of reflectance data will be widely available in the near future, in machine-readable form. Such databases will be either computed using an elaborate reflectance model or measured on actual samples of materials. Precise input data is a necessary condition for the widespread use of physically based simulation methods. The issue of realistic input data is addressed in more detail in Section A.1.5 of the Appendix.

2.2 A model of global illumination

All future discussion in this book will use spectral quantities (radiance and reflectance). However, for simplicity, the superscript λ will be omitted in the rest of the text. In this section, a general equation is presented that describes all energy exchanges between surfaces, and a formal solution is discussed that helps explain some of the simulation algorithms introduced in subsequent chapters.

2.2.1 Energy balance equation

In the general case, the energy equilibrium for a set of radiating surfaces is expressed by the following integral equation:

$$\underbrace{L(x,\theta_0,\phi_0)}_{\text{total radiance}} = \underbrace{L_e(x,\theta_0,\phi_0)}_{\text{emitted radiance}} + \underbrace{\int_\Omega \rho_{bd}(x,\theta_0,\phi_0,\theta,\phi)L_i(x,\theta,\phi)\cos\theta d\omega}_{\text{reflected radiance}} \quad \textbf{(2.30)}$$

(with the notation from Figure 2.7). Equation 2.30 appears under different names (*mutual illumination equation, scattering equation*, and others) in a variety of domains, such as computer vision or thermal engineering. In this text it will be referred to as the *global illumination equation*. Recall the following definitions from the previous section:

- $L(x,\theta_0,\phi_0)$ is the radiance leaving point x in direction (θ_0,ϕ_0);
- $L_e(x,\theta_0,\phi_0)$ is the emitted radiance, a property of the surface at point x;
- $L_i(x,\theta,\phi)$ is the incident radiance impinging on point x from direction θ,ϕ;
- Ω is the set of directions (θ,ϕ) in the hemisphere covering the surface at point x;
- $\rho_{bd}(\theta_0,\phi_0,\theta,\phi)$ is the bidirectional reflectance distribution function (BRDF) describing the reflective properties of the surface at point x.

Equation 2.30 models the energy balance at point x, as it expresses the outgoing radiance in terms of the various sources of radiant energy. The first term on the right-hand side is the emissivity of the surface. This term is non-zero only for surfaces that generate light themselves, even if no other surface is present. For visible light this is only the case for light sources.[8] For heat transfer simulations all surfaces usually exhibit some emissivity, which depends on their temperature. The second term on the right-hand side of Equation 2.30 expresses the effect of light reflection: the reflected radiance is an integral over all possible incoming directions of the incoming flux density (or irradiance, $L_i \cos\theta d\omega$) times the bidirectional reflectance distribution function.

The global illumination equation is an *integral equation*: the unknown radiance function L appears under an integral on the right-hand side, as well as on the left-hand side. Thus Equation 2.30 is difficult to solve, since the computation of the radiance at a particular point requires the knowledge of the incoming radiances from all directions. In general, integral equations can rarely be solved analytically, and numerical methods are used instead to compute approximate solutions. The radiosity and Monte Carlo methods presented in this book are examples of such numerical approximations.

[8]Depending on the precision of the underlying geometric model, the light-emitting part of an incandescent lighting fixture can be represented, for example, by a light bulb, or by the incandescent filament alone.

2.2.2 Formal solution of the global illumination equation

Although an analytic solution of Equation 2.30 cannot be computed in general, a formal manipulation of the equation reveals some interesting properties of the global illumination problem. This operation can in fact be conducted with most integral equations of the same form, and was first presented in the context of computer graphics using a slightly different form of Equation 2.30 called the "rendering equation" [95].

The unknown of the global illumination equation is the distribution of radiance in the scene, L, a function of several variables including position on the surfaces and direction of propagation. The global illumination equation can be rewritten using *integral operators* that act on the radiance distribution to yield a modified distribution. A *reflection operator* $\mathcal{R}$ is defined, which represents the effect on a given radiance distribution of one reflection on all the surfaces:

$$(\mathcal{R}L)(x, \theta_0, \phi_0) = \int_{\Omega} \rho_{bd}(x, \theta_0, \phi_0, \theta, \phi) L_i(x, \theta, \phi) \cos\theta d\omega \,. \tag{2.31}$$

Equation 2.30 then reduces to

$$L = L_e + \mathcal{R}L \,, \tag{2.32}$$

which can be formally inverted using a *Neumann series* [95]:

$$L = [I - \mathcal{R}]^{-1} L_e \tag{2.33}$$

$$= \sum_{n=0}^{\infty} (\mathcal{R})^n L_e \,. \tag{2.34}$$

The expression of the radiance distribution L as a Neumann series in Equation 2.34 has a very simple physical explanation. Since the integral operator $\mathcal{R}$ represents the effect of one reflection on all surfaces of the scene, the infinite series expresses the fact that the radiance distribution is the sum of the "intrinsic" radiance (the emitted radiance L_e), the radiance reflected *once* on the surfaces ($\mathcal{R}L_e$), the radiance reflected *twice* on the surfaces ($\mathcal{R}^2 L_e$), and so on. Thus each term in the series represents the effect of a given number of successive reflections of the emitted radiance. Convergence of the Neumann series is guaranteed for a certain class of integral operators that includes the reflection operator. Conservation of energy ensures that the amount of energy reflected from all surfaces in the scene is less than the incident amount, therefore the *spectral radius* of the reflection operator can be shown to be less than unity. This condition is sufficient to establish convergence.

CHAPTER 3

The basic radiosity method

The radiosity method was originally introduced in the 1950s as a method for computing radiant heat exchanges between surfaces [85, 54]. The beginning of space exploration prompted a renewed interest in the problem of radiant heat transfer, because engineers realized that the absence of atmosphere rendered other means of heat transfer—conduction and convection—ineffective. A satellite can only rely on radiation to dissipate heat absorbed from the sun or generated by onboard equipment. Severe restrictions on size and weight combined with the intense heat flux from the sun make it necessary to carefully engineer spacecraft to maximize surface area of the heat radiators while minimizing weight. Thus elaborate radiators consisting of fins or blades were designed, and their efficiency had to be evaluated. In such assemblies with complex geometries, the interreflection of heat played a major role, and a computational method was needed that could handle all these effects efficiently.

This book is concerned mostly with the application of the radiosity method to the simulation of light transfer, which is somewhat simpler than the simulation of heat transfer. The two problems differ, since when heat is received at a surface, it is usually absorbed, influencing the body's temperature. The reemission of heat, and in particular its spectral distribution, is governed by temperature [160]. Therefore, there is a complex coupling between the incident and emitted energy fluxes. The case of visible light is usually simpler, as temperature plays no significant role in the reemission of light by a surface.

This chapter presents the radiosity method as it applies to computer graphics. A *radiosity equation* is first derived from the general global illumination equation introduced in Section 2.2, based on the assumption that all surfaces are ideal diffuse. Analytic solutions to the radiosity equation are only known for the simplest scenes, and numerical methods are needed to compute approximate solutions. In particular, a discrete version of the radiosity equation is derived, where a matrix of *form factors* expresses the coupling between the discrete variables.

A standard strategy to produce simulations and images using this approach is outlined, and a technique for the computation of form factors is presented.

3.1 The radiosity equation

This section shows how the general global illumination equation (Equation 2.30) can be simplified so that it can be solved in special cases. First, the ideal diffuse assumption makes it possible to establish a simple relationship between the energy received at a surface and the energy emitted by that surface. Then the link between the irradiance at one surface and the emitted radiance at other surfaces is expressed. The result is a simplified integral equation for the radiosity leaving a surface.

3.1.1 Assumptions of the radiosity method

The radiosity method solves a simplified problem, that is, the interreflection of light in an enclosure made up of ideal diffuse surfaces. For such a problem, radiosity can be used instead of radiance as the relevant variable; more importantly, the global illumination equation reduces to a simpler energy balance equation.

Radiosity and radiance

Recall from Section 2.1.2 that radiosity is the total power leaving a surface at a given point, per unit area on the surface. In terms of the radiance leaving the surface, radiosity is described by the following integral (Equation 2.13):

$$B(x) = \int_{\Omega} L(x, \theta, \phi) \cos\theta d\omega .$$

In the case of an ideal diffuse surface, radiance is a function of position only

$$L(x, \theta, \phi) \equiv L(x) \quad \textbf{(3.1)}$$

and can therefore be moved outside the integral; thus

$$B(x) = L(x) \int_{\Omega} \cos\theta d\omega \quad \textbf{(3.2)}$$

$$= L(x) \int_0^{\pi} \int_0^{2\pi} \cos\theta \sin\theta d\theta d\phi \quad \textbf{(3.3)}$$

$$= \pi L(x) . \quad \textbf{(3.4)}$$

Thus radiosity and radiance can be used interchangeably to characterize the light leaving diffuse surfaces.

Simple energy balance equation

As shown in Section 2.1.4, the bidirectional reflectance distribution function (BRDF) becomes independent of directions in the case of ideal diffuse reflectors, and is linked to the diffuse reflectance by Equation 2.23:

$$\rho_{bd}(x, \theta_0, \phi_0, \theta, \phi) = \frac{\rho_d(x)}{\pi}.$$

The general global illumination equation 2.30 can therefore be greatly simplified by moving the reflectance term outside the integral:

$$L(x, \theta_0, \phi_0) = L_e(x, \theta_0, \phi_0) + \frac{\rho_d(x)}{\pi} \int_\Omega L_i(x, \theta, \phi) \cos\theta d\omega. \qquad \textbf{(3.5)}$$

As stated earlier, for diffuse surfaces the radiance $L(x, \theta, \phi) \equiv L(x)$ does not depend on the outgoing direction. Note that the incoming radiance, $L_i(x, \theta, \phi)$, still depends on incoming direction. Here we are also assuming diffuse emitters, so $L_e(x, \theta, \phi) \equiv L_e(x)$.

The integral in Equation 3.5 expresses the incident flux density at point x. Recall that flux density is power per unit area and is expressed in units of W/m^2. If we define

$$H(x) = \int_\Omega L_i(x, \theta, \phi) \cos\theta d\omega, \qquad \textbf{(3.6)}$$

Equation 3.5 becomes

$$L(x) = L_e(x) + \frac{\rho_d(x)}{\pi} H(x). \qquad \textbf{(3.7)}$$

Recall from Equation 3.4 that radiances and radiosities are proportional. The radiosity of point x is obtained by multiplying both sides of Equation 3.7 by π:

$$B(x) = E(x) + \rho_d(x) H(x). \qquad \textbf{(3.8)}$$

In Equation 3.8 $E(x)$ is the exitance defined in the previous chapter by Equation 2.14. Equation 3.8 can be understood this way: since radiosity expresses the total amount of power reflected from a surface, it is the sum of two terms, a "source" term describing the emission of light sources, and the local reflectivity multiplied by the amount of power received from the environment.

Another way to understand the simplification introduced in the illumination equation is to say that at each reflection we need not know which direction the reflected light came from, since it is reflected equally regardless of direction. All that is needed to compute the radiosity leaving a surface is the total incident flux density.

3.1.2 The diffuse illumination equation

The difficulty in solving Equation 3.8 for the radiosity at a surface is that the incident flux density H depends on the radiosities of all other surfaces. This dependence is included in the $H(x)$ term and can be made more explicit by transforming the hemispherical integral in Equation 3.6 into a surface integral. Recall that

$$H(x) = \int_{\Omega} L_i(x, \theta, \phi) \cos\theta d\omega \,. \tag{3.9}$$

If y is the point visible from x in direction (θ, ϕ), then x is also visible from y in a direction (θ', ϕ') (see Figure 3.1). The invariance of radiance along a line of sight (Equation 2.8 in Section 2.1.2) states that

$$L_i(x, \theta, \phi) = L(y, \theta', \phi') \,.$$

Point y lies on a diffuse surface, therefore

$$L(y, \theta', \phi') = \frac{B(y)}{\pi} \,.$$

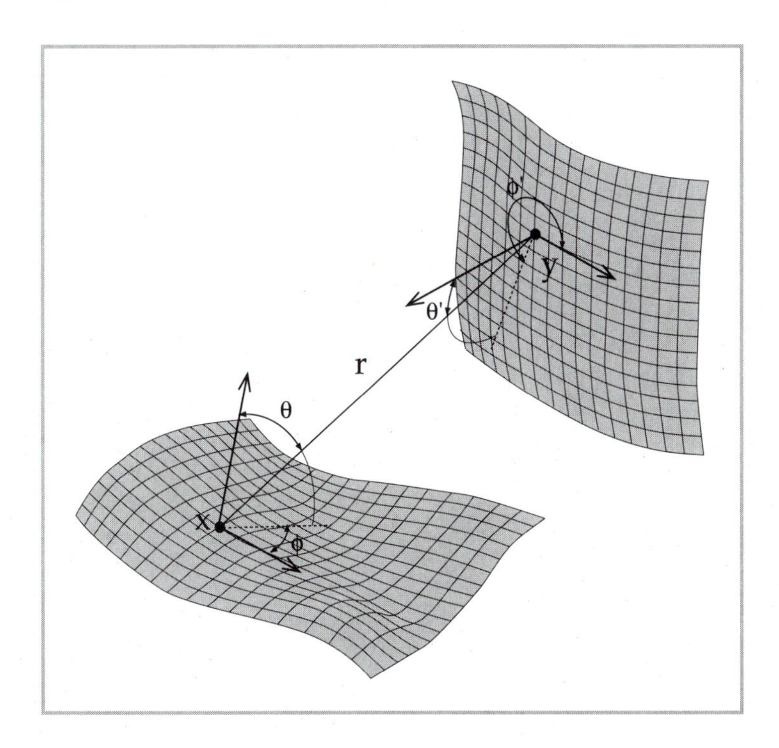

FIGURE 3.1 Using the invariance of radiance to express the coupling of radiosities.

The integral in Equation 3.9 can be written as an area integral over all surfaces in the scene by expanding the differential solid angle

$$d\omega = \frac{\cos\theta' dy}{r^2}$$

and setting the integration domain for the area integral to be the set of surfaces in the scene visible from point x. This is more easily achieved by carrying out the integration over the entire area of the scene while including in the integrand a binary *visibility function* $V(x, y)$, such that

$$V(x, y) = \begin{cases} 1 & \text{if } x \text{ and } y \text{ are mutually visible} \\ 0 & \text{otherwise} . \end{cases}$$

With these modifications $H(x)$ can be expressed as

$$H(x) = \frac{1}{\pi} \int_{y \in S} B(y) \frac{\cos\theta \cos\theta'}{r^2} V(x, y) dy . \tag{3.10}$$

Using the above expression for $H(x)$ in the energy balance equation (Equation 3.8),

$$B(x) = E(x) + \rho_d(x) H(x) ,$$

the radiosity at point x is expressed as a function of the radiosities of all points in the scene, yielding a continuous equation for diffuse illumination:

$$B(x) = E(x) + \rho_d(x) \int_{y \in S} B(y) \frac{\cos\theta \cos\theta'}{\pi r^2} V(x, y) dy . \tag{3.11}$$

Derivation of the radiosity equation

Equation 3.11 is still an integral equation for which no analytic solution is available in general. An example of a situation for which an analytic solution is available is the interior of a uniformly emitting body. While studying such a system can be of great value for thermal analysis, it has little interest for image synthesis! It is interesting to note that even in the case of very simple geometrical arrangements, the inherent complexity of the diffuse illumination equation usually precludes any closed-form solution.

As an example let us consider the simple case of two long planar surfaces forming a corner along the v direction, shown in Figure 3.2. If the surfaces are considered infinitely long in the v direction, the scene is invariant under any translation along v. Therefore the radiosity on each of the patches is independent of v and can be expressed as $B_1(u)$ in the horizontal plane and $B_2(w)$ in the vertical plane. A simple symmetry argument shows that these two functions are identical, provided the emission terms are the same on both surfaces.

In this simple configuration we can express the terms of Equation 3.11 as

$$r = \sqrt{u^2 + v^2 + w^2}$$

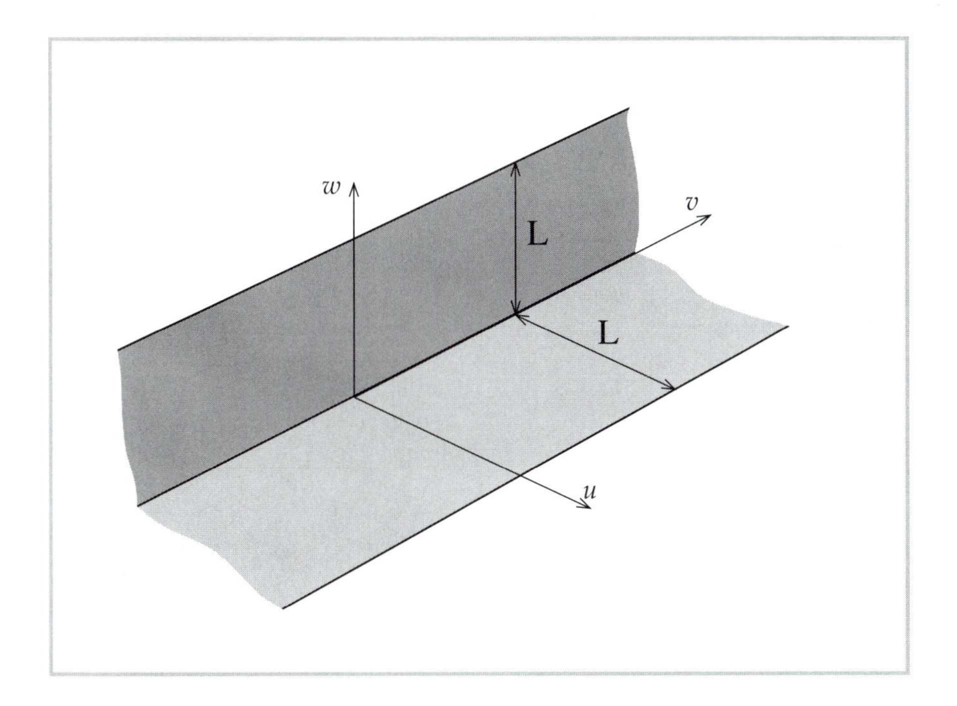

FIGURE 3.2 A simple scene with no known analytic solution.

$$\cos\theta = \frac{w}{r}$$
$$\cos\theta' = \frac{u}{r}.$$

The diffuse illumination equation in this case becomes

$$B(u) = E(u) + \frac{\rho_d(u)}{\pi} \int_{-\infty}^{\infty} \int_0^L B(w) \frac{uw}{(u^2 + v^2 + w^2)^2} dv dw. \tag{3.12}$$

The integration with respect to v can be carried out to yield

$$\int_{-\infty}^{\infty} \frac{dv}{(u^2 + v^2 + w^2)^2} = \frac{\pi}{2(u^2 + w^2)^{\frac{3}{2}}}$$

resulting in the following integral equation for $B(u)$:

$$B(u) = E(u) + \frac{\rho_d(u)}{2} \int_0^L B(w) \frac{uw}{(u^2 + w^2)^{\frac{3}{2}}} dw. \tag{3.13}$$

There exists no closed-form solution to Equation 3.13, even if the source term $E(u)$ is a constant function. This example shows that even in extremely simple cases there is no known analytic solution to the diffuse illumination equation.

3.1.3 Discrete formulation

The heart of the radiosity method is the idea of breaking down the surfaces in the environment into a finite number of patches and solving a discrete version of Equation 3.11 for the radiosities of these patches [170].

In order to further simplify the problem, the assumption is made that radiosity takes a uniform value across the surface of each patch. In other words the radiosity function $B(x)$ is considered to be piecewise constant, or a linear combination of constant basis functions. Figure 3.3 represents such a combination of "box" functions, whose value is 1 over the surface of a given patch and 0 elsewhere, approximating a continuous radiosity function. This rather crude approximation can be refined by considering more elaborate basis functions, as explained later in Section 5.2, but in this presentation the simpler constant functions are used. The diffuse reflectance ρ_d is also assumed to be a constant over the area of each patch. Note that this last assumption is less questionable since a patch usually represents some portion of an object that is made of a uniform material.

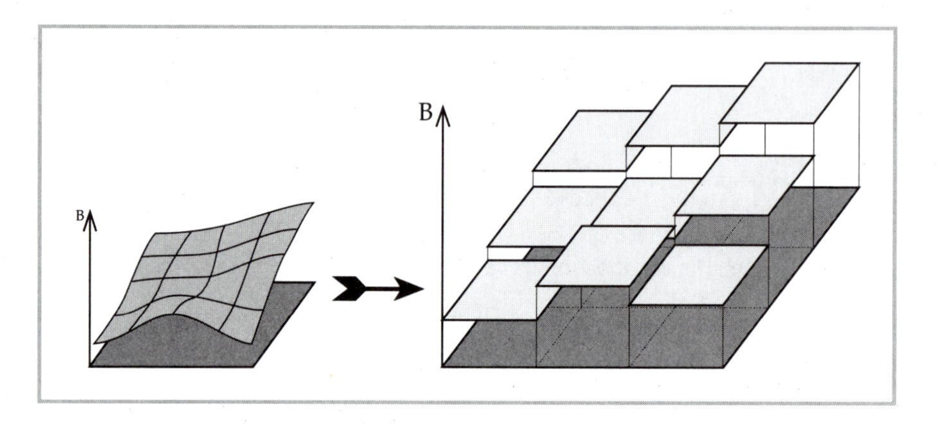

FIGURE 3.3 Radiosity seen as a linear combination of constant functions. Each patch has a uniform radiosity.

Suppose, for now, that the surfaces of the environment are subdivided into a collection of N disjoint patches $\left(P_j\right)_{j=1...N}$. The surface area of patch P_j will be denoted by A_j. Notations are shown in Figure 3.4.

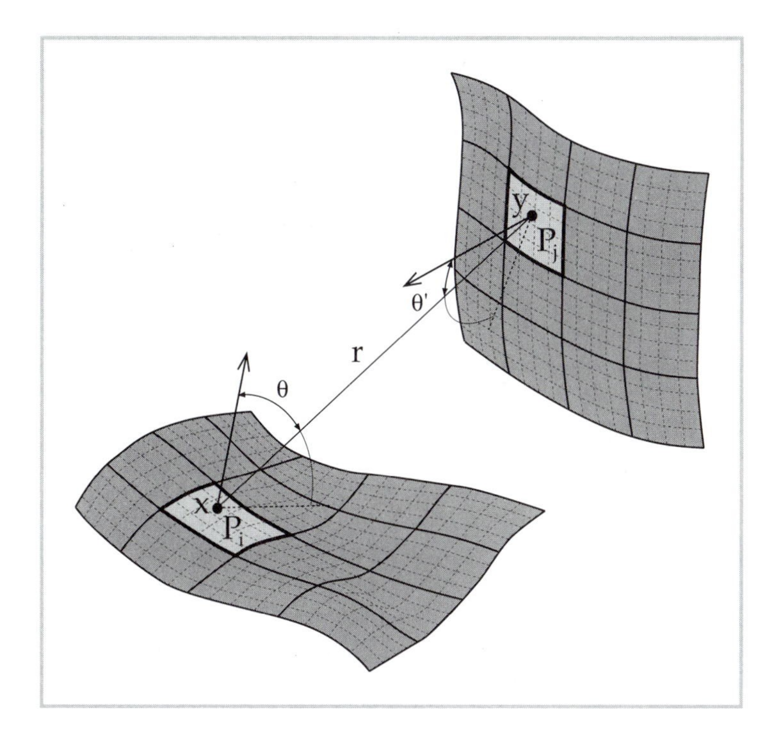

FIGURE 3.4 Notation for the radiosity equation.

The integral over all surfaces of the scene in Equation 3.11 is simply broken into N pieces, each corresponding to a discrete patch:

$$B(x) = E(x) + \rho_d(x) \sum_{j=1}^{N} \int_{y \in P_j} B(y) \frac{\cos\theta \cos\theta'}{\pi r^2} V(x, y) dy .$$

Each patch is assumed to have a uniform radiosity therefore at each point y in P_j, $B(y) = B_j$, and the radiosity can be moved outside the integral:

$$B(x) = E(x) + \rho_d(x) \sum_{j=1}^{N} B_j \int_{y \in P_j} \frac{\cos\theta \cos\theta'}{\pi r^2} V(x, y) dy . \quad \textbf{(3.14)}$$

A rather subtle point raised by Equation 3.14 is the fact that $B(x)$ is likely to vary as x spans the area of a given patch P_i. This is a paradox because of the assumption of a constant radiosity across each patch. The apparent contradiction is resolved by considering B as constant over a patch only for the purpose of illuminating the other surfaces. The constant radiosity value is computed for each patch as an area-weighted average of the pointwise radiosities using the following formula:

$$B_i = \frac{1}{A_i} \int_{x \in P_i} B(x) dx \,. \tag{3.15}$$

Likewise the exitance of a patch is considered to be uniform and is given by

$$E_i = \frac{1}{A_i} \int_{x \in P_i} E(x) dx \,. \tag{3.16}$$

The assumption of a constant reflectance across each patch is expressed by the fact that for each point x in P_i, $\rho_d(x) = \rho_i$. Using the expression of $B(x)$ from Equation 3.14 in Equation 3.15, we obtain

$$B_i = E_i + \rho_i \sum_{j=1}^{N} B_j \frac{1}{A_i} \int_{x \in P_i} \int_{y \in P_j} \frac{\cos\theta \cos\theta'}{\pi r^2} V(x, y) dy dx \,. \tag{3.17}$$

More concisely,

$$B_i = E_i + \rho_i \sum_{j=1}^{N} F_{ij} B_j \,, \tag{3.18}$$

where

$$F_{ij} = \frac{1}{A_i} \int_{x \in P_i} \int_{y \in P_j} \frac{\cos\theta \cos\theta'}{\pi r^2} V(x, y) dy dx \,. \tag{3.19}$$

Here F_{ij} is a very important quantity called the *form factor* between patches P_i and P_j. Equation 3.18 is called the *radiosity equation*.

3.1.4 The form factor

The form factor (sometimes called *view factor*, *angle factor*, or *configuration factor* in the heat transfer literature [18]) has a very simple physical interpretation:

> F_{ij} is the proportion of the total power leaving patch P_i that is received by patch P_j.

To prove this, let us consider the power transferred from a differential area dx around point x towards a visible differential area dy. By the definition of radiance (Equation 2.4), it is

$$\begin{aligned} d^2 P &= L(x) \cos\theta \, d\omega \, dx \\ &= L(x) \frac{\cos\theta \cos\theta'}{r^2} dy dx \,. \end{aligned} \tag{3.20}$$

The power transferred from dx to patch j is the integral of the above quantity over the visible portion of the patch:

$$dP = L(x)dx \int_{y \in P_j} \frac{\cos\theta \cos\theta'}{r^2} V(x, y)dy \,. \tag{3.21}$$

Since the radiosity is constant over patch P_i, we have $L(x) = B_i/\pi$ (Equation 3.4), and the power transferred from patch P_i to patch P_j is

$$P = \frac{B_i}{\pi} \int_{x \in P_i} \int_{y \in P_j} \frac{\cos\theta \cos\theta'}{r^2} V(x, y)dydx \,. \tag{3.22}$$

Since radiosity is defined per unit area, the total power leaving patch P_i is obtained by multiplying by the area of the patch, yielding $A_i B_i$. Thus the proportion of power leaving patch P_i and reaching patch P_j is exactly

$$\frac{P}{A_i B_i} = \frac{1}{A_i} \int_{x \in P_i} \int_{y \in P_j} \frac{\cos\theta \cos\theta'}{\pi r^2} V(x, y)dydx \tag{3.23}$$

$$= F_{ij} \,. \tag{3.24}$$

3.1.5 Notation

In general the form factor between two surface patches P and Q will be denoted by $F_{P,Q}$. As a convenience and to simplify notation, the form factor between patches P_i and P_j will be denoted by F_{ij} (instead of F_{P_i,P_j}).

The notion of form factor between a point x on a surface and a surface patch P will appear in subsequent sections. Such a form factor can be thought of as the limit of the usual form factor when the area of one of the patches goes to zero. Its mathematical expression is simply the inner integral of Equation 3.19:

$$F_{x,P} = \int_{y \in P} \frac{\cos\theta \cos\theta'}{\pi r^2} V(x, y)dy \,. \tag{3.25}$$

3.1.6 Properties of the form factor

The form factor is a strictly geometric quantity: its value depends only on the shape and relative location of surfaces in the scene. This property will prove very useful when computing simulations corresponding to different illumination conditions, since the same form factors will be used in the computation. In fact, the computation of form factors is often the most time-consuming part of any radiosity algorithm, but several tricks can be used to eliminate unnecessary computations.

Reciprocity

Multiplying Equation 3.19 by the area of patch P_i, we see that

$$A_i F_{ij} = \int_{x \in P_i} \int_{y \in P_j} \frac{\cos\theta \cos\theta'}{\pi r^2} V(x, y) dy dx$$

is a symmetrical expression with respect to i and j; that is, the following relationship holds:

$$\forall (i, j) \qquad A_i F_{ij} = A_j F_{ji} . \tag{3.26}$$

This reciprocity relation can be used to derive an unknown form factor from a known one. It also helps understand the definition of the form factor in terms of power transfer given in Section 3.1.4, which often seems unnatural or even contradictory to the radiosity equation 3.18:

$$B_i = E_i + \rho_i \sum_{j=1}^{N} F_{ij} B_j .$$

Most people at first expect to find on the right-hand side F_{ji} instead of F_{ij}, since power is transferred from P_j to P_i. The apparent contradiction comes from the fact that Equation 3.18 is written in terms of radiosities, which have units of power per unit area. If both sides of the equation are multiplied by the area of patch P_i, we obtain

$$A_i B_i = A_i E_i + \rho_i \sum_{j=1}^{N} A_i F_{ij} B_j \tag{3.27}$$

$$A_i B_i = A_i E_i + \rho_i \sum_{j=1}^{N} \frac{A_i}{A_j} F_{ij} A_j B_j \tag{3.28}$$

$$A_i B_i = A_i E_i + \rho_i \sum_{j=1}^{N} F_{ji} (A_j B_j) \tag{3.29}$$

because of the reciprocity relationship.

This last equation involves actual power, and the power emitted by patch j, $A_j B_j$, is multiplied by F_{ji}, as expected.

Additivity

Since the form factor is defined as the proportion of the power emitted by one patch that reaches another, it is clear that given three *disjoint* patches P_i, P_j, P_k, the power received by the union of patches P_j and P_k is the sum of the powers received by each of these patches. Therefore the form factor from P_i to the union of P_j and P_k is the sum of the individual form factors

$$F_{i(j \cup k)} = F_{ij} + F_{ik} . \tag{3.30}$$

Note that in general the reverse is not true. Using the reciprocity relation, we see that

$$F_{(j \cup k)i} = \frac{A_i}{A_j + A_k} F_{i(j \cup k)} \tag{3.31}$$

$$= \frac{A_i}{A_j + A_k} \left(F_{ij} + F_{ik} \right) \tag{3.32}$$

$$= \frac{A_i}{A_j + A_k} \left(\frac{A_j}{A_i} F_{ji} + \frac{A_k}{A_i} F_{ki} \right) \tag{3.33}$$

$$= \frac{A_j F_{ji} + A_k F_{ki}}{A_j + A_k} \neq F_{ji} + F_{ki} \,. \tag{3.34}$$

Thus the form factor from the union of patches P_j and P_k to patch P_i is an area-weighted average of the individual form factors, and not simply their sum. For example, in the special case shown in Figure 3.5, patches j and k are arranged symmetrically. Therefore $F_{(j \cup k)i} = F_{ji} = F_{ki}$.

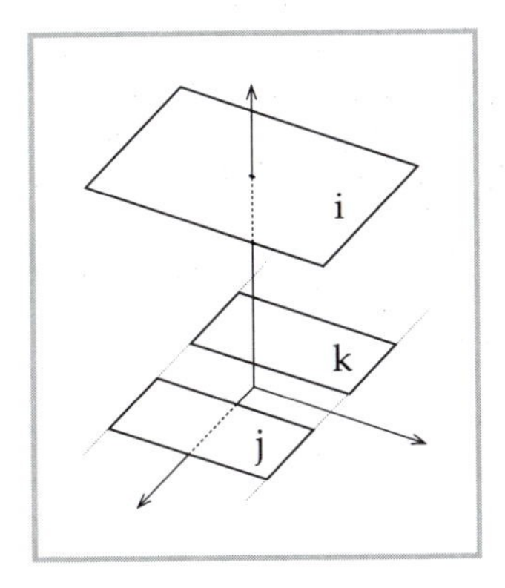

FIGURE 3.5 Additivity of the form factors (in one direction).

The definition of the form factor as an energy ratio implies that in a closed environment, the sum of all form factors from a given patch is unity. This sum represents the proportion of the power emitted from patch P_i, which reaches *any* other patch in the scene. In a closed environment no energy is lost, therefore the sum equals one:

$$\forall i, \qquad \sum_{j=1}^{N} F_{ij} = 1 \,. \tag{3.35}$$

If two patches, P_j and P_k, intersect, the simple argument of energy transfers mentioned earlier shows that the energy radiated towards the intersection of P_j and P_k must be subtracted; otherwise it would be counted twice:

$$F_{i(j \cup k)} = F_{ij} + F_{ik} - F_{i(j \cap k)} . \qquad \textbf{(3.36)}$$

3.2 Solution to the radiosity equation

Since the radiosity equation 3.18 is written for a single patch P_i, there exist a number of similar equations, resulting in a system of N linear equations with N unknowns (the radiosities of each of the N patches that partition the surfaces of the objects in the scene). Assuming all the coefficients of these equations are known, any linear equation solver can be used to extract the radiosity values from the system.

The N instances of Equation 3.18, obtained by considering all possible values for i, can be grouped to form the following matrix equation:

$$\begin{pmatrix} B_1 \\ B_2 \\ \vdots \\ B_n \end{pmatrix} = \begin{pmatrix} E_1 \\ E_2 \\ \vdots \\ E_n \end{pmatrix} + \begin{pmatrix} \rho_1 F_{11} \rho_1 F_{12} \cdots \rho_1 F_{1n} \\ \rho_2 F_{21} \rho_2 F_{22} \quad \vdots \\ \vdots \quad\quad \vdots \\ \rho_n F_{n1} \cdots \cdots \rho_n F_{nn} \end{pmatrix} \begin{pmatrix} B_1 \\ B_2 \\ \vdots \\ B_n \end{pmatrix} \qquad \textbf{(3.37)}$$

or equivalently

$$\begin{pmatrix} 1-\rho_1 F_{11} & -\rho_1 F_{12} & \cdots & -\rho_1 F_{1n} \\ -\rho_2 F_{21} & 1-\rho_2 F_{22} & & \vdots \\ \vdots & & \ddots & \vdots \\ -\rho_n F_{n1} & \cdots & \cdots & 1-\rho_n F_{nn} \end{pmatrix} \begin{pmatrix} B_1 \\ B_2 \\ \vdots \\ B_n \end{pmatrix} = \begin{pmatrix} E_1 \\ E_2 \\ \vdots \\ E_n \end{pmatrix} \qquad \textbf{(3.38)}$$

This system of radiosity equations can be written as[1]

$$\boldsymbol{MB} = \boldsymbol{E} \qquad \textbf{(3.39)}$$

where

$$M_{ij} = \delta_{ij} - \rho_i F_{ij} . \qquad \textbf{(3.40)}$$

Here δ_{ij} is the Kronecker symbol, whose value is one if and only if $i = j$, and zero otherwise. Obtaining a solution to the matrix equation is equivalent to inverting $\boldsymbol{M}$. A

[1] Throughout this text, matrices and vectors will appear in boldface characters, to distinguish them from their components that appear with one or several subscripts.

simple radiosity algorithm for image synthesis that follows from this formulation consists of the following three steps.

1 Compute the matrix elements M_{ij}.
2 Solve the system of linear equations.
3 Display the results.

Figure 3.6 shows what input information is being processed at each step. The matrix elements are functions of both geometric information (for the form factors) and the physical properties of the materials used (for the reflectances and exitances). Since the reflectances and exitances are given as input to the simulation, the first step, computing the matrix elements, amounts to the evaluation of the form factors. Thus form factors are first computed based on the geometrical information supplied in the scene description. The computation of these form factors can be very involved because of the inherent complexity of their expression. This complexity is mostly due to the presence of the visibility term. Several computation algorithms for form factors are presented in Sections 3.3 and 5.1.

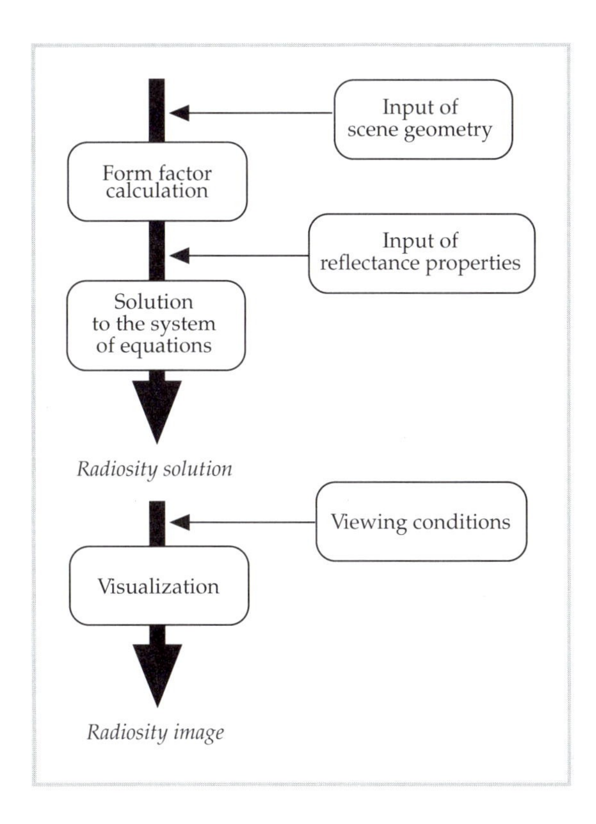

FIGURE 3.6 The radiosity algorithm for image synthesis.

Once all the form factors are known, exitances and reflectances are used to construct the actual system of equations to be solved, and a linear solver is used to obtain the vector $\boldsymbol{B}$ of radiosity values [68]. Note that exitances are non-zero only for light sources and are used to specify the emission characteristics of each light source. One major benefit of the radiosity formulation is that there is no distinction between light sources and other patches: any patch in the scene can be made a light source by appropriately setting its exitance.

A *radiosity solution* consists of a set of patch radiosities, as obtained from this process. Although these numerical values can be used for a variety of purposes, for image synthesis applications the goal is to create a displayable image. This is accomplished by a *rendering* step: a view of the environment is computed where each patch is assigned a color based on its radiosity. This process is detailed in Section 3.2.3.

3.2.1 Iterative solution

A number of numerical algorithms are available to solve linear systems of equations, but the system of radiosity equations has certain mathematical characteristics that make it particularly amenable to an iterative solution technique known as *Gauss-Seidel relaxation* [37]. In particular the property of *diagonal dominance* established below ensures that the relaxation algorithm converges.

As a general rule, relaxation techniques work by iteratively computing an approximate solution of a matrix equation, based each time on the previous approximation. More specifically, in order to solve Equation 3.39, $\boldsymbol{MB} = \boldsymbol{E}$, it is first written as

$$\sum_{j=1}^{N} M_{ij} B_j = E_i, \qquad 1 \leq i \leq N. \tag{3.41}$$

The definition of $\boldsymbol{M}$ in Equation 3.40, gives $M_{ii} = 1 - \rho_i F_{ii}$ for all i. From the properties of diffuse reflectance (Section 2.1.4) we can state $0 \leq \rho_i < 1$ (a reflectance of 1 is physically impossible to realize). Furthermore, form factors are such that $0 \leq F_{ii} \leq 1$; and in most practical cases, such as for planar patches, $F_{ii} = 0$ since the patch cannot see itself. Therefore $M_{ii} > 0$ for all i, and Equation 3.41 can be used to compute the value of B_i for any given i, as a function of all other variables:

$$B_i = -\sum_{\substack{j=1 \\ j \neq i}}^{N} \frac{M_{ij}}{M_{ii}} B_j + \frac{E_i}{M_{ii}} \qquad 1 \leq i \leq N. \tag{3.42}$$

Jacobi relaxation The simplest iterative solution method, known as Jacobi relaxation, proceeds as follows: An initial guess is first chosen, which is a vector

$$\boldsymbol{B}^{(0)} = \begin{bmatrix} B_1^{(0)} \\ B_2^{(0)} \\ \vdots \\ B_n^{(0)} \end{bmatrix}.$$

At each iteration step $m > 0$, a new approximation to the solution is computed using Equation 3.42 for each value of i in turn

$$B_i^{(m)} = -\sum_{\substack{j=1 \\ j \neq i}}^{N} \frac{M_{ij}}{M_{ii}} B_j^{(m-1)} + \frac{E_i}{M_{ii}} \qquad 1 \leq i \leq N . \tag{3.43}$$

Gauss-Seidel relaxation Gauss-Seidel relaxation is a slightly different form of this iterative method, where the values already computed in the current iteration cycle are used in Equation 3.43 instead of the previous approximations:

$$B_i^{(m)} = -\sum_{j=1}^{i-1} \frac{M_{ij}}{M_{ii}} B_j^{(m)} - \sum_{j=i+1}^{N} \frac{M_{ij}}{M_{ii}} B_j^{(m-1)} + \frac{E_i}{M_{ii}} \qquad 1 \leq i \leq N . \tag{3.44}$$

The advantage of this formulation over simple Jacobi relaxation is that a single vector of radiosity estimates can be used, which is updated in place during the computation. Also it can be shown that the asymptotic convergence rate of Gauss-Seidel relaxation is better than that of Jacobi relaxation. Finally, Gauss-Seidel relaxation always converges when matrix $\boldsymbol{M}$ is *strictly diagonally dominant* [182], that is, when the diagonal terms M_{ii} all dominate their entire row of the matrix in the following sense:

$$|M_{ii}| > \sum_{\substack{j=1 \\ j \neq i}}^{N} |M_{ij}|, \qquad 1 \leq i \leq N . \tag{3.45}$$

The particular matrix $\boldsymbol{M}$ used in radiosity computations is always strictly diagonally dominant, as shown by the following reasoning. As mentioned above, the diagonal terms of $\boldsymbol{M}$ are given by

$$M_{ii} = 1 - \rho_i F_{ii} .$$

Recall from Equation 3.35 that all form factors sum to one, that is, $\sum_{j=1}^{N} F_{ij} = 1$. Therefore

$$|M_{ii}| = \sum_{j=1}^{N} F_{ij} - \rho_i F_{ii} .$$

Since $\rho_i < 1$, for all i we have $F_{ij} > \rho_i F_{ij}$, and

$$|M_{ii}| > \sum_{j=1}^{N} \rho_i F_{ij} - \rho_i F_{ii} = \sum_{\substack{j=1 \\ j \neq i}}^{N} \rho_i F_{ij} \tag{3.46}$$

$$|M_{ii}| > \sum_{\substack{j=1 \\ j \neq i}}^{N} |M_{ij}| \tag{3.47}$$

This last inequality is obtained simply by noting that when $i \neq j$, $M_{ij} = -\rho_i F_{ij}$. Therefore the radiosity matrix is always strictly diagonally dominant, and Gauss-Seidel relaxation will converge for any choice of the vector of initial radiosities $\boldsymbol{B}^{(0)}$. A common choice is to use the exitance value of a patch as a first guess for its radiosity

$$B_i^{(0)} = E_i \,.$$

The property of diagonal dominance will also prove very useful in Section 4.1 when considering the convergence of alternate formulations of the solution process.

3.2.2 Treatment of color

The discussion so far has considered a single wavelength λ. However, radiances and radiosities in the preceding text are actually spectral quantities, defined per unit wavelength. In fact, as mentioned in Section 2.1.2, all relevant quantities generally have some dependence on wavelength.

However, for radiation in the visible spectrum of light, there is usually no exchange of energy between different wavelengths; that is, light received at one particular wavelength is not reemitted at another wavelength. *Fluorescence*, the ability to reflect light in a different wavelength, does exist in nature but is not considered in the radiosity method.

The usual way to solve for the complete spectral radiosities is to discretize the spectrum of interest—that is, the range of relevant wavelengths—into a number of wavelength bands, within which a constant spectral radiosity is assumed. A whole system of equations such as 3.18 can then be assembled for each selected wavelength, using the specific values of the reflectances and exitances for that wavelength.

The solution obtained after solving all the systems of equations is a vector of radiosity values for each patch. These vectors represent the spectrum of the radiosity function for the patch. There are several ways of mapping such a spectrum to a color that can be displayed on a monitor, some of which are described in the Appendix (Section A.1.3). Most implementations use three wavelength channels and map these channels directly to the red, green, and blue input channels of the display monitors.

Note that the form factors can be shared by all wavelength channels, as they depend solely on the geometry of the scene.

Color bleeding

As mentioned in Section 2.1.4, the radiosity method can simulate an effect called color bleeding, which is the transfer of color via reflection on a colored surface [68]. Since all patches in the scene have the same status with respect to the simulation, they all play the role of light emitters. The color of the reflected light depends directly upon the spectral characteristics of the material; therefore objects are seen as colored light sources for the purpose of illuminating other objects. For instance, in Color Plate 6, a reddish tint can be observed on the white wall in the back, due to the light reflected from the red wall. Similarly the presence of the green wall on the right creates a greenish coloration towards the right of the small box.

3.2.3 Display and image generation

The last step of the radiosity process, displaying the results, can take many different forms. A view of the scene can be generated given viewing parameters, and using the radiosities as input to a variety of shaders. The simplest one is a *flat shader*, which in effect paints each patch with the appropriate color, based on the radiosity value. However, for image synthesis applications, more elaborate shaders are generally desired. For example, the appearance of the image can be greatly enhanced by computing a continuous shading across the surfaces, even though the computation was carried out under the assumption of a constant radiosity per patch.

Obtaining a continuous shading from the radiosities

When the patches are arranged in a regular mesh, radiosity values can be generated at the vertices of the mesh, which can then be interpolated across the area of the patches. In fact, simple bilinear interpolation is even performed in hardware on most modern graphics-oriented computers (a functionality called *Gouraud shading*).

Consider the example shown in Figure 3.7. A radiosity value can be computed for all internal vertices of the mesh using straightforward averaging between neighboring patches. However, external vertices, those lying on the border of the surface, require a little more attention. One possibility is to use the average radiosity of the available neighboring patches. An alternative would be to extrapolate a value based on neighboring patches and the values computed for internal vertices. Care must then be taken that the resulting value still represents a valid radiosity, which, for instance, must be a positive number.

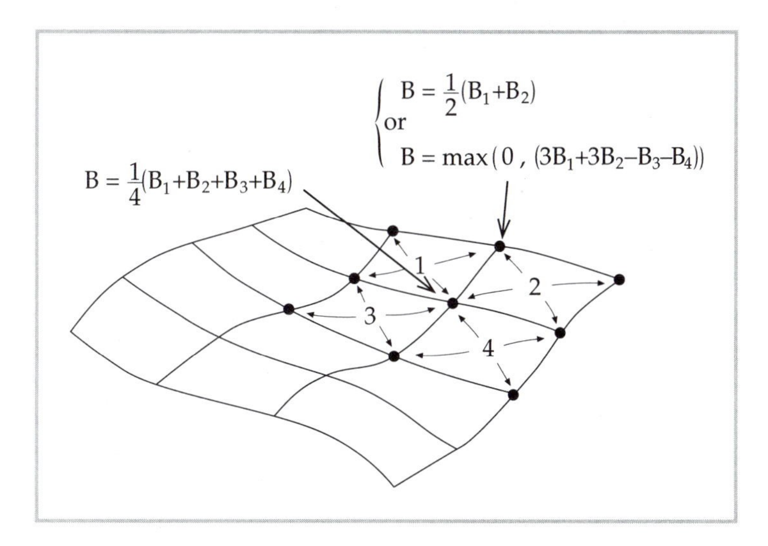

FIGURE 3.7 Obtaining radiosities at mesh vertices.

Although the image may look better, no additional information has been gained from continuous shading, and the results cannot be considered more accurate. A detailed study of the reconstruction process—the creation of a continuous radiosity function from a finite number of computed values—is presented in Section 5.4.

3.2.4 Cost considerations

It is easy to see that for a scene consisting of N patches, there are on the order of N^2 form factors, even though the actual number of independent form factors can be somewhat reduced by using, for example, the reciprocity relation (Equation 3.26). For each of the $\mathcal{O}(N^2)$ form factors, Equation 3.19 is used and requires the evaluation of the visibility function V. Simple occlusion testing can easily have $\mathcal{O}(N)$ complexity if the visibility of each patch is tested against all others. The computation of the form factor matrix has a high-degree polynomial time complexity and is likely to be a time-consuming process. In fact, the time needed for this computation is typically the major part of the total computation time. Even though the solution phase, consisting of solving the linear system, also has nontrivial complexity, the computational expense of the solution of the visibility problem dominates all other costs.

In addition, should one object be moved or have its geometry altered, all the form factors may have to be recomputed, because the change can alter the visibility between any two other patches. Incremental techniques permitting a minimal recomputation to deal with such modifications are presented in Chapter 6.

Fortunately the form factors are independent of all material properties and illumination conditions. Solutions of different illumination problems can be computed using the same set of form factors, as long as the geometry is not altered.

Even better, the radiosity solution is totally independent from the observer. We call the solution *view-independent* to emphasize that the results can be viewed from any position without further computation. The only effort consists of generating an image using the patches visible from a particular viewpoint and set of viewing conditions. This feature of the radiosity algorithm provides for interactive exploration programs where a user can "walk through" a virtual scene, as explained in Section 6.1.1.

Recall the simple flow chart shown in Figure 3.6, where inputs to the process are shown at the right. From that figure it is clear that once a radiosity solution has been computed, it is often possible to generate new solutions without having to redo all of the computation. If reflectances of exitances are modified, as is the case when a light source is switched on or off, a new system of radiosity equations is assembled using the preexisting form factors, and solved using Gauss-Seidel relaxation or another linear system solver. Viewing conditions, on the other hand, can be modified without having to recompute the radiosity solution. This property can be seen as a reward for the massive amount of computation carried out during the solution process.

On the other hand, it could also be argued that there is some waste in this huge amount of computation if only one view is desired. In that case, some of the computations might be more important than others since some patches will be far away or not visible at all. The notion of *importance* can be given a precise technical meaning, which will be developed in Section 4.5.

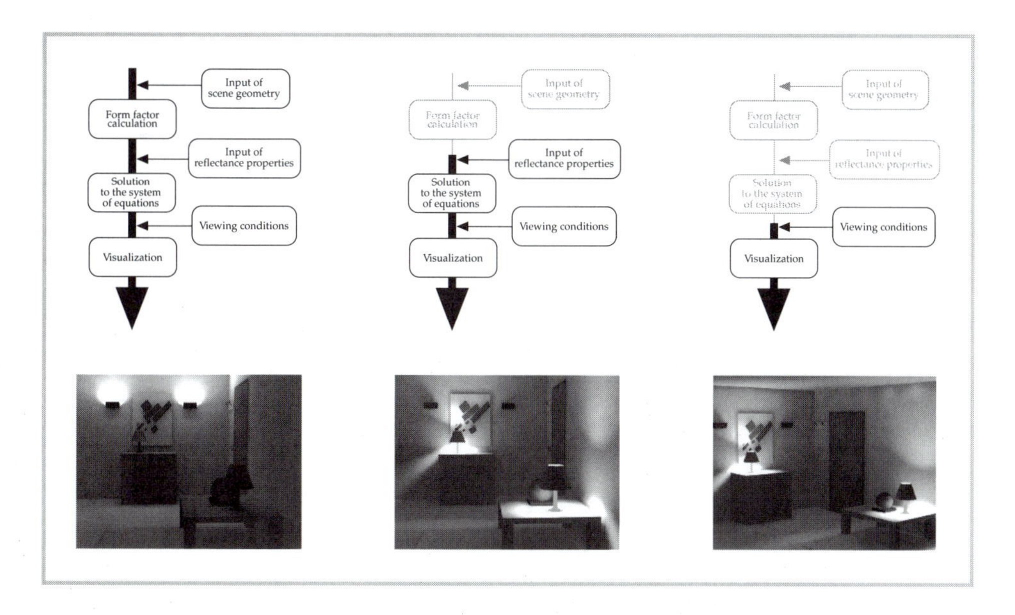

FIGURE 3.8 Computation required for Color Plates 1–3.

Figure 3.8 shows what computations were carried out to generate three images of a simple room (color versions can be found in the color section). The image on the left (Color Plate 1) was computed by running a complete radiosity algorithm. The middle image (Color Plate 2) required only a new radiosity solution and display, and the image on the right (Color Plate 3) only required the display step.

3.3 Computing the form factor

This section presents some common techniques for the computation of the form factor. As indicated in Section 3.2.4, such computations usually constitute the bulk of the computational effort in a radiosity simulation. Consequently the search for faster algorithms is an area of active research.

3.3.1 Unoccluded case

When two patches, P_i and P_j, are fully visible to each other, the form factor has the following expression, obtained by setting the visibility term to 1 in Equation 3.19

$$F_{ij} = \frac{1}{A_i} \int_{x \in P_i} \int_{y \in P_j} \frac{\cos\theta \cos\theta'}{\pi r^2} dy dx \,. \tag{3.48}$$

Direct integration

The integral in Equation 3.48 can only be computed directly for very simple arrangements. Tables of form factor expressions have been computed for many simple configurations and are available in the literature [87]. In most cases these integrals are obtained between primitive shapes such as axis-aligned rectangles, discs, and cylinders. However, it should be noted that even the conceptually simple case of two isolated polygons in space results in a very complex expression for the form factor [151]. For the simple arrangements shown in Figure 3.9, the form factors are given by the following expressions, using the notation

$$X = \frac{u}{w} \qquad Y = \frac{v}{w}.$$

Figure 3.9a shows a "pointwise" form factor from a point x to a disc perpendicular to the direction joining x to its center:

$$F_{x,\text{disc}} = \frac{u^2}{u^2 + v^2}. \tag{3.49}$$

Figure 3.9b shows a form factor between a surface element at point x and a parallel rectangle perpendicular to the direction joining x to one of its corners:

$$F_{x,\text{rect}} = \frac{1}{2\pi}\left[\frac{X}{\sqrt{1+X^2}}\tan^{-1}\left(\frac{Y}{\sqrt{1+X^2}}\right) + \frac{Y}{\sqrt{1+Y^2}}\tan^{-1}\left(\frac{X}{\sqrt{1+Y^2}}\right)\right]. \tag{3.50}$$

Figure 3.9c shows a form factor between two perpendicular rectangles having a common edge:[2]

$$\begin{aligned} F_{\perp} = \frac{1}{\pi X}\Bigg\{ & X\tan^{-1}\left(\frac{1}{X}\right) + Y\tan^{-1}\left(\frac{1}{Y}\right) \\ & - \sqrt{X^2+Y^2}\tan^{-1}\left(\frac{1}{\sqrt{X^2+Y^2}}\right)\Bigg\} \\ + \frac{1}{4\pi X}\Bigg\{ & \ln\left[\frac{(1+X^2)(1+Y^2)}{1+X^2+Y^2}\right] + X^2\ln\left[\frac{X^2(1+X^2+Y^2)}{(1+X^2)(X^2+Y^2)}\right] \\ + Y^2 & \ln\left[\frac{Y^2(1+X^2+Y^2)}{(1+Y^2)(X^2+Y^2)}\right]\Bigg\}. \end{aligned} \tag{3.51}$$

[2]Note that this situation is similar to the one presented earlier in Figure 3.2, where no analytic solution was available for the radiosity function. The difference here is that the radiosity function is assumed constant, which makes it possible to compute the geometric integral representing the form factor.

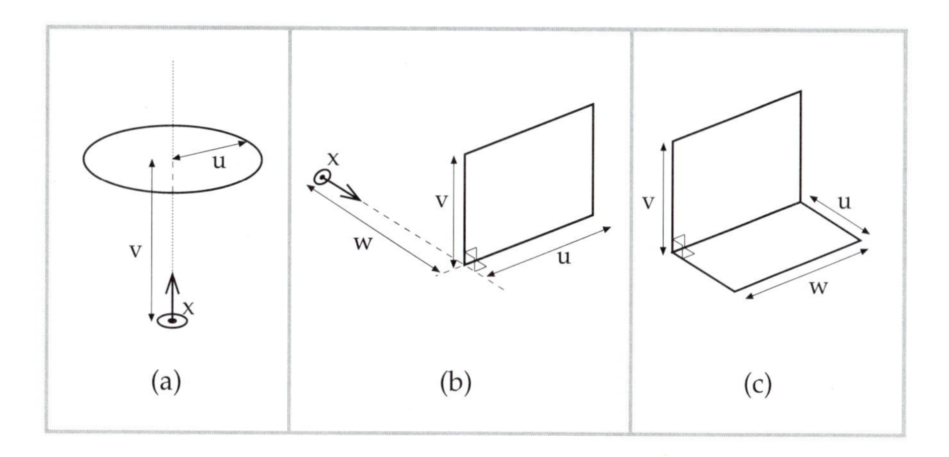

FIGURE 3.9 Some examples for which the form factor integral can be computed analytically.

Contour integration

Using Stokes' theorem, the area integrals in Equation 3.48 can be transformed into contour integrals over the boundaries of the two patches. The actual derivation is not repeated here, which yields the following expression for the form factor [86]:

$$F_{ij} = \frac{1}{2\pi A_i} \oint_{C_i} \oint_{C_j} \ln r \quad d\vec{x} \cdot d\vec{y} \,. \tag{3.52}$$

C_i and C_j are the contours of patches P_i and P_j, and $d\vec{x}$ and $d\vec{y}$ are differential vectors along these contours, as shown on Figure 3.10. The above integral can be evaluated relatively easily using quadrature methods in the case of polygonal contours, particularly for special situations such as those with parallel or perpendicular polygons.

The integration in Equation 3.52 must be carried out carefully to avoid the singularity as $r \to 0$. This occurs when two surface patches are in contact with each other. In this case, although the kernel of the integral can diverge, the integral itself is always defined [148].

Angle formula

In the case of polygonal patches, contour integration can be carried out explicitly along polygon edges. When estimating the radiosity at a particular point x on a surface, the "point-to-patch" form factors introduced in Section 3.1.5 are used, and can be computed using the following formula

$$F_{x,P} = \frac{1}{2\pi} \sum_{g \in G} \vec{n} \cdot \vec{\Gamma}_g \,, \tag{3.53}$$

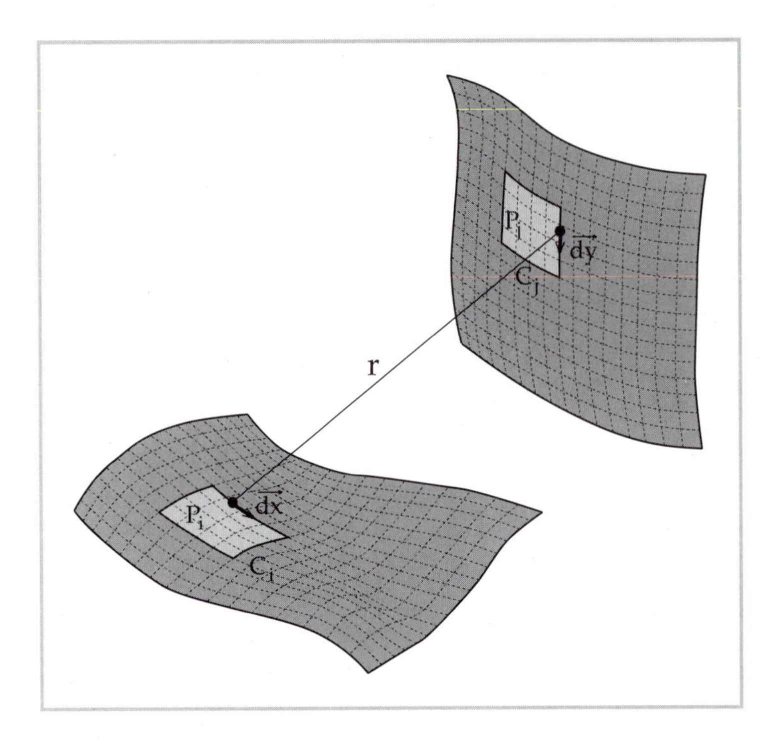

FIGURE 3.10 Contours used to integrate the form factor.

where $\vec{n}$ is the normal vector of the surface at point x, G is the set of vertices of the polygon, $\vec{R}_g$ is a vector from x to vertex number g of patch P, and $\vec{\Gamma}_g$ is a vector oriented in the direction of the cross product $\vec{R}_g \wedge \vec{R}_{g+1}$, with magnitude equal to the angle γ_g (notations are shown in Figure 3.11). To obtain this formula, a single contour integral is computed around patch P, as a sum of integrals along each edge of P [86].

Formula 3.53 can be used to compute the form factor to an arbitrarily oriented polygon. Note however that only the pointwise form factor from x to the polygon is given, and that no such closed-form expression is available for the form factor between two polygons.

Form factor algebra

Form factors between surfaces are not all independent. They are linked by several relations discussed in Section 3.1.6, such as reciprocity (Equation 3.26) and additivity (Equation 3.35). Furthermore the structure of the form factor integral implies other symmetry relationships. In some symmetrical arrangements it is possible to establish a one-to-one correspondence between differential elements in two different form factor integrals. A simple relationship between the corresponding form factors follows. In the situations depicted in Figure 3.12, a simple exchange of integration variables shows that the double integrals

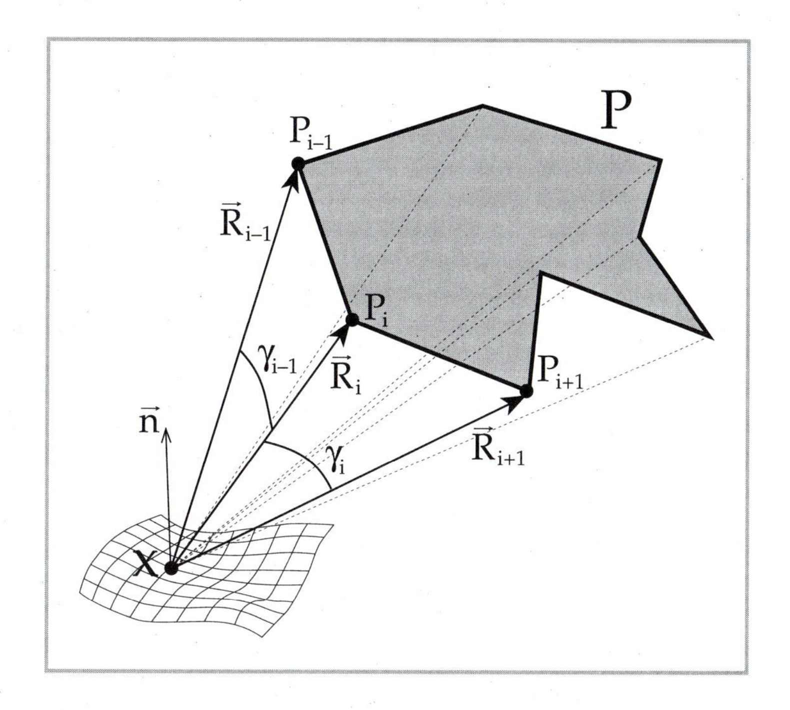

FIGURE 3.11 Analytic formula for the unoccluded form factor between a point and a polygonal patch.

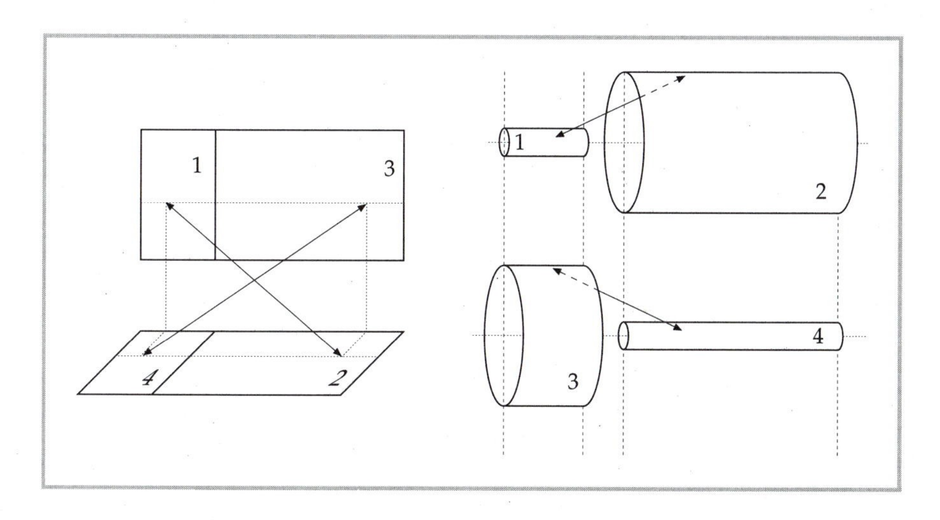

FIGURE 3.12 The Yamauti principle exploits the symmetry of the form factor integral (after Brewster [18]).

in the form factor expressions for F_{12} and F_{34} are equal. Thus

$$A_1 F_{12} = A_3 F_{34}\,. \tag{3.54}$$

This way of using the symmetry between two form factor integrals is known as the *Yamauti principle* or the *reciprocity theorem* [86]. It can be used to compute unknown form factors from known ones, a process commonly referred to as *form factor algebra.* As an example, consider the computation of the form factor F_{12} between the two rectangles in Figure 3.12. We start by introducing two new rectangles, numbered 5 and 6 in Figure 3.13, and computing the form factor F_{52}. Note that the form factor between two rectangles in perpendicular planes that share a common edge is known (from Equation 3.51). Therefore a number of form factors are readily obtained: in particular F_{87}, F_{54}, and F_{62} since patch 8 is the union of patches 4 and 2, and patch 7 is the union of patches 5 and 6.

Using the simple properties of the form factor, the following transformations can be applied to the known form factor F_{87}:

$$F_{87} = F_{85} + F_{86} \tag{3.55}$$

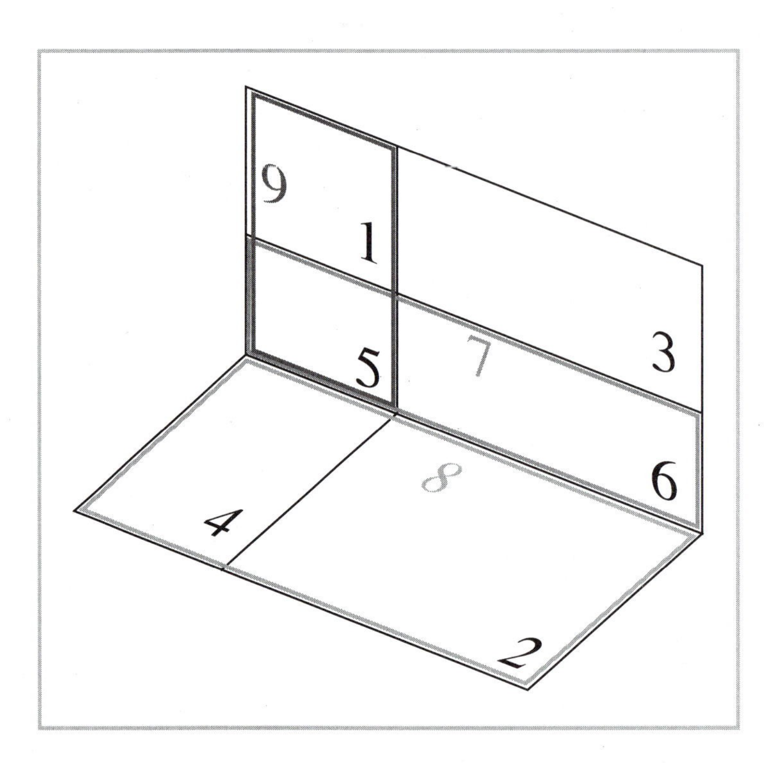

FIGURE 3.13 An example of form factor algebra. Larger patches are defined by $7 = 5 \cup 6$, $8 = 4 \cup 2$, and $9 = 1 \cup 5$.

$$= \frac{A_5}{A_8} F_{58} + \frac{A_6}{A_8} F_{68} \quad (3.56)$$

$$= \frac{A_5}{A_8} (F_{54} + F_{52}) + \frac{A_6}{A_8} (F_{62} + F_{64}) \,. \quad (3.57)$$

Using Equation 3.54 to relate F_{64} and F_{52}, an equation is formed where all form factors but F_{52} are known. This equation is easily solved for F_{52} to yield

$$F_{52} = \frac{A_8 F_{87} - A_5 F_{54} - A_6 F_{62}}{A_5} \,. \quad (3.58)$$

The form factor between the union of patches 1 and 5, called patch 9, and patch 2, can be computed in the same manner. The final result is obtained by combining these two factors using Equation 3.34 to yield

$$F_{12} = \frac{A_9 F_{92} - A_5 F_{52}}{A_1} \,.$$

Although the Yamauti principle and form factor algebra provide interesting alternatives to the brute force computation of form factors, a careful analysis of the involved symmetries must be carried out, making it difficult to apply them automatically.

3.3.2 Projection methods

In the general case, the visibility function V must be present in the expression of the form factor, and must somehow be evaluated. In this evaluation, an interesting geometrical property of the form factor, used for a long time in the context of thermal analysis, can provide an advantage.

When two surface patches are distant from each other, relative to their size, the inner integral in the form factor definition (Equation 3.19),

$$F_{ij} = \frac{1}{A_i} \int_{x \in P_i} \int_{y \in P_j} \frac{\cos\theta \cos\theta'}{\pi r^2} V(x, y) dy dx \,,$$

varies very little across the surface of patch P_i, so that the effect of the outer integral is merely a multiplication by 1. In such a case, the form factor can be computed as that from a point (a differential area) to a finite area.

When the above assumption does not hold, one can imagine subdividing patch P_i into smaller subpatches to enforce the condition, and then combining the results using the area-weighted average of Equation 3.34. In this way the problem of computing form factors between distant finite areas is reduced to the somewhat simpler problem of computing form factors between points and finite areas.

Nusselt's Analogy

An alternate formulation of the form factor can be obtained by looking back at the definition of the incident flux density H on a surface, given by Equation 3.6,

$$H(x) = \int_{\Omega} L_i(x, \theta, \phi) \cos\theta d\omega .$$

Comparing the simple energy balance equation (Equation 3.8)

$$B(x) = E(x) + \rho_d(x) H(x)$$

with the expanded equation (Equation 3.14)

$$B(x) = E(x) + \rho_d(x) \sum_{j=1}^{N} B_j \int_{y \in P_j} \frac{\cos\theta \cos\theta'}{\pi r^2} V(x, y) dy ,$$

we obtain an expression for the pointwise form factor (introduced in Section 3.1.5) from point x to a given patch P. It is the following integral over the solid angle subtended by patch P:

$$F_{x,P} = \frac{1}{\pi} \int_{\Omega_P} \cos\theta d\omega . \tag{3.59}$$

Here Ω_P represents the set of directions that allow x to see a point on P.

A simple geometrical construction can be derived from Equation 3.59. A solid angle was defined in Chapter 2 as the surface area on the unit sphere centered at the origin that is covered by the projection of the surface of interest (Section 2.1.1). For a given infinitesimal area on the unit sphere, multiplication by $\cos\theta$ yields the projected area onto the base plane (Figure 3.14). Division by π can be interpreted as division by the area of the unit disc. This construction leads to an alternate definition of the form factor from a point to a finite surface patch, called *Nusselt's analogy* [126]:

> $F_{x,P}$ is the fraction of the area of the unit disc in the base plane obtained by projecting surface patch P onto the unit hemisphere Ω centered at point x, and then orthogonally down onto the base plane.

Here the "base plane" is simply the tangent plane of the surface at point x.

It follows from the above definition that two surfaces sharing the same projection on Ω share the same form factor from x. In other words, the form factor from x to a given surface depends only on the projection of that surface onto the hemisphere Ω. Figure 3.14 shows Nusselt's construction, and a set of surfaces that would all result in the same form factor from x.

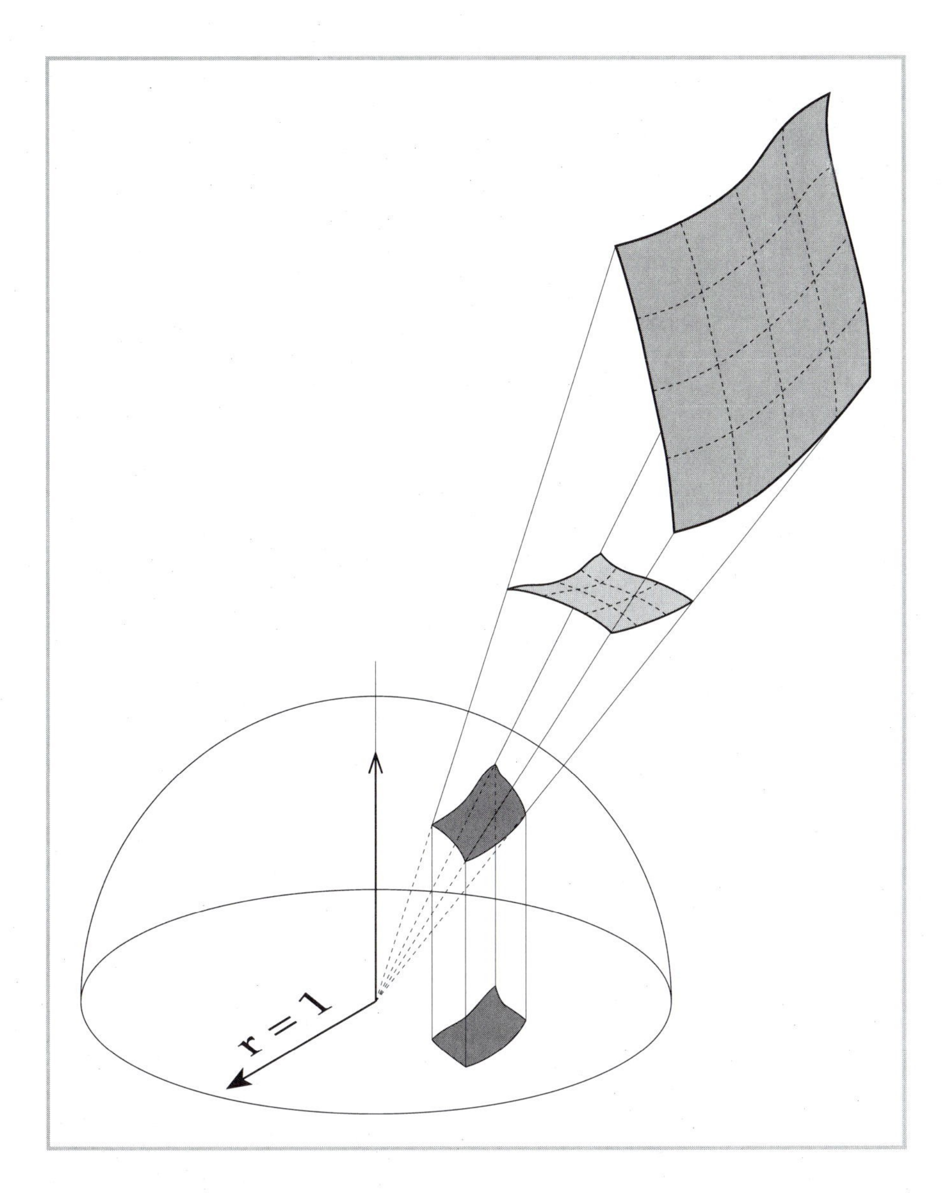

FIGURE 3.14 Nusselt's analogy provides a geometrical illustration of the form factor.

Algorithms based on Nusselt's analogy

Several algorithms have been developed to take direct advantage of Nusselt's analogy. In particular, before the advent of computers, photographic methods were introduced whereby a fish-eye lens was used to account for the spherical projection. Form factors were then determined from the area occupied by each object on the photograph. Since then, computer simulations of this process have been proposed [115]. One such process generates random positions on the unit disc, then fires rays from the origin through the point on the unit hemisphere that projects onto the disc point. The first surface encountered by the ray is the one that is visible in that direction.

Perhaps the main benefit of Nusselt's analogy is that it helps understand that any surface can be used for projection to determine the visible areas, not necessarily a hemisphere. In particular, the *hemi-cube* formulation presented in the next section makes the projection particularly easy since planar faces are used.

3.3.3 The hemi-cube

Nusselt's construction can be transformed into a computational algorithm by assuming that the unit hemisphere is discretized into a number of "cells," corresponding to small areas on its surface. Then a small contribution to the form factor can be computed for each cell, called a *delta-form factor*. This is simply the area of the cell multiplied by $\cos\theta$ and divided by π. If a surface is projected onto the hemisphere, the corresponding point-to-patch form factor is obtained by adding together the delta-form factors of all cells within the projection.

The direct implementation of the above idea is not very practical due to the problem of sphere discretization and the computation of the visibility function. The first computational algorithm introduced in computer graphics, the hemi-cube, solves both of these problems at once [37]. Consider a cube centered around the point from which form factors are to be computed. As shown in Figure 3.14, any two surfaces sharing the same projection on this cube will also share the same projection on the unit hemisphere, and therefore the same form factor. Since only the half-space above the surface of interest is relevant, a half-cube or hemi-cube is used as a projection surface, as shown in Figure 3.15.

The faces of the hemi-cube are easily discretized into a number of square cells, for which a delta-form factor ΔF can be computed analytically. In practice an approximation can be used safely since the area ΔA of a cell is usually very small compared to unity. With the notation of Figure 3.16, the following formulas are derived from Equation 3.25 by assuming a constant integrand.

- For a cell on the top face of the hemi-cube:

$$\Delta F = \frac{\Delta A}{\pi(1 + x^2 + y^2)^2} . \tag{3.60}$$

- For a cell on a side face of the hemi-cube:

$$\Delta F = \frac{z\Delta A}{\pi(1 + z^2 + y^2)^2} . \tag{3.61}$$

Each face of the hemi-cube is used in turn as a projection surface to determine visibility, by means of an *item buffer*. An item buffer is an array of patch identifiers—one

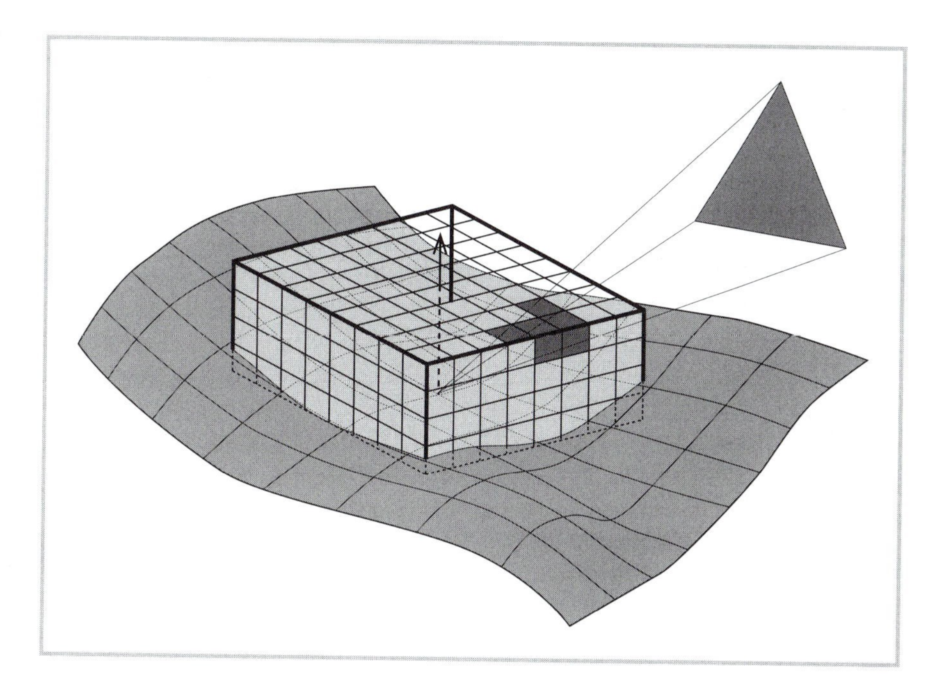

FIGURE 3.15 The hemi-cube.

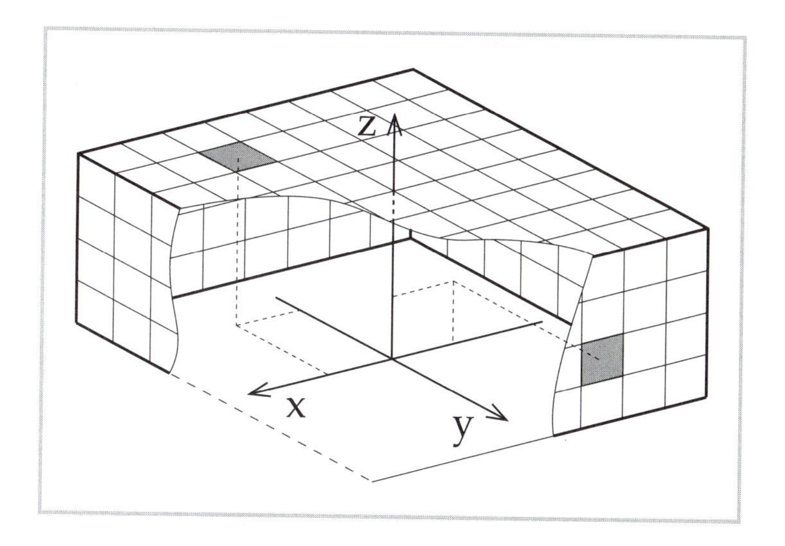

FIGURE 3.16 Computation of the delta-form factors.

for each hemi-cube cell—that records the visible surface for the direction of each cell. It is constructed by following the common z-buffer strategy, whereby all surfaces are projected in turn onto the face. For each cell intersected by the projection, the distance to the projected surface is computed and compared to the distance previously recorded for that cell. Each patch is given a number from 1 to N. If the patch being projected is closer than the recorded distance, its number is recorded in the item buffer and its distance in the z-buffer. The sole difference with the usual z-buffer technique is that the patch (or "item") number of the nearest patch is kept rather than the patch color. The closest surface patch visible through each cell is thus determined, and after all patches have been projected, the item buffers contain all the relevant visibility information. The accuracy of this information naturally depends on the hemi-cube resolution.

The form factors to all surfaces are then computed at once. Each hemi-cube cell contributes its delta-form factor to the form factor with its visible patch. The form factor to a given patch is obtained by summing the delta-form factors corresponding to all the cells covered by the projection of the patch. In other words, if $C(j)$ is the set of hemi-cube cells through which patch P_j is visible, then

$$F_{x,P_j} = \sum_{q \in C(j)} \Delta F_q .$$

Pros and cons of the hemi-cube

The main problem with the hemi-cube is its limited resolution. Whatever the complexity of the scene, if there are N_c hemi-cube cells, no more than N_c patches will have a non-zero form factor from any given point since only N_c delta-form factors can be assigned. This quantization problem can lead to severe inaccuracies. Note that the use of a regular sampling pattern on the faces of the hemi-cube is not necessarily optimal, and other sampling strategies can produce more accurate results for a given number of cells [113]. Other deficiencies of the hemi-cube algorithm are listed in Section 5.1.1.

Despite this drawback, the hemi-cube is appealing because of its simplicity. Furthermore, hidden-surface elimination algorithms implemented in hardware can be used to compute the item buffer for the faces of the hemi-cube quickly at the cost of limited precision (because of the limited resolutions of the hemi-cube itself and of the hardware z-buffer). Section 5.1.2 reviews some of the other choices for the computation of form factors.

❐ ❐ ❐

This chapter presented the essence of the radiosity method. This basic formulation offers a solution to the restricted problem of global illumination with ideal diffuse reflectors, and introduces all the concepts that will be built upon to derive more elaborate simulation techniques. The key notion of form factor was introduced, and the formulation of the global illumination problem as a matrix equation was proposed. The computational strategy for radiosity simulation follows naturally, whereby form factors are computed first to assemble the matrix, an iterative solution technique is then used to compute radiosity values, and finally the results are displayed. Simple techniques for the computation of form factors were presented, including the widely used hemi-cube algorithm. More accurate methods will be discussed in Chapter 5.

CHAPTER 4

Managing the complexity

The basic radiosity method is a computationally intensive process, especially since it requires the entire matrix of form factors to be computed before a solution can be obtained. Alternative strategies that reduce the size and complexity of the problem are presented in this chapter. Since computation of the form factor matrix constitutes the bulk of the work, useful variations of the algorithm attempt to reduce the number of form factors that need to be computed.

One possible avenue consists of reducing the number of surface patches in the scene. However, as the next chapter explains, the accuracy of the radiosity computation is directly dependent on the number and placement of the discrete patches used to represent the surfaces. Improved meshing techniques can be viewed as an attempt to reduce the number of patches needed to arrive at a solution within a given error bound, and these are also discussed in Chapter 5. In this chapter another approach is taken to reduce the complexity of the calculation: given a particular discretization of the surfaces, means are sought that simplify the representation of energy transfers.

The *progressive refinement* technique considers the emission of energy from each individual patch in turn, producing a useful image at each iteration. The granularity of the calculation is reduced since the form factor matrix is computed one row at a time. *Substructuring* and *adaptive refinement* techniques attempt to simplify the radiosity problem for a given number of elements, by computing energy exchanges with groups of patches at once. The result is a smaller, rectangular form factor matrix. *Hierarchical* methods extend this idea by computing energy exchanges at various hierarchical levels and condensing entire blocks of the form factor matrix for even greater simplification.

Finally, the consideration of how the simulation will be used allows further simplifications of the radiosity process. *Importance methods* allow selective refinement of the calculation in view of a particular goal.

Most techniques presented in this chapter have an impact on both the complexity of the algorithm and its accuracy; therefore there is a strong coupling between this chapter and the following one.

4.1 Progressive refinement radiosity solution

One problem with the radiosity computational process introduced in Chapter 3 is that the entire matrix of form factors must be computed and stored before the Gauss-Seidel iteration method can produce a solution. Thus the basic radiosity algorithm requires $O(N^3)$ computation time and $O(N^2)$ storage space. Fortunately other matrix solution techniques are available. A particular reformulation of the solution process has become very popular because it generates intermediate solutions that let the user monitor the progress of the simulation. This formulation is based on the *Southwell relaxation* method and yields a progressive refinement radiosity algorithm, where an approximate solution is continually updated to smoothly converge towards the expected solution [36, 121]. Note however that convergence to the actual solution is not any faster than with the Gauss-Seidel solution method.

4.1.1 The radiosity solution process revisited

Recall that the radiosity equation has the form

$$\boldsymbol{MB} = \boldsymbol{E} \qquad \text{with} \quad M_{ij} = \delta_{ij} - \rho_i F_{ij} . \tag{4.1}$$

The use of Gauss-Seidel relaxation in Chapter 3 was justified from a numerical point of view because the radiosity matrix is diagonally dominant, a property that guarantees fast convergence. However, in the case of radiosity calculations, the most expensive portion of the computation is the evaluation of the form factors F_{ij}. The iterative solution typically takes up only a relatively small fraction (say a few percent) of the total computation time.

Other numerical solution techniques are available; some are better suited to the radiosity problem, since they can produce approximate solutions without computing the entire matrix. An example is the Southwell relaxation technique, which attempts to maximize the efficiency of each iteration step in order to increase the initial rate of convergence. While Gauss-Seidel iteration is widely used and thoroughly documented, Southwell relaxation is less known, and is presented in detail below.

Southwell relaxation

Recall that Gauss-Seidel relaxation repeatedly computes a new estimate of the radiosities by extracting from each of the N linear radiosity equations a new approximation for the radiosity value at a single patch. Southwell relaxation also computes new approximations of the radiosities by repeatedly solving one linear equation at a time, but the choice of the particular equation to use is based on a comparison of the estimated efficiency of all possible choices. In the case of radiosity exchanges, these comparisons are most meaningful if performed on energy values (emitted by the whole patch), as opposed to radiosity values (energy per unit area).[1] Therefore we start by rewriting the radiosity equation in terms of energy values per patch. We define new vectors β and ε such that

$$\beta_i = A_i B_i \qquad \text{total energy leaving patch } i$$
$$\varepsilon_i = A_i E_i \qquad \text{energy emitted by patch } i\,.$$

The radiosity equation can now be written

$$\boldsymbol{K}\beta = \varepsilon\,, \qquad \text{with} \quad K_{ij} = \frac{A_i}{A_j} M_{ij} = \delta_{ij} - \rho_i F_{ji}\,. \tag{4.2}$$

Note that the expression for the elements of matrix $\boldsymbol{K}$ involves F_{ji} instead of F_{ij} as in matrix $\boldsymbol{M}$. This transposition of indices is possible because of the reciprocity relation (Section 3.1.6). The Southwell and Gauss-Seidel relaxation procedures both belong to a general class of iterative techniques known as *relaxation methods*. These methods work by iteratively computing a series of approximations to the actual solution β, denoted by $\beta^{(k)}$. Since $\beta^{(k)}$ is only an approximation of the exact solution, a *residual* vector can be defined as

$$\boldsymbol{r}^{(k)} = \varepsilon - \boldsymbol{K}\beta^{(k)}\,, \tag{4.3}$$

which allows us to assess the quality of the approximation $\beta^{(k)}$. If $\beta^{(k)}$ converges towards the actual solution as $k \to \infty$, the residual will vanish.

Relaxation methods compute a new approximation vector $\beta^{(k+1)}$ at each step by modifying a single component of the vector $\beta^{(k)}$ in such a way that one of the components of the residual becomes zero. Even though the other components of the residual vector might increase in magnitude during this operation, the hope is that eventually all elements of the residual will converge to zero. Relaxation thus means adjusting the value of a selected component of the variable vector so that the associated residual cancels out.

Gauss-Seidel relaxation relaxes each coordinate in turn, sweeping through all indices in a regular manner. Thus one global iteration of the Gauss-Seidel method (the sequence of operations needed to update all variables) consists of N relaxation steps.[2]

---

[1] All dimensions should be understood as per unit time, since, strictly speaking, either *power* or *flux density* (power per unit area) values are used in the physical equations. The term *energy* is used here because of its intuitive meaning, without prejudice, since time plays no role in the radiosity process we are interested in.

[2] The notation adopted here is slightly different from that of Section 3.2.1, where the index k measured the number of global iterations performed.

In contrast, Southwell relaxation always chooses the coordinate i, which corresponds to the largest residual component, and relaxes the corresponding variable $\beta_i^{(k)}$. Therefore variables are updated in a different order, and in fact it is difficult to predict when a particular variable will be updated. Suppose that at step k, the largest residual component is $r_i^{(k)}$ for a particular i. Requiring that this component of the residual must vanish at step $k+1$ yields an equation on the vector of variables $\beta^{(k)}$:

$$0 = r_i^{(k+1)} \tag{4.4}$$

$$= \varepsilon_i - \sum_{j=1}^{N} K_{ij} \beta_j^{(k+1)} . \tag{4.5}$$

Since only one component β_i of the vector β is modified, we have for all $j \neq i$ $\beta_j^{(k+1)} = \beta_j^{(k)}$. Thus the new value of $\beta_i^{(k+1)}$ can be extracted from Equation 4.5:

$$\beta_i^{(k+1)} = \frac{1}{K_{ii}} \left(\varepsilon_i - \sum_{j \neq i} K_{ij} \beta_j^{(k)} \right) . \tag{4.6}$$

The equivalent formula

$$\beta_i^{(k+1)} = \beta_i^{(k)} + \frac{r_i^{(k)}}{K_{ii}} \tag{4.7}$$

is found by factoring out the definition of the residual from Equation 4.3. The effect of this relaxation step on the residual, in addition to setting its ith component to zero, is a modification of all other components. The definition of the residual shows that

$$\boldsymbol{r}^{(k+1)} = \varepsilon - \boldsymbol{K}\beta^{(k+1)} \tag{4.8}$$

$$= \boldsymbol{r}^{(k)} - \boldsymbol{K}(\beta^{(k+1)} - \beta^{(k)}) \tag{4.9}$$

since $\boldsymbol{r}^{(k)} = \varepsilon - \boldsymbol{K}\beta^{(k)}$. Only one component of $\beta^{(k)}$ was modified by the relaxation step, thus $(\beta^{(k+1)} - \beta^{(k)})$ has only one non-zero component (that with index i), and only one column of matrix $\boldsymbol{K}$ is needed to update all residual values. Combining Equations 4.7 and 4.9, the expression of the new residual becomes

$$r_j^{(k+1)} = r_j^{(k)} - \frac{K_{ji}}{K_{ii}} r_i^{(k)} . \tag{4.10}$$

In summary, the Southwell relaxation procedure functions as follows. Given a current estimate of the solution $\beta^{(k)}$ and the associated residual $\boldsymbol{r}^{(k)}$, the index i of the residual component with greatest absolute value is identified. The solution estimate $\beta_i^{(k+1)}$ is then computed according to Equation 4.7, and all residual components are updated using Equation 4.10. During each iteration, a single column of the matrix $\boldsymbol{K}$ is needed; thus only one row of form factors must be computed.

An initial approximation vector $\beta^{(0)}$ must be chosen before the relaxation procedure is started. A simple choice is to use a vector with all coordinates set to zero. As a consequence the initial residual $\boldsymbol{r}^{(0)}$ is equal to the vector of emitted energies, which allows a fruitful physical interpretation explained later in Section 4.1.3. However, the choice of the initial conditions is in fact arbitrary; the next section will show that the relaxation procedure converges for all possible initial vectors [69].

4.1.2 Proof of convergence

Consider the vector norm (1-norm) defined by

$$\|\boldsymbol{r}^{(k)}\| = \sum_{j=1}^{N} |r_j^{(k)}| .$$

In order to prove that Southwell relaxation converges for radiosity matrices, it suffices to establish that

$$\lim_{k \to \infty} \|\boldsymbol{r}^{(k)}\| = 0 .$$

Equation 4.10 shows that

$$\|\boldsymbol{r}^{(k+1)}\| = \sum_{j \neq i} |r_j^{(k)} - \frac{K_{ji}}{K_{ii}} r_i^{(k)}| \qquad \text{since } r_i^{(k+1)} = 0 . \tag{4.11}$$

Therefore

$$\|\boldsymbol{r}^{(k+1)}\| \leq \sum_{j \neq i} |r_j^{(k)}| + \sum_{j \neq i} |\frac{K_{ji}}{K_{ii}} r_i^{(k)}| \tag{4.12}$$

$$\leq \|\boldsymbol{r}^{(k)}\| - |r_i^{(k)}| + |r_i^{(k)}| \sum_{j \neq i} |\frac{K_{ji}}{K_{ii}}| . \tag{4.13}$$

Using the derivation of the diagonal dominance property of matrix $\boldsymbol{M}$, presented in Section 3.2.1, a similar property concerning the columns of matrix $\boldsymbol{K}$ is easily established:

$$|K_{ii}| > \sum_{\substack{j=1 \\ j \neq i}}^{N} |K_{ji}| \qquad 1 \leq i \leq N . \tag{4.14}$$

Therefore a scalar value t exists such that

$$0 < t < 1 \qquad \text{and} \quad \sum_{j \neq i} \frac{K_{ji}}{K_{ii}} < t \quad \text{for} \quad 1 \leq i \leq N ,$$

and continuing from Equation 4.13

$$\|\boldsymbol{r}^{(k+1)}\| \leq \|\boldsymbol{r}^{(k)}\| - (1-t)|r_i^{(k)}| \,. \tag{4.15}$$

The index i was chosen so that $r_i^{(k)}$ is the largest component of the residual vector, therefore

$$\|\boldsymbol{r}^{(k)}\| \leq N|r_i^{(k)}| \,.$$

Multiplying both sides by $(1-t)$ and dividing by N yields

$$(1-t)|r_i^{(k)}| \geq \frac{1-t}{N}\|\boldsymbol{r}^{(k)}\| \,. \tag{4.16}$$

Substituting Equation 4.16 into Equation 4.15, we have

$$\|\boldsymbol{r}^{(k+1)}\| \leq \left(1 - \frac{1-t}{N}\right)\|\boldsymbol{r}^{(k)}\| \,. \tag{4.17}$$

Let

$$T = 1 - \frac{1-t}{N} \,,$$

clearly $T < 1$, and

$$\|\boldsymbol{r}^{(k+1)}\| \leq T^{k+1}\|\boldsymbol{r}^{(0)}\| \,. \tag{4.18}$$

Since $\lim_{k\to\infty} T^{k+1}\|\boldsymbol{r}^{(0)}\| = 0$, we have established that $\lim_{k\to\infty}\|\boldsymbol{r}^{(k)}\| = 0$. This means that $\beta^{(k)}$ converges to a solution of the radiosity equation (Equation 4.2). Note that this proof is independent from the choice of the initial estimate $\beta^{(0)}$. Therefore the Southwell relaxation process applied to radiosity equations converges for all possible choices of initial conditions.

4.1.3 Physical interpretation of the Southwell relaxation process: propagating energy

Having shown that Southwell relaxation converges in the case of radiosity equations, let us rephrase this procedure using more familiar radiosity terminology. This will explain some of the important advantages of this approach.

It may not be obvious at this point why Southwell relaxation should be preferred to Gauss-Seidel relaxation. In both cases a single component of the solution estimate is updated by a relaxation step. However, in the case of Southwell relaxation, the residual $\boldsymbol{r}^{(k)}$ has an interesting physical meaning, and can be used to obtain a new approximation of all patch radiosities at each step.

Assume that the Southwell iterative process starts with an approximate solution vector consisting of null values. In that case the initial residual as given by Equation 4.3 is equal to the vector of emitted energies.[3] The first iteration selects the patch with the greatest residual component, that is, the patch with the most energy to emit. This first relaxation step computes a new estimate of the total energy value for that patch, such that the associated residual component becomes null. In addition, all patches that are visible from the selected patch see their residual change.

Looking back at Equation 4.10, and assuming for simplicity that form factors from a patch to itself are zero, the change in the residual value for all patches can be expressed as

$$r_j^{(k+1)} = r_j^{(k)} + \rho_j F_{ij} r_i^{(k)} \qquad j = 1 \ldots N . \tag{4.19}$$

Observing the difference between $r_j^{(k+1)}$ and $r_j^{(k)}$ for all patches P_j, it becomes apparent that the residual value of the selected patch i is "distributed" among all other patches according to the appropriate form factor and reflectivity values. Since the residual represents energy, an iteration simulates the propagation of energy from the selected patch.

The residual value for each patch can be interpreted as a measure of the energy that should be radiated from that patch in the environment. Initially this is simply the exitance term, multiplied by the patch's area. However, for each relaxation step, one patch radiates this energy into the environment, and as a consequence all other patches receive some new energy to be radiated. These energy values accumulate in the residual until the patch is selected for relaxation, at which point the residual is zeroed and the "total energy" value is updated to reflect the amount of energy radiated.

In other words, patches can be considered to exchange packets of energy to mimic the actual propagation process. Received energy contributions, attenuated by reflectance coefficients, are accumulated in the residual component to be radiated during a later iteration. Note that the selection of the radiating patch at each iteration is based on the amount of energy that each patch has accumulated *since it was last selected.*

Progressive refinement

The value of this physical interpretation is that it makes apparent the relevant information contained in the residual vector. Although the computation of all the total energy values β_i to high accuracy still requires many iterations, an estimate of the final values can be obtained at any time by considering the sum of β_i and its residual r_i. Equation 4.7 states that when an energy value is modified by a relaxation step, it is simply increased by the former residual (assuming $K_{ii} = 1$; in other words, that the form factor from a patch to itself is zero). Thus β_i represents the energy whose propagation has already been modeled by previous relaxation steps. Adding the energy that has not yet been propagated in the course of the

[3]The careful reader might have noticed that the initial vector of radiosities used in the Gauss-Seidel relaxation procedure in Section 3.2.1 was the vector of exitance values, whereas the initial radiosities here are all set to zero. According to the above proof of convergence, all possible initial conditions will produce the same solution. The particular choice made here affords a simple physical interpretation of the process.

relaxation procedure results in an improved estimate of the total energy radiated by the patch:

$$\beta_i'^{(k)} = \beta_i^{(k)} + r_i^{(k)} . \quad \textbf{(4.20)}$$

The values $\beta_i'^{(k)}$ and the corresponding radiosity estimate

$$B_i^{(k)} = \beta_i'^{(k)} / A_i$$

have been shown to converge rapidly towards the final solution in the early stages of the computation [36]. Note that all residual values are modified by a relaxation step. Thus a new estimate of the radiosity is obtained for all patches at each step. These can be used to continuously display a rendered scene as the solution is progressing. This is an example of a progressive refinement strategy for image rendering [16], whereby a crude estimate of the image is continuously improved over time until user input requires a restart of the solution process.

Gathering and shooting

In contrast to the Southwell relaxation procedure just described, the Gauss-Seidel technique solves for one radiosity value B_i at a time, based on the radiosities of all other patches, according to the following formula (first presented as Equation 3.43):

$$B_i^{(k+1)} = E_i + \rho_i \sum_{j=1}^{N} F_{ij} B_j^{(k)} . \quad \textbf{(4.21)}$$

This can be described as "gathering" light incoming from all other surfaces on patch P_i, since the summation considers the radiosity at all other patches. The Southwell relaxation technique updates the energy estimates of all patches according to the following formula, derived from Equation 4.19 (assuming patch P_i is selected for relaxation):

$$\beta_j'^{(k+1)} = \beta_j'^{(k)} + \rho_j F_{ij} r_i^{(k)} . \quad \textbf{(4.22)}$$

This time the procedure amounts to "shooting" energy from patch P_i towards all other patches. Thus instead of evaluating the contribution of all patches to the radiosity of one particular surface, the impact of one selected patch on all the surfaces is assessed. Figure 4.1 depicts how gathering and shooting use, respectively, a row of matrix $\boldsymbol{M}$ or a column of matrix $\boldsymbol{K}$. Note that because of reciprocity the same row of form factors $\left(F_{ij}\right)_{i=1,N}$ is used in both cases.

A *progressive refinement radiosity algorithm* therefore consists of performing the Southwell relaxation procedure, starting with an initial vector of null values. Although the above presentation was done using energy variables, the radiosity computation algorithms usually are expressed in terms of radiosity values, so as to be consistent with other

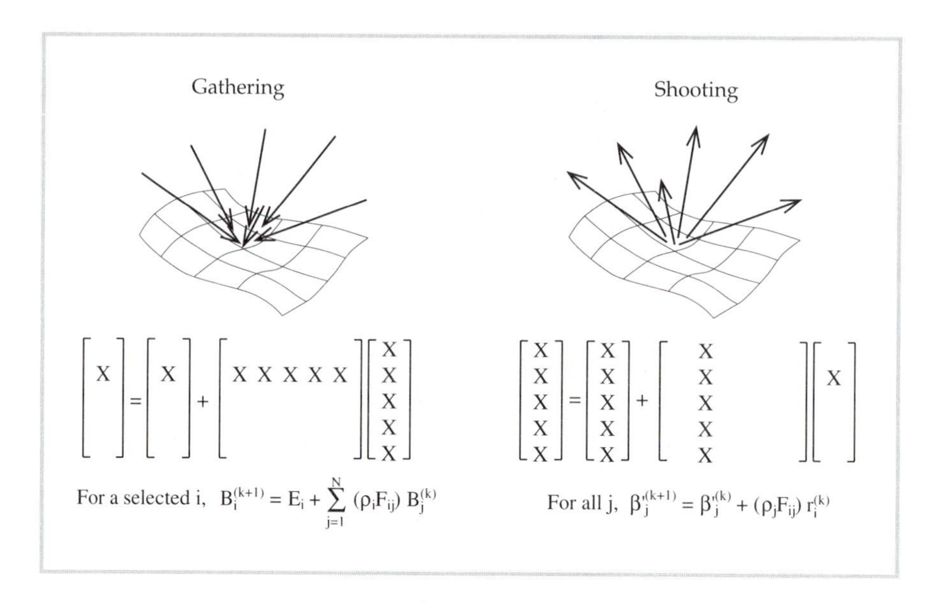

FIGURE 4.1 Gathering vs. shooting (after Cohen et al. [36]).

formulations. This is easily accomplished by dividing all relevant variables by the corresponding patch's area. Two variables are maintained for each patch, a radiosity

$$B_i \equiv \frac{\beta_i'^{(k)}}{A_i} = \frac{\beta_i^{(k)} + r_i^{(k)}}{A_i}$$

representing the current estimate of the final radiosity for that patch, and an "unshot radiosity"

$$\Delta B_i \equiv r_i^{(k)} / A_i \,,$$

which represents the amount of energy waiting to be propagated from that patch per unit area. A relaxation step thus comprises the following operations:

1 Select the next "shooting patch" P_i, that is, the one with the greatest residual $r_i^{(k)} = A_i \Delta B_i$.

2 Compute a row of form factors, for example, using a hemi-cube centered on P_i.

3 Update all radiosities and unshot radiosities using a modified version of Equation 4.19 that considers energy per unit area:

$$\Delta B_j \leftarrow \Delta B_j + \rho_j F_{ij} \frac{A_i}{A_j} \Delta B_i \qquad j = 1 \ldots N, j \neq i \tag{4.23}$$

$$\Delta B_i \leftarrow 0 \tag{4.24}$$

$$B_j \leftarrow B_j + \rho_j F_{ij} \frac{A_i}{A_j} \Delta B_i \qquad j = 1 \ldots N, j \neq i. \qquad \textbf{(4.25)}$$

Note that total radiosities are increased by the same amount as the unshot radiosities, since they represent the sum of an "already shot" radiosity portion (which remains unchanged) and the unshot radiosity term.

4 (optional) Display current estimate using the B_i values.

The ability to perform this last operation is one of the main benefits of this method. Since a new estimate of all radiosity values is computed at each step, a new image can be displayed after each iteration.The progress of the simulation can thus be monitored. Color Plate 9 shows intermediate images produced by the progressive refinement radiosity algorithm, after 1, 2, 24, and 100 iterations, respectively. The sequence of images gives a feel for the propagation of light starting from the light sources. Note that displaying an image is typically much faster than a relaxation step, and can often be performed in real time on a computer equipped with accelerated graphics hardware.

Equation 4.25 shows how the unshot radiosity values are updated using a row of the form factor matrix. It is worth noting that the reciprocity property of the form factors (Section 3.1.6) allows this equation to be rewritten using the form factor from the receiving patch to the shooting patch, in a manner more consistent with the traditional formulation presented in Equation 3.18:

$$\Delta B_j \leftarrow \Delta B_j + \rho_j F_{ji} \Delta B_i \qquad j = 1 \ldots N. \qquad \textbf{(4.26)}$$

The value of this expression is that it corresponds exactly to the formulation of the radiosity equation (with i and j swapped). The slightly different form of Equation 4.25 is closer to the actual computation, since in fact what is being computed at each iteration is a row of form factors $\{F_{ij}\}_{j=1..N}$.

The limit of the physical analogy

The presentation of the relaxation process as a simulation of light propagation is useful to acquire a feeling for how the algorithm works, but the analogy should not be pushed too far. For example, an examination of the energy exchanges modeled by this process seems to reveal a disturbing imbalance. Consider a scene containing a single primary emitter of light, with an initial energy value of E. The first relaxation step will consist of distributing this energy among all other surfaces, each of which will reflect some of it (that is, will add some of it, multiplied by its reflectance, to its *unshot energy* value). Thus some of this energy will reappear as unshot energy because of the first reflection. A fraction of this unshot energy will itself be reflected, and so on.

If the set of surfaces in the scene has an average reflectance of ρ_{ave}, then the unshot energy created on the surfaces by the first reflection will be on the order of $\rho_{\text{ave}} E$. On the second reflection, an average amount of $\rho_{\text{ave}}^2 E$ will be added to the unshot energy. After n reflections, an average of $\rho_{\text{ave}}^n E$ will be added. A global interreflection factor can be computed, based on the average reflectance of the scene, to account for all of these reflections:

$$R = 1 + \rho_{\text{ave}} + \rho_{\text{ave}}^2 + \rho_{\text{ave}}^3 + \ldots = \frac{1}{1 - \rho_{\text{ave}}}. \tag{4.27}$$

The total amount of energy distributed over the entire course of the relaxation procedure will be roughly RE, which is greater than the initial energy E since $R > 1$. This apparent contradiction stems from the fact that all of the computation is carried out on steady-state variables, which are all defined per unit time (power or flux density) and are assumed not to vary over time. A correct energy balance can only be carried out with time-integrated quantities, over some time interval.

Note that the "time" of the relaxation process (the sequence of relaxation steps) does not represent real time. In reality, propagation and reflection on all surfaces happen simultaneously. However, light is not reflected by a surface at the same time it is being emitted by the light source, since propagation occurs with a finite speed. Therefore, at any given time there is energy bouncing around the scene that has been emitted by the light source at various times in the past. There can be much more energy present in the scene than that emitted by the light source during a given time interval, because it has been introduced earlier (since we are assuming a steady state, energy has been received since "the beginning of time").

Adding an "ambient" correction

An additional adjustment can be used to enhance the appearance of the intermediate images produced by the progressive refinement algorithm, especially in the early stages of computation. The analogy with the physical process of light propagation shows that the energy estimates, and consequently the radiosity values, continuously increase during the relaxation procedure: starting with the local emitted energy and smoothly converging towards final values that take into account all interreflections of light. Therefore, if the approximate radiosities are used to display the scene during the solution, the image will be very dark in the beginning, progressively becoming brighter as more areas become illuminated. In particular, areas of the scene that are not directly visible from the light sources must rely on reflections to receive their illumination and may appear dramatically too dark during the early stages of the solution.

A clever suggestion to remedy this situation is to introduce an additional term in the radiosities used for display. The new term represents an estimate of the effect of subsequent shooting operations [36].

The total amount of unshot energy in the scene at a given stage of the solution is simply the sum of all residual terms,

$$U = \sum_{j=1}^{N} r_j^{(k)}.$$

An average reflectance for the environment is also computed. This is done by weighting each patch's reflectance according to its area:

$$\rho_{\text{ave}} = \frac{\sum_{i=1}^{N} A_i \rho_i}{\sum_{i=1}^{N} A_i} . \tag{4.28}$$

Since by definition the unshot energy has not yet been propagated into the scene, its effect on other surfaces has not been accounted for. Furthermore this energy, once released into the scene, will undergo several reflections. The global interreflection factor R defined by Equation 4.27 can be used to obtain an estimate, RU, of the total amount of energy that will be propagated in the scene during the later stages of the computation.

Ambient lighting has been used with success in a variety of rendering models to provide a minimal illumination to surfaces that are not directly visible from the light sources. This illumination acts as a crude estimate of the impact of global illumination effects such as multiple reflections. A similar idea is to "spread" the total unshot energy across all surfaces in the scene, to approximate the impact of the upcoming computation. Assuming this energy is "spread" equally across all surfaces in the scene, an average *ambient flux density* is computed by dividing the ambient energy by the total surface area of the scene,

$$H = \frac{RU}{\sum_{i=1}^{N} A_i} .$$

Each patch is then considered to be subjected to this ambient illumination, resulting in a radiosity correction ΔB_i given by

$$\Delta B_i = \rho_i H . \tag{4.29}$$

This correction is used profitably when displaying the intermediate results of the progressive refinement algorithm, as demonstrated in Color Plate 10. However it is only used for display and should not be included in the radiosity estimate output by the simulation.

Note that the amount of unshot energy U goes to zero as the solution progresses; thus the magnitude of the ambient term also decreases to zero. In other words the difference between the displayed image using the ambient correction and the one computed by the progressive refinement technique decreases to zero as the computation progresses. This adjustment is most helpful in the very early stages of the relaxation process, when little energy has actually been distributed. Visually the use of the ambient term results in an image that initially looks flat, that is, evenly illuminated everywhere. Successive relaxation steps do not significantly change the overall brightness of the displayed image, but instead modify the distribution of the light, as energy is removed from the shadowed areas and propagated to the more strongly lit areas.

4.2 Substructuring

In the radiosity algorithm, a single wavelength-dependent radiosity value is assigned to each patch, under the assumption that the actual radiosity function does not vary across the patch. This amounts to computing an average radiosity value over the surface of each patch. This practice is quite acceptable for evaluating the balance of energy between patches, but can lead to some visual artifacts when computing images.

The choice of the particular mesh of patches used during the calculation has a dramatic impact on the appearance of the picture. This goes far beyond the quantitative accuracy of the results. In particular, the scale of illumination details captured by the radiosity calculation is directly linked to the size of the patches used. The next chapter will address meshing in detail, but it should be clear that smaller patches are needed in areas where the illumination varies over a small area, such as around shadow boundaries. If patches are too large compared to the scale of the illumination changes, illumination details will appear blurred, as they will be averaged across too large an area.

Unfortunately, decreasing the size of the patches also means increasing their number, and thus the complexity of the whole radiosity process. If a full matrix of form factors is computed, storage needs grow as N^2, where N is the number of patches. Furthermore, uniform subdivision of the surfaces results in a number of patches that is inversely proportional to the square of the linear size of a patch. Halving the length of the sides of all patches in a uniform mesh would then result in a 16-fold increase in the number of form factors!

The conflicting demands for smaller patches and manageable complexity can be reconciled by recognizing that small patches are really needed as *receivers* of light, so as to capture the details of illumination. However, large patches with average radiosities are usually acceptable to act as *emitters* of light. In fact, for the purpose of illuminating a distant patch, there will be little gain in replacing an average-radiosity "source" patch with the combination of a small dark patch and a small bright patch.

4.2.1 Using various levels of subdivision: patches and elements

The two roles assumed by surface patches, that of emitter or receiver of light, can be somewhat separated by introducing several levels of discretization in the tessellation of surfaces [38]. Let us call pieces of the surfaces that are used as emitters of energy *patches* (this corresponds to the earlier definition of patches), and smaller pieces used as receivers *elements*. A patch can be considered an element itself, or it can be broken down into several elements, as shown in Figure 4.2. The concept of substructuring, used for example in engineering mechanics, consists of using the results of a coarse calculation (in this case a radiosity solution obtained with the larger patches) to compute a more refined solution (the radiosity of the smaller elements).

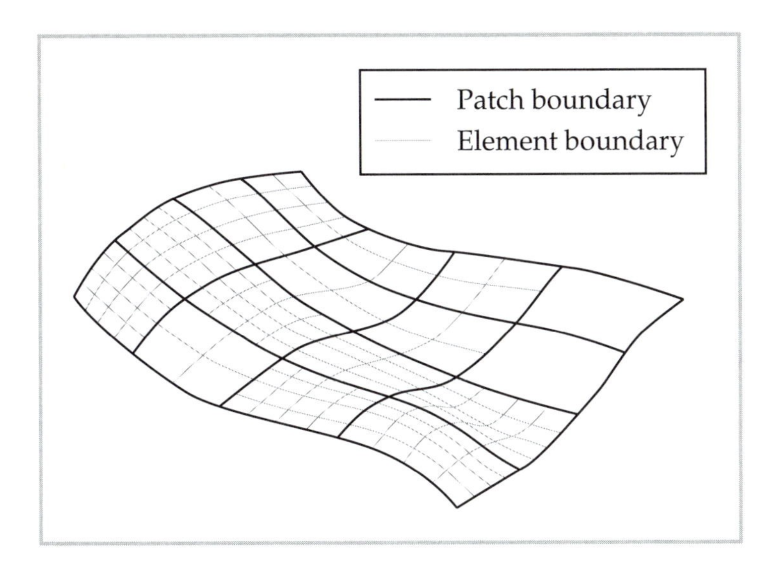

FIGURE 4.2 Patches and elements on a surface.

Consider a patch P_i, subdivided into m_i elements denoted by p_q, where the index q ranges from 1 to m_i. To avoid any confusion between patches and elements sharing the same index, we shall use an index $\bar{q}$ when referring to properties of element p_q, such that no "collision" of indices is possible. The radiosity equation can be used to express the operation of gathering light energy onto a particular surface element p_q. If only the patches are considered to be emitters of light, the summation in the radiosity equation is performed over the patches alone:

$$B_{\bar{q}} = E_{\bar{q}} + \rho_{\bar{q}} \sum_{j=1}^{N} F_{p_q, P_j} B_j \,. \tag{4.30}$$

Equation 4.30 can be used to obtain a radiosity value for each element, provided a coarse radiosity solution is available for the patches and all element-to-patch form factors, F_{p_q, P_j}, have been computed. These form factors can be computed in the same way as patch-to-patch form factors; for example, by placing a hemi-cube at the center of each element and projecting only the patches onto its faces. The total number of elements is

$$M = \sum_{i=1}^{N} m_i \geq N \,,$$

therefore a rectangular $M \times N$ matrix of form factors is obtained.

Each element inside patch P_i has a distinct radiosity value given by Equation 4.30. For the purpose of acting as an illuminator, patch P_i must also have an associated radiosity. This patch radiosity can be obtained as an area-weighted average of the element radiosities:

$$B_i = \frac{1}{A_i} \sum_{q=1}^{m_i} B_{\bar{q}} A_{\bar{q}} . \tag{4.31}$$

Substituting the expression of $B_{\bar{q}}$ from Equation 4.30, and assuming that the exitance and reflectance of all elements inside P_i are the same, an alternate form of the radiosity equation for patch P_i is obtained:

$$B_i = E_i + \rho_i \sum_{j=1}^{N} \left[\frac{1}{A_i} \sum_{q=1}^{m_i} F_{p_q, P_j} A_{\bar{q}} \right] B_j . \tag{4.32}$$

Comparing Equation 4.32 to the radiosity equation (Equation 3.18) shows that the patch-to-patch form factor F_{ij} is obtained as an area average of element-to-patch form factors:

$$F_{ij} = \frac{1}{A_i} \sum_{q=1}^{m_i} F_{p_q, P_j} . \tag{4.33}$$

Note that the patch-to-patch form factor obtained in this way is a more accurate estimate than that given by a single hemi-cube calculation, since in effect a discrete approximation of the outer integral in the defining equation of the form factor (Equation 3.19) is being computed; whereas the use of a single hemi-cube placed at the center of the patch amounts to assuming the inner integral is a constant across the patch.

A practical algorithm for computing element radiosity values using the substructuring strategy is as follows:

1. The rectangular $M \times N$ matrix of element-to-patch form factors is computed, for example, using the hemi-cube. This step is more time-consuming than the usual form factor computation step since there are more elements than patches ($M > N$), but less time-consuming than the computation of form factors between all pairs of elements. Note that the computation time for a single hemi-cube is not increased, since only patches are being projected. M hemi-cubes are computed, yielding an $M \times N$ matrix of form factors.
2. A square ($N \times N$) matrix of patch-to-patch form factors is computed by area-averaging all rows of the rectangular matrix corresponding to elements within the same patch.
3. A coarse radiosity solution is found for the patches using the $N \times N$ form factor matrix. Note that the complexity of this solution step is not increased compared to the usual patch-only solution.
4. All element radiosities are obtained by substituting the patch radiosities in Equation 4.30, in effect gathering light from the patches.

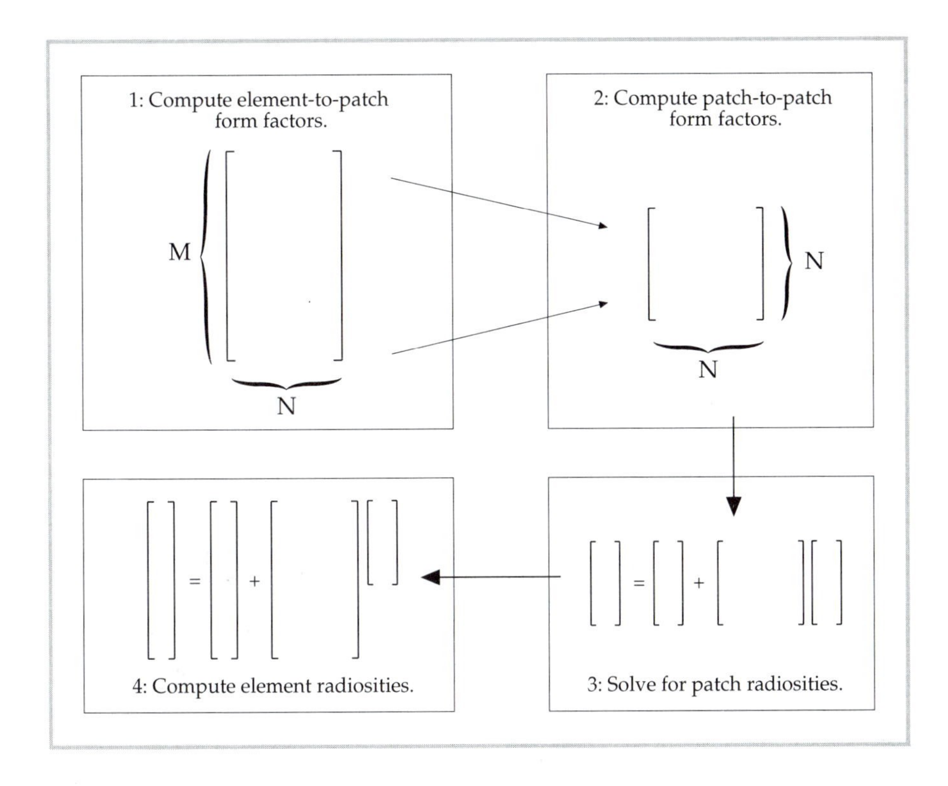

FIGURE 4.3 Form factor matrices used for substructuring.

In summary, the above algorithm allows the computation of a much more accurate radiosity solution, by representing intensity variations inside the patches using small surface elements. The complexity of the calculation is somewhat increased since M rows of form factors are computed with the hemi-cube instead of just N. However, solving for the patch radiosities is done using an $N \times N$ matrix—thus with no added cost—and the solution obtained after the final substitution is comparable to the result of a complete solution involving only elements, with an $M \times M$ matrix. In this regard the savings are quite significant.

The rectangular form factor matrix can be seen as the result of a compression of the larger, complete $M \times M$ matrix, where successive columns that represent a single patch are collapsed into one. Figure 4.3 depicts the transformation of the various matrices.

4.2.2 Substructuring and progressive refinement

The strategy of using a coarse solution to compute the radiosities of smaller elements can also be used in the context of the progressive refinement radiosity algorithm of Section 4.1. Since patches are used as emitters of light, they are the ones used for *shooting*. Each radiosity shot, or Southwell relaxation step, is performed by computing the patch-to-element form

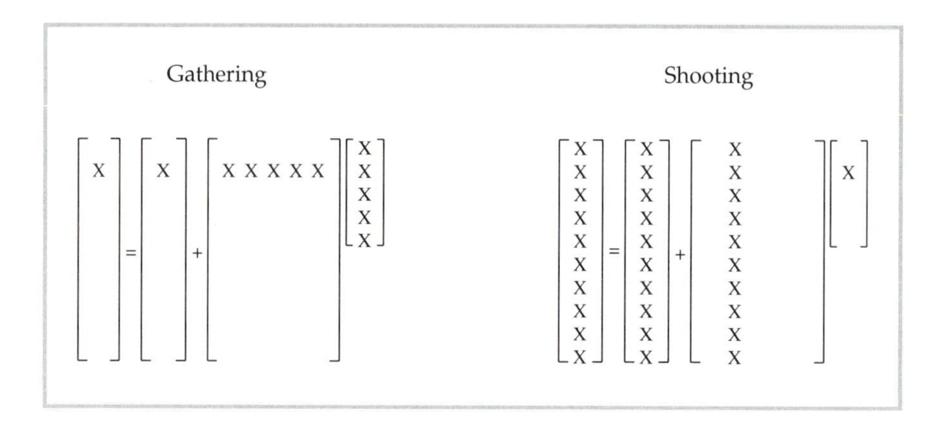

FIGURE 4.4 Gathering and shooting with rectangular matrices.

factors from the shooting patch to all receiving elements, and distributing the patch's "unshot energy" among them, as explained in Section 4.1.3.

Note that in this situation, each step of the process entails the computation of M form factors, from the shooting patch to all receiving elements. This is in contrast to the previous algorithm, where the N form factors from receiving elements to all patches were computed. Thus as might have been expected, the symmetry between the shooting and gathering operations is somewhat broken by the substructuring scheme and the use of different numbers of emitters and receivers. Figure 4.4 is a modified version of Figure 4.1 adapted to the case of rectangular matrices, which demonstrates this loss of symmetry.

After each shooting step, new residual (unshot energy) values are available for all elements, and these values are averaged across each patch to yield a patch residual. The patch residuals are sorted and the next shooting patch is chosen to be the one with the largest residual.

Substructuring successively improves the efficiency of the progressive refinement algorithm, in the same proportion as that of the traditional radiosity algorithm. However, the combination of substructuring and progressive refinement results in an algorithm that is less numerically stable. Since in that case energy is shot towards smaller elements, the accuracy limitations of the hemi-cube are emphasized by the asymmetric formulation. This problem is discussed in more detail in the next chapter (Section 5.1.1).

4.3 Adaptive mesh refinement

The rationale for using small receiving elements in the radiosity computation is to try to capture rapid variations of radiosity values across the surfaces. A denser mesh of elements is needed in areas where the illumination changes rapidly, since the assumption of a constant radiosity per element imposes that the radiosity function across a surface be treated as a piecewise constant function.

The substructuring strategy recognizes that it is infeasible to use a uniformly fine mesh of elements on all surfaces, and replaces it by a dual mesh of patches and elements. Still, the choice of a particular mesh remains a very difficult issue. The selection of the number, size, and location of patches and elements is crucial to the quality of the results.

4.3.1 Automatic meshing

It is desirable that the mesh follows the distribution of light in the environment, with a higher density of elements in areas where the illumination changes rapidly. Since the distribution of illumination is precisely the unknown of the problem, it is unrealistic to rely on the user to guess where and how the mesh elements should be placed. Instead the mesh should be generated automatically by the simulation program, based on the properties of the environment. Since the illumination is not known in advance, heuristic methods are employed to drive the meshing algorithm.

Two approaches can be considered for the generation of the mesh. The first avenue consists of predicting where relevant illumination features (such as shadow boundaries) fall on the surfaces, and basing the mesh on the predicted location of these features. This a priori meshing strategy requires geometric calculations that will be presented in detail in Section 5.3.3.

A simpler idea consists of having the mesh evolve as the solution progresses. In this case, the simulation process generates more elements in areas where a rapid change of the radiosity function has been detected. This second strategy works by considering partial results of the simulation, obtained using a simple initial mesh. The results are used to draw conclusions regarding the desirable density of the mesh. It can be characterized as a posteriori meshing.

The substructuring algorithm outlined in Section 4.2.1 can be transformed into an iterative algorithm, which repeatedly evaluates the current radiosity solution and makes new meshing decisions. New elements are generated in areas where a high radiosity variation is found, but the set of patches remains unchanged. Assume that a radiosity solution has been computed using a given mesh and the associated rectangular matrix of element-to-patch form factors. The rate of change in radiosity across a surface element, or radiosity gradient, can be estimated by looking at the neighboring element radiosities. A new mesh is then generated by subdividing all elements for which the gradient exceeds some preset threshold. At this point a new estimate of the radiosity solution is computed with the improved mesh, and the whole process iterates until no large radiosity gradients can be identified.

4.3.2 Adaptive subdivision and Gauss-Seidel solution

The refined mesh of elements that is constructed based on the estimated radiosity variations need not be a uniform subdivision of each patch, and instead the density of the mesh can adapt locally to the complexity of the illumination. This can be accomplished using a hierarchical subdivision structure for each patch, in which each element can be subdivided independently of its neighbors. An example of a hierarchical mesh of elements is presented in Figure 4.5, using a *quadtree* to represent the hierarchical structure. In the quadtree data structure, a *node* represents a surface patch and points to four children nodes representing a partition of that patch [146]. Quadtrees are well suited to the representation of rectangles, and can also be easily adapted for parametric surfaces that employ a regular subdivision of parameter space.

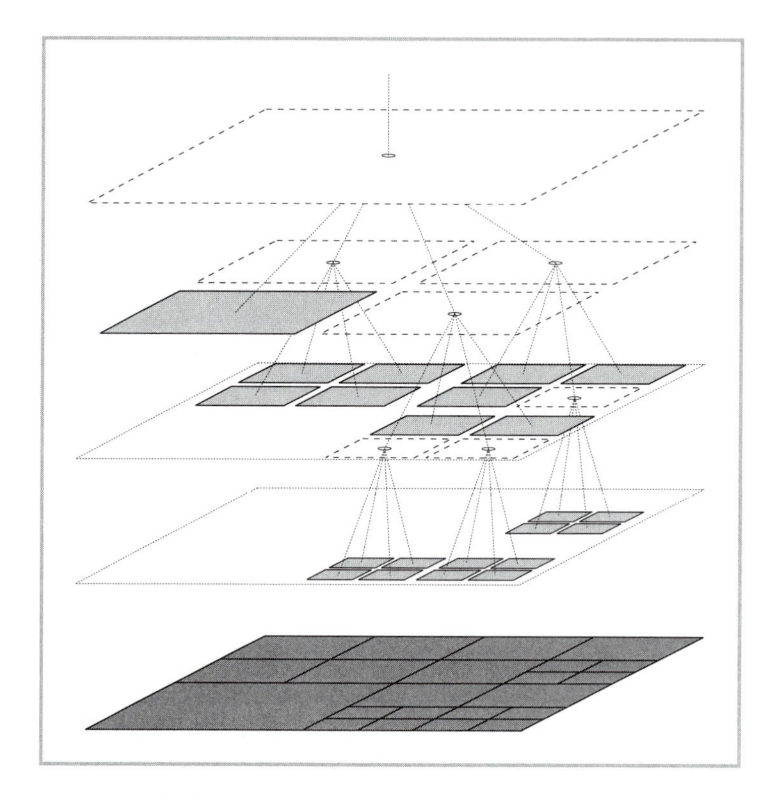

FIGURE 4.5 Adaptive subdivision of the element mesh using a quadtree.

When a quadtree is used to represent the subdivision of a surface, the leaves of the tree correspond to elements that together completely cover the original surface.

Adaptive subdivision of the mesh requires a method for deciding whether an element should be subdivided further. As mentioned above, this criterion can be based on the estimated rate of variation of the radiosity across the element: an element for which the radiosity doesn't vary significantly need not be subdivided. Note that it is not possible to directly measure the radiosity variation; an approximation must be used instead. A very simple criterion compares the element radiosity value to the neighboring radiosity values. Most hierarchical data structures such as the quadtree provide easy access to neighboring elements. A sufficiently large difference with any one neighbor will then trigger the subdivision of the element. Figure 4.6 illustrates a possible subdivision resulting from a shadow cast onto a surface.

FIGURE 4.6 Adaptive subdivision generated along a shadow boundary.

More elaborate criteria can be developed, for example, by computing radiosity values at the vertices of the elements as a weighted average of the neighboring elements' radiosities. This allows the varying level of subdivision of the neighboring elements to be accounted for: a very small element sharing a vertex with a large element will have more influence on that vertex's radiosity. The vertex radiosity values can then be used to estimate the radiosity gradient. More details on the reconstruction of radiosity values at selected vertices can be found in Section 5.4. In general more elaborate reconstruction techniques will give rise to better subdivision criteria, but will be more expensive to compute.

We now consider the practical implications of the subdivision of an element. First the element must be replaced in the mesh by several smaller elements (four in the case of a quadtree). Then the element-to-patch form factors are computed from all the newly introduced elements. The net effect on the rectangular matrix of form factors is to replace one of its rows by several rows, corresponding to the new elements. At this point, new element radiosities can be computed by performing the final gathering operation with the new form factors, and a decision can be made immediately concerning further subdivision. Alternatively, the new form factor matrix can be used to initiate a new solution cycle and compute more accurate radiosity estimates at all elements. Further subdivision is then based upon the new, more accurate element radiosity values.

4.3.3 Adaptive subdivision and progressive refinement

Adaptive subdivision is also possible with the progressive refinement algorithm, since after each refinement step the various energy contributions on the receiving surfaces can be analyzed to decide on further element subdivision.

During the course of the progressive refinement algorithm, several pieces of information are available about the illumination of the surfaces and can be used to develop various subdivision criteria. For instance, the current estimate of the final energy value ($\beta_i'^{(k)} = \beta_i^{(k)} + r_i^{(k)}$ in the language of Section 4.1) is updated after each relaxation step, and the contribution of the last step to the residual value can also be isolated. This contribution represents the effect of the direct illumination by the current emitter. Subdivision can therefore be controlled based on the impact of each individual emitter.

Adaptive mesh subdivision can be performed at each radiosity step in the following way: a subdivision criterion is evaluated for each element just as in the matrix solution method, based on some estimate of the radiosity gradient. Note that this radiosity gradient can be computed based solely on the contribution of the current emitter, so that the subdivision only depends on the illumination variations created by that patch. All elements that are found to require subdivision are split, and the variables are restored to what they were prior to the shot, effectively canceling the shot. A new shot is then performed from the same emitter, this time using the new set of elements.

This simple subdivision strategy works best if the criterion is based only on the impact of the current shooting patch. In this case the subdivision will follow the shadow boundaries created by that patch. Interestingly, since all radiosity steps are independent of each other, the subdivision criterion can be varied for different surfaces. For example, emitting patches specifically identified as light sources can use a specific threshold on the radiosity gradient to ensure that their associated shadows are finely subdivided. This is particularly useful since shadows from primary light sources usually constitute important features of the illumination in a scene.

The operation of splitting the receiving elements raises a new question. All elements possess a current set of variables, such as their estimated shot energy ($\beta_i^{(k)}$) or their current unshot energy ($r_i^{(k)}$), representing the effect of all previous refinement operations. But what values should be associated with the newly created elements that do not have a history of received contributions?

In order to obtain an accurate value for these new elements, all previous radiosity shots could be recomputed. This would in fact be equivalent to the computation of a totally new radiosity solution. This is not desirable since it simply discards all the preceding computation.

A simpler alternative consists of interpolating the shot and unshot energy values of former elements to obtain the values for the new elements. This practice can be justified by the observation that if no subdivision occurred for a particular element during previous iterations, the resulting accumulated energy is likely to vary smoothly across the element, and can be represented to some degree of accuracy using simple interpolation.

This simple remark can also be carried further by noting that if previous iterations did not generate large radiosity variations across an element, subsequent iterations might also be able to operate accurately with a coarser mesh. With the method just described, once an element has been refined, the finer mesh is used for all subsequent operations regardless of what is actually needed. Based on this observation, a possible improvement of this method is to reconsider the need for element subdivision at each shot. Suppose an element has already been subdivided but that no subdivision is deemed necessary for the current shot. The radiosity values for all subelements can be interpolated, instead of being computed with the full form factor calculation. This process is illustrated in Figure 4.7.

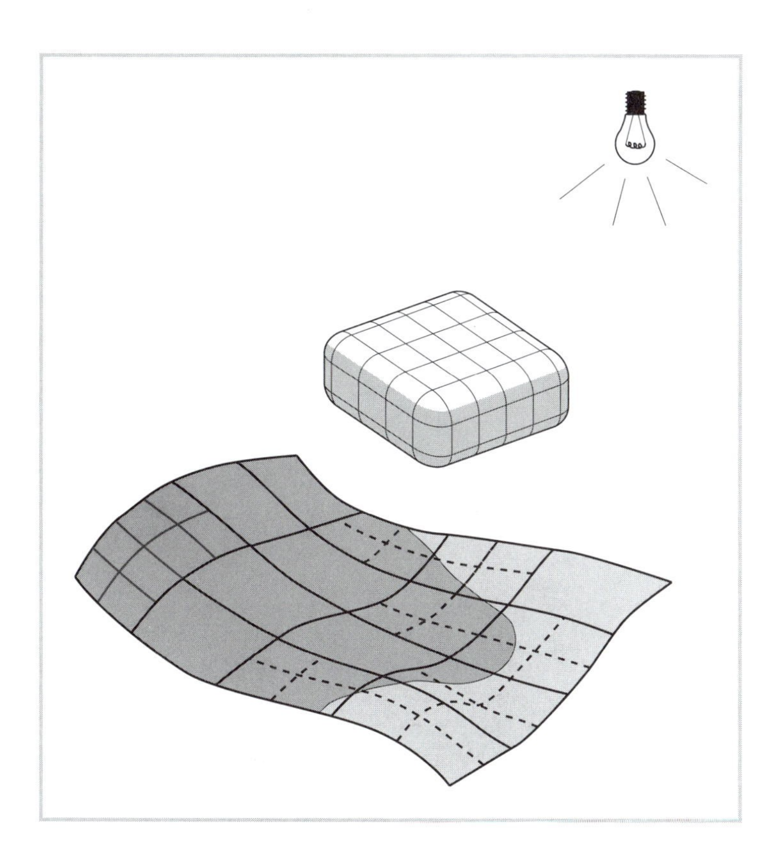

FIGURE 4.7 The current shot produces the subdivision marked by dotted lines. Elements in the lower-left corner result from a previous shot, and their new radiosity is obtained by interpolation.

The next section goes beyond this simple improvement of the adaptive subdivision scheme. It evaluates each transfer of energy between a pair of patches at the appropriate subdivision level, not only on the receiving side but on the emitting side as well.

4.4 Hierarchical radiosity formulation

The preceding discussion of adaptive mesh refinement reveals one of the main difficulties in designing an effective meshing strategy: for any particular area of the scene, a fine mesh is sometimes needed to capture the impact of a few radiosity emitters accurately, but a coarser subdivision level is acceptable for most other emitters. Emitters in the second category include those that do not generate a shadow boundary in the region of interest.

The simple substructuring technique mentioned in Section 4.2 is too rigid to accommodate such a variable subdivision, in the sense that the same patches are used to compute energy exchanges with all surfaces. In this section, the radiosity method is reformulated as a hierarchical algorithm [76, 77]. The idea of adaptive mesh refinement is extended by removing the arbitrary separation of patches and elements, replacing them by a continuum of hierarchical elements. Radiosity exchanges are then computed between various levels of the hierarchy. For any pair of surfaces, an appropriate subdivision level on both surfaces is determined and then used to compute the energy exchange. Therefore the energy received by a given surface from several others will in general be computed using several different subdivision levels.

This hierarchical algorithm was inspired by advances in the context of N-body simulation problems, where the influence of a group of elements is approximated by the influence of a single, composite element for interactions taking place at a significant distance [3, 72]. For radiosity applications this amounts to dividing the form factor matrix into a number of blocks, each of which represents an interaction between patches or groups of patches. The advantage of this formulation is that, as explained below, the number of blocks in the matrix is $O(N)$ (where N is the total number of elements), to be compared with the $O(N^2)$ entries in the regular form factor matrix [77].

4.4.1 Hierarchical representation of surfaces

The substructuring technique from Section 4.2 reduces the size of the form factor matrix by grouping adjacent columns to express the impact of several elements as that of a single emitting patch. However, a complete column of form factors is still used for each patch, which means that a form factor is computed with each individual receiving element. All form factors are typically computed to within the same error tolerance, regardless of their magnitude, resulting in wasted computation time as well as storage space. Hierarchical algorithms attempt to avoid devoting resources to the computation of form factors that represent insignificant energy exchanges.

The key idea behind *hierarchical radiosity* is that the effort spent computing a form factor should be commensurate with its significance with respect to the global energy balance. Since digital computation is inherently approximate, and display devices have a limited precision, there is a limit to the precision of the simulation results. Recognizing that an approximate solution is all that can be obtained, the hierarchical algorithm seeks to perform a minimal amount of work to compute energy transfers within a specified error bound. The subdivision used in the calculation should always be the coarsest one that delivers the desired level of precision.

A hierarchical view of energy exchanges

The need for a hierarchical representation of radiosity exchanges is illustrated by the following example: Consider a patch P, resulting from the subdivision of a wall, and its interaction with some other surface patch S in the scene. As the wall exchanges energy with a number of other surfaces of varying size and distance, P is not necessarily always an adequate level of representation. Several cases are presented in Figure 4.8, corresponding to increasing distances between P and S:

(a) For the purpose of illuminating a nearby surface S_1, whose size is comparable to its distance to P, such as the cover of the book on the chest of drawers, P should be

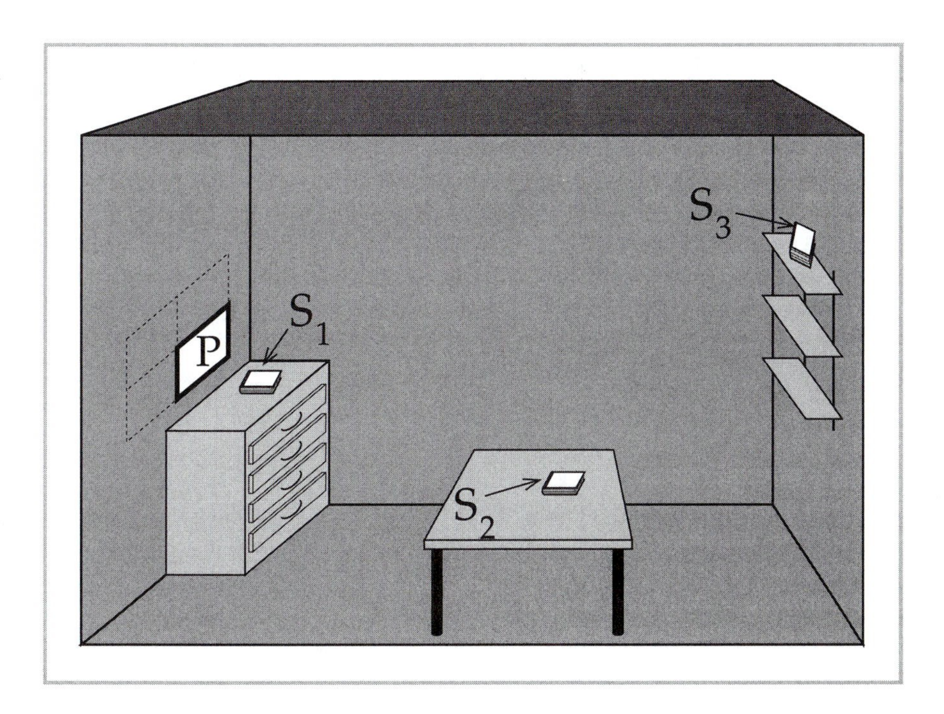

FIGURE 4.8 Interactions between a reference patch and a variety of surfaces.

subdivided into smaller pieces. This is necessary in order to represent the small-scale illumination changes on its surface, which can dramatically alter the illumination of the book.

(b) For a more distant surface S_2, such as the cover of the book on the table, P is likely to be an appropriate size; thus the corresponding form factor is estimated with reasonable precision without further subdivision.

(c) When the distance between S and P becomes so large that the form factor between P and S is very small (as for a book S_3 on the shelf across the room), P could be merged with neighboring patches into a single entity, with little impact on the resulting solution.

This example shows that, for any given surface S, there is only a limited range of distances for which patch P is an appropriate level of representation for the computation of the energy transfer with S. If the two surfaces are close to each other relative to their size, the form factor between them is typically large and further subdivision is needed to obtain a precise estimate. However, if the surfaces are distant and their form factor is very small, there is no need to compute it with great relative precision, and P represents an unnecessary subdivision of the underlying surface. In that case the interaction of S with P's supporting surface should be represented higher up in the hierarchy.

4.4.2 Constructing the hierarchy

A hierarchical representation of the surfaces is easily constructed using a *top-down* approach. Starting with a small number of "large" surfaces composing the scene, a hierarchical mesh of elements is built by recursively splitting the surfaces according to a simple rule. For each pair of surfaces, the algorithm decides whether the current level of subdivision is sufficient, and subdivides them if not. The interaction of two surfaces exchanging energy is recorded at the appropriate level of the hierarchy at both ends, in the form of a *link* between the two surfaces.

Subdivision criterion

The hierarchical subdivision of surfaces is driven by a simple criterion that attempts to establish whether or not the current subdivision level captures the essence of the energy transfers. In the example of Figure 4.8 the magnitude of the form factor between the two surfaces was used as the discriminating parameter. The hierarchical algorithm is largely independent of the particular criterion used, and it is presented here with a simple threshold on the form factor value. Other criteria can also be used to assess the appropriateness of a given subdivision level. In particular a brightness-based criterion is discussed in Section 4.4.4.

Note that, since the core of the hierarchical algorithm consists of repeatedly evaluating the subdivision criterion, it is essential that the particular criterion chosen be easily computed. A simple and effective criterion is obtained by considering a crude estimate of the form factor and requiring further subdivision whenever that estimate exceeds a user-supplied threshold. A useful form factor estimate is the geometrical expression inside the form factor integral (defined in Equation 3.19):

$$\frac{\cos\theta\cos\theta'}{\pi r^2}.$$

This estimate is computed for two particular points chosen on the surfaces, and does not consider the effect of possible occlusion between the surfaces.

Note that the relative error incurred in such an approximation is proportional to the magnitude of the estimated form factor [76]; thus the estimate can be used directly as a measure of the error of the computation.

While such a crude form factor estimate is useful to quickly identify surfaces that require subdivision, it cannot be used in the actual calculation of energy transfers, where occlusion can play a significant role. Section 4.4.4 explains how to take occlusion into account in the form factor between two hierarchical surfaces.

Hierarchical data structure

A practical example of a hierarchical representation of surfaces is the quadtree structure mentioned in Section 4.3.2. Recall that the leaves of the tree correspond to the finest level of elements in the subdivision and form a partition of the original surface. On the other hand, interior nodes in the quadtree correspond to larger patches. Thus the hierarchical radiosity algorithm uses all nodes of a quadtree to represent surfaces with varying levels of detail.

The top-down hierarchical algorithm operates by recursively applying the following sequence of operations for each pair of "top-level" surfaces.

1. Estimate the form factor between the two surfaces using a quick and approximate formula.
2. If the estimated form factor is below the threshold, or if the surfaces are too small to be subdivided, record their interaction at the current level.
3. Otherwise, subdivide one of the surfaces and recurse.

As mentioned above this algorithm relies on the fact that the form factor error is commensurate with the form factor itself. Thus the test on the form factor actually measures the quality of the approximation at the current subdivision level.

Block representation of the form factor matrix

The example of the wall patch in Figure 4.8 showed that a given surface must be represented at varying levels of detail depending on the energy transfer being considered. In contrast to the traditional radiosity algorithm, the set of relationships between a surface and the rest of the environment cannot simply be represented by a vector of form factors. Instead the form factor matrix is divided into "blocks" that represent the interactions between aggregate surfaces, each representing the average behavior of several elements.

Each of the links generated by the above algorithm represents such a block that can be viewed as an average form factor between all underlying elements on both sides. In Figure 4.9 a hypothetical one-dimensional example is constructed, with two line segments playing the roles of top-level patches. The subdivision of each segment is pictured using a binary tree, and the links established during the subdivision process are shown both as labeled arcs and as blocks in the matrix. Note that in general the blocks are not necessarily square, although they are for this simple example.

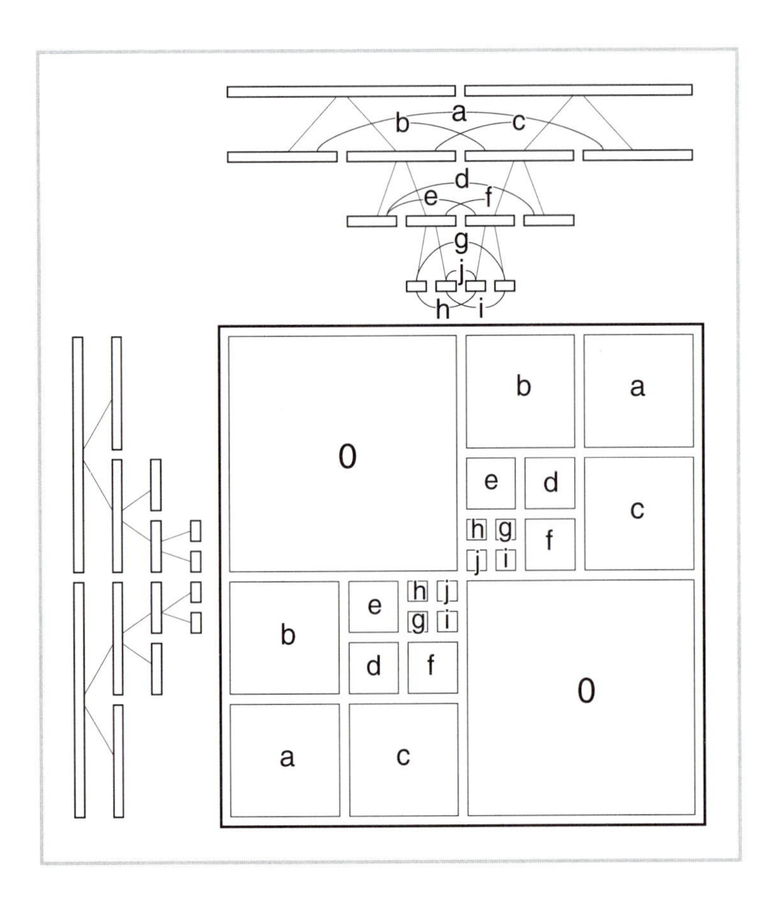

FIGURE 4.9 Hierarchical representation of the form factor matrix. (*Courtesy of P. Hanrahan, Princeton University.*)

Size of the hierarchical problem

An example of the hierarchical subdivision induced by the algorithm is presented in Figure 4.10. Note that there appears to be the same number of links leaving each patch, at all levels of the hierarchy. This property is quite general, as demonstrated in reference [77]. The number of links is proportional to the number of nodes in the hierarchical structure,

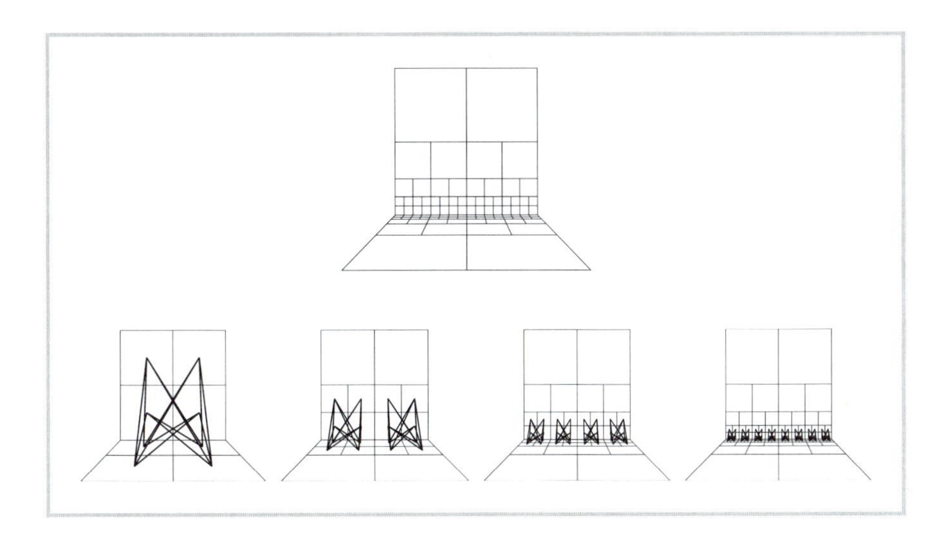

FIGURE 4.10 Hierarchical subdivision obtained for two perpendicular polygons. (*Courtesy of P. Hanrahan, Princeton University.*)

which is itself proportional to the number of leaves in the tree. Thus the total number of links is $O(N)$ where N is the number of elements that would be obtained if all surfaces were fully subdivided. This is in contrast to the $O(N^2)$ entries in the complete form factor matrix.

The reduction of the number of "form factors" to $O(N)$ results in a substantial improvement in the computational demands of the radiosity algorithm. However, it should be noted that if the algorithm reduces the number of links by limiting the subdivision of large polygons, it must always start by establishing a link for each pair of top-level surfaces. Therefore, there is an additional $O(k^2)$ cost, where k is the number of top-level surfaces in the scene. Unfortunately the relationship between N and k is difficult to express in general. In a worst-case situation, where all surfaces are small and far apart, no subdivision is needed and $N = k$. Conversely, the savings are enormous in the situation where a small number of large polygons are hierarchically subdivided into many more elements ($N \gg k$).

In order to guarantee a lower complexity, a hierarchical algorithm should incorporate a *clustering* mechanism, whereby disjoint patches are joined and treated as a single entity. Clustering can eliminate the $O(k^2)$ term in the algorithm complexity since all original surfaces do not necessarily interact directly. The issue of clustering is currently an active area of research, and it is expected that general hierarchical methods, working in both bottom-up and top-down fashion, will become prominent in the coming years. One of the few clustering algorithms already described operates by replacing groups of surfaces by simple boxes for the purpose of computing indirect illumination. The boxes are assigned diffuse reflectance values based on the optical characteristics of their contents, to make them *optically equivalent* to the set of surfaces that they replace [141]. Note that the simplified representation is used only for the computation of the illumination that is not directly received from light sources. Direct illumination is computed using the detailed description of the scene to maintain a good definition of shadows. A desirable extension of this simple scheme would be a more precise characterization of the reflective behavior of surface clusters, going beyond the ideal diffuse approximation. Current research investigates how error bounds can be established for the transfer of energy between clusters, in order to drive the subdivision efficiently.

4.4.3 Solution of the hierarchical problem

Once a hierarchical representation of the form factor matrix is constructed, the actual computation of the energy transfers is as follows: for a given node in the hierarchy, energy is "gathered" by following all the links originating at that node and multiplying the associated form factor by the radiosity found at the other end of the link.

Care must be taken that a meaningful radiosity value is maintained at all levels of the hierarchy. Since links can be established at all levels, the radiosity of the patch associated with a given node depends on the links of its ancestors as well as the links of its descendents. To ensure that all nodes in the hierarchy have a complete view of the energy transfers at all levels, a complete bidirectional traversal of the structure is needed. First, accurate radiosity values are computed at the lowest level of the structure, by propagating contributions down the tree using simple replication. Starting from the top of the tree, a node's reflected radiosity is simply added to each of its children's radiosity. This in effect *pushes* correct radiosity values to the leaves, where all contributions are adequately considered.

All internal nodes must then be updated to reflect the appropriate radiosity based on their descendents. Since radiosity is defined per unit area, the correct radiosity value for a parent node is the area average of its children radiosities. Thus radiosity values are *pulled* up the tree, starting at the leaves, and averaged at each step to yield a correct radiosity value at all levels of the tree. The entire *push/pull* process is illustrated in Figure 4.11.

The radiosity solution process thus consists of repeatedly executing the following sequence of operations.

1. Determine complete radiosity values for each node of the hierarchy:
   a. Push radiosity values down to the leaves.
   b. Pull radiosity values up the hierarchy.
2. Propagate energy along all links.

The second operation, propagating energy along the links, can be seen as a gathering operation, since all the radiosity impinging on a particular node is computed. Note that the gathered radiosity cannot directly replace the current radiosity estimate for subsequent gathering iterations, since it only includes the radiosity arriving at a given level of the hierarchy. Thus a bidirectional sweep is performed before each gathering step, to obtain new estimates of all radiosities.

It should be noted that links are bidirectional in essence, as energy can be exchanged in both directions between any two surfaces. Therefore an alternate solution process, based on shooting, can be proposed. However, its usefulness is limited by the following factors.

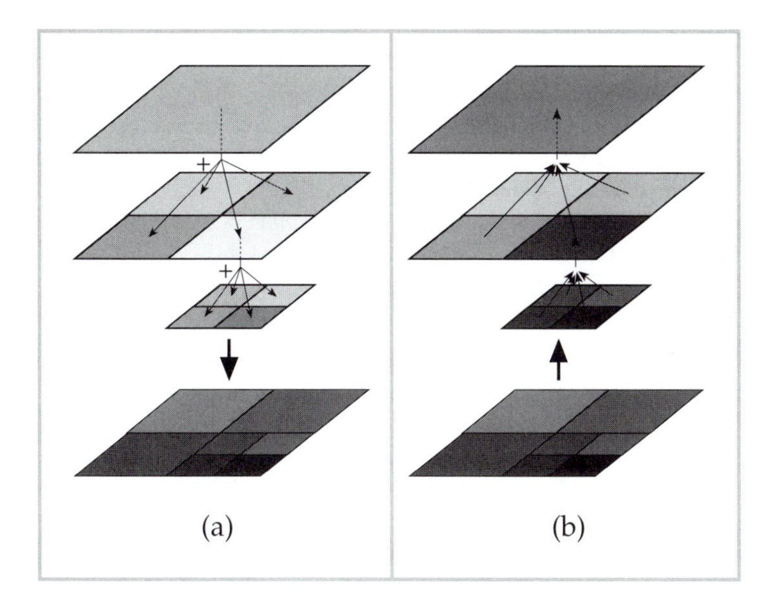

FIGURE 4.11 Combination of radiosity exchanges at all levels of the hierarchy. Note that darker patches here indicate greater radiosity values. (a) Radiosity values are pushed to the leaves and added along the way. (b) Radiosity values are pulled up the tree and averaged at each level. As a result each level has a correct representation of the radiosity received at levels both higher and lower in the tree. For example, the lower-right corner of the second level has seen its radiosity increase to reflect the energy received by its parent and by its children.

First, it would possess a much finer grain than the progressive refinement procedure of Section 4.1. Instead of the complete contribution of some surface patch, each relaxation step would correspond to a particular level of the hierarchy. Thus if a surface has established links at different hierarchical levels, several shots will be needed to propagate its reflected energy. Second, each shot would only propagate light to the nodes that are directly linked to the shooter. Finally, the sorting phase needed to select the best shooting candidate would require that the total radiosity be known at each level of the hierarchy, which implies that a bidirectional traversal of the structure is needed after each shot. Thus the shooting strategy offers no advantage over the gathering strategy in the context of the hierarchical algorithm.

Color Plate 20 shows all links established in a scene, at various hierarchical levels. Notice how links tend to connect surfaces of similar size. In those images the links are color-coded to indicate visibility between surfaces. Dark blue links connect fully occluded surfaces, white links represent fully visible pairs, and green links indicate partial visibility. The final image is shown in Color Plate 21.

4.4.4 Refinement criteria and error control

Brightness-weighted refinement

The above presentation of the hierarchical radiosity formulation is based on the idea that the error in the form factor estimate can be used to control the subdivision. An alternative criterion uses the product of the calculated radiosity and the form factor to drive the subdivision, in an attempt to consider the actual impact of the proposed link on the radiosity distribution. This criterion is called *BF refinement* since it uses the product of a radiosity B by the form factor estimate F [77]. In simple terms this criterion expresses the fact that large errors can be tolerated in the form factor as long as little or no energy is being transported across the corresponding link.

Multi-gridding

Since the radiosity distribution is not known in advance (it is the result we are looking for) BF refinement works best when integrated into a multi-scale resolution approach inspired by multi-gridding techniques, as explained below.

The hierarchical subdivision process is controlled by a threshold on the BF product. Using a fairly large value for this threshold allows a very rapid computation of a coarse solution. This solution can serve as the basis for a subsequent subdivision stage. Several such cycles can follow with decreasing values for the threshold, resulting each time in a better solution.

The resulting computation algorithm alternates the two phases of the hierarchical method, first refining the subdivision and establishing links, and then solving for radiosities. The error threshold is decreased after each solution phase to ensure convergence towards an accurate solution.

Computation of form factors

The form factor value used in the gathering step of the radiosity solution cannot simply be the crude estimate computed during the subdivision stage. In particular, this estimate makes no effort to represent the effect of occlusion by intervening surfaces between the two nodes of interest.

A simple correction of the form factor estimate can be computed in the form of a multiplicative factor (a scalar value between 0 and 1) expressing the relative fraction of a node visible from the other. An important fact that should be considered when computing this occlusion factor is that since the form factor is being computed with limited accuracy, the occlusion factor itself need only be known with limited precision.

The hemi-cube algorithm is not suited to the calculation of individual occlusion factors, since it requires the projection of all surfaces in the scene. Other form factor computation methods will be proposed in Chapter 5, and many of them can be adapted to the computation of the occlusion factor of a link. One possibility that is particularly interesting for the simpler problem at hand is to fire a fixed number of rays between the two patches to test for visibility. Those that do not intersect other objects contribute to the visibility of the link, while the others account for the occlusion. Endpoints for the visibility rays must be distributed across the area of the patches, either randomly, as discussed in Chapter 8, or using a pseudorandom distribution grid [77].

Error control

In the hierarchical radiosity algorithm it is possible to control the accuracy of individual links. However, it is difficult to control the accuracy of the global solution since the total number of links is not known in advance. This number can grow very rapidly when the error threshold for individual links is lowered. Although the number of links is always proportional to the final number of elements, both are dependent on the particular subdivision criterion chosen.

Enforcing a small error threshold in the subdivision stage can obviously result in unnecessary subdivision, and does not even guarantee an accurate solution. In particular, quadtree leaves accumulate radiosity contributions from all levels of the hierarchy, with a corresponding accumulation of error. A noticeable artifact can result when adjacent low-level elements belong to two different branches of the quadtree, since their radiosities sometimes appear to differ significantly. Although all contributions to these radiosities may be very similar on both sides, the resulting sum exhibits a disturbing disparity.

Thus one possible avenue for improvement of the hierarchical radiosity algorithm concerns the definition of proper subdivision criteria. For example, subdivision must be encouraged when partial visibility is detected, since this corresponds to a shadow transition across the surface. Visibility preprocessing techniques will be discussed in the Appendix (Section A.1.2). They classify visibility situations as being either fully visible, partially visible, or fully invisible, thus making it easier to adapt subdivision strategies.

Another possibility is to use other hierarchical representations for radiosity, such as *wavelets*, that allow a more precise characterization of errors and approximations. This idea is explored in Section 5.2.4.

4.5 Adjoint radiosity formulation and importance

The complexity of the radiosity computation process is largely caused by the view-independent nature of the algorithm: the interaction between any pair of surfaces is always computed to a certain accuracy to ensure a correct result. However, in most practical applications, only a limited subset of radiosity values are really of interest. These may be, for example, the radiosities of visible surfaces for a given view of the scene.

In such a case, when a single static image must be produced from the radiosity simulation, there should not be much effort spent in computing the radiosities of surfaces that have little impact on the appearance of the final picture. Even when a sequence of images is eventually produced, corresponding to a virtual walkthrough, it may well be the case that only a fraction of all surfaces have a significant impact on the result. Without loss of generality we will now refer to the end result of the simulation as "the final picture," as in the case of a single static image.

4.5.1 The notion of importance

The notion of *potential*, or *importance*, was recently introduced in computer graphics to help in determining the effective accuracy needed in the evaluation of different radiosity exchanges [130, 167]. This concept was inspired by work conducted on Monte Carlo simulations of neutron transport, and the underlying theory can in fact be applied to all transport equations.

Suppose that all visible surfaces are identified for a given set of viewing conditions.[4] Obviously these surfaces are important for the computation of a picture. They receive their illumination from other surfaces, which therefore also have some degree of importance. This process continues so that importance propagates "backwards" from the visible surfaces into the scene. This is pictured in Figure 4.12.

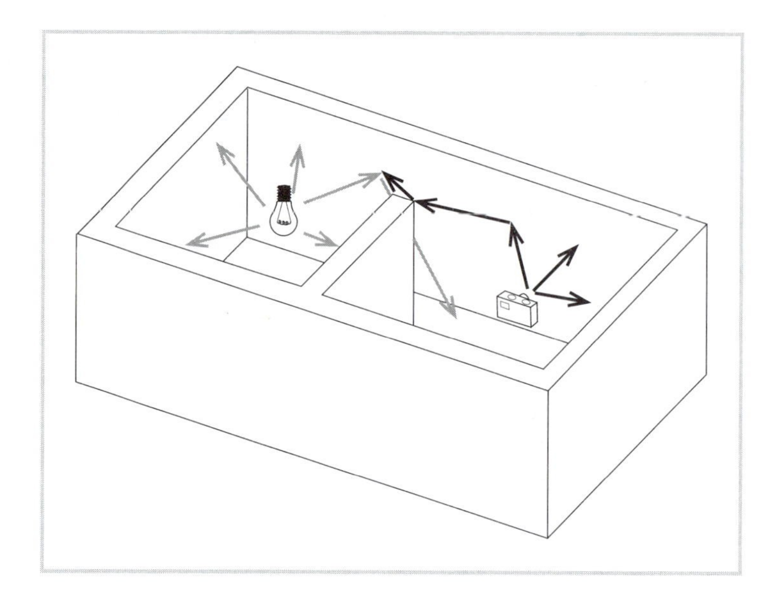

FIGURE 4.12 Light and importance travel in opposite directions.

Let us define the importance, or potential, of a surface patch as a measure of the impact on the final picture of a unit radiosity on that surface. This definition is intentionally

[4]When a sequence of images is being produced, a visibility preprocessing technique can be used to generate a list of the surfaces that are visible from any point along the camera path. One such technique is described in Section 6.1.2.

ambiguous, as many different measures of importance are possible. The point of this discussion is merely to describe the general properties of such a quantity.

Consider a pair of mutually visible patches P_i and P_j, and suppose that P_i's importance is I_i. Since energy can propagate from P_j to P_i, the radiosity of P_j influences that of P_i, and also, necessarily, the final picture. Therefore the existence of an energy transfer from P_j to P_i implies that importance is also transported in the reverse direction.

The exact amount of importance "propagated" from P_i to P_j is computed as follows. Consider a unit radiosity at patch P_j. Setting $B_j = 1$ in Equation 3.18 and ignoring the existence of all other patches, its influence on the radiosity at patch P_i is given by

$$B_{i \leftarrow j} = \rho_i F_{ij} B_j = \rho_i F_{ij}.$$

By the above definition of importance, the impact on the final picture is the product of $B_{i \leftarrow j}$ by P_i's importance. Since we started with a unit radiosity on P_j, it is also precisely the importance of P_j due to the existence of P_i, or in other words, the importance $I_{j \leftarrow i}$ transferred from P_i to P_j:

$$I_{j \leftarrow i} = \rho_i F_{ij} I_i \,. \tag{4.34}$$

An *importance equation* can be formed from Equation 4.34 by expressing the total importance of patch P_i as the sum of an "intrinsic importance" R_i and that contributed by all other patches:

$$I_i = R_i + \sum_{j=1}^{N} \rho_j F_{ji} I_j \,. \tag{4.35}$$

At first sight the importance equation appears very similar to the radiosity equation (Equation 3.18), with the major difference that the indices of the reflectance and the form factors are changed. R_i, called a *receiver term* by analogy with the *source term* E_i of the radiosity equation, expresses the intrinsic importance of various surface patches regardless of light interreflection. A non-zero R_i term indicates that a given surface patch has some effect on the final picture, even if all other patches are removed. As explained in the next section, with a proper choice of the receiver terms, the solution of the importance equation can be used in place of the radiosity solution to generate the picture.

4.5.2 Adjoint radiosity equation

In mathematical terms the similarity between the radiosity and importance equations is expressed by saying that they form a set of *adjoint equations*. In fact, the theory of linear operators and adjoint equations will be used below to derive a more formal definition of importance, based on the actual goal of the computation.

Recall that the radiosity equation can be expressed in matrix form as in Equation 4.1:

$$\boldsymbol{MB} = \boldsymbol{E} \qquad \text{with} \quad M_{ij} = \delta_{ij} - \rho_i F_{ij} \,.$$

$\boldsymbol{M}$ is a matrix representing the effect of a linear operator that transforms radiosity vectors. The *adjoint* of a linear operator $\boldsymbol{M}$ is another linear operator $\boldsymbol{M}^*$ such that the following property holds for any two vectors $\boldsymbol{X}$ and $\boldsymbol{Y}$

$$\langle \boldsymbol{X}, \boldsymbol{MY} \rangle = \langle \boldsymbol{M}^* \boldsymbol{X}, \boldsymbol{Y} \rangle \,, \tag{4.36}$$

where $\langle \boldsymbol{X}, \boldsymbol{Y} \rangle = \sum_{i=1}^{N} X_i Y_i$ denotes the inner product of two vectors. The adjoint of a real-valued matrix such as the radiosity matrix $\boldsymbol{M}$ is simply its transpose $\boldsymbol{M}^\top$ defined by $M_{ij}^\top = M_{ji}$, $1 \leq i, j \leq N$.

Careful examination of Equation 4.35 shows that it involves the adjoint (or transpose) of the radiosity operator $\boldsymbol{M}$, which means that importance is a solution of the adjoint equation,

$$\boldsymbol{M}^* \boldsymbol{I} = \boldsymbol{R} \,. \tag{4.37}$$

The value of what amounts so far to a formal mathematical manipulation appears with the choice of the receiver term. Suppose that the result of the calculation is expressed as a scalar function $v(\boldsymbol{B})$ of the radiosity vector $\boldsymbol{B}$ (this could be, for example, the value of a single pixel of the final image). Since any linear function of $\boldsymbol{B}$ can be expressed as an inner product, v defines a vector $\boldsymbol{R}$ such that $v(\boldsymbol{B}) = \langle \boldsymbol{R}, \boldsymbol{B} \rangle = \sum_{i=1}^{N} R_i B_i$.

Then using the definition of the adjoint property,

$$v(\boldsymbol{B}) = \langle \boldsymbol{R}, \boldsymbol{B} \rangle = \langle \boldsymbol{M}^* \boldsymbol{I}, \boldsymbol{B} \rangle = \langle \boldsymbol{I}, \boldsymbol{MB} \rangle = \langle \boldsymbol{I}, \boldsymbol{E} \rangle \,,$$

the result of the calculation is expressed as the inner product of the radiosity source term and the solution of the adjoint equation using the vector $\boldsymbol{R}$ as a source of importance. Thus the illumination can be obtained by solving either one of the two adjoint equations. This equation also explains how to assign the "intrinsic" importance terms R_i.

For example, consider the case where the goal of the calculation is to obtain the radiosity of a single patch P_k: the "result function" is expressed as $v(\boldsymbol{B}) = B_k$ with a corresponding vector of receiver terms defined by

$$R_i = \delta_{ik} \qquad 1 \leq i \leq N \,.$$

So far we have established that the adjoint equation, and its solution the importance function, can be used to compute a picture instead of the traditional radiosity equation. However, this property in itself does not improve the situation, since importance is just as hard to compute as radiosity: the governing equations are based on the same form factors. The real benefits of the importance formulation stem from a property of adjoint systems first established by nuclear engineers in the study of neutron transport problems: if approximate solutions are available for both adjoint equations (radiosity and importance), they can be combined into a new solution with higher accuracy than either component alone.

This property is adapted to the case of radiosity algorithms by computing simultaneous solutions for radiosity and importance, and basing the refinement of a hierarchical representation on the combination of both quantities.

4.5.3 Simultaneous solution for radiosity and importance

An importance-driven variation of the hierarchical radiosity algorithm presented in Section 4.4 is obtained by using a new subdivision criterion to control the hierarchical refinement. The new criterion compares the product BIF (radiosity times importance times estimate of the form factor) for a proposed link, to a user-specified threshold.

Compared to the BF refinement criterion introduced in Section 4.4.4, the rationale behind this BIF refinement is that large errors can be tolerated on the form factor—even if a lot of energy is transferred across the link—as long as that energy has little impact on the final picture. Thus refinement will concentrate in areas where significant energy transfers occur, which have an actual influence on the final results.

Estimates for both the radiosity and the importance of a patch are needed to evaluate the subdivision criterion; thus the hierarchical radiosity algorithm is extended to compute an importance solution as well as the radiosity solution. Note that this is practical since the error criterion is symmetric in both quantities, and both are refined to the same precision: a single hierarchical representation of surfaces can then be used for the calculation.

The "solution" stage of the algorithm is modified so that importance is shot at the same time radiosity is gathered across the links. Figure 4.13 shows an example for a pair of patches, where links have been recorded at different hierarchical levels. A single link, at a high level in the hierarchy, suffices to represent the transport of radiosity from P_i to P_j, and the transport of importance from P_j to P_i. However, the transfers in the opposite direction have more impact on the error because the corresponding radiosity and importance values are larger. Thus they are represented at a finer level of subdivision.

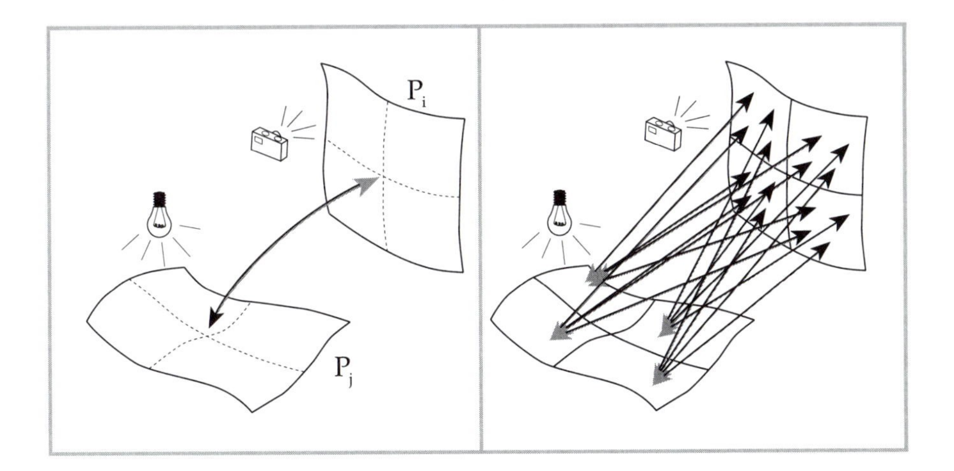

FIGURE 4.13 Simultaneous transport of importance and radiosity. Each link carries energy in one direction (black arrow) and importance in the reverse direction (gray arrow).

There is one noticeable difference in the treatment of radiosity and importance in the hierarchical algorithm. Recall that radiosity is defined as power per unit area, whereas importance is a dimensionless quantity. This subtle difference becomes apparent in the consolidation mechanism, whereby contributions from all levels are distributed throughout the hierarchy. As explained before, radiosity values are pushed down the tree unchanged and area-averaged when pulled upwards. Importance values, on the other hand, are split among the children of a node according to their relative area, and are simply summed when pulled up the hierarchy.

Color Plates 11 to 13 provide a visual representation of importance-driven refinement. A radiosity solution is computed for a simple maze environment and shown in red in the first image. The next image represents a solution of the adjoint equation with a single source of importance at the eye point, where each surface is colored in green according to the resulting importance. The third image shows a superposition of both solutions. Note that the areas with large radiosity *and* importance appear in various shades of yellow and orange. These correspond to the areas where the error criterion is high, therefore they require a finer subdivision. Areas that are either red, green, or black do not receive enough radiosity and importance to warrant much subdivision.

The idea of importance-based refinement leads to very significant savings when only a small fraction of the total scene contributes to the final results. This is useful for example in architecture, since many models consist of numerous distinct regions with limited light exchanges between them—different floors of a building or different rooms on a floor. Color Plates 14 to 19 show an example in which hierarchical subdivision is effectively confined around the visible portion of the scene.

Thus importance methods allow a tremendous simplification of the radiosity calculation and a much better adaptation of the accuracy of the final picture. Since only the most significant energy exchanges are computed to high accuracy, using a stricter bound does not generate the usual complexity explosion. In that regard, the progression from a criterion based on the form factor alone (F refinement) to BF refinement, and on to BIF refinement can be viewed as a natural progression of hierarchical radiosity systems, where the effort is increasingly focused to avoid unnecessary computation.

❒ ❒ ❒

This chapter focused on various methods for reducing the computational burden of radiosity simulations. The goal of these techniques is to avoid the computation and manipulation of large form factor matrices. The progressive refinement strategy does not really reduce the complexity of the complete simulation, since many iterations are still needed before convergence, but it provides useful results after only a very short time and therefore allows better interaction with the simulation process. The substructuring technique and its extension to hierarchical algorithms are the major avenues for actually reducing the size of the problem. Hierarchical methods are clearly needed for the simulation of realistic environments comprising millions of surfaces. Note however that the hierarchical algorithm described here does not offer a progressive solution: interactions are established first, and the propagation of energy across the links is performed later. The notion of importance offers a very convenient tool for evaluating the need for accuracy in various parts of a scene. Its usefulness increases when nondiffuse reflectors are simulated, as will be explained in Chapter 7.

CHAPTER 5

Improving the accuracy of the simulation

As mentioned before, the radiosity method was originally introduced in the heat transfer field. The recent application of this method to simulate visible light and produce images has emphasized several potential difficulties that were not relevant previously. In particular a much finer scale of detail is needed in the resolution of the energy transfers when visible images are produced, compared to thermal simulations. In fact, images computed using the radiosity method are often easy to recognize, since they exhibit some characteristic artifacts such as blocky shadow edges.

All inaccuracies in the computed radiosity values should of course be avoided, since ideally one would like to treat the results of the simulation as reliable estimates of actual illumination; but the most significant difficulties arise from the perceptual impact of certain kinds of inaccuracies in a radiosity solution. This chapter presents some of the improvements introduced in recent years to make radiosity a more reliable simulation method for image synthesis.

It should be emphasized that the notion of accuracy is ambiguous in the context of global illumination for image synthesis. Various, sometimes contradictory, error metrics can be used to evaluate the success or failure of different approaches. When the end result is a displayed image, its accuracy cannot be evaluated without considering the impact of perceptual issues. In general, a quantitative, viewer-independent measure of accuracy will be used together with a more perceptual measure, usually more qualitative, that attempts to assess the *visual* quality of the pictures.

The first group of algorithms presented in this chapter is concerned with the accuracy of the radiosity values themselves. Numerous applications such as engineering simulations do not require "pretty pictures" but rather numerically reliable results. One obvious source of error is the numerical computation of the form factor, and improved computational methods are discussed below. However, even with a set of accurate form factors, the solution of the radiosity equation is not necessarily close to a solution of the continuous illumination equation. The discretization process that led to the radiosity equation can be refined by using more elaborate basis functions in a finite-element framework. Therefore the important question of the choice of the basis functions and of the discretization of the surfaces is also studied.

Even when an accurate radiosity solution is obtained in terms of radiometric quantities, the production of an image for display is subject to more errors in the visual and perceptual domain. Thus a final section is devoted to the subject of reconstructing continuous radiosity functions from the radiosity values and avoiding visual artifacts.

5.1 Accurate computation of the form factors

The hemi-cube algorithm suffers from a variety of problems that make it unreliable if precise results are desired. Furthermore, most of these problems become worse when the progressive refinement approach is used. This section presents an analysis of the weaknesses of the hemi-cube, particularly in the context of progressive refinement radiosity, and then shows how to alleviate most of the accuracy problems. Possible strategies include selectively improving the hemi-cube, and choosing a different method for visibility determination.

5.1.1 Problems with the hemi-cube

We begin by clearly stating the drawbacks of the hemi-cube technique. The implicit underlying assumptions and conditions of validity of the method are more easily violated in the context of the progressive refinement approach. The following analysis is inspired by reference [14].

Implicit assumptions of the hemi-cube

Recall the definition of the form factor given in Equation 3.19:

$$F_{ij} = \frac{1}{A_i} \int_{x \in P_i} \int_{y \in P_j} \frac{\cos\theta \cos\theta'}{\pi r^2} V(x, y) dx dy .$$

A common practice in hemi-cube implementations is to ignore the outer integral in this formula, thereby replacing the area form factor by the pointwise form factor introduced in Section 3.1.5. The point that is chosen for the placement of the hemi-cube is usually the center of the patch. The implicit assumption contained in this practice is that the value of the inner integral does not change "too much" across the area of the patch. Upon closer examination, it appears that this assumption holds only if the following two conditions are met.

- **Proximity assumption:** Surfaces are far away from each other, relative to their size. This ensures that the fraction

$$\frac{\cos\theta\cos\theta'}{\pi r^2}$$

in Equation 3.19 varies very little over the area of the reference patch.
- **Visibility assumption:** The visibility of other surfaces does not change across the patch. This ensures that the V term in Equation 3.19 remains constant.

Another source of error in hemi-cube implementations is limited resolution. Regular point sampling on the faces of the hemi-cube is subject to aliasing, in a manner similar to raster display algorithms. Most surfaces, once projected on the hemi-cube, do not cover an exact number of cells, so depending on the origin of projection, the form factor may vary considerably. Even worse, some surfaces may be missed altogether if their projection on

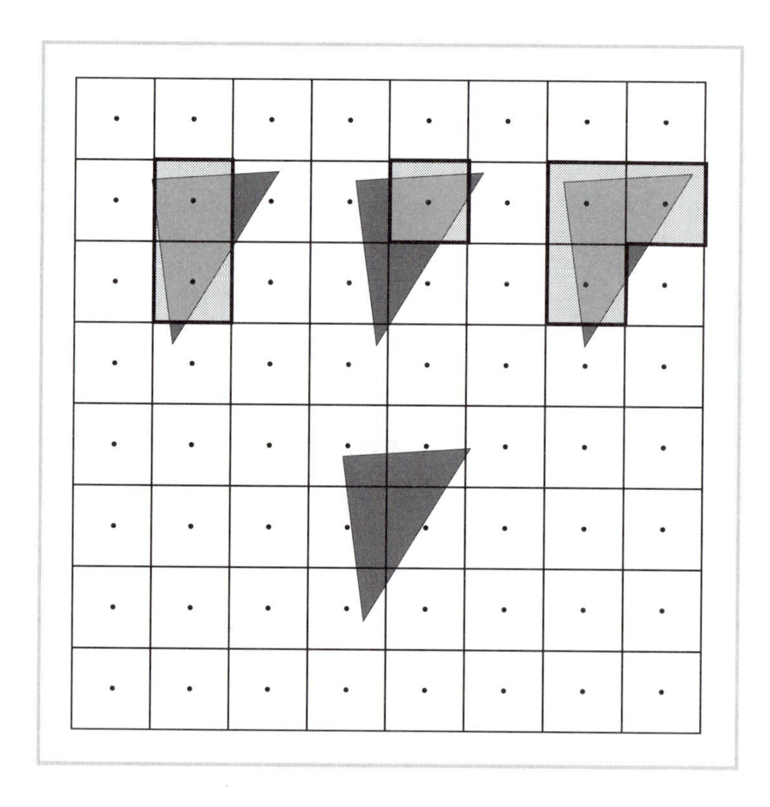

FIGURE 5.1 Four identical surfaces have been projected onto the top face of the hemi-cube. Centers of hemi-cube cells are marked by black dots. Each projection covers a different number of hemi-cube cell centers, resulting in a wide variance in the associated form factors.

the hemi-cube is small enough to fall entirely in between the centers of hemi-cube cells. These problems are illustrated in Figure 5.1.

Finally, it is clear that if the hemi-cube faces are divided into N_C cells, at most N_C surfaces in the environment will be assigned a non-zero form factor. This happens because at most N_C *delta-form factors* are assigned. This simple argument shows that the choice of hemi-cube resolution should depend on the complexity of the scene.

A common result of this resolution error is the emergence of plaid patterns on the surfaces, as demonstrated in Figure 5.2. The sampling rate of the hemi-cube "beats" with the regular mesh on the receiving surface to produce a regular, undesirable pattern.

A closer look at progressive refinement radiosity

Recall that in the progressive refinement radiosity method, the hemi-cube is used to *shoot* light from emitters, as opposed to *gathering* light on receivers. This reformulation is perfectly valid on a theoretic level, but turns out to be much more sensitive to numerical problems posed by the hemi-cube.

The impact of the progressive refinement algorithm is most easily understood when considering the portion of the original algorithm that is not symmetrical with respect to the exchange of emitters and receivers; that is, the substructuring scheme of Section 4.2.

As described in Section 4.2, substructuring amounts to setting up a distinction between patches (used as emitters of light) and elements (used as receivers), where patches are typically much larger than elements. In the progressive refinement approach the hemi-cube is placed on patches, not elements. Replacing the area integral by a single sample point

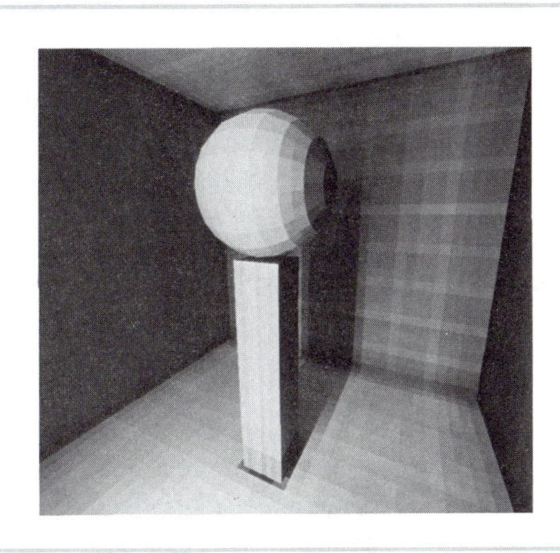

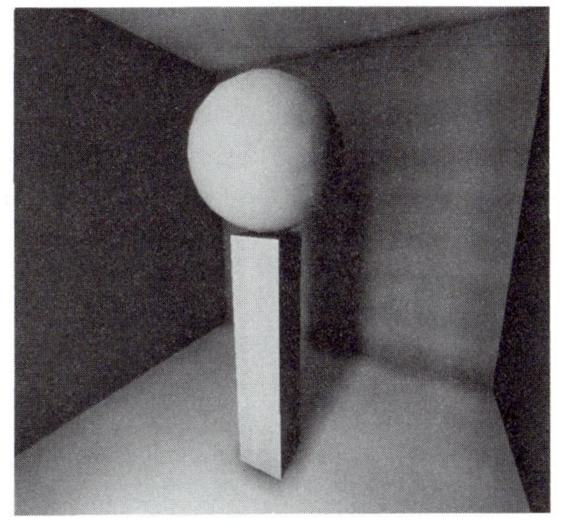

FIGURE 5.2 Plaid pattern caused by hemi-cube aliasing. The image on the left shows the resulting radiosity at each element, while the image on the right uses bilinear interpolation to obtain continuous radiosity variations. (*Courtesy of Daniel R. Baum, Silicon Graphics.*)

across the larger structure is more likely to introduce errors, by violating either the proximity or visibility assumption.

In addition, since elements are smaller and more numerous than patches, the projection on the hemi-cube is more likely to suffer from aliasing and "plaiding." In the traditional gathering approach, such aliasing occurs much less frequently, mainly when light sources (large patches) appear too small as seen from a given surface.

A second effect of the progressive refinement procedure is that form factors are not computed directly but through the use of the reciprocity relation. Unfortunately, most hemi-cube implementations compute point-to-patch form factors, for which the reciprocity relation does not hold.

The hemi-cube computes form factors *from* a given patch; that is, if placed on patch P_i, a row of the form factor matrix $\{F_{ij}\}_{j=1..N}$ is obtained. What is needed for a "shot" of progressive refinement radiosity is a column of the form factor matrix $\{F_{ji}\}_{j=1..N}$, as shown in Equation 4.26. As explained in the previous chapter these form factors are typically obtained using the reciprocity relation $A_i F_{ij} = A_j F_{ji}$. This calculation does not introduce much error by itself, since the areas are usually known with good precision, but it emphasizes errors due to the use of a single hemi-cube centered on the patch. This error is not a result of the numerical calculation but instead results from a violation of the reciprocity relation. To better understand why this is the case, let us consider the following (rather exaggerated) situation: a large patch almost completely covered by a plate that has a pinhole in its center. The center of this patch has an unobstructed view of the environment through the pinhole, while the patch itself is not visible from anywhere. Thus a point-to-patch form factor computed from the center cannot be used reliably to derive form factors to that patch.

Indeed the reciprocity relation is derived from the double integral formulation of the form factor, and when a single integral is used, as in the point-to-patch form factor, reciprocity does not hold anymore.

In search of better solutions

Some of the issues mentioned above are not really due to the hemi-cube, but to the use of a single point-to-patch form factor to represent the area form factor. One obvious remedy consists of approximating the outer area integral in the form factor by a weighted average of a number of sample hemi-cubes distributed across the surface of the patch. This was suggested in the original article on the hemi-cube [37]. However, this simple workaround also has some drawbacks: since the hemi-cube computes the form factors to all surfaces of the scene at the same time, the same sample points on the source patch are used to compute all form factors from that patch. Although some optimization is possible, the total cost of the form factor calculation stage is roughly multiplied by the number of samples used.

At this point, it is worth noting that the hemi-cube actually fulfills two duties at the same time: on the one hand it is a visibility-checking device, as it identifies the visible surfaces from a point, and on the other hand it is used to compute the value of the form factor by adding together the appropriate delta-form factors. To obtain more accurate algorithms, alternative techniques can be used for one or both of these duties. For instance, visibility can be determined using the hemi-cube or ray casting, while the computation of the actual form factors can either be done analytically or by point sampling.

5.1.2 Avoiding accuracy problems with the hemi-cube

The hemi-cube algorithm can be enhanced in the following manner: violations of the proximity and visibility assumptions are identified, and trigger the use of a more robust analytical computation for the form factor [13]. In essence, the algorithm relies on the hemi-cube to test the visibility of elements in the scene, but uses a more accurate method to obtain the numerical value of the form factor in some cases. Heuristic criteria are used to decide where the improved calculation method should be used.

Suppose that element P_e is visible through the center of a particular hemi-cube cell q on patch P_i. The conventional hemi-cube technique assigns the delta-form factor ΔF_q of that cell to the form factor F_{P_i,P_e}.[1] The reciprocity relation is then used to obtain F_{P_e,P_i}.

As an alternative, for polygonal patches, direct calculation of the point-to-patch form factor F_{x_e,P_i} is possible using Equation 3.53. However, this calculation is only valid if point x_e has a complete view of patch P_i. The final area-to-area form factor F_{P_e,P_i} is then computed by area-averaging all available point-to-patch form factors for element P_e, corresponding to different hemi-cube cells. For that average, the projected area of each hemi-cube cell onto the element is used, as shown in Figure 5.3.

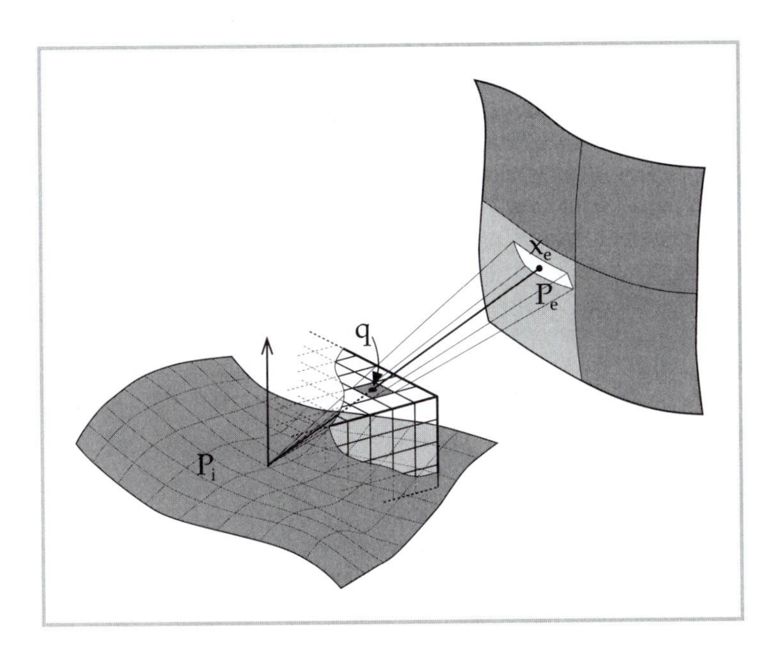

FIGURE 5.3 An element with a point seen through a hemi-cube cell.

[1]Although in reality the pointwise form factor F_{x_i,P_e} from the center of patch P_i is being computed, it is considered identical to the patch-to-patch form factor.

Because of its relatively high cost, this direct calculation is only performed when one of the validity assumptions is violated, in particular the proximity assumption, which is the easiest to check. The resolution issue is not addressed by this algorithm, since elements that are missed by the hemi-cube are ignored. The visibility issue is resolved by recursively subdividing the source patch until the hemi-cubes from all subpatches return similar visibility information.

One consequence of this treatment of visibility is that the subdivision of a particular source patch is the same for all receiving elements. It may be argued that a very distant element would require much less subdivision of the source patch than a close one, since visibility is less likely to change across the patch. The algorithm explained in the following section offers the ability to vary the subdivision of the source patch based on the particular receiving element being considered.

5.1.3 Direct computation at the vertices using ray casting

Looking back at the various hemi-cube methods, the following observation can be made: shooting energy from a patch using the hemi-cube is far less effective than the conventional method of gathering energy with the hemi-cube. As mentioned earlier, the hemi-cube is typically used to compute a point-to-area form factor, but using this point as a source produces more noticeable error than using it as a receiver. Conversely, receivers are treated as areas, which can be missed by the hemi-cube if their projection is too small. Considering that in the end a radiosity value is needed at mesh vertices for display and shading purposes, the use of area receivers is even more questionable.

In essence, the propagation of radiosity should be modeled from areas to points rather than the reverse. This is what the hemi-cube achieves when used to gather energy, but a better method is needed for shooting.

An elegant algorithm uses *ray casting* both to solve the visibility problem and to directly compute form factors from receiving vertices to the source patch [185]. This allows computed radiosities to be used directly for display, without the extrapolation stage described in Section 3.2.3.

Computing the form factor integral

Let us consider a step of the progressive refinement radiosity algorithm, in which the source patch is P_i. Instead of computing a number of form factors from P_i and using the reciprocity relation to obtain the desired reverse factors, a point-to-patch form factor can be directly computed from each vertex of the mesh using the following formula (Equation 3.25):

$$F_{y,P_i} = \int_{x \in P_i} \frac{\cos\theta' \cos\theta}{\pi r^2} V(y,x) dx \,. \qquad \textbf{(5.1)}$$

The radiosity received at each vertex is then obtained by multiplying this form factor by the source patch's radiosity. The integral in Equation 5.1 can be evaluated numerically by breaking down the surface of patch P_i into a number of N_f fragments P_i^k $(k = 1 \ldots N_f)$, as shown in Figure 5.4, and summing the integrals corresponding to all visible fragments. This assumes that each fragment has a uniform visibility from point y. If the (binary) visibility of fragment P_i^k is denoted by $V_k \in \{0, 1\}$, then an estimate of F_{y,P_i} is

$$\hat{F}_{y,P_i} = \sum_{k=1}^{n_i} V_k \, \delta F_k \,, \tag{5.2}$$

where

$$\delta F_k = \int_{x \in P_i^k} \frac{\cos\theta \cos\theta'}{\pi r^2} dx \,.$$

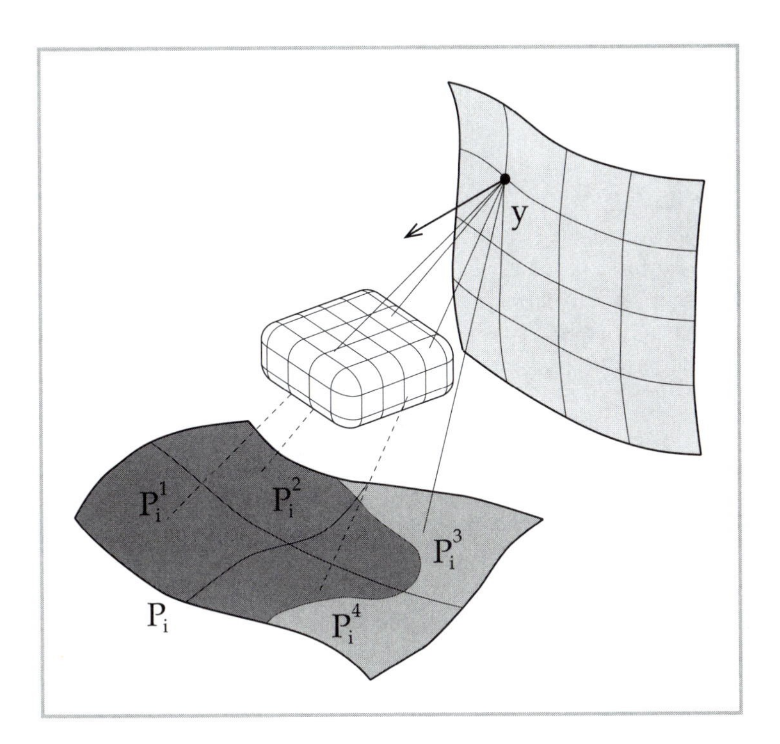

FIGURE 5.4 Source patch subdivision for the computation of a form factor.

Thus the visibility issue and the actual calculation of the form factor are effectively decoupled: visibility is determined for each fragment by casting one or several rays, and the integral for each visible fragment can be computed in a number of ways. The simplest scheme consists of computing the value of the integrand at the center of the fragment and multiplying it by the fragment's area, effectively assuming a constant integrand over the fragment. However, very severe inaccuracies (and even divergence) can occur using this point sampling technique for surfaces that are close together, due to the $1/r^2$ term in the integrand. It is therefore preferable to obtain a more accurate value for each fragment, taking into account its actual area. To this end more elaborate quadrature methods can be employed [148].

One possibility, assuming polygonal environment, is to use the analytical formula introduced in the previous section to compute the form factor to each fragment. The sole remaining possible source of error in that case will be the assumption that each fragment is entirely visible or entirely invisible. However, the amount of computation is very substantial, and a better compromise between accuracy and speed is the following: each fragment is approximated by a disc with the same area and orientation, for which an analytical expression of the form factor is available.

The form factor from a differential area to a parallel disc of radius a was given in Section 3.3.1:

$$F_{x,\mathrm{disc}} = \frac{a^2}{a^2 + r^2} . \tag{5.3}$$

If a fragment P_i^k has area A_i^k, Equation 5.3 is used with a defined such that $\pi a^2 = A_i^k$. The effect of the respective orientations of the source and receiving surfaces is taken into account by multiplying the form factor by the cosines of the relevant angles. This represents an approximation since, strictly speaking, the angles can vary across the fragment. However, as long as the distance between patches is large relative to their size, this remains a second-order approximation. The corresponding form factor is thus

$$\delta F_k = \frac{A_i^k \cos\theta \cos\theta'}{A_i^k + \pi r^2} . \tag{5.4}$$

Note that as $r \to 0$, $\delta F_k \to \cos\theta\cos\theta'$ and the fraction always has a finite value. Thus divergence is avoided even for patches that are very close together.

Choice of the sample points on the source patch

An important question is that of the selection of the source fragments to be used in Equation 5.2. Several strategies can be used and in fact a different one can even be used for each receiving point.

The first and simplest strategy is to subdivide the source patch regularly (either in 3D space or in parameter space). This is adequate if the integrand does not vary steeply across the source patch, since it basically corresponds to a low-order quadrature method. Note that the level of subdivision can still be chosen independently for each particular receiver.

When the receiver is close to the source patch relative to the patch's size, the point-to-point form factor varies greatly across the source patch, and low-order quadratures do not suffice to obtain an accurate value. The approximation of a fragment's form factor using a disc is valid only for very small fragments in regions with a rapid variation of the integrand. A hierarchical decomposition of the source patch can give much better results than a uniform one, by concentrating the fragments where the integrand varies the most. Such a decomposition is readily computed by comparing the form factor estimate obtained by using the disc approximation to that obtained using four smaller discs, and subdividing where the difference exceeds a specified threshold. Figure 5.5 shows examples of uniform and hierarchical sampling patterns.

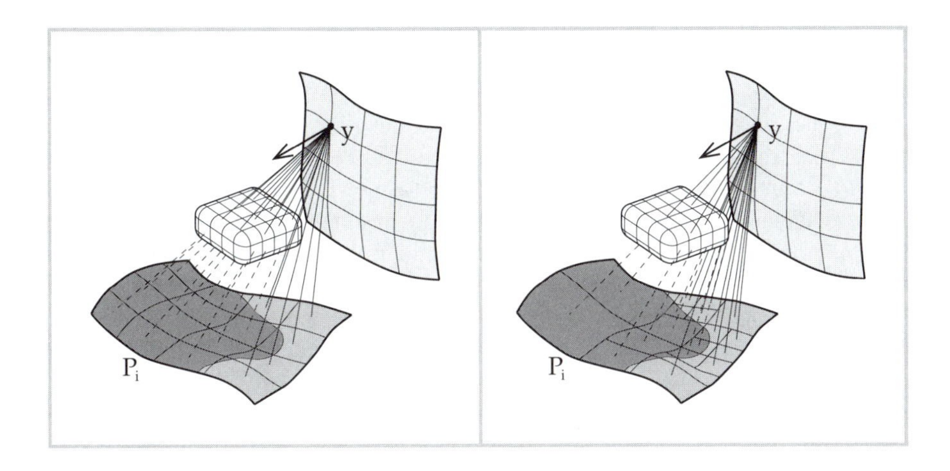

FIGURE 5.5 Uniform vs. adaptive sampling of the source patch.

Choice of the sample points on receiving patches

The ray casting method has other benefits than the computation of accurate form factors: *shooting*, or the operation of sending power from a source patch to a receiving sample point, is performed for all receiving sample points in turn, simulating a step of the progressive refinement radiosity method. The flexibility of ray casting allows the effort devoted to the computation of these form factors to be distributed at will among the surfaces of interest. Sample points can be selected on the receiving surfaces based on any criteria, with the assurance that all sample points will receive an estimate of their form factor to the current source patch. This was not the case for the hemi-cube because of its limited resolution.

Furthermore, adaptive refinement of the mesh of sample points is easily performed, since form factors can be computed for newly introduced points independently of the existing mesh. A subdivision criterion can be established, based for example on radiosity gradients: after all receiving sample points have gathered their new radiosity, a decision is made for each pair of neighboring samples. New vertices are introduced where indicated by the subdivision criterion, and their radiosity (or rather their form factor to the source) is computed directly at very little cost.

Discussion of the ray casting approach

The main benefit of the ray casting approach for the computation of form factors is the greater flexibility offered in contrast to the hemi-cube method. In particular, since a separate computation is carried out for each receiving vertex of the scene, algorithmic parameters can be fine-tuned according to each specific situation. For example, the sampling pattern on the source patch can be refined depending on the receiving vertex's distance or on the source patch's radiosity. Receiving patches that are deemed important can use finer sampling on the source. Another example of ray casting's flexibility concerns the possibility of adaptive subdivision during a radiosity shot. A variety of subdivision criteria can be devised, each to be used in particular situations. When the source patch is deemed a significant light source, a more stringent criterion can be selected that compares the visibility of the light source from neighboring vertices. This information is available from the visibility tests for all fragments. Subdivision can then be triggered as soon as visibility differs significantly [161].

The aliasing problems inherent in the fixed sampling of the hemi-cube are completely absent from the ray casting method, since all receiving vertices are guaranteed to obtain an estimate of their form factor to the source. The improved accuracy comes at higher computational cost, and as expected ray casting is typically slower than the hemi-cube, even without considering the fact that the latter can take advantage of special-purpose graphics hardware. Outside of speed considerations, the ray casting method represents a marked improvement over the hemi-cube approach, and has the additional advantage of being easily implemented, since efficient ray tracing algorithms are readily available.

Finally, note that the form factor from a sample point in the scene to the "shooting patch" can be computed to great accuracy (with a price to pay in the form of a great many sample points on the source patch) using the ray casting approach outlined above, which is a remarkable improvement over the hemi-cube approach. But care must be taken not to lose this increased precision because of other approximations: the radiosity of the shooting patch is no longer a relevant variable in this process, since radiosity values are computed only at the vertices of the mesh. Thus patch radiosities must be computed as a weighted average of the vertex radiosities, which entails some degree of approximation. In other words, it is probably unnecessary to devote too much effort to the computation of a very accurate form factor, since that form factor is later multiplied by a single patch radiosity value whose computation also suffers some error.

5.2 Finite-element formulation of radiosity

A fundamental and somewhat provoking question should be considered at this point. In the previous section the issue of accurate computation of the form factor was addressed, but do accurate form factors guarantee an accurate solution? If the numerical techniques used to solve the radiosity equation converge, an accurate solution of this discrete radiosity equation will be obtained. But recall that the discrete radiosity formulation was derived under strict assumptions that severely limit the range of problems accurately modeled. In particular, radiosity was assumed to take a constant value across each patch of the scene. This assumption can be stated in other words by saying that the radiosity function was expressed as a sum of constant basis functions.

The point here is that performing an accurate computation of the form factors will not help in obtaining a solution that is "close" to the true continuous solution if that true solution cannot be represented properly by a sum of constant functions. In such cases, the constant radiosity assumption can be replaced by the assumption that the approximate radiosity solution is a linear combination of some other basis functions. This is the basic principle of *finite-element* methods, where a discrete equation is formed to link the scalar coefficients or coordinates of the solution in the set of basis functions.

The finite-element procedure is a general technique to obtain approximate solutions of continuous integral equations such as the diffuse illumination equation. In finite-element language, a number of *nodes* are chosen on the surfaces, each with an associated *shape function* (denoted by $N_j(x),\quad j = 1 \ldots N$). An approximate radiosity function across the surfaces is then sought as a linear combination of these shape functions:

$$\tilde{B}(x) = \sum_{j=1}^{N} B_j N_j(x)\,, \tag{5.5}$$

the variables being the N scalars B_j, also known as *nodal values*. A variety of shape functions can be chosen, including constant, linear, quadratic, and other polynomial functions. The shape functions form a basis of the set of obtainable solutions, and are often referred to as basis functions. Therefore the search for approximate solutions is limited to a finite-dimensional subspace of functions. Shape functions usually have compact support, that is, they take non-zero values only over a (small) number of surface elements. The condition that

$$N_j(x_i) = \delta_{ij}$$

is often imposed on the system of nodes and shape functions, so that

$$\forall i \quad \tilde{B}(x_i) = B_i\,.$$

The ambiguity between area values and point values noted in Section 5.1.3 is also resolved elegantly by the finite-element formulation, since all variables are computed at nodes.

In order to solve the diffuse illumination equation, first introduced as Equation 3.11:

$$B(x) = E(x) + \frac{\rho_d(x)}{\pi} \int_{y \in S} B(y) \frac{\cos\theta \cos\theta'}{r^2} V(x, y) dy\,,$$

let us define a kernel function

$$\kappa(x, y) = \rho_d(x)\frac{\cos\theta\cos\theta'}{\pi r^2}V(x, y) \tag{5.6}$$

so that the illumination equation can be written

$$B(x) = E(x) + \int_{y\in S} \kappa(x, y)B(y)dy\,. \tag{5.7}$$

This type of equation is known as a Fredholm integral equation of the second kind. Note that the unknown radiosity function, B, appears both outside and inside the integral.

To measure the quality of the approximation, a residual function r is defined as

$$r(x) = \tilde{B}(x) - E(x) - \int_{y\in S} \kappa(x, y)\tilde{B}(y)dy\,. \tag{5.8}$$

This residual function is the continuous analog of the residual vector used with relaxation methods in Section 4.1. Ideally the residual should be zero. Since the domain of approximate solutions is restricted by the choice of the shape functions, however, the residual is not identically zero and should instead be "minimized" in some sense. Several minimization constraints can be imposed on the solution; two are presented below.

5.2.1 Galerkin method

For mathematical convenience, let us denote by $\mathcal{F}$ the space of radiosity functions defined over the surfaces of the scene. Since we are considering solutions that are linear combinations of a finite number of shape functions, the domain of possible solutions is restricted to a finite-dimensional subspace $\mathcal{F}_0$ of the entire function space, spanned by the set of shape functions. Unfortunately the true solution in general is not contained in $\mathcal{F}_0$.

The problem can thus be formulated as a search for the function in the subspace $\mathcal{F}_0$ that is "closest" to the actual solution, in a sense that is clarified below.

$\mathcal{F}$ can be equipped with an inner product defined by

$$\langle f, g\rangle = \int_{x\in S} f(x)g(x)dx\,. \tag{5.9}$$

The "closest function in subspace" condition is then expressed as the constraint that the residual be orthogonal to all basis functions in $\mathcal{F}_0$.

$$\forall i \quad \langle r, N_i\rangle = 0\,. \tag{5.10}$$

Using the definition of the residual in Equation 5.8, Equation 5.10 expands into

$$\forall i \quad \langle\tilde{B}, N_i\rangle - \langle E, N_i\rangle - \langle\int_{y\in S} \kappa(x, y)\tilde{B}(y)dy, N_i\rangle = 0$$

$$\langle \sum_{j=1}^{N} B_j N_j, N_i \rangle - \langle E, N_i \rangle - \langle \int_{y \in S} \kappa(x, y) \sum_{j=1}^{N} B_j N_j(y) dy, N_i \rangle = 0$$

$$\sum_{j=1}^{N} B_j \langle N_j, N_i \rangle - \langle E, N_i \rangle - \sum_{j=1}^{N} B_j \langle \int_{y \in S} \kappa(x, y) N_j(y) dy, N_i \rangle = 0 .$$

Using the shorthand notations

$$\epsilon_i = \langle E, N_i \rangle ,$$

and

$$\Delta_{ij} = \langle N_i, N_j \rangle ,$$

and expressing the inner product as an integral (Equation 5.9), the Galerkin condition becomes

$$\forall i \quad \epsilon_i = \sum_{j=1}^{N} B_j \left(\Delta_{ij} - \int_{x \in S} N_i(x) dx \int_{y \in S} \kappa(x, y) N_j(y) dy \right) . \tag{5.11}$$

Although it appears to be more complex, Equation 5.11 is comparable to the traditional radiosity equation. In particular it can be expressed as a matrix equation similar to Equation 3.39,

$$\boldsymbol{MB} = \varepsilon ,$$

with

$$M_{ij} = \Delta_{ij} - \int_{x \in S} N_i(x) dx \int_{y \in S} \kappa(x, y) N_j(y) dy . \tag{5.12}$$

The radiosity equation: Galerkin method with constant elements

In this section, we show that the diffuse radiosity equation that was originally derived from a number of simplifying assumptions is a special case of the more general Galerkin formulation.

Consider the very simple case of constant basis functions. One node is placed in each patch, for example in the center, and the shape functions are disjoint "box" functions, as shown in Figure 5.6. These are defined by

$$N_j(x) = \begin{cases} 1 & \text{if } x \in P_j \\ 0 & \text{if } x \notin P_j \end{cases} . \tag{5.13}$$

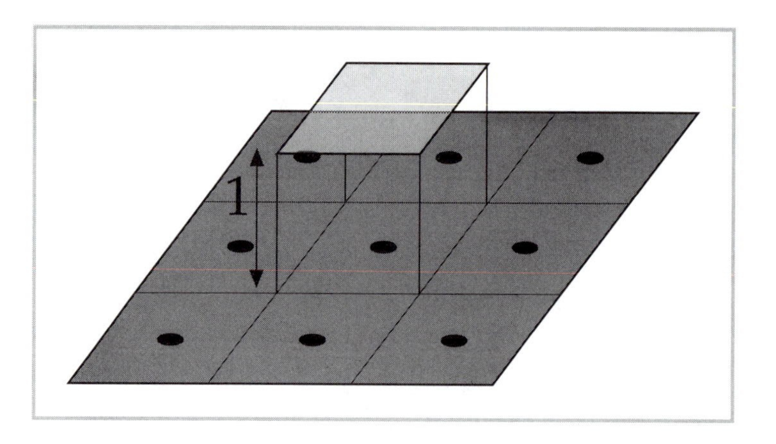

FIGURE 5.6 Constant basis function defined over a rectangular element.

It is easy to see that in that case $\Delta_{ij} = A_i \delta_{ij}$, where δ_{ij} is the Kronecker symbol, and Equation 5.11 becomes

$$\forall i \quad A_i E_i = A_i B_i - \sum_{j=1}^{N} B_j \int_{x \in P_i} dx \int_{y \in P_j} \kappa(x, y) dy . \tag{5.14}$$

Note that the integrals are computed over the areas of patches P_i and P_j, since the shape functions are non-zero only for points inside these patches. Dividing by A_i and reorganizing the terms, the radiosity equation (Equation 3.18) is found:

$$\forall i \quad B_i = E_i + \sum_{j=1}^{N} B_j \rho_{di} \left(\frac{1}{A_i} \int_{x \in P_i} \int_{y \in P_j} \frac{\cos\theta \cos\theta'}{\pi r^2} V(x, y) dx dy \right) .$$

This identity is significant since it indicates an avenue for the development of better algorithms. The use of more sophisticated shape functions allows a more accurate representation of the radiosity functions, effectively getting rid of the "constant radiosity" assumption.

5.2.2 Point collocation method

An alternative to the Galerkin constraint is to impose on the residual that it vanishes at all nodal points, that is,

$$\forall i \quad r(x_i) = 0 . \tag{5.15}$$

This condition expands into

$$\forall i \quad E(x_i) = \sum_{j=1}^{N} B_j \left(N_j(x_i) - \int_{y \in S} \kappa(x_i, y) N_j(y) dy \right) . \qquad \textbf{(5.16)}$$

The collocation technique only evaluates the kernel at fixed locations x_i with respect to the first variable, whereas the Galerkin technique uses an integral of the entire kernel. Therefore Galerkin techniques "extract" more information from the kernel, at the cost of a more complex calculation.

Using a single hemi-cube per patch: point collocation method with constant elements

In the case of constant elements (Section 5.2.1), $N_j(x_i) = \delta_{ij}$ for all i and j, and Equation 5.16 reduces to

$$\forall i \quad B_i = E_i + \sum_{j=1}^{N} B_j \int_{y \in P_j} \kappa(x_i, y) dy \qquad \textbf{(5.17)}$$

$$B_i = E_i + \sum_{j=1}^{N} B_j \rho_i F_{x_i, P_j} . \qquad \textbf{(5.18)}$$

This is equivalent to the radiosity equation, with the form factor replaced by the pointwise "form factor"

$$F_{x_i, P_j} = \int_{y \in P_j} \frac{\cos\theta \cos\theta'}{\pi r^2} V(x_i, y) dy . \qquad \textbf{(5.19)}$$

Since the hemi-cube technique effectively computes pointwise form factors as explained in Section 5.1.1, the "one hemi-cube per patch" technique is exactly equivalent to point collocation with constant basis functions.

5.2.3 Computing the form factors

We have seen that in general the finite-element formulation produces a system of linear equations that are similar to the original radiosity equations. By analogy with this standard equation, a "form factor" can be defined in this case as well. This form factor, however, is not a simple fraction of the total energy radiated by one patch that is received by the other. In this more general sense there exists a form factor for each pair of nodes, which quantifies the strength of the coupling between the two associated shape functions. For example, with the Galerkin method, the equivalent of the form factor is the quantity

$$\hat{F}_{ij} = \int_{x \in S} N_i(x) dx \int_{y \in S} \kappa(x, y) N_j(y) dy . \qquad \textbf{(5.20)}$$

The presence of shape functions N_i and N_j inside the integrals makes this factor more difficult to compute than the standard form factor. However, it should be noted that it is still a purely geometrical quantity. As shown above this factor reduces to the usual form factor in the case of constant shape functions. Even when more elaborate shape functions are used, the integrals can generally be computed over a restricted subset of the surfaces in the scene, that is, the set of elements over which N_i and N_j take non-zero values. This typically represents a small number of elements around nodes i and j.

Shape functions are often chosen to be piecewise polynomial functions, therefore they exhibit smooth variations over the elements. Unfortunately the kernel function $\kappa(x, y)$ has a much more complex behavior. It varies very quickly when surfaces are close together, and exhibits discontinuities due to the visibility term. Thus no simple quadrature rule can guarantee an accurate evaluation of the form factor integral in all cases.

An example of non-constant shape functions: linear elements

Let us first consider the case of linear shape functions: suppose a set of elements is given, realizing a tessellation of the surfaces in the scene. For simplicity assume that all elements are triangles, although bilinear shape functions can easily be defined on quadrilaterals as well. For such a configuration, nodes are positioned at the vertices of the mesh. The corresponding shape functions are "tents" with a single pole at the corresponding node, thus taking the value 1 at the node and zero at all neighboring nodes, as shown in Figure 5.7.

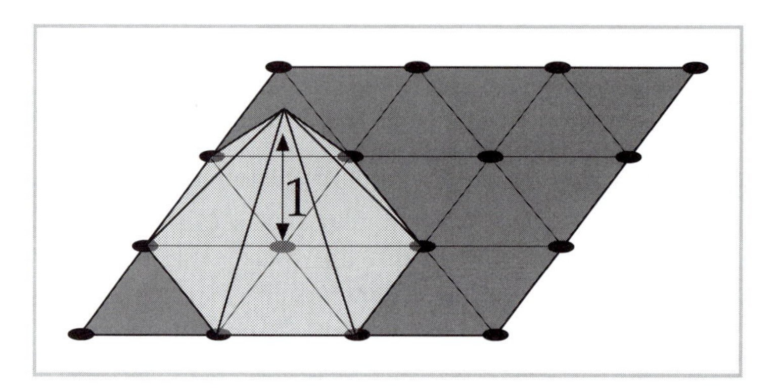

FIGURE 5.7 Linear shape function defined over triangular elements.

The hemi-cube technique can be adapted to compute the form factor integral for linear shape functions, by taking advantage of interpolation hardware when projecting onto the hemi-cube faces [114]. As each triangular element is projected, the value of its three vertices' shape functions is interpolated across its area. This can be performed automatically with hardware interpolation engines.

Note that the use of linear shape functions is not equivalent to the use of bilinear interpolation of the vertex radiosities during the rendering phase, following a traditional radiosity step with constant basis functions. By taking into account the variation of radiosity across the elements during the calculation of energy exchanges, a more accurate representation of the illumination is obtained with linear shape functions.

Since the hemi-cube suffers from severe limitations, as outlined in Section 5.1.1, more accurate techniques based on ray casting can be employed to evaluate the form factor integral. In particular, stochastic methods such as *Monte Carlo quadrature* (discussed in Section 8.3.1) provide statistical estimates of the integral by computing the kernel and shape functions for random pairs of points on two elements.

Higher-order elements

The choice of shape functions and element shapes could be regarded as a black art by nonspecialists. The infinite number of possible combinations and their complicated impact on quality and speed make it almost impossible to formulate a definitive recommendation.

Consider the relative merits of a large number of elements with low-order polynomial shape functions, versus a small number of elements with high-order polynomial shape functions. In the former case the computation of the form factors is relatively simple but there are many such factors, while in the latter case there are far fewer factors but they are computed at a higher cost [180].

When large elements are used together with high-order polynomials, the variations of the visibility function across the area of the elements are unlikely to be captured accurately by simple quadrature methods. The typical result of these errors is ringing in the solution estimates. One proposed workaround consists of separating the computation of the visibility term from that of the coupling factor between shape functions. The visibility term is obtained using a high-resolution "shadow mask," while the unoccluded form factor is computed using Gauss quadrature points [203].

Note that in general it is perfectly valid practice to mix various types of shape functions in a single scene. In fact, if certain features of the final radiosity functions are known in advance, it is possible to make an educated guess concerning the order of the shape functions needed on various surfaces. In particular, this should be done when using *predictive* meshing techniques such as the ones described in Section 5.3.3.

5.2.4 Hierarchical elements and wavelets

A particular class of shape functions has recently received a lot of attention for the representation of radiosity functions. These are the *hierarchical basis functions*. For example, the hierarchical radiosity algorithm of Section 4.4 can be considered to decompose radiosity over a set of hierarchical "box" functions: contributions stored at various levels of the hierarchy are the coordinates of the radiosity function on the corresponding basis functions. Note that this particular set of hierarchical box functions is redundant, in that several combinations of hierarchical contributions can yield the same overall radiosity function; the basis functions are not linearly independent.

This framework sheds new light on the hierarchical radiosity process introduced in Section 4.4: recall that the form factor matrix was represented in the form of a block matrix, each block representing a link. The size of that matrix, N, was the number of elements at the finest subdivision level, and the hierarchical linking process was considered a means of compressing the matrix. In light of the preceding discussion of finite-element methods, another representation suggests itself. Consider the hypothetical one-dimensional example used earlier in Figure 4.9: if there are N basis functions at the finest level of subdivision, then the total number of basis functions in the hierarchical set is $N + \frac{N}{2} + \frac{N}{4} + \ldots + 1 \approx 2N$. Thus a $2N \times 2N$ matrix can be assembled to represent the "form factors" given by Equation 5.20 over the set of hierarchical basis functions. Both matrix representations are shown in Figure 5.8. For the larger matrix the basis functions are arranged in breadth-first order, with all finest-level basis functions grouped to the left. Thus the lower-left quadrant of that matrix corresponds to the usual radiosity matrix. Note that an entry of the larger matrix that is not in the lower-left quadrant represents a block in the previous matrix, since an interaction is taking place higher up in the hierarchy.

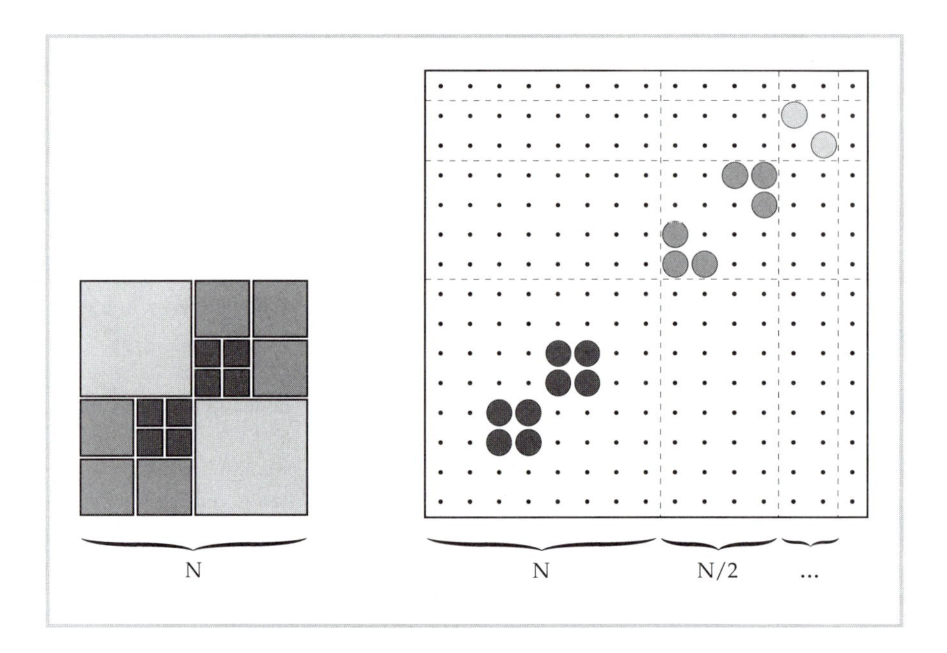

FIGURE 5.8 Two possible representations of hierarchical radiosity matrices. An element in the larger matrix corresponds to a block in the smaller matrix.

In the hierarchical radiosity algorithm, compression is realized by choosing (in a non-unique manner) a limited number of non-zero entries, such that the corresponding blocks completely cover the original matrix, as shown in Figure 5.8. The set of hierarchical box functions is not well suited to a finite-element formulation, since the functions are not linearly independent. Other sets of hierarchical basis functions can be constructed using the recently established theory of wavelets.

Wavelet bases for radiosity

A comprehensive discussion of wavelets and their possible applications in solving integral equations is beyond the scope of this book. However, wavelet bases have recently been shown to provide a natural extension of hierarchical radiosity, and the following presentation aims at providing a flavor of the technique. The interested reader will find a wealth of literature on wavelets, and can consult [70, 150] for a good introductory presentation.

Consider a one-dimensional scene treated by hierarchical radiosity: the push and pull operations described in Section 4.4.3 create a complete representation of the radiosity function at all levels of the hierarchy, where the value at any given level represents an area average of the radiosity across the corresponding element. The radiosity function can thus be approximated at various levels of detail, by using only the basis functions at the desired level.

Wavelets are hierarchical functions that are used to produce and manipulate such multi-scale representations. Contrary to box functions that always compute an average of the radiosity function across some element, wavelets at a given hierarchical level actually encode the "difference" between the representation at the current level and that of the previous level. Therefore wavelets encode the *detail* information, or the correction that must be added to the higher-level representation of a function. A full wavelet basis thus consists of a base function (used to represent the smooth component of the function), and a hierarchical set of detail functions obtained by scaling, dilating, and translating a given wavelet.

In practice, the projection of a given (one-dimensional) function onto a wavelet basis is done in a bottom-up fashion: a set of two filters can be associated with a particular wavelet basis, one of them being a low-pass filter that encodes *smooth* information, the other being a high-pass filter that encodes *detail* information. By convolving these filters with the function at a number of N points and throwing away every other result, two sets of $\frac{N}{2}$ numbers are obtained, representing the smooth information and detail information, respectively. The latter can be understood as a number of coordinates on the finest-level wavelets. The process is then iterated on the smooth representation (that is, it is convolved with the filters corresponding to the next hierarchical level), until the smooth component is reduced to a single number, which is the coordinate for the base function. Thus smooth information about the function is stored high in the hierarchy, whereas very fine details are stored in coefficients for wavelets towards the bottom of the hierarchy.

The main feature of wavelets is that they offer a very natural means of compressing information: since wavelets represent detail information at a given scale, the projection of a function over a particular wavelet will only be significant if there is indeed a significant variation of the function at the corresponding location and at the corresponding level of detail. In other words, wavelet coefficients will tend to be very small where the function is smooth and has little "detail." This property can be given a precise technical meaning using the concept of *vanishing moments*: a wavelet has k vanishing moments if any polynomial of degree strictly less than k integrates to zero against the wavelet. Thus the higher the number of vanishing moments, the fewer non-zero wavelet coefficients there will be, since more of the function's behavior will be well approximated by piecewise polynomials of degree $k - 1$. Many different wavelet bases can be defined, with varying numbers of vanishing moments.

Wavelets can be used like any other shape functions to derive a finite element equation, using for example the Galerkin method. In particular they are easily extended to higher dimensions. The matrix of kernel coefficients (the "form factors" computed from Equation 5.20) is compressed by using only the most significant entries: depending on the particular wavelet basis used, the matrix entries will be very small where the kernel can be approximated by a polynomial of low enough order. Figure 5.9 shows the matrix of the radiosity kernel for the case of two parallel line segments, expressed in a wavelet basis with two vanishing moments, and compares it to a traditional matrix representation. The size of the dots indicates the magnitude of the corresponding entry.

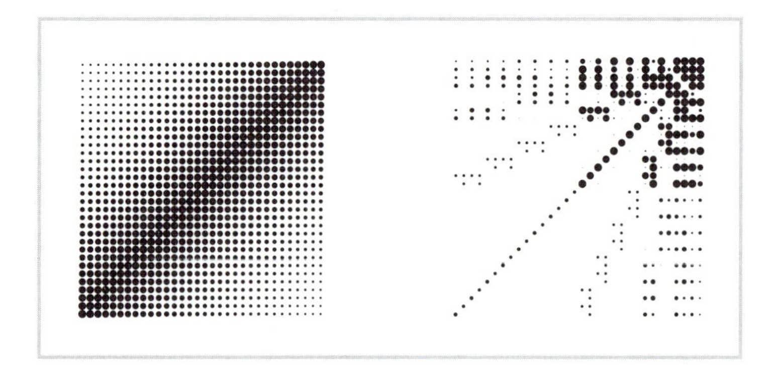

FIGURE 5.9 Radiosity kernel for two parallel lines (in a two-dimensional world), represented with a uniform set of box functions (left), and with a set of wavelets (right). Note the sparsity of the wavelet representation. (*Courtesy of S. Gortler, P. Schröder, M. Cohen, and P. Hanrahan, Princeton University.*)

Note that the above discussion of wavelet projection assumed that the function was known (to allow convolution with high- and low-pass filters). This bottom-up approach is not suitable for radiosity applications, since it would entail computing all form factors and then selecting the most significant ones. Instead, as in the previous hierarchical algorithm, a top-down approach is required, where form factors are computed at the next level only when necessary. The determination of this necessity can be based on the number of vanishing moments of the wavelet basis: if the kernel can be approximated by a polynomial of low enough order across a pair of elements, there is no need to subdivide further.

A more detailed discussion of wavelets and their application for solving the radiosity equation can be found in reference [39]. The key benefit of wavelet bases is that they provide an effective means of reducing the complexity of the kernel matrix, based on mathematical properties of the wavelets and kernel functions.

5.3 Avoiding geometrical problems with the mesh

Many visual artifacts present in radiosity images can be traced to problems with the mesh of elements on the surfaces. Some of these artifacts only present problems for imaging applications and do not reveal major inaccuracies of the simulation, but still appear to be visually distracting because they are emphasized by the human visual system. Undesirable discontinuities in the final radiosity across a surface are typical of this group, and can result from some specific properties of the mesh.

Early radiosity applications concentrated on the difficult problem of form factor computation and used very simple algorithms to come up with an initial mesh on each surface, which was sometimes refined adaptively. Typical difficulties experienced using simplistic meshes are reviewed below. Possible cures are then discussed, most of which take the form of some kind of preprocessing. More involved mesh construction techniques are also discussed. In these, the location of the key features of the illumination functions (such as discontinuity curves) is *predicted*.

5.3.1 Simple meshing and common problems

Let us consider a simple meshing algorithm for radiosity, and study some of the possible consequences on the displayed radiosity functions. We shall see that it is often difficult to separate the question of how to subdivide surfaces and that of the reconstruction of the radiosity function across the surfaces. For example, several of the problems mentioned below, including light and shadow *leaks*, appear when simple Gouraud shading is used to display the mesh elements (as suggested in Section 3.2.3), in effect performing bilinear interpolation of the radiosity values at the vertices.

Meshing with a regular grid

A common meshing technique, used extensively because of its simplicity, consists of superimposing a regular grid onto the surface to be meshed or onto some parameter space representing the surface. Figure 5.10 shows an example of this process for a planar polygon. Grid elements that are found to lie completely inside the polygon are added to the mesh, and grid elements intersecting the boundary of the polygon are cut along the lines of intersection.

This simple "slice-and-dice" algorithm is fairly robust but has one major drawback: it generates a mesh whose density is determined across all surfaces by the underlying grid. This is a problem because it means that the small mesh elements needed to capture fine

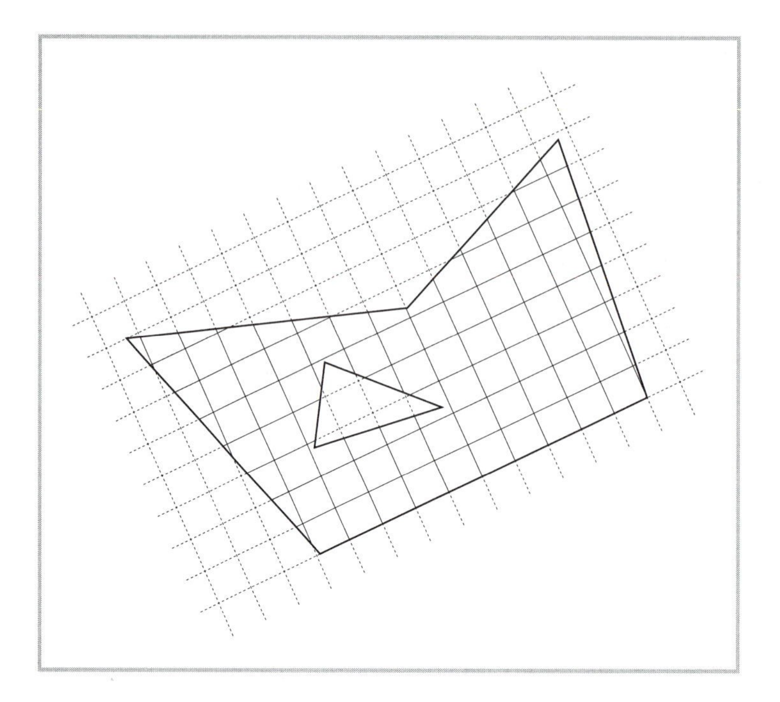

FIGURE 5.10 Simple mesh for a polygon. The direction of the grid has been chosen to be aligned with the longest polygon edge.

illumination details such as shadow boundaries impose unnecessary subdivision of the entire scene, resulting in more form factors to compute. Most implementations therefore include an algorithm for adaptive subdivision of this uniform mesh, such as the one described in Section 4.3. Figures 5.11 and 5.12 show two radiosity solutions for the same environment. Figure 5.11 was computed using a uniform mesh, and Figure 5.12 was computed using an adaptively refined version of the same mesh. The resolution of illumination features is better using the adaptive mesh, for a lower cost than that of a full fine-scale subdivision of all surfaces.

Still, the fact that the mesh is derived purely from geometrical considerations leaves it prone to several deficiencies for representing radiosity functions. These are detailed below, and possible solutions will be presented in the following sections.

Staircase effect

Because of the regular nature of the uniform mesh, oblique shadow boundaries give rise to blocky patterns reminiscent of the staircase effect observed when drawing oblique lines on raster displays [56]. This effect can be observed in Figure 5.11, where the shadow cast by the table has a blocky appearance. Note that although adaptive refinement of the

COLOR PLATES

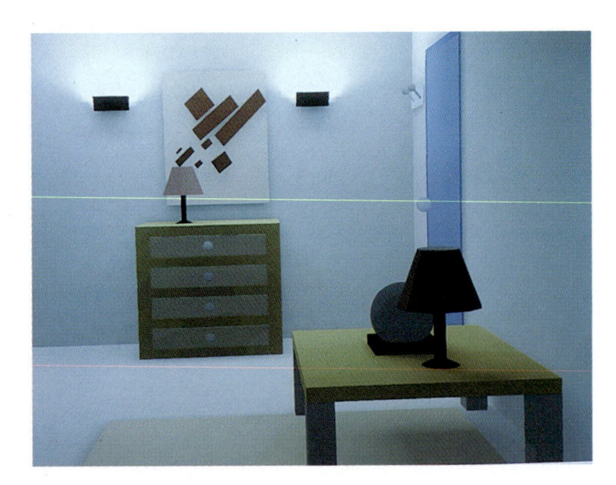

PLATE 1

PLATE 2

PLATE 3

PLATE 4

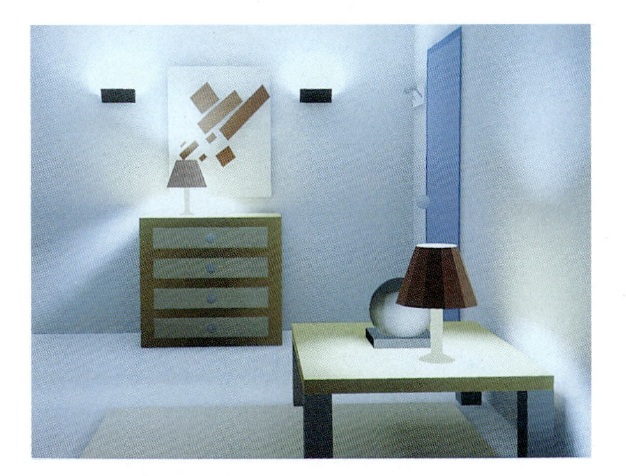

PLATE 5

PLATES 1-5: A series of lighting simulations of a room using the radiosity method. Different lighting conditions can be evaluated from a variety of viewpoints. *(Courtesy of F. Sillion, Ecole Normale Supérieure.)*

PLATE 6: A simple environment demonstrating some important interreflection effects. Note in particular the color bleeding from the walls. *(Courtesy of F. Sillion, Program of Computer Graphics, Cornell University.)*

PLATE 7: Radiosity simulation with texture-mapped paintings and light source. *(Courtesy of M. Cohen, Program of Computer Graphics, Cornell University.)*

PLATE 8: Isolux contours superimposed on a synthetic image to represent irradiance levels. The image was computed with the Radiance program. *(Courtesy of G. Ward, Lawrence Berkeley Laboratory.)*

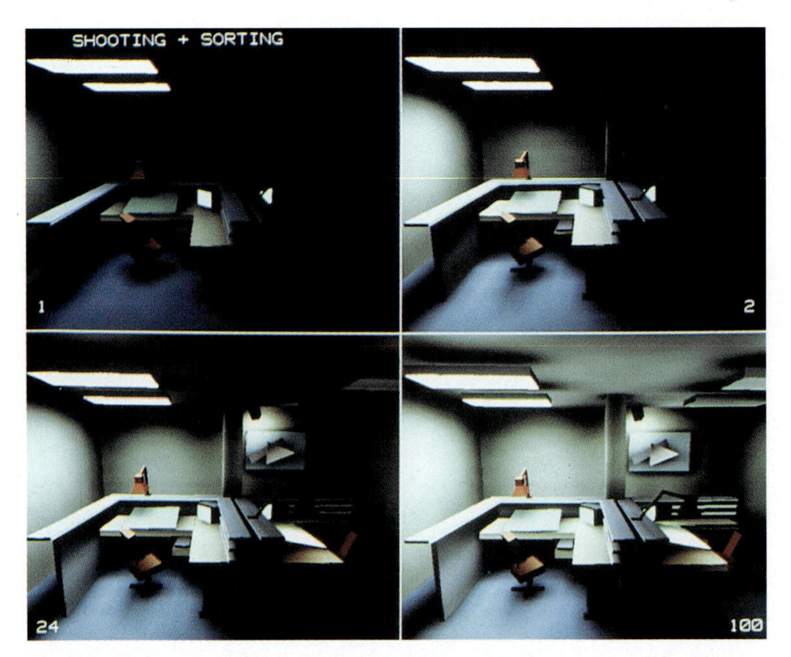

PLATE 9: The progressive refinement radiosity algorithm in action: images obtained after 1, 2, 24, and 100 iterations. *(Courtesy of M. Cohen, Program of Computer Graphics, Cornell University.)*

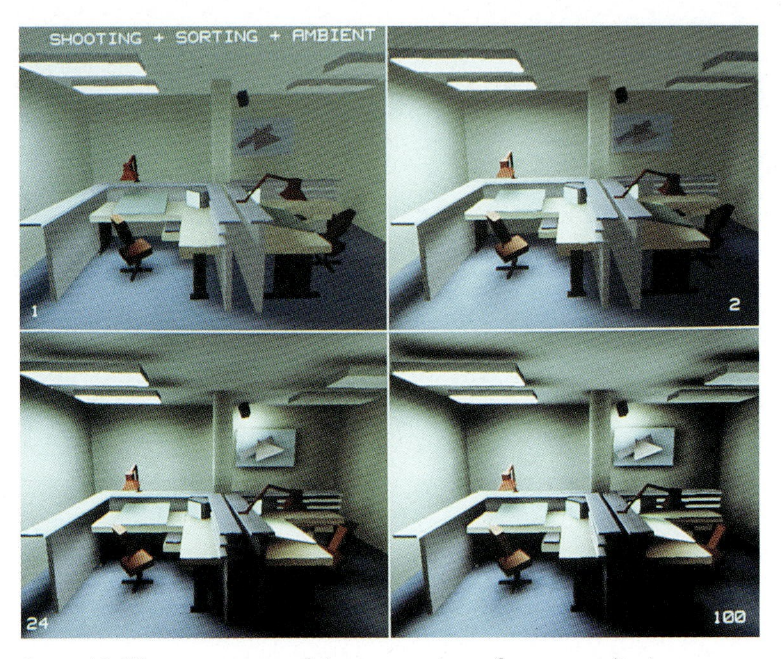

PLATE 10: The same stages of the progressive refinement radiosity algorithm, with the ambient term added for display. *(Courtesy of M. Cohen, Program of Computer Graphics, Cornell University.)*

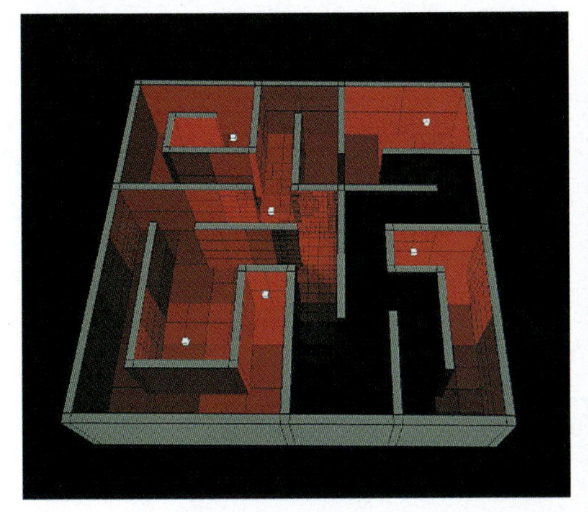

PLATE 11: Radiosity solution.

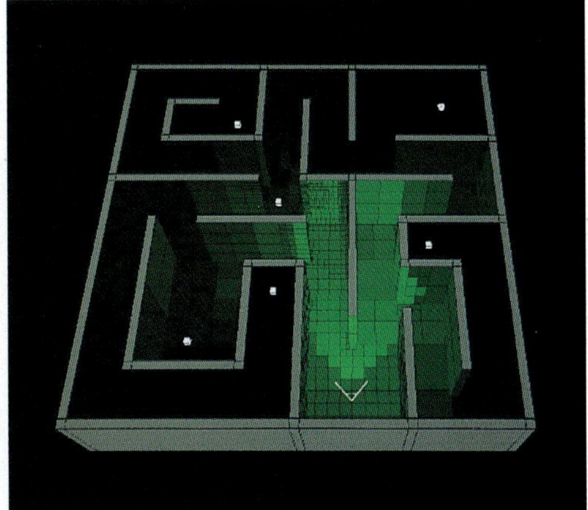

PLATE 12: Importance solution.

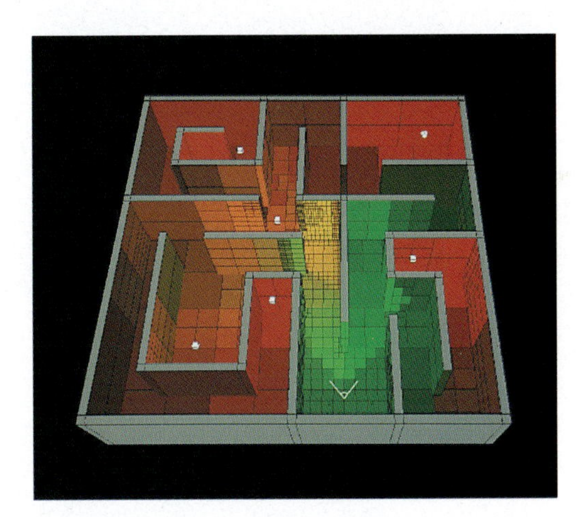

PLATE 13: Superposition of radiosity and importance solutions. Regions with both significant radiosity and importance values appear in yellow.

Visual illustration of importance-driven refinement. *(Courtesy of B. Smits, J. Arvo, and D. Salesin, Program of Computer Graphics, Cornell University.)*

A sequence of images showing the results of the importance-driven hierarchical algorithm in a maze environment. Notice in particular how little subdivision occurs in areas far away from the center of interest. *(Courtesy of B. Smits, J. Arvo, and D. Salesin, Program of Computer Graphics, Cornell University.)*

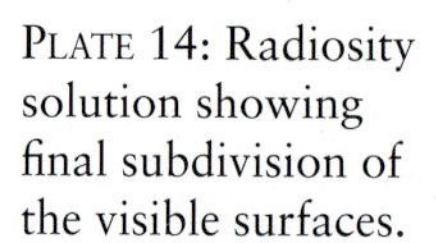

PLATE 14: Radiosity solution showing final subdivision of the visible surfaces.

PLATE 15: Final image after smooth reconstruction.

PLATE 16: Radiosity solution from farther back.

PLATE 17: Importance solution from farther back.

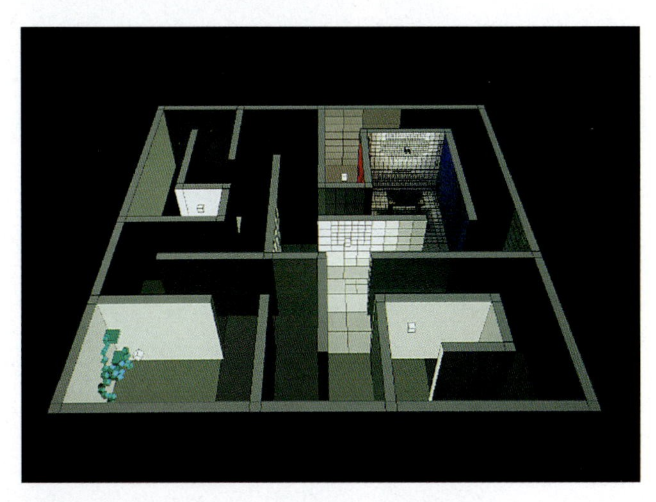

PLATE 18: Radiosity solution from even farther back.

PLATE 19: Importance solution from even farther back.

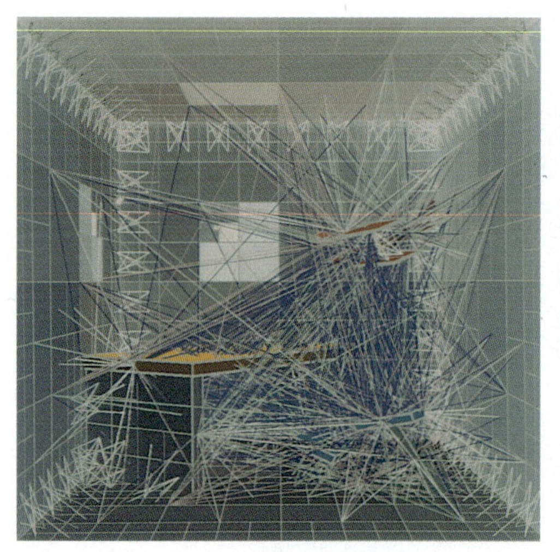

Plate 20A

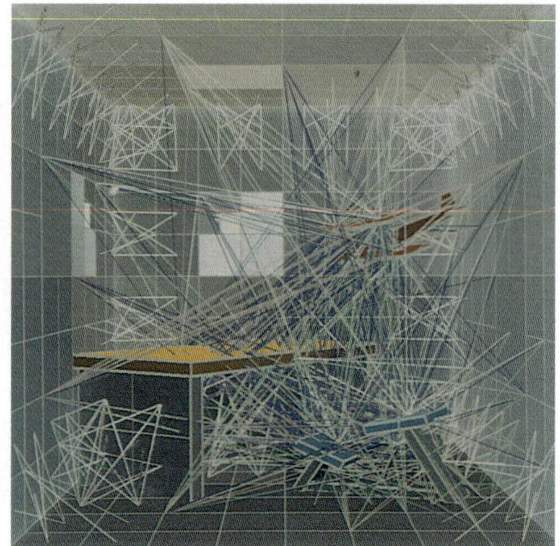

Plate 20B

Plate 20C

Plate 20D

Hierarchical radiosity: representation of the links established in a simple environment at different hierarchical levels. *(Courtesy of P. Hanrahan, Princeton University.)*

PLATE 21: Final image produced by the hierarchical radiosity algorithm. *(Courtesy of P. Hanrahan, Princeton University.)*

PLATE 22: An image with non-diffuse reflectors, computed using a hierarchical algorithm to solve for three-point interactions. *(Courtesy of P. Hanrahan, Princeton University.)*

PLATE 23: Detail of a radiosity solution computed with an adaptively refined mesh. The very fine shadows cast by the window frame are incorrectly reproduced.

PLATE 24: Solution for the same environment using discontinuity meshing to ensure that all significant discontinuities are aligned with mesh lines.

PLATE 25: Very detailed shadows are captured by the discontinuity mesh.

Illustration of the discontinuity meshing technique. *(Courtesy of D. Lischinski, F. Tampieri, and D. P. Greenberg, Program of Computer Graphics, Cornell University.)*

PLATE 26: A ship's boiler room. Highlights were added to a diffuse radiosity solution as a post-process. *(Courtesy of J. Wallace, 3D/Eye, Inc.)*

Plate 27: Simulation of a scene with directional-diffuse reflectors. *(Courtesy of F. Sillion, J. Arvo, S. Westin, and D. Greenberg, Program of Computer Graphics, Cornell University.)*

Plate 28: Another view of the same scene. Notice how the directional highlights have changed. These highlights are described by the directional radiance distributions attached to the surfaces. *(Courtesy of F. Sillion, J. Arvo, S. Westin, and D. Greenberg, Program of Computer Graphics, Cornell University.)*

Series of images demonstrating a range of reflectance behaviors. The roughness of the tall box is increased from left to right, producing an increasingly diffuse BRDF. *(Courtesy of F. Sillion, J. Arvo, S. Westin, and D. Greenberg, Program of Computer Graphics, Cornell University.)*

PLATE 29A

PLATE 29B

Plate 29c

Plate 29d

PLATE 30: Simulation of a participating medium: a room with smoke at sunset. *(Courtesy of H. Rushmeier, Program of Computer Graphics, Cornell University.)*

PLATE 31: Simulation of the Ontario legislature building. *(Courtesy of Stuart Feldman, Lightscape Graphics Software Ltd. Design by A. J. Diamond, Donald Schmitt & Company. Rendered using the Lightscape Visualization System on a Silicon Graphics computer.)*

PLATE 32: The Ontario legislature building, side view. *(Courtesy of Stuart Feldman, Lightscape Graphics Software Ltd. Design by A. J. Diamond, Donald Schmitt & Company. Rendered using the Lightscape Visualization System on a Silicon Graphics computer.)*

PLATE 33: A radiosity solution computed incrementally after the robot was added to the scene. *(Courtesy of D. George, Program of Computer Graphics, Cornell University.)*

PLATE 34: A simulated stage set for the canal scene of the opera *Les contes d'Hoffman. (Courtesy of J. O'Brien Dorsey, Program of Computer Graphics, Cornell University.)*

PLATE 35: Simulation of Luther's tavern in *Les contes d'Hoffman. (Courtesy of J. O'Brien Dorsey, Program of Computer Graphics, Cornell University.)*

Plate 36: Simulation using Monte Carlo Path Tracing. *(Courtesy of John Mardaljevic, ECADAP Group, School of the Built Environment, De Montfort University, Leicester, UK.)*

Plate 37: Visualization of an office, produced by CRL for Thorn Lighting, illustrating the SENSA range of light fittings. *(Courtesy of Campbell McKellar, Central Research Laboratories Ltd.)*

PLATE 38: An image computed using Monte Carlo Path Tracing. Sixty-four rays were traced per pixel. Indirect illumination was obtained from a radiosity solution computed on a simplified environment. *(Courtesy of C. Wang and P. Shirley, University of Indiana.)*

PLATE 39: Hybrid radiosity simulation (12 minutes). *(Courtesy of Eric Chen, Apple Computer.)*

PLATE 40: Multipass simulation (4.5 hours). *(Courtesy of Eric Chen, Apple Computer.)*

PLATE 41: Interreflections computed by Progressive Radiosity. *(Courtesy of Eric Chen, Apple Computer.)*

PLATE 42: Direct illumination computed by Monte Carlo Path Tracing. *(Courtesy of Eric Chen, Apple Computer.)*

PLATE 43: Caustics computed by Light Ray Tracing. *(Courtesy of Eric Chen, Apple Computer.)*

PLATE 44: Using radiosity for lighting design: light source specifications were computed automatically to achieve a feeling of *visual clarity* (left) or *privateness* (right). *(Courtesy of J. Kawai, University of Utah.)*

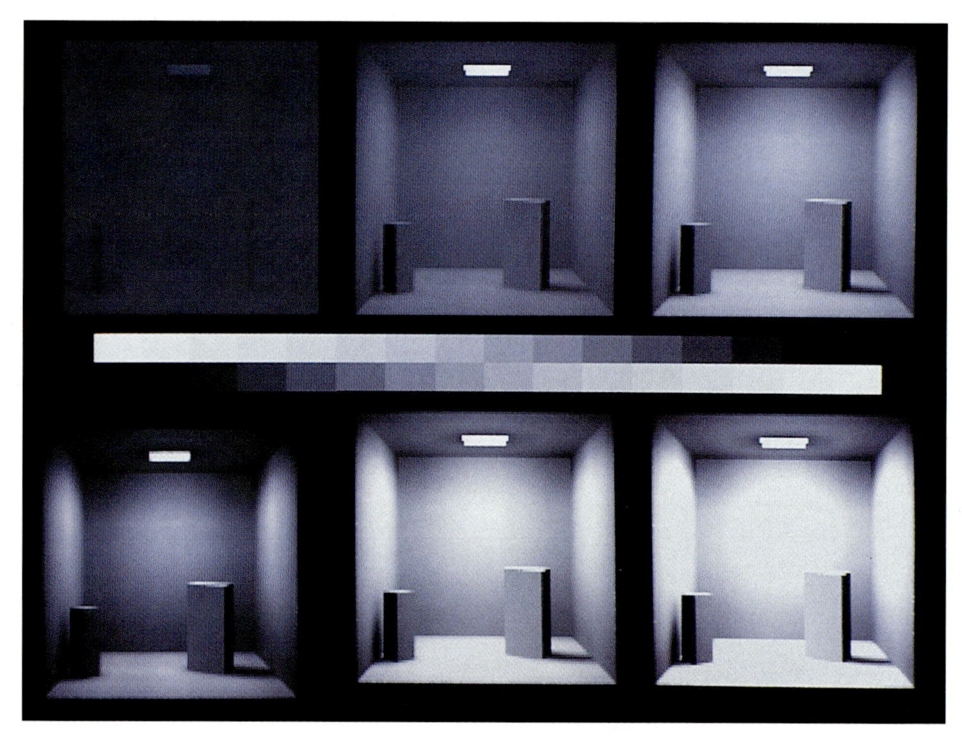

PLATE 45: Images of a simple environment illuminated by a light source of varying strength. For each image the adaptation level of the eyes is taken into account to perform adequate nonlinear luminance scaling and make the best use of the limited display's dynamic range. Light source strengths are in a maximum ratio of 10^8 : 1 between the upper-left and lower-right images. *(Courtesy of J. Tumblin, Georgia Institute of Technology.)*

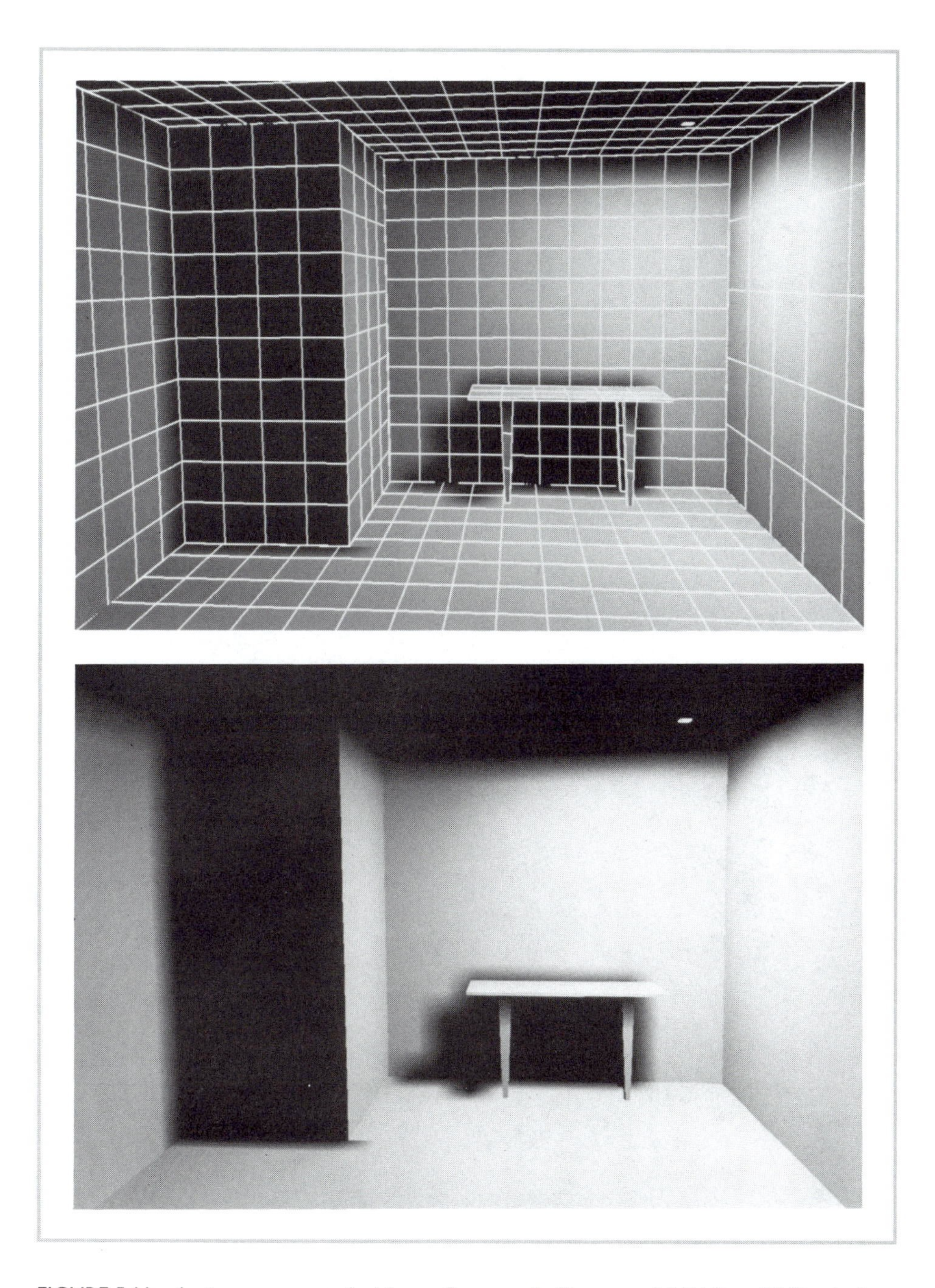

FIGURE 5.11 An image computed with a uniform mesh. (*Courtesy of J. Wallace, 3D/Eye, Inc.*)

FIGURE 5.12 An image of the same scene, where the mesh is adaptively refined. (*Courtesy of J. Wallace, 3D/Eye, Inc.*)

mesh improves the appearance of the shadow, as shown in Figure 5.12, the staircase effect cannot be totally eliminated unless the elements are subdivided down to a level where they cover less than a pixel on the final image. Considering that this heavy amount of subdivision is needed for each shadow boundary in the image, this is a prohibitively expensive way of dealing with the staircase problem.

Light and shadow leaks

An artifact frequently found in radiosity images is the so-called leaking problem. This problem is encountered when two surfaces meet but their respective meshes do not coincide. Consider the situation depicted in Figure 5.13, where radiosity is computed using the ray casting method of Section 5.1.3, that is, shooting energy from the source patch to all vertices of the mesh. Vertices a and b receive some light from the source, while vertices c and d are in the shadow of the wall. When patch P is displayed, bilinear interpolation "spreads" the radiosity from the illuminated points across the patch, resulting in a surface that is too bright near c or d, and too dark near a or b. The wall appears to float above the floor because of the apparent light leak.

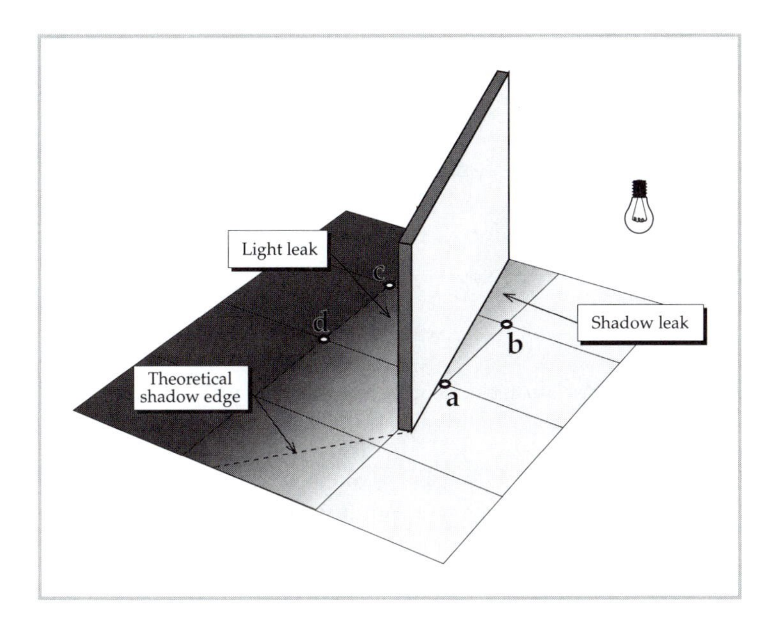

FIGURE 5.13 Light leaking under a wall.

This effect appears whenever a mesh element spans an area where very fast illumination changes occur, in particular when a discontinuity in the radiosity function is created by the contact of several objects. Sometimes it takes the form of a *shadow leak*. This can be observed in Figure 5.11, where the table touches the wall: the shadow from under the table seems to creep up along the wall. Note that *light leaks* are usually interpreted by our visual system to suggest that the touching surfaces are in fact separated by some distance, thus allowing some light to pass through. Shadow leaks such as the one just described are even more distracting to the eye, since no simple physical interpretation is available: they simply look wrong.

Interpolation artifacts

Concave polygons result in discontinuous shading across a patch when bilinear Gouraud interpolation is used [71], as shown in the left-hand side of Figure 5.14. Since the interpolation is carried out along a scanline, the radiosity of a point immediately above point d is totally independent of the radiosity at d. However, for all points below d, the interpolated radiosity value is affected by its radiosity. Thus the interpolated radiosity is discontinuous across the horizontal line passing through point d.

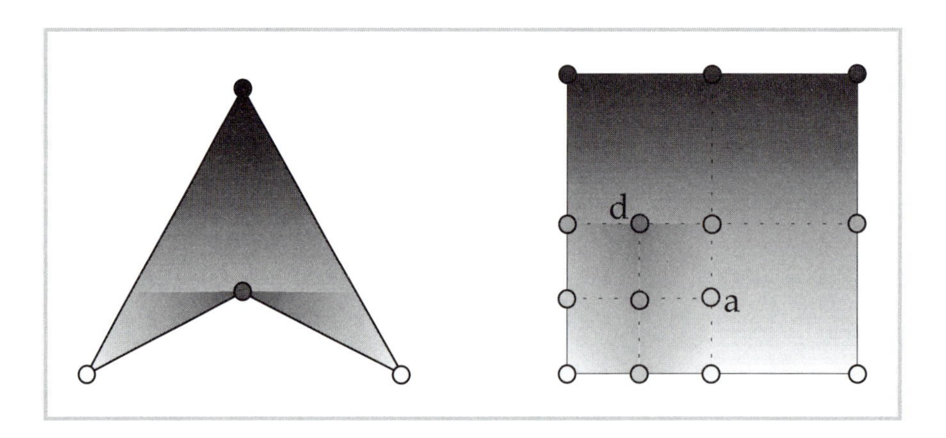

FIGURE 5.14 Shading discontinuities: concave polygon (left) and T-vertex (right).

Since the shading discontinuity happens along a scanline of the display device, its location relative to the shaded surface will appear to change when the viewing conditions are modified. The resulting movement of the discontinuity lines can be very distracting during interactive walkthrough applications.

T-vertices

T-vertices are vertices appearing only on one side of an edge common to two elements. They are commonly introduced by adaptive subdivision techniques, since an element can be subdivided while its neighbor remains unchanged. Such vertices also result in shading discontinuities, since radiosity values are interpolated from different sets of vertices on both sides of the edge. The right-hand side of Figure 5.14 shows an example with a discontinuity along the horizontal line through vertex d. In this particular example, no discontinuity is created by T-vertex a, since its computed radiosity value is consistent with the interpolated value. Note that these particular shading discontinuities appear at fixed locations with respect to the surfaces since they are intrinsically tied to the mesh.

5.3.2 Mesh cleaning as a preprocess

From the above presentation of typical meshing problems it appears that the mesh must be designed very carefully before the radiosity computation can take place. One difficulty is that the geometric models of the scenes to be rendered are produced using a variety of modeling or computer-aided design (CAD) packages, which usually do not ensure any topological or physical consistency.

It is therefore unrealistic to expect geometric meshes to be available in a form suitable for artifact-free radiosity computations. An additional processing step can be employed to correct some of the most serious problems of the mesh before the radiosity calculation begins. A series of such cleanup operations are described below. These operations are applied to a mesh to make it suitable for radiosity processing [13].

Resolving consistency issues

In the physical world all solid objects have a well-defined boundary between the "inside" and "outside" regions of space. Similarly, two different objects cannot be at the same location in space. Unfortunately, most geometric modelers allow these simple properties to be violated. For example, the geometry of a scene is rarely composed of solid models. For the sake of simplicity many objects are described using incomplete surface representations such as open single-sided surfaces, called *facades*.

Facades can be the source of several problems. First they can only participate in energy transfers on one side, defined as the outward-facing side. Light coming in from the wrong direction will not be received by a facade since the surface will be considered back-facing and ignored in the calculation of the form factor. In addition, since facades are not solid objects and have no width, they can coincide with other surfaces that belong to other objects. A typical problem occurs when a carpet on a floor is modeled as a single-sided polygon positioned at the height of the floor. Such a situation is likely to generate errors and artifacts both in the computation of the form factors and in the rendering phase, since the determination of the visible surface will be unpredictable. Sometimes the carpet will appear to be on top of the floor and sometimes below it.

Since geometric models are often created without physical consistency in mind, complicated shapes are frequently represented by several simpler surface patches with the same overall geometry. To avoid inconsistencies and discontinuities that result from such situations, the first operation performed on a model is to group all connected surfaces representing the same object into a single maximal surface. This can be done by identifying shared vertices and edges.

To avoid light and shadow leaks, an additional processing step consists of checking all pairs of surfaces for intersection and cutting them if necessary along their intersection line. The main difficulty in this operation is to produce consistent results with limited numerical precision. It is also an expensive $O(N^2)$ process since all pairs of surfaces must be considered.

Finally, coincident surfaces such as the carpet-on-floor just mentioned can be avoided by discarding one of the surfaces. Note that it is impossible to predict automatically which surface should be removed. A possible heuristic recommendation consists of discarding the one coming originally from the larger surface. This works well in the case of the carpet since the fragment of the floor under the carpet will be removed.

Avoiding concave elements and T-vertices

Once the set of surfaces has been improved using the above operations, an initial radiosity mesh can be created for each surface. Concave elements, which produce unwanted shading discontinuities, must be avoided in this mesh. This is accomplished by adding an extra step to the simple slice-and-dice meshing algorithm of Section 5.3.1. After the regular grid has been superimposed, the grid elements that are not entirely contained in the polygon are *triangulated*. This is shown in Figure 5.15.

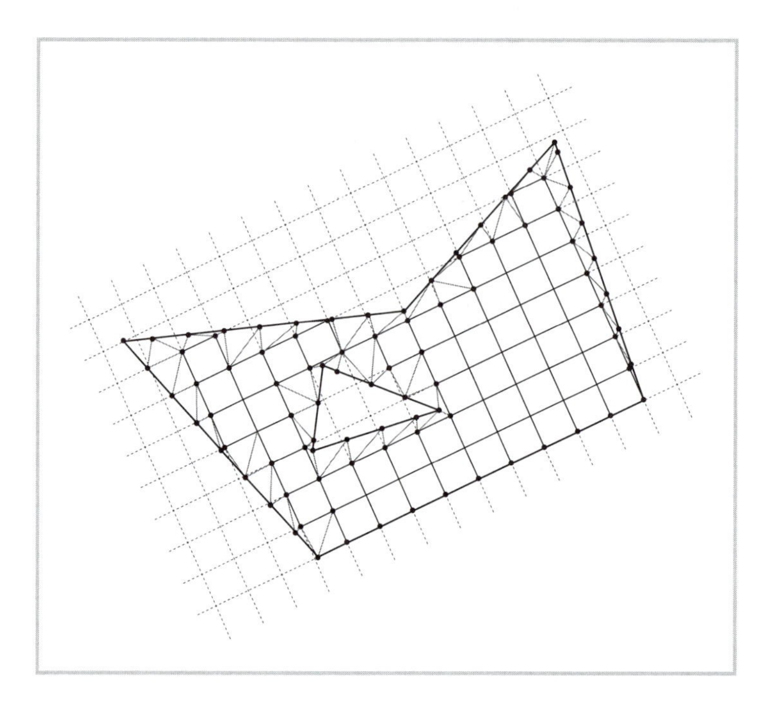

FIGURE 5.15 A mesh with no concave polygons, obtained after triangulating the set of marked (•) vertices. Those are obtained by considering a regular subdivision of all polygon edges and adding the vertices of all grid elements that are partially covered by the polygon.

A variety of triangulation algorithms are available [133] and typically operate on a set of vertices. The initial vertices for the mesh can be obtained, for example, by subdividing the edges of the initial polygon in a regular manner and adding some of the grid vertices.

Another source of undesirable shading discontinuities are the T-vertices created by the adaptive subdivision process. Consider the case of a hierarchical subdivision using a quadtree. The severity of the T-vertex problem can be greatly reduced by enforcing the condition that the subdivision levels of two neighboring elements should never differ by more than one level. The resulting structure is called a *restricted quadtree* [146]. The advantage of using a restricted quadtree is that it is possible to post-process the radiosity results to generate a consistent interpolation.

One post-processing algorithm performs one pass through the quadtree just before display, enforcing for each element the subdivision of the immediate neighbors that are less subdivided. Note that this subdivision is not propagated in the structure, thus it might break the restricted nature of the tree. The radiosity of newly created vertices is simply interpolated from the edge endpoints, thus no new radiosity calculation is performed. This is shown in Figure 5.16a. The net result of this algorithm is that bilinear interpolation yields consistent results along the border between two adjacent elements.

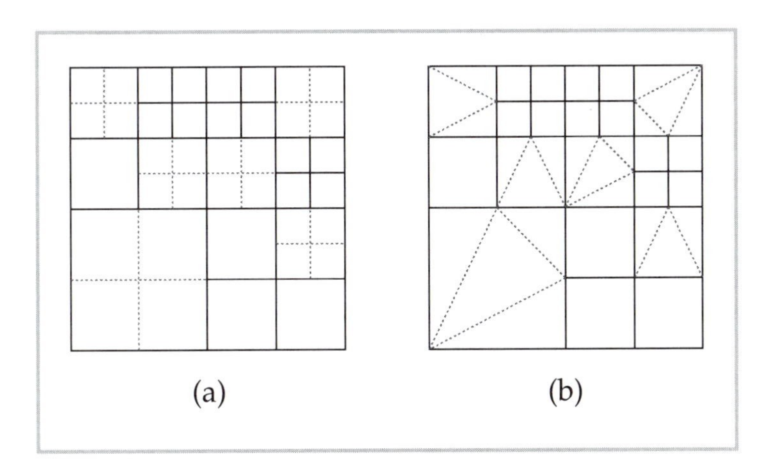

FIGURE 5.16 Treatment of T-vertices in a restricted quadtree: (a) extra subdivision and (b) anchored tree.

Another post-processing option for the display of a restricted quadtree is to *anchor* each element that has a neighbor with greater subdivision level [13]. This operation consists of triangulating the element to ensure that all T-vertices are connected either to other T-vertices or to element corners. This is illustrated in Figure 5.16b.

Both these techniques are performed immediately before display and do not actually modify the mesh used for radiosity calculations.

5.3.3 Discontinuity meshing

The creation of a mesh on the surfaces of a scene can be viewed as a sampling operation, where the goal is to reduce the continuous problem to a discrete problem while still allowing accurate reconstruction. Using this terminology emphasizes the fact that the regularity of the radiosity function should play a major role in determining the appropriate meshing strategy. Sampling theory shows that discontinuities in the radiosity function cannot be represented by a uniform mesh, however fine it may be, since they correspond to arbitrarily high frequencies in the function's spectrum. However, if all discontinuities happen to lie on mesh lines, appropriate reconstruction techniques can be used to represent the exact radiosity function. Thus it is worth at this point taking a closer look at the properties of radiosity functions, in terms of their discontinuities of various orders. *Discontinuity meshing* refers to the algorithms that generate a mesh according to the predicted location of the radiosity discontinuities. Some discontinuity meshing methods are reviewed below. Note that the current discontinuity meshing algorithms are restricted to planar polygonal surfaces: this constraint is adopted throughout this section.

Different types of discontinuities

The illumination of a surface by a single light source is described by a formula similar to the point-to-patch form factor given in Equation 3.25. In fact, for a source with uniform radiance, the radiosity received on another surface is directly proportional to this form factor. The form factor kernel is composed of continuous functions except for the visibility term, and as a result discontinuities in the radiosity function can be produced by changes in visibility. We use the notation that a function has a D^k discontinuity at a given point if the function is C^{k-1} but not C^k at that point [80].

D^0 discontinuities The simplest type of discontinuity is one where a finite portion of the source becomes abruptly visible as we move from one point to its neighbor. This happens either when two objects are in contact (imagine crossing the contact line) or across the shadow boundaries created by a point light source. An example of a D^0 discontinuity appears in the scene pictured in Figure 5.11. A linear D^0 discontinuity should be present, for example, where the table touches the wall. Note that the discontinuity is not properly displayed.

D^0 discontinuities are difficult to represent since the radiosity function can take several different values at the same point in space. Thus the data structure used to hold radiosity functions must allow the storage of multiple values.

D^1 and D^2 discontinuities Higher-order discontinuities can also appear in the radiosity function. They are the result of more subtle visibility changes called *visual events*. Events were originally studied for computer vision applications, and two categories were identified for polygonal scenes: vertex-edge (VE) events and edge-edge-edge (EEE) events [64].

VE events are created when a vertex and an edge in the scene are at least partially mutually visible. The *critical surface* along which the visibility change occurs is a portion of the plane containing the vertex and the edge, that is, the set of points from which the vertex is seen to coincide with the edge. The intersection of this critical surface with other surfaces creates *critical curves* where derivative discontinuities of the radiosity function are found. The boundary of the penumbra region created by an extended light source is an example of a critical curve. For polygonal environments the critical "curves" are line segments. Figure 5.17 shows an example of the critical lines generated on a floor polygon by a triangular light source and a rectangular occluder, considering only VE events.

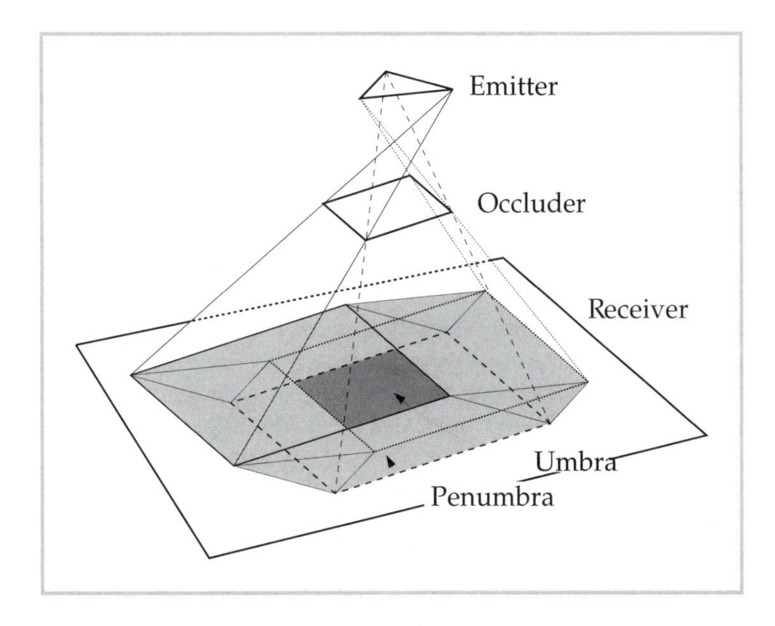

FIGURE 5.17 Discontinuities of the radiosity function for a single source and occluder. (*Courtesy of P. Heckbert, Carnegie Mellon University—after Nishita and Nakamae [123].*)

In general the discontinuities associated with these critical lines are D^2 discontinuities. That is, both the radiosity function and its derivative are continuous, but the rate of change of the derivative varies abruptly when the critical line is crossed. However, as shown in Figure 5.18, a D^1 discontinuity occurs for some particular orientations of the source and the occluder. This happens when an edge containing the event's vertex is parallel to the event's edge.

EEE events occur in the presence of three skew edges, each visible to the others. The critical surface is the set of points from which all three edges are seen as intersecting at one point, and is a subset of a quadric. The resulting critical curves are conics and usually correspond to D^2 discontinuities.

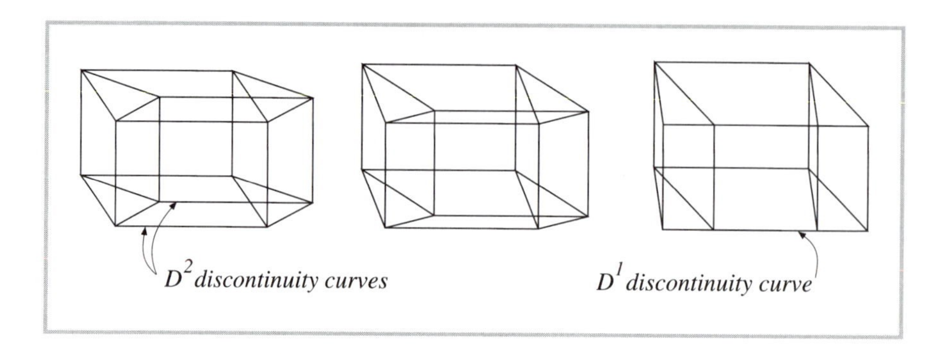

FIGURE 5.18 Two D^2 discontinuities can coincide to yield a D^1 discontinuity. (*Courtesy of P. Heckbert, Carnegie Mellon University.*)

Building a discontinuity mesh

There can be an infinite number of discontinuities of various orders in a scene. The number of visual events is already large, since for a scene consisting of m edges, there are $O(m^2)$ critical surfaces for VE events and $O(m^3)$ critical surfaces for EEE events. Each of these critical surfaces can result in $O(m)$ critical curves.

Furthermore, the existence of radiosity discontinuities on the light source itself creates other discontinuities on the receiving surfaces. This is expressed by the Discontinuity Propagation Law: D^k discontinuities on the source result in D^{k+1} and D^{k+2} discontinuities on the receivers [80].

Fortunately, the importance of the discontinuities decreases as their order increases: D^0 and D^1 discontinuities are the most perceptually significant, and although some D^2 discontinuities are noticeable, higher-order discontinuities can be ignored safely.

Recognizing the importance of the discontinuities of the radiosity functions, discontinuity meshing attempts to include in a polygonal mesh all critical lines associated with "significant" discontinuities.

D^0 discontinuities can be found by identifying all pairs of intersecting surfaces and computing their intersection curve, as explained in the previous section. D^0 discontinuities created by point light sources are in fact associated with VE events where the vertex is the point light source.

VE events are relatively easy to take into account, since the critical surfaces are subsets of planes. VE events are generated either by a vertex of the source and an edge of an occluder, or a vertex of an occluder and an edge of the source. Events are deemed significant based on the expected order of the discontinuity and on the strength of the light source. For each of these significant events, a critical surface is constructed and critical lines are recorded on all intersecting surfaces.

The first algorithm that was proposed to generate a discontinuity mesh constructs a BSP tree to hold all object surfaces as well as the critical surfaces, and splits the objects in the scene accordingly [21, 29]. Other suggestions include using an extended winged-edge data structure (see Section A.1.2 in the Appendix) to store critical segments on the surface of the objects [79] and maintaining a two-dimensional BSP tree on each surface [107].

No matter how critical lines are represented, the final mesh is generated by further refining the mesh of critical lines. There exist variations on the Delaunay triangulation algorithms that allow the inclusion of a set of predefined edges into the triangle set [27, 28]. Color Plates 23 and 24 show how the inclusion of critical curves in the radiosity mesh can dramatically improve the quality of the radiosity solution.

EEE events are much more difficult to capture because of the complex shape of the critical surfaces. Representations for these critical curves have been developed for visibility processing [172]. However, since these events correspond to D^2 discontinuities, they are often neglected. Recent advances in discontinuity meshing include the possibility of building a *complete* discontinuity mesh that partitions the surface of the receivers into regions with a similar view of a light source. Accurate radiosity reconstruction is then facilitated inside each region [48].

On the use of discontinuity meshing

Discontinuity meshing creates meshes that are well suited to accurate radiosity computation. Although the essence of the algorithm is fairly simple, the complexity of the calculation often renders discontinuity meshing prohibitively expensive to use. In practice critical surfaces and curves should only be computed for a small number of significant events. Since there is no way to determine automatically whether the discontinuity associated with a given critical line will be visible in the rendered image, heuristics can be based on the predicted order of the discontinuities (favoring D^0 and D^1 discontinuities) and on the strength of the light source. Color Plate 25 shows an image with very high quality shadows, obtained by considering discontinuities created by the main light sources.

In any case, the mesh data structure must be modified to store new information, such as multiple radiosity values in the case of D^0 discontinuities. The radiosity computation itself must also be modified to take into account the variations of the radiosity function across the source patch. In addition, the effort spent for discontinuity meshing should not be wasted by employing poor reconstruction. There is no use in explicitly representing all D^1 discontinuities if the final reconstruction is performed using Gouraud shading, with its automatic creation of spurious D^1 discontinuities at patch boundaries (see below). Accurate reconstruction techniques for use with discontinuity meshing are discussed later in this chapter.

An interesting development consists of using the critical lines predicted by the discontinuity meshing algorithm to perform the surface subdivision in the hierarchical radiosity algorithm that was introduced in Section 4.4 instead of a quadtree [108]. Since critical lines bound areas of constant visibility, the error in the form factor estimation is reduced and fewer levels of subdivision are needed. In the end, the time spent computing the discontinuity mesh is regained by a much faster hierarchical analysis stage.

Finally, a different approach to representing radiosity discontinuities consists of deforming a given mesh to align mesh lines with appropriate features of the radiosity function. This a posteriori method uses the information from a low-accuracy radiosity solution to decide how the mesh points should be moved [1].

5.4 Reconstruction of the radiosity functions

Let us assume that the radiosities at mesh points can be computed to an arbitrary degree of accuracy, using any of the techniques already mentioned for the generation of the mesh or the computation of form factors. In order to produce an image or display, a radiosity function must be reconstructed for all visible points of the scene based on the computed radiosities.

5.4.1 Bilinear interpolation and Gouraud shading

In Section 3.2.3 a simple reconstruction scheme was presented that uses bilinear interpolation across polygons to produce a continuous shading of the surfaces. This approach is widely used, mainly because of the ability of graphics acceleration hardware to perform bilinear interpolation very quickly. As mentioned earlier, radiosity values must be known at the mesh vertices in order to provide the polygon renderer with color values to interpolate.

However, a distracting artifact produced by bilinear interpolation is the production of first-derivative discontinuities of the radiosity function across patch boundaries. In general the rate of change of the radiosity function will be different on both sides of a patch edge, and these derivative discontinuities produce "Mach banding" that is readily noticeable [56]. Mach bands can be noticed in Figure 5.11 in the bright area of the wall.

Furthermore, using bilinear interpolation to obtain a continuous shading of the surfaces from radiosities that are computed using constant basis functions merely improves the appearance of the image, but does not significantly reduce the error of the solution [80]. Improved reconstruction methods are outlined below.

5.4.2 Higher-order reconstruction

A first avenue towards improving the appearance of the computed radiosity functions is to generate a smoother function from the radiosity values. Numerous techniques have been devised to interpolate scattered data values [22], and they can be adapted to the interpolation of radiosity functions [12]. The basic idea is to use neighboring radiosity values to come up with a higher-order polynomial interpolant. Note however that this amounts to forcing the radiosity function to be smooth (say C^1 or even C^2) even though some discontinuities are naturally present in these functions and should be preserved.

When the computation is carried out with non-constant basis functions, as suggested in Section 5.2, a continuous radiosity solution is actually obtained as a linear combination of continuous basis functions, and no interpolation is necessary. Instead the radiosity can be computed at any surface location by evaluating the basis functions at that point using Equation 5.5.

5.4.3 Reconstruction with discontinuities

A better approach to the reconstruction problem is to couple it with the discontinuity meshing technique. Since some discontinuities are naturally present in the radiosity function, as shown in Section 5.3.3, the effort of the reconstruction should concentrate on obtaining a smooth radiosity function in the regions bounded by discontinuity lines, while preserving the correct discontinuities along these lines.

A $\mathcal{C}^1$ reconstruction technique can be adapted to allow the preservation of selected discontinuities [145]. During the construction of the mesh, information regarding the order of the various discontinuities is stored with the mesh elements. This information is used to selectively eliminate some of the constraints driving the computation of a Bézier interpolant.

5.4.4 Reconstruction without polygons

Using a discrete mesh to represent the surfaces of the scene can present difficulties, especially when curved surfaces are present, since a polygonal approximation can be either difficult to compute or very inaccurate. When ray casting is used for all visibility computations there is actually no need for an explicit polygonal decomposition of the objects.

An alternate representation of the radiosity function is in the form of a *radiosity texture*, that is, a function defined in some parameter space that is then mapped onto the surface. The advantage of this representation is that no complex data structure is needed to represent a mesh of elements with its associated geometry and topology. The radiosity values are not explicitly associated with a point or vertex in 3D space, but this association is performed indirectly through the mapping operation. This representation was successfully used in a probabilistic algorithm for the simulation of light exchanges, which will be presented in Section 8.4 [81].

Another alternative is to compute radiosity values at a number of selected points on the surfaces, without constructing a mesh of elements. These points can be represented in a hierarchical data structure in parameter space [183]. Reconstruction is then performed by considering a reconstruction kernel at each of these sample points and computing a weighted sum of all sample values according to the kernel values at the point of interest. Further refinement of this idea is possible by using kernels whose shape varies according to the direction of the radiosity gradient.

Finally the reconstruction stage could be replaced altogether by an image-space radiosity computation: for all visible points, radiosity can be gathered from all surfaces (using any of the form factor calculation methods presented earlier). This expensive technique ensures that the correct radiosity is associated with each pixel [137, 93].

❐ ❐ ❐

This chapter dealt with the problem of controlling the accuracy of the simulation results. One potential source of inaccuracies is the computation of form factors. The hemi-cube algorithm is improved in that respect by identifying situations that cause severe aliasing and using a more accurate analytic method in those cases. The ray casting approach for the computation of form factors offers an excellent alternative since it is both easy to implement and flexible. However, it cannot make use of z-buffer hardware.

Another source of inaccuracy is the assumption of constant radiosity functions across each patch. The formulation of the global illumination problem as a finite-element system generalizes the basic presentation of Chapter 3. Within this framework extensions can be derived by using appropriate basis functions, such as wavelets or polynomials. The use of low-degree polynomials is especially interesting considering that the reconstruction of radiosity functions is often accomplished with such polynomials. Computing polynomial radiosity functions is therefore a more consistent approach. Note that the algorithms presented in this chapter for the computation of form factors were designed for constant basis functions. For higher-order functions, a more general computation method is presented in Chapter 8.

CHAPTER 6

Controlling the simulation

In previous chapters the radiosity method was considered as a numerical simulation tool, but little attention was paid to actual application domains of the method. This chapter takes a closer look at practical situations that benefit from the radiosity technique. Consideration of the user's point of view in this chapter reveals a need for a versatile simulation tool, with easy and efficient control of the various features of the algorithm.

A benefit of radiosity, when compared to other rendering techniques, is that it correctly models and takes into account the subtle interreflection effects that are responsible for the atmosphere of a scene. This valuable capability helps in the understanding of the three-dimensional nature of the objects represented, as well as their spatial relationships [33]. Another salient feature of the radiosity method is the view-independent character of the results: a *radiosity solution* is a set of radiosity values, possibly a spectrum of values corresponding to different wavelengths, attached to the points or surface elements in a scene. Given such a solution, images can be rendered from any viewpoint.

These two features make radiosity a useful tool in the hands of end-users who might need to obtain a good three-dimensional perception of a scene and to view the results from a variety of viewpoints. Architectural simulation has been cited as the premier application field for the method, but it may be argued that radiosity will prove as useful in general computer-aided design (CAD) applications to provide a first-pass approximation to complex illumination conditions, including shadows.

An obvious requirement for a design or modeling tool is that the user is able to alter the scene or the model in real time, and otherwise interact with the simulation process.

Unfortunately, the radiosity method typically requires several minutes, if not hours, to compute complete radiosity images. One way to provide the necessary feedback rates is to advance the concept of progressive refinement, with an emphasis placed on obtaining faster results, possibly at the expense of accuracy. Most of the techniques reviewed in this chapter have to do with minimizing the reaction time of the simulation in response to user intervention.

6.1 Interactive display of the results

Since the classic radiosity method produces a list of radiosity values independently of the viewer's characteristics, it is possible to render an image of the simulated scene (or otherwise extract view-dependent information from it) using any viewing conditions.

6.1.1 Walking through the scene

One way to use the view-independent nature of the radiosity algorithm is to implement an interactive walkthrough algorithm for scenes with a precomputed radiosity solution. At each step the camera position and orientation, as well as its other characteristics, are updated according to the user's control, and surfaces of objects are displayed with colors determined by examining the results of the radiosity computation. This is made particularly easy using the specialized capabilities of a graphics accelerator, with hardware support for hidden-surface elimination and color interpolation. In this case a walkthrough program need only specify the viewing conditions at each step and feed a polygonal description of the scene into the rendering pipeline.

Better yet, the progressive refinement radiosity formulation introduced in Section 4.1 produces intermediate results that can be used to render images at various stages of the computation. These images can themselves be computed with any viewing conditions, which means that a user can interactively explore the scene *while the computation is taking place*.

The user's control of navigation through the scene is a difficult problem, and extensive research is being conducted on the subject of human interfaces for three-dimensional interaction [194]. Most currently available systems rely on a two-dimensional input device (mouse or tablet) or on a collection of one-dimensional devices (rotating knobs or sliders), and consequently offer a navigation model that is counterintuitive. A discussion of the available input devices is beyond the scope of this book. However, it should be noted that three-dimensional input capabilities are developing rapidly, with the advent of *virtual reality* systems. Such systems rely on actual three-dimensional motion for input, using for example a magnetic tracker attached to the head or hand of the user. The tracker can have up to six degrees of freedom, considering position and orientation. Visualization is typically performed using a head-mounted display, with two small video screens presenting a pair of collimated stereo images to the eyes.

6.1.2 Visibility preprocessing

Walkthrough applications require real-time image updates but also usually make use of scenes that are large enough to be impossible to render rapidly. These conflicting requirements have motivated research efforts in *visibility processing*. Here the idea is to build a spatial data structure that allows for easy determination of the set of potentially visible objects for the given viewing conditions.

For example, a two-dimensional map of a building floor can be preprocessed to generate lists of candidate objects that should be tested for visibility, effectively excluding most of the scene database for any given viewpoint [174]. This work was extended to three dimensions to determine the volume visible for an observer looking through a sequence of openings through walls or floors [172]. An incremental construction of the visibility graph, which allows easy classification of interpatch visibility situations, is also possible [173].

6.1.3 Levels of detail

If interactive motion is of great importance to the user, a lower-resolution geometrical description of the scene is usually acceptable, and allows faster updates as the viewing conditions change. In fact, while the user is controlling motion in the simulated environment, even a rather poor definition of the illumination characteristics, with no fine-scale details, suffices to provide a good three-dimensional perception.

When a hierarchical description of the surfaces is available, a variable amount of geometry can be used, depending on the constraints imposed by the interactive display. This is the case in particular when the hierarchical radiosity formulation of Section 4.4 is used, but such a description can also be obtained for most other environments. For instance, most radiosity implementations rely on a meshing module to subdivide large surface elements into smaller entities. Several descriptions of each object, with varying levels of detail, can be stored for use in the interactive walkthrough phase [2, 60, 59].

6.1.4 Data exploration and interactive steering

The ability to explore the radiosity solution by moving through the scene is clearly a major advantage of this approach over other advanced rendering techniques such as ray tracing. However, the argument can be made that this advantage is only the positive side of a major drawback, that is, the view-independent nature of the computation, which potentially wastes a lot of effort. Importance-driven radiosity, introduced in Section 4.5, offers an interesting compromise: if importance is properly attributed to the various surfaces according to their visibility in a final image or in a sequence of images, no computation is wasted on invisible portions of the environment.

Still, there are cases where it is impossible to predict in advance what portions of the scene the user is most interested in. In some virtual reality applications especially, the user is "immersed" in the virtual world and may develop an interest in any of the features of the environment. In such cases, a truly view-independent radiosity solution is clearly needed. Many virtual reality demonstrations make use of a precomputed radiosity solution to shade the surfaces. In addition to the view-independence just mentioned, two other properties make radiosity an apt technique for virtual reality. First, it offers a high degree of perceptual realism thanks to the subtle interreflection effects that are taken into account. Second, all the illumination information is contained in the radiosity solution. Although this solution is obtained at considerable expense, it greatly simplifies the display of the scene, thus allowing fast update rates. The only operation required for display is the interpolation of color across the surfaces, which is typically much faster than doing even a simple shading calculation for each surface.

Being able to explore the data, especially as the solution is progressing, inevitably creates a desire to be able to influence the computation itself as it progresses. In the scientific visualization domain this paradigm is referred to as *interactive steering*. A user should be offered the means to not only explore the data and the results of the simulation, but also to modify some parameters, change the focus of interest, and otherwise refine the simulation to more closely satisfy his or her goals.

In the case of radiosity, this means being able to change the model or the lighting parameters during the computation and immediately visualize the effects of the change. This issue is examined in the next section.

6.2 Incremental computation

Some characteristics of the radiosity method as presented above are not compatible with its use in a general modeling environment. For instance radiosity considers a static environment, in which the number of objects, as well as their shape and location, are fixed during the simulation. The problem is that if an object of the scene is modified, as might happen during a modeling session, all form factors could potentially be affected, since all pairs of surfaces in the scene could see their mutual visibility change as a result of the modification. Two surfaces that see each other can have their visibility blocked by a newly introduced object, and two objects that cannot see each other can become mutually visible if the obstructing object is removed.

It is possible, however, to express the radiosity simulation as an incremental process, enhancing the progressive refinement algorithm from Section 4.1. In essence a computation is performed that produces an incremental correction to the radiosity solution in response to a modification [135, 25, 62]. Throughout this section we assume that a radiosity solution has been computed using the progressive refinement algorithm, and must be updated to reflect changes made by the user.

6.2.1 Some simple examples

Before looking at the practical algorithm for incremental computation and its formal justification, let us first examine two simple cases and attempt to acquire a feeling for the extent of the modification to a global radiosity solution induced by a simple change to the scene. We shall see that all modeling operations can be expressed as a sequence of elementary operations similar to the two examples chosen.

Fixed geometry

Suppose that the geometry of the environment is not altered, but some illumination properties, such as exitances or reflectances, are changed. For example a light source might be switched on or off, or the color of an object might be changed. To accomplish this the user modifies the balance of the spectral reflectivities for that object.

As mentioned in Section 3.2.4, if a full matrix of form factors is already available, the impact of the change on the radiosity solution is obtained by computing a new solution to the linear system of radiosity equations. In the case of the hierarchical radiosity formulation of Section 4.4, the matrix is actually stored in a compact manner using links, and similarly, a new radiosity solution is obtained quickly by iteratively propagating energy along the links. Recomputing a radiosity solution typically requires only a few seconds.

If form factors or links have not been stored, and all that is available is a former radiosity solution, an incremental correction can be applied so that the algorithm automatically and smoothly converges to the correct solution, taking into account the modification.

Consider a particular surface patch P_i. During the course of the previous radiosity solution, this patch has distributed its radiosity among the other objects using one or more radiosity shots. If the exitance and/or reflectance of patch P_i is changed, then the amount of energy distributed in the radiosity solution becomes incorrect and must be adjusted. Fortunately the required correction is easy to compute: it is composed in part of the change in exitance, and in part of the change in reflectance, multiplied by the incident flux on P_i. The incident flux itself is derived from the radiosity, exitance, and reflectance values, as shown later. Therefore a new progressive radiosity step can be performed, in effect shooting the radiosity correction into the environment. This correction must be shot for all surfaces whose characteristics are altered. Note that the correction can be either positive, such as when the exitance or reflectance is increased, or negative, for a decreased exitance or reflectance.

The correction procedure is not sufficient to produce a valid radiosity solution. As an example consider an environment with a single light source. After the initial radiosity solution, even surfaces that do not have a direct view of the light source may have a non-zero radiosity, due to light interreflection. If the light source is now switched off, the correction just described only affects the surfaces directly visible from it. In order for all light in the scene to disappear, the changes must be propagated further. These simple ideas are formalized in Section 6.2.2.

Adding an object

In the case where the geometry of the scene is allowed to change, more complex modifications are needed. Some visibility relationships are modified, hence the form factors are changed. Let us consider the simple case where a new object is added to the scene.

All surfaces visible from that object have distributed their energy during the radiosity solution to the surfaces they could see. After the new object is introduced, these surfaces should redistribute their energy, so that the new object receives its share, and the surfaces obscured by the new object are properly shadowed. This is illustrated in Figure 6.1.

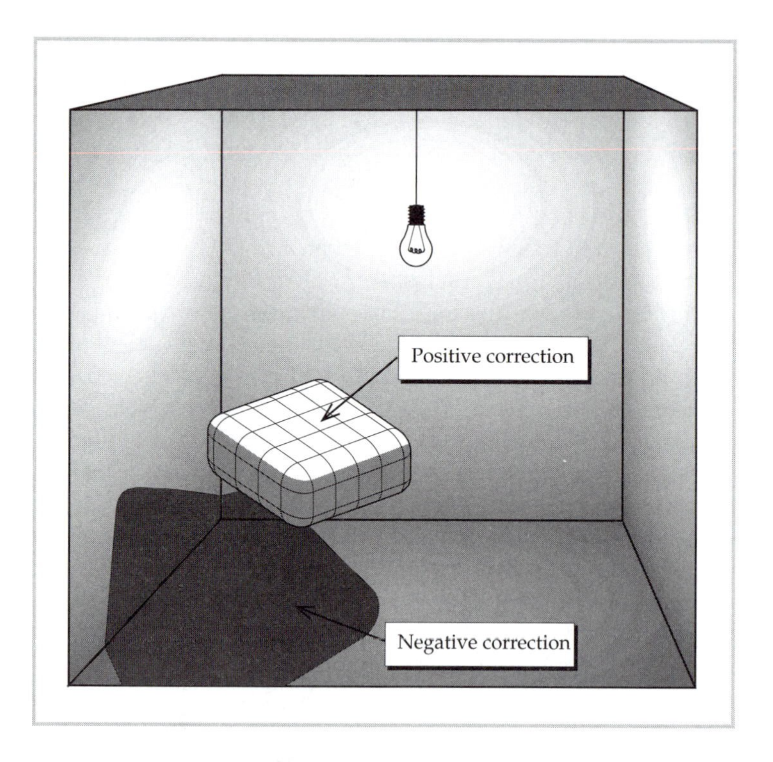

FIGURE 6.1 Adding an object to the scene. Energy must be redistributed between the object and its shadow.

The case where an object is removed from the scene is a symmetric operation; a positive correction is distributed to the patches that were in shadow, but have become exposed to illuminating patches due to the removal of the object. Moving an object or altering its shape can be seen as a combination of removal and addition operations: the object is first removed from its original position, modified in any way desired, and reintroduced in the scene with its new shape and position.

6.2.2 Incremental formulation

Let us consider the situation where a radiosity solution is available from a previous calculation, and some part of the environment is modified. To better understand the impact of the modification on the radiosity distribution, we express the change of all radiosities by first writing the two radiosity equations side by side, before the change, at time t, and after the change, at time $t + \Delta t$:

$$B_i^t = E_i^t + \rho_i^t \sum_{j=1}^{N} F_{ij}^t B_j^t \tag{6.1}$$

$$B_i^{t+\Delta t} = E_i^{t+\Delta t} + \rho_i^{t+\Delta t} \sum_{j=1}^{N} F_{ij}^{t+\Delta t} B_j^{t+\Delta t} . \tag{6.2}$$

Subtracting 6.1 from 6.2, and denoting by superscript Δt the difference between a given quantity at times $t + \Delta t$ and t, results in the following expression for the change in radiosity $B_i^{\Delta t}$:

$$B_i^{\Delta t} = E_i^{\Delta t} + \rho_i^{t+\Delta t} \sum_{j=1}^{N} F_{ij}^{\Delta t} B_j^t + \rho_i^{\Delta t} \sum_{j=1}^{N} F_{ij}^t B_j^t + \rho_i^{t+\Delta t} \sum_{j=1}^{N} F_{ij}^{t+\Delta t} B_j^{\Delta t} . \tag{6.3}$$

Equation 6.1 shows that

$$\sum_{j=1}^{N} F_{ij}^t B_j^t = \frac{B_i^t - E_i^t}{\rho_i^t} \tag{6.4}$$

as long as $\rho_i^t \neq 0$. This condition is verified in all practical cases, so we shall assume it is always true in the remainder of this chapter. Note that the above quantity represents the incident flux density on patch P_i in the original solution. Equation 6.3 can now be rewritten as

$$B_i^{\Delta t} = E_i^{\Delta t} + \rho^{\Delta t} \frac{B_i^t - E_i^t}{\rho_i^t} + \rho_i^{t+\Delta t} \sum_{j=1}^{N} F_{ij}^{\Delta t} B_j^t + \rho_i^{t+\Delta t} \sum_{j=1}^{N} F_{ij}^{t+\Delta t} B_j^{\Delta t} . \tag{6.5}$$

The first three terms define a *redistribution term*:

$$R_i = E_i^{\Delta t} + \rho^{\Delta t} \frac{B_i^t - E_i^t}{\rho_i^t} + \rho_i^{t+\Delta t} \sum_{j=1}^{N} F_{ij}^{\Delta t} B_j^t . \tag{6.6}$$

Equation 6.5 becomes equivalent to the usual radiosity equation, with only a modified *source term*:

$$B_i^{\Delta t} = R_i + \rho_i^{t+\Delta t} \sum_{j=1}^{N} F_{ij}^{t+\Delta t} B_j^{\Delta t} . \tag{6.7}$$

The name *redistribution* is used because the different terms in Equation 6.6 express the radiosity correction mentioned in the qualitative discussion of Section 6.2.1. Note that they depend only on the radiosity values at time step t and the new simulation parameters. The first term represents the change in exitance, while the second term models the effect of a change in reflectance: the amount of radiosity that was previously reflected is reevaluated using the variation in reflectance. The third term expresses the effect of the change in irradiance, or incident light on patch P_i, due to the changes of visibility from P_i.

Equation 6.7 states that the total change in radiosity is not limited to the redistribution term, but must take into account higher-order reflection terms. Thanks to its similarity to the normal radiosity equation, an algorithm to obtain the new radiosity solution from the old one is easily derived. Assuming the redistribution term is known for all patches, all radiosity changes can be obtained by following the usual progressive refinement procedure, which in effect propagates the redistributed energy into the environment. Thus a simple approach consists of a *redistribution* phase, where all R_i terms are computed, followed by a *propagation* phase, where the final answer is obtained.

Equations 6.6 and 6.7 are complicated because they are written for the most general case, where all parameters—position, shape, reflectance, exitance—are allowed to change between time steps t and $t + \Delta t$. For the two simple cases considered earlier, these equations can be further simplified.

Fixed geometry

If the geometry of the objects in the scene remains fixed, no form factors are changed. Therefore, for all pairs of indices (i, j), $F_{ij}^{t+\Delta t} = F_{ij}^t$ or, equivalently, $F_{ij}^{\Delta t} = 0$. Therefore the redistribution term becomes

$$R_i = E_i^{\Delta t} + \rho^{\Delta t} \frac{B_i^t - E_i^t}{\rho_i^t}, \tag{6.8}$$

and the change in radiosity is given by

$$B_i^{\Delta t} = R_i + \rho_i^{t+\Delta t} \sum_{j=1}^{N} F_{ij}^t B_j^{\Delta t}. \tag{6.9}$$

Note that the redistribution term depends only on available parameters: radiosities at time step t, exitances, and reflectances. As already mentioned, if all form factors are still available from a previous computation, Equation 6.9 is readily solved using iterative methods. When form factors are not known, the progressive refinement approach is used to propagate the most important redistribution terms first.

Variable geometry

We shall restrict ourselves to the case where a single geometry modification happens between time steps t and $t + \Delta t$. Since exitances and reflectances do not vary between t and $t + \Delta t$, the redistribution term reduces to

$$R_i = \rho_i^t \sum_{j=1}^{N} F_{ij}^{\Delta t} B_j^t. \tag{6.10}$$

Note that R_i depends on the change of form factor from P_i to all other surfaces. Therefore computing all redistribution terms prior to a new progressive refinement solution phase is a very expensive operation, since all form factors must be recomputed. If the form factors corresponding to the old configuration are not available, they must be computed as well.

In order for the incremental formulation to yield an efficient algorithm, with fast convergence towards the new solution, another solution scheme must be devised. It is simply too costly to compute all redistribution terms using Formula 6.10; therefore a progressive refinement approach must be used for that computation as well. The actual organization of the computation is examined in the next section.

6.2.3 Organizing the computation

If we concentrate on the case where the geometry of the scene has been modified, the redistribution term depends on the change in form factors between all pairs of patches. For simplicity we shall deal only with the case of the addition of a new object, knowing that other cases can be treated similarly.

Another level of progressive refinement

A redistribution term must be computed for each patch P_i, according to Equation 6.6. Similar to the computation of static form factors, two strategies can be envisioned: computing a row of form factor changes at a time, or computing a column of form factor changes at a time. These correspond to gathering and shooting redistribution contributions, respectively.

For all but trivially simple scenes, an operation such as the addition or removal of an object will have a limited impact on the total illumination. More precisely the impact on the illumination will be concentrated in the areas near the relevant object and its shadow areas. Only a small number of form factor changes $F_{ij}^{\Delta t}$ are significant, and many patches will actually receive very little redistributed energy. An important goal for a practical algorithm is to quickly identify the non-zero form factor changes and to efficiently compute only those values.

The sources of illumination that are most influential on the illumination of the new object, or on the creation of its shadows, are responsible for the major portion of the redistribution energy in the scene. Therefore the shooting approach seems better tuned to the problem of rapidly computing a good approximation of the redistribution terms. A patch P_j that is deemed an important redistributor shoots out its contribution by adding to all relevant receiving patches the contribution

$$\rho_i^{t+\Delta t} F_{ij}^{\Delta t} B_j^t \,.$$

Since only a limited number of patches P_i are actually affected by the redistribution operation, computation can be significantly reduced by restricting the effort to the patches that are on the added object and in its shadow.

This can be accomplished in a variety of ways, depending on how the form factors are being computed. When a projection method such as the hemi-cube is used, both the *old* and the *new* form factors are computed by projecting all patches, except those on the new object, only once on the hemi-cube, and then compositing the new object in the item buffers [25]. Note that only the fraction of the hemi-cube that bounds the extent of the projection of the new object is used, as shown in Figure 6.2.

If ray casting is used to compute pointwise form factors, as in Section 5.1.3, several approaches are possible. Patches that cannot possibly require a new form factor can be culled away, using a *shadow volume* [123] or a *shaft* [73], as shown in Figure 6.3. Alternatively, a simple intersection test can be added to the calculation, in order to limit the expensive occlusion tests to rays that actually touch the new object [162].

Ordering the computation

So far we have seen how the change in the radiosity distribution can be computed in reaction to a modification of the scene. The simple approach outlined above first computes all redistribution terms R_i, and then uses these values as substitutes to the normal exitance terms in a progressive refinement radiosity phase.

As shown in the previous section, however, it is very inefficient in terms of providing rapid feedback to compute all redistribution terms before starting the propagation phase. Even if the redistribution phase is terminated when redistribution terms become sufficiently

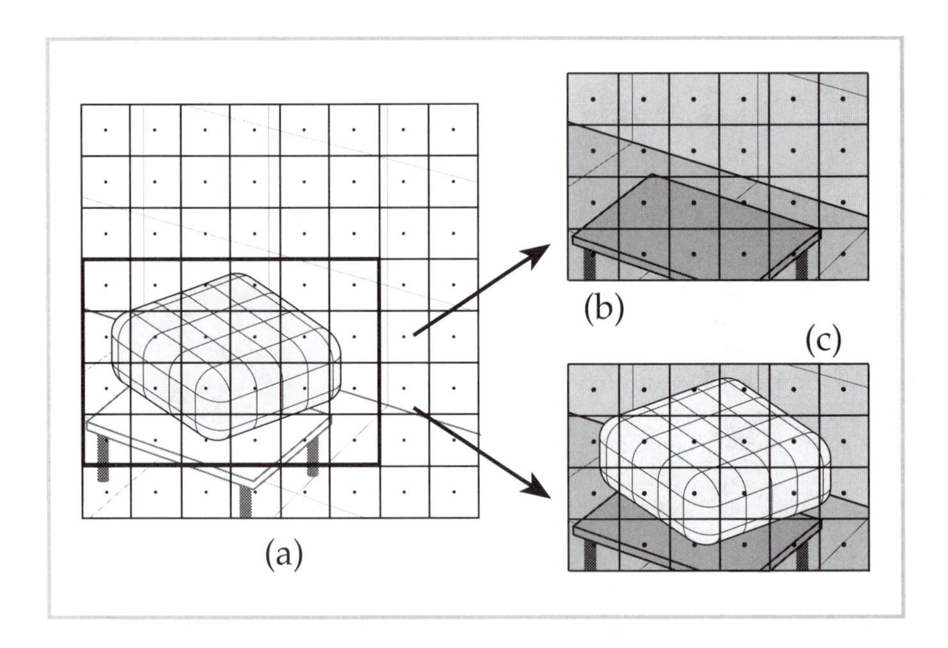

FIGURE 6.2 A single hemi-cube is used to compute the change in form factors. First, the extent of the projection of the new object on the hemi-cube is found (a). The static part of the scene is projected onto the hemi-cube (b). Finally, the new object is composited in the item buffers (c).

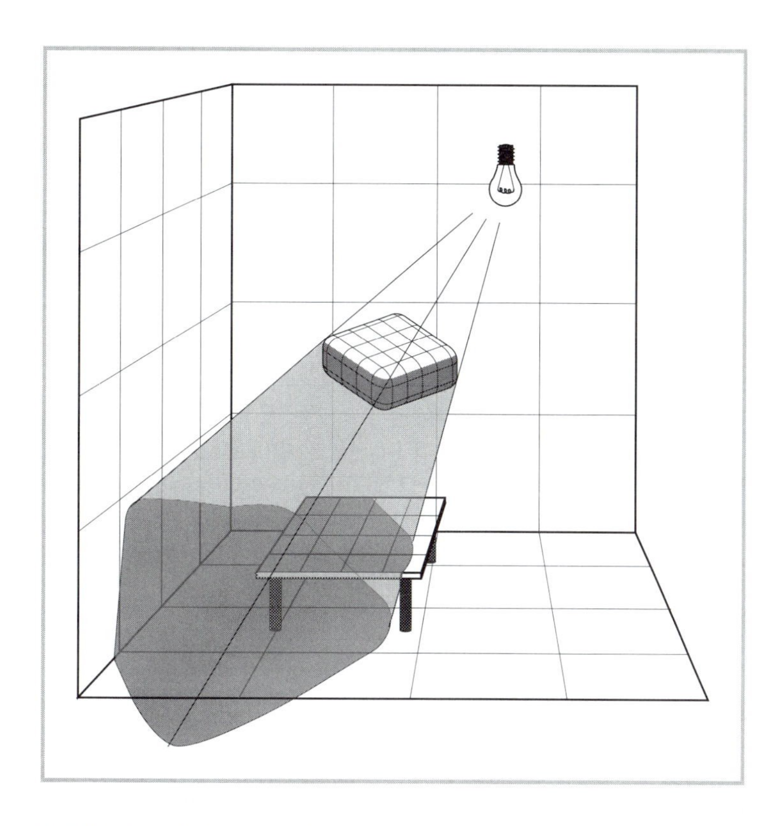

FIGURE 6.3 A shadow volume aids in the determination of patches that are affected by redistribution.

small, it is often the case that some effects of the propagation are more significant and should be computed and displayed early on. A natural idea is therefore to interleave redistribution steps and propagation steps, by always selecting the next action based on its estimated impact on the final solution. In the case of a propagation step, the impact on the scene can be quantified by the amount of energy distributed. This impact can be expressed as the radiosity of the shooting patch multiplied by its area. In the case of redistribution steps, the impact is more difficult to measure since it depends on the energy sent in the direction of the new object. A patch with large radiosity values can end up redistributing very little energy, if the new object occupies only a small fraction of the patch's field of view. Simple heuristic tests can be used to obtain a rough estimate of the importance of a particular patch for redistribution without imposing a heavy computational burden [62].

As long as such an estimate is available, interleaving redistribution and propagation steps is very easy, and allows propagation effects to be treated very early on, if they are likely to have a strong impact on the resulting radiosity solution. An example of a significant propagation step occurs when a new object is added to a scene with a very powerful light source. The redistribution step from the light source will illuminate the new object and create a shadow. Further redistribution steps would account for the effects of secondary illumination of the object, but it is also very important to propagate the energy received on the object, as well as to propagate its shadow.

Color Plate 33 shows a radiosity simulation that was computed incrementally after the robot in the center was added to the scene. A converged radiosity solution was used as a starting point, and a meaningful solution including shadows was obtained in less than a minute. This should be compared to the several hours required for a new radiosity solution.

Handling successive modifications

So far, we have considered the case of a single modification of the scene between time steps t and $t + \Delta t$. We have seen that it is possible to incrementally update the radiosity solution, and to compute and display the most significant changes first. This is not sufficient in a modeling environment where the user is likely to request modifications before previous modifications have been completely processed; in other words, the incremental process does not have a chance to converge to the new solution in between changes.

When a change in the environment occurs before the redistribution and propagation of light has converged, the situation is more complex, since no accurate solution is available as a starting point for computing a new incremental correction.

One approach to solving this problem is to try to process as much of the incremental correction as possible before a new modification occurs, and to delay the rest of the computation until later, when user input pauses and more processing time becomes available. An entry can be made in a data structure that indicates that further action is required to complete the processing of previous modifications [62]. Although conceptually simple, this approach leaves many implementation questions unanswered.

The first question concerns the information to be stored in order to allow the computation to resume at a later time. The incremental correction due to a given modification must be computed using the scene that is current at the time of the modification. If the computation is delayed and the scene undergoes further changes, there needs to be a way to access the previous state of the scene. This particular problem can be addressed by using a *geometry queue*, which describes the succession of changes made to the scene [25].

Another problem is that of the significance of partial solutions: if incremental corrections are not computed up to a certain accuracy before new changes are made, errors in the radiosity solution presented to the user can rapidly render the solution useless. For practical use there needs to be a way to estimate the error in the current solution due to incomplete computation. This could be used by the user to estimate the reliability of the solution being displayed.

Finally, if a number of modifications are made, it may become more practical to start a solution from the beginning, instead of accumulating incremental corrections and their associated errors. CAD users frequently make several changes to the same object before moving on to other parts of the scene. To prevent the size of the "modifications queue" from growing too rapidly, a simple selection scheme can be used. The particular object is selected by the user before any modification can be done, at which time it is removed from the radiosity solution. While the user is modifying the object, the incremental corrections are always recomputed from that solution, instead of being accumulated and generating more log entries. Only when the object is deselected is a new log entry recorded, corresponding to the addition of the modified object to the scene.

6.2.4 Convergence

Starting from a converged solution

Equation 6.7, which controls the variation of radiosity caused by a change in the environment, has the exact same form as the classic radiosity equation (Equation 3.18). Therefore, the progressive refinement algorithm presented in Section 4.1 can be successfully applied to the problem of incrementally updating the radiosity solution, provided the redistribution terms R_i are all known. In this case the convergence of the Southwell relaxation scheme is guaranteed, as shown in Section 4.1.2.

Since the progressive refinement algorithm converges and produces a solution for the $B_i^{\Delta t}$s, the total radiosity solution corresponding to the new scene conditions is obtained by summing this correction and the previous solution.

Starting from a partially converged solution

If the incremental radiosity algorithm is used in an interactive system, it is unlikely that a converged radiosity solution will be available before each modification of the scene. In general a change to the scene will occur while the progressive refinement process is in progress. Here we show that the properties of Southwell relaxation guarantee that the redistribution process will still converge to the true solution.

A partial solution of the Southwell relaxation procedure corresponds to a vector of energy estimates β and an associated residual vector given by $\boldsymbol{r} = \epsilon - \boldsymbol{K}\beta$. If changes are made to the geometry of the scene or lighting conditions, ϵ and $\boldsymbol{K}$ are modified accordingly.

The discussion of the Southwell relaxation technique in Section 4.1.2 shows that the progressive refinement algorithm converges for all possible choices of the initial energy estimate. The redistribution algorithm of Section 6.2.3 amounts to starting such a progressive refinement procedure, with the new geometry and lighting conditions, but with an initial energy vector $\beta^{(0)}$ equal to the last energy estimate computed in the previous (partial) solution.

The redistribution term can be retrieved by expressing the residual vector corresponding to the choice of this initial estimate. If the defining equation for the residual vector (Equation 4.3) is written immediately before and after the change in the scene, noting that, by definition, the radiosity estimates just before and after the change are equal; that is,

$$\beta^{t+\Delta t\,(0)} = \beta^{t\,(k)} = \beta\,,$$

we have

$$\boldsymbol{r}^{t\,(k)} = \epsilon^t - \boldsymbol{K}^t \beta \tag{6.11}$$

and

$$\boldsymbol{r}^{t+\Delta t\,(0)} = \epsilon^{t+\Delta t} - \boldsymbol{K}^{t+\Delta t} \beta \,. \tag{6.12}$$

Thus the "initial" residual, with respect to the progressive refinement that happens after the modification of the scene, is obtained using

$$\boldsymbol{r}^{t+\Delta t\,(0)} = \boldsymbol{r}^{t\,(k)} + \epsilon^{\Delta t} - \boldsymbol{K}^{\Delta t} \beta \tag{6.13}$$

and the definition of matrix $\boldsymbol{K}$ (Equation 4.2),

$$r_i^{t+\Delta t\,(0)} = r_i^{t\,(k)} + A_i \left(E_i^{\Delta t} + \rho_i^{t+\Delta t} \sum_{j=1}^{N} F_{ij}^{\Delta t} \frac{\beta_j^t}{A_j} + \rho_i^{\Delta t} \sum_{j=1}^{N} F_{ij}^{t} \frac{\beta_j^t}{A_j} \right) \qquad 1 \le i \le N \,. \tag{6.14}$$

Looking back at equations 6.4 and 6.6, we see that

$$r_i^{t+\Delta t\,(0)} = r_i^{t\,(k)} + A_i R_i \qquad 1 \le i \le N \,. \tag{6.15}$$

Thus the redistribution term is exactly what is added to the residual to ensure proper convergence of the progressive refinement algorithm.

6.3 Radiosity acceleration

Accelerating the radiosity computation is another means of improving the response time of the simulation. Acceleration can be obtained by devoting more powerful resources to the computational phase of the radiosity solution, or alternatively by using approximate solutions that are obtained with simpler and faster algorithms.

6.3.1 Software architecture for interactive display

Let us reconsider the case of a radiosity simulation process that allows the user to walk through the scene interactively. There are several update rates to consider. The scene refresh rate depends on the time it takes to render the objects of the scene. This should be on the order of several frames per second, depending on the complexity of the scene and the graphics performance available. For the simulation, another update rate is defined as the time needed to complete one step of the progressive refinement computation. Typically this simulation rate is much lower than the display rate, on the order of several seconds per frame. Given this situation it makes sense to try to make the interaction loop as independent as possible from the simulation.

Fortunately, the computation involved in solving the radiosity equation is completely separate from rendering, thus making it easy to decouple the two processes. The computation process and the visualization process can in fact be separate processes. The only requirements are that both processes have complete knowledge of the scene geometry and that there is a mechanism for transmitting a set of radiosity values at any given time [135]. This interface can be realized using an area of shared memory, accessed on one side for writing by the simulation process, and from the other side for reading by the visualization process, as shown in Figure 6.4. The use of other interprocess communication constructs such as message-passing is also possible.

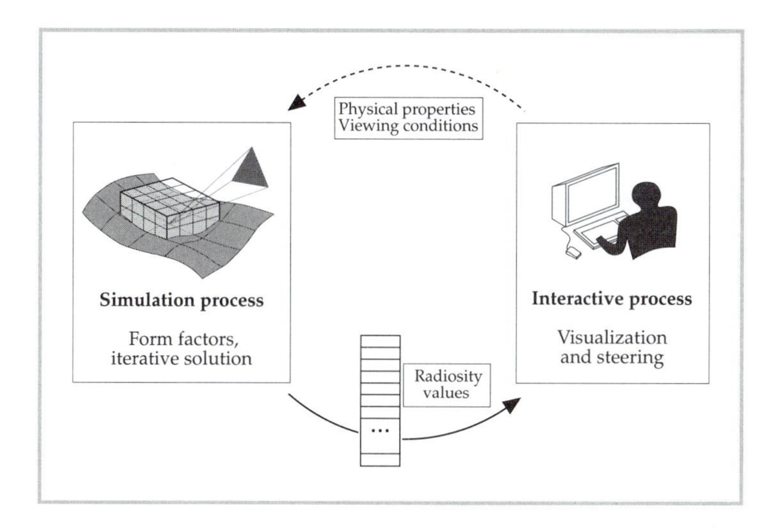

FIGURE 6.4 The lighting simulation process communicates a list of radiosity values to the visualization process.

The two processes can be decoupled further by executing them on different processors or on different machines. The radiosity computation can thus be transferred to a more powerful machine, while the graphics-intensive viewing operation takes place on a computer with special-purpose graphics hardware. This is represented in Figure 6.5. When the only interaction granted to the user consists in being able to "walk around" in the scene, the geometry of the objects never changes and a display list can be used to improve performance [56]. An efficient mechanism must be provided to update the colors of the objects in response to the generation of new radiosities from the simulation.

6.3.2 Using parallelism

Another method for speeding up the radiosity computation is to use some sort of parallelism. The progressive refinement radiosity algorithm lends itself to a simple parallel

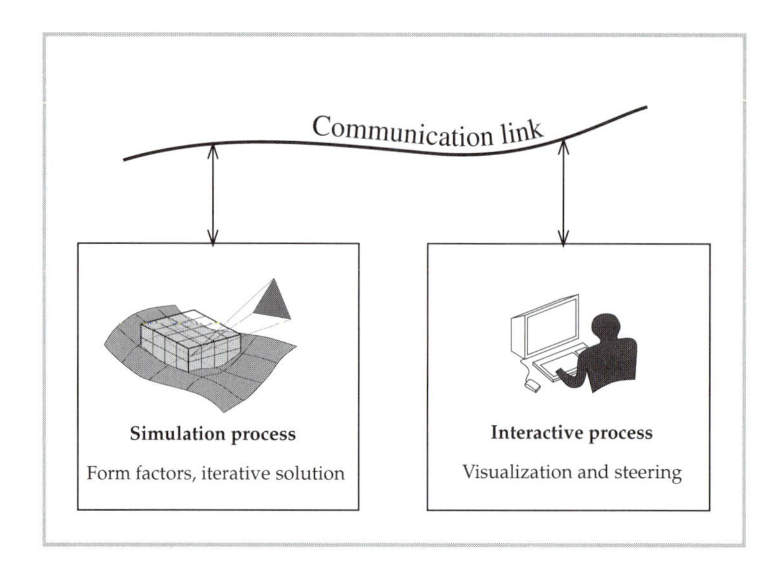

FIGURE 6.5 Using a compute node and a display node.

formulation, where all processing elements work independently of each other and communicate only with one particular processing element. This element is sometimes called the *master* or *server*. The master process distributes work to the other processes by requesting complete rows of the form factor matrix at a time. These rows are then used to perform a shooting step of the progressive refinement algorithm. Figure 6.6 illustrates this procedure.

This simple algorithm has been published in various forms, using either multiprocessor machines [15] or individual computers linked by a local area network [135, 136]. In the latter case the relatively low communication bandwidth severely limits the usefulness of the approach since, even for moderately complex scenes, the interprocess communication overhead increases rapidly with the number of processors.

Even on a multiprocessor machine with faster communication, the simple algorithm outlined above will be limited in both number of processors and complexity of the scene. The first and most important problem is that the entire scene description must be replicated at each processor. Thus a very desirable feature of a parallel implementation is violated, namely that larger problems should be treated simply by adding more processors to the system. For complex scenes the simple master-slave approach is therefore not practical, unless shared memory is available between all processors. Another limitation, linked to the requirement that each processor hold a copy of the scene, is that adaptive refinement of the mesh becomes very difficult to implement.

If large-scale performance increases are sought, without any limitation on the size of the problems to solve, a data-parallel architecture must be used, where the data is distributed among the processors. A vast body of research has been devoted to the similar problem of

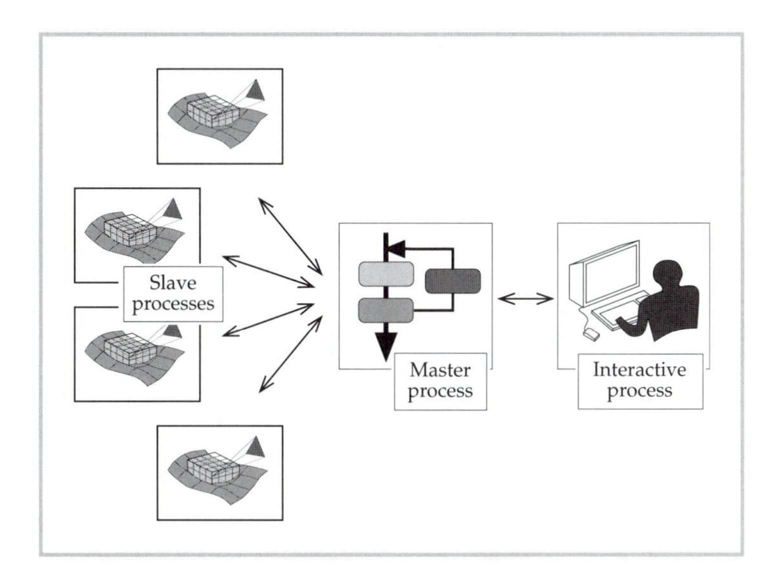

FIGURE 6.6 Master-slave organization of the radiosity simulation.

ray tracing. This work can be drawn upon to design a parallel radiosity implementation. In particular if ray casting is used for the computation of form factors, most published methods can be easily adapted [45, 119, 127, 52, 92].

6.3.3 Improved progressive refinement

Two means of accelerating the perceived improvement rate of a radiosity solution are to either try to obtain a better solution in the same amount of time, or reduce the time needed to achieve a given quality. Another approach consists of allowing some degradation of the solution's quality, in exchange for a much larger reduction of the computation time. This is particularly useful if the full-precision radiosity solutions can be obtained at a later time.

Since form factor computation dominates the radiosity process, this last idea can be implemented by selecting an alternative algorithm for the computation of form factors. One alternative uses a single projection plane to determine the visibility of other patches, instead of the five hemi-cube faces [165, 136]. This plane is positioned to account for the major portion of the energy diffusely reflected from a surface, as shown in Figure 6.7. The energy sent in directions that do not intersect the plane can either be neglected entirely or accounted for at a later stage by reintroducing the "missing" hemi-cube faces and projecting the environment onto them.

When the ray casting algorithm of Section 5.1.3 is used, the number of sample points used on the source patch is an easily controllable parameter, with a direct relation to computation time and an inverse relation to solution quality [185].

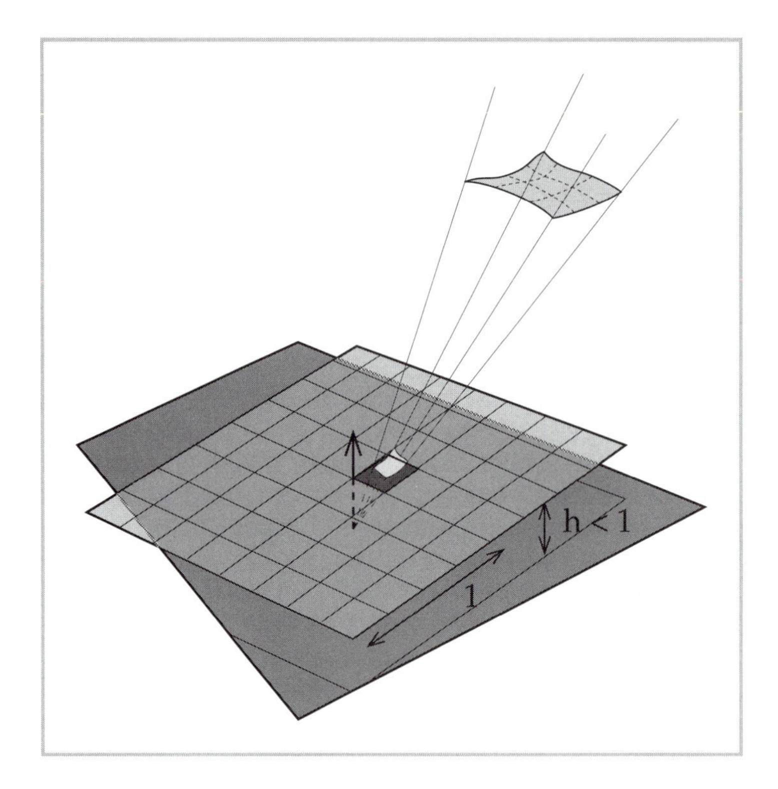

FIGURE 6.7 Using a single projection plane to quickly compute approximate form factors. Energy exchanges at grazing angles are ignored by this algorithm, but account for a relatively small fraction of the total flux.

6.3.4 Interactive accuracy control

Although the user of an interactive system usually wants to obtain good performance, in the case of radiosity simulations it is often very important to control the accuracy of the results. Since many applications require quantitative results, obtaining faster results at the cost of precision is not always satisfactory. While the computation of a very fast, lower accuracy solution is almost certainly necessary in order to provide basic interaction capabilities, the concept of interactive steering must also be applied to enable some user control over the precision of the results.

Possible means of control include the interactive refinement of the underlying geometrical mesh, or interactive specification of areas of interest, when using the importance-driven algorithm of Section 4.5. The radiosity solution can be updated quickly in response to mesh refinement by gathering radiosity at the newly introduced sample points. Importance is not necessarily assigned to surfaces based on their visibility from a particular set of viewpoints, but can be explicitly assigned using a variety of criteria, depending on the goals of the simulation.

6.4 Radiosity as a tool for lighting design

The radiosity method is often presented as a tool that helps the user to simulate the lighting conditions in an environment. Given a scene geometry and all reflectivities and light source settings, a distribution of radiosity is computed and displayed. For *lighting design* applications however, the goal is not merely to visualize a proposed set of lighting conditions, but to decide what fixtures and lighting properties achieve the desired effect.

Extensions to the radiosity method have been proposed to address some of the specific needs of design applications [46]. For example, in theatrical lighting, special effects are often realized using filters and masks in front of light sources. The directional characteristics of the light sources must be accurately modeled for these applications. A discussion of directional light sources can be found in the Appendix (Section A.1.5). Slide projection techniques are also used for stage lighting to provide a background scene, and must also be simulated. Examples of simulated images for opera productions are shown in Color Plates 34 and 35. Note that the background scene in Plate 35 is projected on a curved backdrop, with appropriate corrections being computed to counter the distortion due to the projection.

The conventional use of lighting simulation for design application involves a trial-and-error process, in which the user investigates the space of possible options by manually selecting parameters and judging simulation results. While this is of course a useful process, it is interesting to investigate how the search in "design space" can be at least partially automated by applying the radiosity technique to solve the *inverse* problem. In other words, given a scene geometry and a specification of the desired lighting conditions, a set of reflectivities and light source characteristics can be computed that would produce these conditions. Looking back at the radiosity equation

$$B_i = E_i + \rho_i \sum_{j=1}^{N} F_{ij} B_j$$

we see that if the radiosities B_i and reflectances ρ_i are specified, and the form factors have been computed, the necessary exitances are immediately obtained:

$$E_i = B_i - \rho_i \sum_{j=1}^{N} F_{ij} B_j \,. \qquad \textbf{(6.16)}$$

Real-world lighting design problems cannot be solved by computing this set of exitance values. One problem is that light sources are not as flexible in terms of position and physical characteristics as their virtual counterparts. In addition, the goal of a lighting designer is not to obtain a predetermined radiosity distribution, but rather to enforce a number of constraints, such as compliance with regulatory standards or creation of a certain atmosphere.

Assuming that these constraints can be expressed in the form of a scalar *objective function* that depends on the distribution of radiosities, the usual radiosity solution process can be seen as a tool to compute this objective as a function of any set of exitances and reflectances. Given such a mapping between lighting characteristics and objective, a solution can be sought by solving a maximization problem, that is, trying to determine the set of properties that yields the best results.

Possible objective functions include specified radiosities for visible surfaces. Least-squares minimization is then used to obtain the set of radiosity values that produces the closest approximation in image space [147]. Other choices include subjective characterizations of lighting distributions [98]. Color Plate 44 shows two examples of lighting conditions in a room that were obtained automatically after specifying different desired high-level properties for the lighting distribution. Notions such as "visual clarity" or "privateness" were first given a technical meaning in an experimental study: a correlation was established between these subjective appreciations and numerical quantities, such as overall illumination and contrast. Goals were then specified, with an emphasis on visual clarity for the left-hand image, and on privateness for the right-hand image. The optimization process controlled the emissive power and direction of the light sources in order to achieve the desired goals.

❒ ❒ ❒

Interaction is becoming a major requirement of computer graphics systems, and the simulation of global illumination is a problem of choice for the application of interactive techniques. Beyond the simple, yet very effective walkthrough capability offered by a view-independent radiosity simulation, the ability to interact with the computational process itself is one of the most challenging current research areas. With the advent of virtual reality applications, users must be able to modify and influence the environment, while retaining a high-quality radiometric simulation. The incremental technique presented in this chapter is a step in this direction, but does not completely solve the accuracy issue raised by successive modifications of the scene.

Radiosity is now being used for lighting design applications, as demonstrated in the examples in the color plates. The combination of physical accuracy and automated computational algorithms places a very powerful tool in the hands of designers. The dissemination of radiosity techniques to this public is likely to increase the pressure for designing truly interactive systems.

CHAPTER 7

Extensions to radiosity

The radiosity method has been successfully applied to the simulation of radiant energy transfers in several application fields, including heat transfer analysis and image synthesis. However, the basic technique contains rather stringent assumptions, some of which prevent its use in solving complex problems in those fields. For example the assumption that all surfaces are ideal diffuse reflectors is rarely met in practice. Deviation from diffuse behavior is necessary for photorealistic image synthesis. Unfortunately, nondiffuse reflectors make the global illumination problem significantly more complex, and algorithmic changes are needed to keep this complexity under control. The assumption of a nonparticipating, transparent medium also limits the use of radiosity in global illumination. The simulation of participating media is important when large-scale scenes are rendered, for which atmospheric effects cannot be neglected. Volume scattering effects also play an important role in thermal simulations. This chapter reviews some extensions to the radiosity method that permit the simulation of more realistic conditions.

7.1 Nondiffuse global illumination

The radiosity method presented so far is valid only for ideal diffuse reflectors. Unfortunately, this is a poor representation of reality. Furthermore, diffuse scenes do not efficiently communicate spatial relations, since the human visual system is very good at detecting and interpreting highlights. Highlights are used by our visual system to identify high-curvature regions on the objects. Thus any attempt to produce photorealistic images must take nondiffuse reflection into account.

When the assumption of ideal diffuse reflection is relaxed, the general form of the global illumination equation must be used, complete with an arbitrary bidirectional reflectance distribution function, or BRDF ρ_{bd}. This term was introduced in Section 1.4. Recall that the global illumination equation for surfaces is

$$L(x, \theta_0, \phi_0) = L_e(x, \theta_0, \phi_0) + \int_\Omega \rho_{bd}(x, \theta_0, \phi_0, \theta, \phi) L_i(x, \theta, \phi) \cos\theta \, d\omega . \qquad \textbf{(7.1)}$$

The presence of $\rho_{bd}(x, \theta_0, \phi_0, \theta, \phi)$ inside the integral makes the scattering problem much more difficult to solve. In integral equations terms (see Section 5.2), the kernel now has an explicit dependence in all variables, since the reflectance cannot be taken out of the integral. Furthermore, these dependences can be very complex, and in particular the kernel is generally not a smooth function. Properties of general reflectance functions are discussed below. The relevant variable of the general global illumination problem is now a *radiance function*, and cannot be represented by a direction-independent radiosity function.

From an algorithmic point of view, more information is needed to obtain the distribution of reflected radiance at some point. Recall that radiosities could be computed if the total incoming flux was known for each surface, as shown by Equation 3.8 in the derivation of the diffuse illumination equation. When ρ_{bd} is not constant this is no longer the case. The directional distribution of irradiance (incident flux density) must be available in addition to the BRDF in order to predict how the energy is reflected.

Before an algorithm can be derived for the computation of solutions to Equation 7.1, a new discrete formulation must be established, in a manner similar to the derivation of the discrete diffuse equation in Section 3.1. The first method we present attempts to extend the discretization technique that worked with diffuse radiosity, that is, the use of simple, constant discrete elements. However, since the reflection kernel is no longer smooth, it is difficult to capture the complexity of the illumination with a small number of simple elements, and this approach tends to produce noticeable artifacts (unless a prohibitively large number of elements is used). We present bidirectional methods as an alternative to a complete discretization. In particular, two-pass strategies are reviewed. These treat the discontinuous portion of the kernel in a separate step. Finally another discretization attempt using global basis functions to represent the directional dependence of radiance is proposed to allow a complete simulation for general BRDFs.

One source of complexity in the treatment of general reflectors is ideal specular reflection. Physical optics models show that ideal specular reflection is a common phenomenon, by no means limited to ideally smooth surfaces: since the ideal specular component of the reflectance experiences an exponential decay with roughness, slightly rough surfaces also exhibit this behavior. For visible light, ideal specular reflectance can be observed on materials with surface irregularities of up to 0.5 μm in size. Such scales of roughnesses are commonly found on manufactured objects. The images in Color Plate 29 show the variation of appearance of an aluminum box as its roughness is increased. For longer wavelengths, ideal specular behavior is even more common since the relevant roughness scales with wavelength. The ideal specular component of the reflectance deserves special attention because it introduces discontinuities in the BRDF and consequently also in the reflected radiance distributions. Special care must also be taken in all numerical solutions because of the resulting singularities in the reflection kernel. For example if a simple discretization scheme is used, it may prove necessary to use a very fine discrete mesh to capture all the details of the radiance functions, thereby creating many variables. Since the matrix of interactions grows as the square of the number of elements, such a discretization might prove too expensive.

Fortunately, in addition to being nonsmooth, the reflection kernel is also sparse. This means that light reflected at a particular point in a given direction only affects a limited subset of all points and directions in space. Consider a point x on a particular surface, and a direction in space. There is only one point y on one other surface that is visible from x in that direction. Alternatively, we can state that given two points x and y, there is only one direction in space connecting them.

Therefore, although the space of relevant variables expands tremendously by gaining two dimensions, the reflection kernel only "connects" very few of these variables.

7.2 Radiosity with nondiffuse reflectors: discretizing both the surfaces and the direction space

The basic idea underlying the development of the radiosity method—that is, replacing the continuous transfer equation by a set of linear equations—can be extended to the nondiffuse case. To this end we define an adequate set of variables, no longer reduced to a single radiosity value per surface patch. Using finite-element terminology, an adequate choice of discrete elements must be chosen to tile the space of variables, together with appropriate shape functions. The main benefit of this approach is that a view-independent solution can be computed that incorporates directional effects.

One choice of variables consists of selecting a number of discrete patches P_i and a finite number of directional elements Ω_j in space. An "element" in the space of variables is a tuple consisting of a patch and a direction, expressed as (P_i, Ω_j). This composite element is used in the derivation of a directional radiosity algorithm developed in the next two sections. Another approach consists of expressing the global illumination equation with *three-point transport* quantities, representing the energy transferred from one point to another after a reflection at the third point. The variables are then represented by triples of points on the surfaces. This representation has been used to derive a hierarchical computation algorithm that extends the one from Section 4.4 [10]. However, its practicality is not yet established because of the huge number of potential three-way interactions. The interested reader will find the details of this very elegant formulation in reference [10]. Color Plate 22 shows an image computed using the hierarchical algorithm to solve for three-point transport variables in the presence of nondiffuse reflectors.

7.2.1 Finite-element formulation

Let us reconsider Equation 7.1 and develop a finite-element formulation using simple shape functions. In Chapter 3 we showed that the global illumination equation can be expressed in one of two forms, with the integral being computed either over the area of the surfaces in the scene, or over the hemisphere of incident angles. Since the relevant variable for nondiffuse reflection is radiance for a position/direction pair, it is convenient to rewrite the illumination equation by integrating over *both* surface and angle.

For simplicity Θ will be used to denote a direction, corresponding to two angles (θ, ϕ), with the convention that $d\Theta \equiv d\omega = \sin\theta d\theta d\phi$. The opposite direction from Θ will be denoted by $-\Theta$. Using this notation the global illumination equation can be stated as

$$L(x, \Theta_0) = L_e(x, \Theta_0) + \int_{y \in S} \int_{\Theta \in \Omega} \rho_{bd}(x, \Theta_0, \Theta) L(y, -\Theta) \cos\theta \, \mathcal{V}(x, y, \Theta) dy d\omega . \quad \textbf{(7.2)}$$

This equation uses a modified visibility function $\mathcal{V}(x, y, \Theta)$ that is non-zero only if x can see y in direction Θ. Thus this function defines an implicit relationship between x, y, and Θ, and makes it easy to switch from an integral over the surfaces in the scene to an integral over the incident directions at x. Strictly speaking, $\mathcal{V}$ is a combination of Dirac distributions such that for any function of direction f,

$$\int_{\Theta \in \Omega} \mathcal{V}(x, y, \Theta) f(\Theta) d\omega = V(x, y) f(\Theta_y) \quad \textbf{(7.3)}$$

if Θ_y is the direction in which x sees y. Similarly, for any function g of position,

$$\int_{y \in S} \mathcal{V}(x, y, \Theta) g(y) dy = g(y_\Theta) \quad \textbf{(7.4)}$$

where y_Θ is the point visible from x in direction Θ. In order to use the finite-element method, we seek a solution of the form

$$\tilde{B}(x, \Theta) = \sum_{i,j=1}^{N} L_{ij} N_{ij}(x, \Theta) ,$$

as explained in Section 5.2. Perhaps the simplest choice for the shape functions in this higher-dimensional space is a tensor product of box functions over surface elements P_i and directional elements Ω_j, as illustrated in Figure 7.1:

$$N_{ij}(x, \Theta) = \psi_i(x) \varphi_j(\Theta) .$$

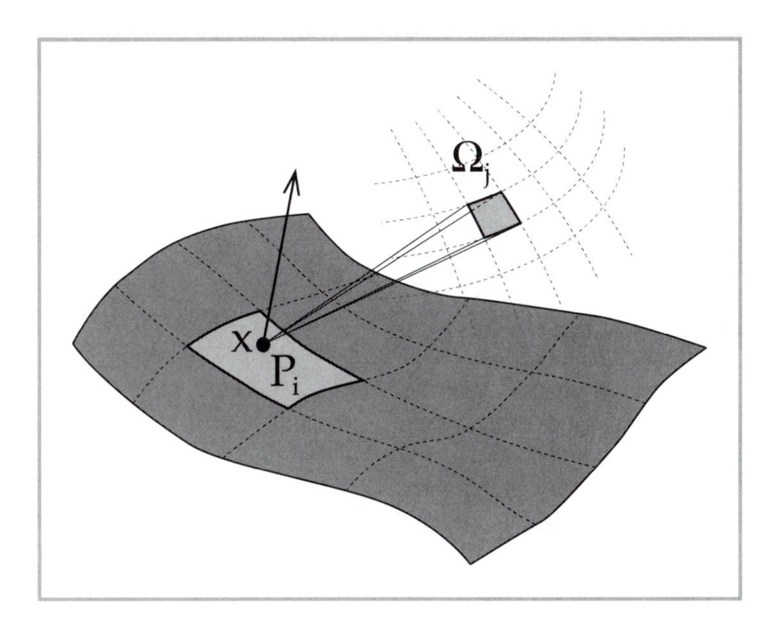

FIGURE 7.1 Simple elements used for directional radiance function.

The unknowns of the problem are the L_{ij}. They represent the average radiance of patch P_i for directions in Ω_j.

The point collocation constraint described in Section 5.2.2 can be used to obtain a set of linear equations. The "residual" must be zero at nodes (x_k, Θ_l). For all pairs (k, l),

$$0 = \sum_{i,j} L_{ij}\psi_i(x_k)\varphi_j(\Theta_l) - L_e(x_k, \Theta_l) \\ - \int_{y\in S}\int_{\Theta\in\Omega} \rho_{bd}(x_k, \Theta_l, \Theta) \sum_{i,j} L_{ij}\psi_i(y)\varphi_j(-\Theta)\cos\theta\mathcal{V}(x, y, \Theta)dyd\omega\,. \quad (7.5)$$

Since φ and ψ are box functions, $\psi_i(x_k) = \delta_{ik}$ and $\varphi_j(\Theta_l) = \delta_{jl}$. Thus the collocation constraint reduces to

$$L_{kl} = L_e(x_k, \Theta_l) + \\ \sum_{i,j} L_{ij} \int_{y\in S}\int_{\Theta\in\Omega} \rho_{bd}(x_k, \Theta_l, \Theta)\psi_i(y)\varphi_j(-\Theta)\cos\theta\mathcal{V}(x, y, \Theta)dyd\omega\,. \quad (7.6)$$

Since φ_j is a box function defined on directional element Ω_j around Θ_j, it is identically 0 outside this element; therefore integration can be restricted to the set of directions Θ such that $-\Theta \in \Omega_j$. We write this set of directions $-\Omega_j$. Thus

$$L_{kl} = L_e(x_k, \Theta_l) + \sum_j \sum_i L_{ij} \int_{\Theta \in -\Omega_j} \int_{y \in S} \rho_{bd}(x_k, \Theta_l, \Theta) \psi_i(y) \cos\theta \mathcal{V}(x, y, \Theta) dy d\omega . \quad \textbf{(7.7)}$$

Using the property of the extended visibility function expressed in Equation 7.4, the integration over the surface is removed to yield

$$L_{kl} = L_e(x_k, \Theta_l) + \sum_j \sum_i L_{ij} \int_{\Theta \in -\Omega_j} \rho_{bd}(x_k, \Theta_l, \Theta) \psi_i(y_\Theta) \cos\theta d\omega . \quad \textbf{(7.8)}$$

Again using box function properties, we can state that $\psi_i(y_\Theta)$ is non-zero only if y_Θ lies on patch P_i. Thus the summation over i should only be conducted over the set of indices such that the corresponding patch be visible from x in the directional element $-\Omega_j$.

7.2.2 Directional radiosity

In this section a computational algorithm is derived from Equation 7.8. Consider a particular pair of indices (k, l), for which the radiance value L_{kl} is to be computed. Apart from the self-emissivity term, the reflected radiance is obtained by summing contributions from all directions. This amounts to a summation over j. Each contribution has the form

$$\sum_i L_{ij} \int_{\Theta \in -\Omega_j} \rho_{bd}(x_k, \Theta_l, \Theta) \psi_i(y_\Theta) \cos\theta d\omega .$$

Two assumptions can be made at this point to simplify the equation. First, it is assumed that there is only a single surface element visible from point x_k through the directions in $-\Omega_j$. Let us denote by $v(j)$ the index of that element. Second, the BRDF $\rho_{bd}(x_k, \Theta_l, \Theta)$ is considered a constant as Θ spans $-\Omega_j$.

Under these assumptions the contribution to L_{kl} from direction Θ_j reduces to

$$\rho_{bd}(x_k, \Theta_l, -\Theta_j) L_{v(j)j} \int_{\Theta \in -\Omega_j} \cos\theta d\omega .$$

This formulation shows that a *directional radiosity* algorithm can use the same computation to determine the visibility relationships and obtain the contributions to the radiance function [91]. Given a surface patch P_k, the visibility information is first obtained by projecting each surface onto a *global cube* centered at point x_k. A global cube is a cube whose faces are subdivided into cells like those of the hemi-cube, with a fixed orientation in space. The visibility information is recorded in the relevant global cube's item buffer.

The cells on the global cube's faces are used as the directional elements Ω_j. Because the cube always has the same orientation, it is particularly easy to access a direction $-\Theta_j$

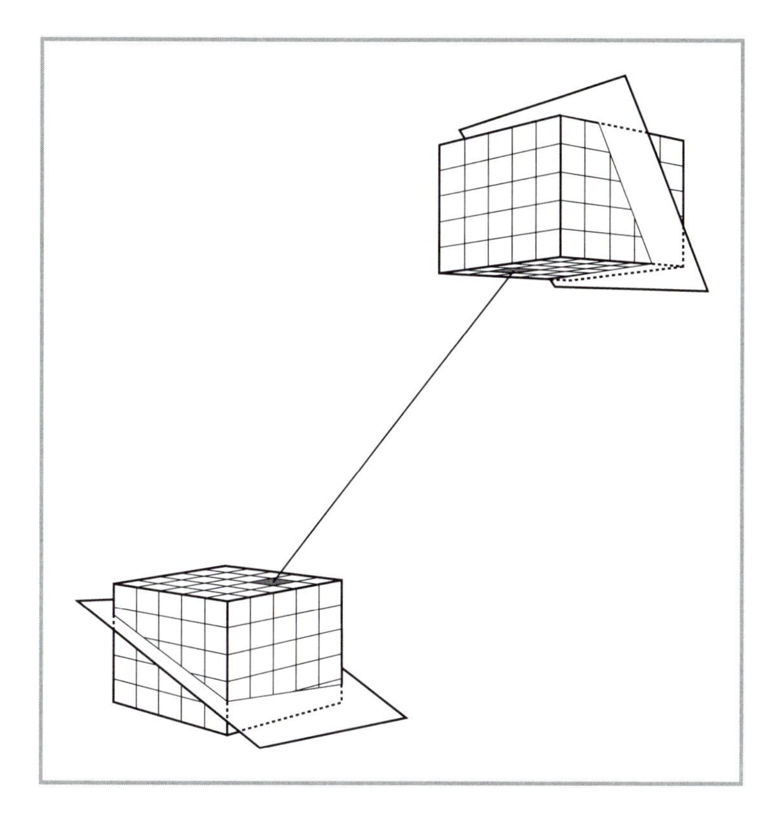

FIGURE 7.2 The global cube.

knowing Θ_j, as shown on Figure 7.2. Thus for each surface patch P_k, an array of radiance values L_{kl} corresponding to the directions of the global cube is maintained.

The system of discrete transfer equations is now

$$\forall k, l \quad L_{kl} = L_e(x_k, \Theta_l) + \sum_j \rho_{bd}(x_k, \Theta_l, -\Theta_j) L_{v(j)j} \int_{\Theta \in -\Omega_j} \cos\theta \, d\omega \,. \tag{7.9}$$

This equation can be solved iteratively as in the progressive refinement formulation of radiosity. Typically, $L_e(x_k, \Theta_l)$ is used as an initial estimate for $L_{kl}^{(0)}$. Once these are available, iterations are executed until convergence. An iteration consists of computing new estimates for all L_{kl} based on Equation 7.9. Note that the integral represents the delta-form factor associated with the cell $-\Omega_j$ and is thus computed only once at the start of the algorithm. The index of the visible surface $v(j)$ is found in the corresponding item buffer.

To render an image, the radiances stored in the global cubes are used in the manner illustrated in Figure 7.3. For each pixel of the image, the visible surface is found. This can be accomplished using ray casting. The nearest nodes on the surface are identified, and the relevant radiance values are extracted from them. The radiance value at the point that is visible under the pixel is then interpolated from these stored values.

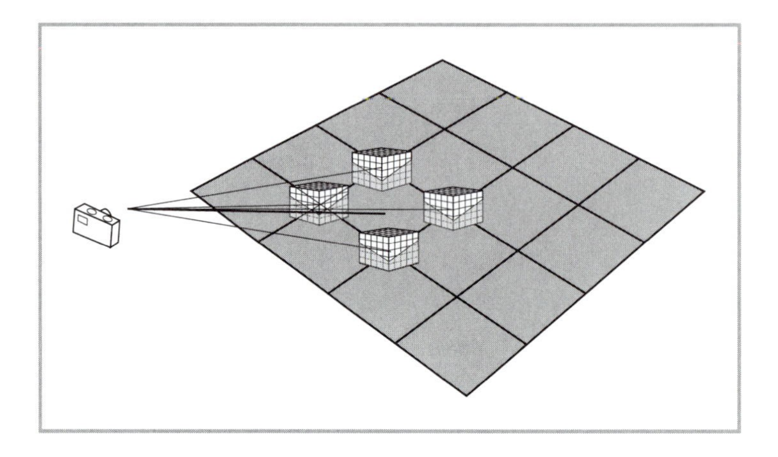

FIGURE 7.3 Radiance reconstruction using the global cubes.

Discussion

This simple method exploits the sparse character of the kernel by only computing energy transfers between mutually visible points and directions. This is achieved by using the visibility information stored in the item buffers as directional transfer information. However, even with this simplification, the technique draws heavily on resources, in particular random-access memory, since an array of radiance values must be stored for each surface element. Computation times are on the order of several months on a 1-MIPS machine.[1]

In addition to these difficulties, the use of a view-independent discrete set of radiance values can result in severe aliasing. In particular, specular effects have high spatial frequencies and thus cannot be reconstructed properly from the low sampling rate imposed by the global cube. Using smaller patches or more discrete directions to reduce aliasing only increases the already heavy computational burden. Thus the choice of these parameters should be made after careful consideration. Figure 7.4 shows an image computed with this directional radiosity algorithm. Note the specular reflections on the floor and the associated aliasing pattern.

The precision problems encountered using this method raise the question: Is it worthwhile to seek an accurate view-independent solution to the global illumination equation, or

[1] 1 MIPS = one million instructions per second.

FIGURE 7.4 An image computed with the global cube technique.

is the effort better spent in achieving high accuracy only in areas important to a given set of views? This question is central to the development of new computational techniques for global illumination, and leads naturally to the study of *view-dependent* methods.

7.3 Hybrid methods

The two major approaches for the simulation of global illumination can be characterized as view-independent, which comprises radiosity and the extension to nondiffuse reflectors just discussed, and view-dependent, which attempts to limit the computation to the visible effects.

This section reviews a number of hybrid alternatives. Most of these are extensions to the basic, view-independent radiosity method, in which some of the directional properties of the radiance distributions are retrieved from a view-dependent analysis.

7.3.1 Bidirectional solution

View-dependent global illumination

When the goal of a global illumination simulation is the production of an image, it makes sense to devote the most effort to the computation of energy transfers that actually have a significant impact on the final picture. This was the rationale behind the development of the importance-driven radiosity algorithm presented in Section 4.5. Here we shall see that this approach carries additional benefits in the presence of nondiffuse reflectors.

Indeed, as mentioned earlier, the human eye is very sensitive to highlights and specular reflections, and these are obviously dependent on the viewing conditions. A mirror, for example, appears very different depending on the direction of sight. It is quite natural to want to simulate these effects while considering the viewpoint. Part of the reason for the success of ray tracing as an image synthesis technique is due to the fact that it easily incorporates some directional reflection effects. The solution to the most general global illumination equation can be computed by tracing rays that originate at the eye point using probabilistic techniques to evaluate the reflection integral of Equation 7.1. These probabilistic, or Monte Carlo, techniques will be presented in the next chapter.

Although energy transfers in the direction of the viewer are important, there exist other important transfers that must be identified to effectively simulate the flow of energy in the scene. These include for example indirect illumination effects due to the reflection of light on a specular surface. Identifying all such transfers is a difficult task when nondiffuse reflectors are present, since they introduce preferred directions of reflection that can result in concentrations of light (sometimes referred to as *caustics*).

Identifying significant energy transfers

The directional radiosity algorithm presented in Section 7.2.2 attempts to solve the complete global illumination equation without any simplifying assumptions on reflection processes. Closer examination shows that directional radiosity and ray tracing algorithms each lack information that is precisely computed by the other: in directional radiosity, great directional precision is required on all surfaces since it is not known in advance which ones will be visible, and with ray tracing important illumination directions are not known, thus many rays are needed to capture all effects.

This observation leads naturally to the idea that an efficient algorithm for computing global illumination should "start from both ends," thus making use of all relevant information. On the one hand, light sources are usually known and deserve special treatment; on the other hand, the viewing parameters help to focus attention on relevant parts of the scene. The computation of the importance of each surface, as explained in Section 4.5, is one possible implementation of this strategy.

Another possibility consists of *storing* illumination information on each surface and *retrieving* this information later during a view-dependent pass. As explained in Section 7.2, it is not practical to store at each surface a complete directional radiance distribution including discontinuities caused by ideal specular reflection. However, it is also a waste to recompute it all for each pixel of the resulting image.

As a compromise, some methods are presented below that only store the diffuse shading component across the surfaces. This is the case in bidirectional ray tracing, a method that ignores the diffuse interreflection of light. A classification of light paths between different types of reflectors is introduced to help explain how this limitation can be overcome. This is accomplished by two-pass algorithms that combine a radiosity calculation and a view-dependent calculation.

Bidirectional ray tracing

A typical bidirectional simulation method first propagates energy from the light sources in a *light-ray tracing* pass, and subsequently retrieves the illumination information deposited on the surfaces in an *eye-ray tracing* pass. Therefore the two passes "meet" on the surfaces, where information is transferred from the light pass to the eye pass.

The diffuse illumination information can be stored on the surfaces using *illumination maps* [5, 196]. These are a special form of the texture maps commonly used in computer graphics. Rays are traced from the light sources into the scene, and follow specular reflections or transmissions along their path. Whenever a diffusely reflecting surface is encountered, a contribution is stored in the surface's illumination map. Thus the illumination map effectively stores the integral term in the global illumination equation. During the eye-ray tracing pass, the radiance diffusely reflected at any given point is then extracted from the illumination maps as needed.

Light reflection paths

The simple strategy outlined above models diffuse reflection in a restrictive manner: light coming from a light source can be diffusely reflected only once along its path from the light source to the viewer. In natural environments, multiple diffuse reflections can and do occur, and are often responsible for visually significant effects such as color bleeding or more generally indirect lighting. They must therefore be simulated.

A classification of the various reflection paths characterizes the complexity of general reflective environments [81]. Each reflection mode along the light's path from the light (L) to the eye (E) can be characterized as diffuse (D) or specular (S). Any path is then expressed as a string in the set given by the *regular expression*[2] $L(D|S)^*E$. Some of these paths are illustrated in Figure 7.5. "Classic" (ideal diffuse) radiosity simulates LD^*E paths, while "classic" ray tracing simulates $LDS^*E|LS^*E$ paths. Bidirectional ray tracing methods only model a single diffuse reflection, thus the simulated paths are $LS^*DS^*E|LS^*E$.

---

[2] A regular expression is a concise representation of a set of words constructed from an alphabet. Special symbols are used to indicate possible repetitions of characters: $*$ denotes any number of repetitions, while $+$ denotes any non-zero number of repetitions. The | represents the logical OR operator and thus denotes the union of two or more expressions [83].

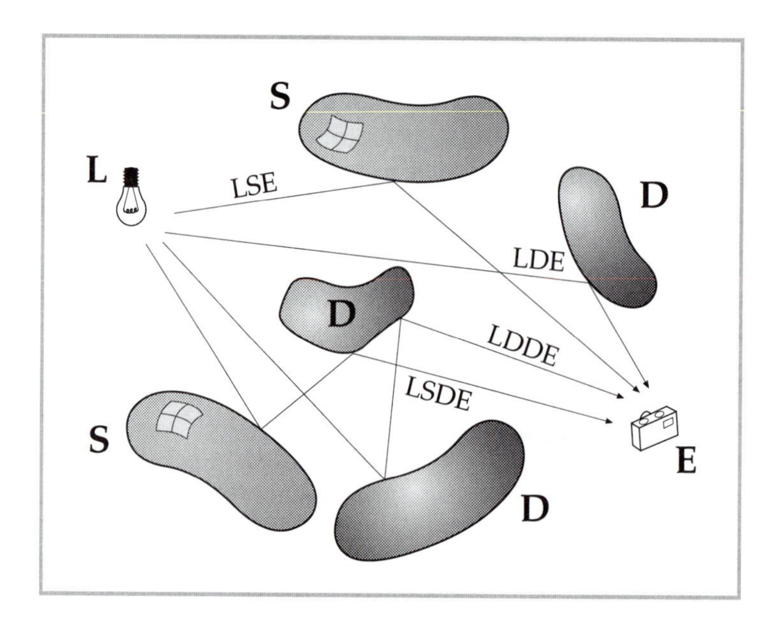

FIGURE 7.5 Classification of light reflection paths.

Adding diffuse interreflection

The bidirectional paradigm outlined above can be extended to incorporate the effects of diffuse interreflection, that is, allowing more than one 'D' term in the regular expressions. The light-ray tracing operation is repeatedly executed, using surface patches as secondary light sources [23, 81]. This makes the light-ray tracing pass equivalent to the complete progressive refinement radiosity method of Section 4.1. The eye-ray tracing phase is unchanged.

7.3.2 A simple two-pass approach

Another approach to incorporating diffuse interreflection in the bidirectional strategy consists of taking advantage of the complementary strengths of radiosity and ray tracing. Practically, this amounts to using radiosity to compute the diffuse interreflection of light between the surfaces, and a view-dependent algorithm to add specular reflections and highlights.

Once the radiosity solution is obtained and a viewpoint has been selected, a picture is easily rendered using a classical ray tracer with the following simplifications:

- No shadow rays are needed, since the radiosity solution already takes into account shadowing between surfaces. Since shadow rays typically account for most of the computation time in conventional ray tracing, the second pass is thus much faster than regular ray tracing.

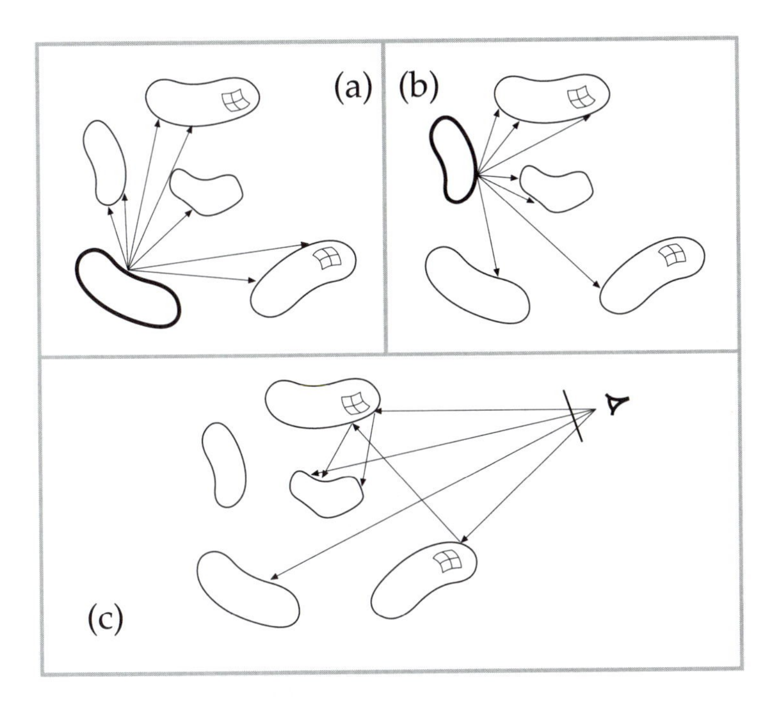

FIGURE 7.6 Separation of the computation into two passes. Diffuse interreflection is first computed, using for example a progressive refinement algorithm. Two iterations are shown in (a) and (b). View-dependent specular reflections are added at a later stage (c).

- The shading model used for the surfaces is trivial: apart from the specular contribution obtained by spawning a reflected ray, it is simply the diffuse radiosity value calculated in the first pass.

Note that the radiosity solution produced in the first pass remains view-independent, so that different views of the scene can be rendered at the sole cost of the second pass. The two passes are illustrated in Figure 7.6.

Alternatively, the second pass could simply consist of a traditional rendering (possibly hardware-assisted) using an elaborate local light reflection model to capture highlights on the surfaces, but without the expense of recursive ray casting. For example a Phong shading model can be used to add specular highlights to the surfaces whose diffuse "color" is obtained by the radiosity pass [135]. Color Plate 26 was computed in this manner.

Discussion

The bidirectional scheme outlined above is based on a separation of the diffuse and specular shading contributions. Unfortunately these components are not independent: light traveling from one point to another is neither diffuse nor specular, as these terms only describe different reflection modes, not different types of energy. Light can encounter any succession of diffuse and nondiffuse reflectors along its path from the light source to the receiver. The diffuse component of the illumination in a scene cannot be determined independently; exchanges between different reflection modes must be taken into account.

Using the formalism of regular expressions, we can characterize the shortcomings of the simple two-pass method. The second pass using eye-ray tracing cannot find paths such as LS^+DE, because when the diffuse surface is found from the eye, there is no information available to compute the illumination of that surface due to specular reflectors. Figure 7.7 shows a scene where such LS^+DE paths can play an important role and should be simulated. The left-hand image shows an ideal diffuse radiosity solution. The black panel is a mirror and therefore has a very low diffuse reflectance. The center image is the result of the simple two-pass scheme in which the radiosity solution is used in the eye-ray tracing phase. The right-hand image shows the complete illumination including *specular-to-diffuse* transfers. Note in particular the light reaching the table and the back of the vase through a specular reflection on the mirror. This example demonstrates the need for more complete methods that take all light transfers into account.

FIGURE 7.7 Specular-to-diffuse (LS^+DE) transfers can produce visible effects, as shown in the right-hand image.

In summary, simple two-pass techniques are often capable of producing highly realistic images. However, they ignore important physical properties of light reflection and offer no guarantee that reflection effects are correctly simulated. Indeed the simple bidirectional ray tracing method does not handle multiple diffuse reflections, while the simple combination of radiosity and ray tracing misses some important effects. When the view-dependent pass is performed using a hardware shader to produce highlights [135], the resulting radiance values are no longer solutions of the global illumination equation since the shading formula is usually inconsistent with the global illumination equation. More comprehensive methods are described below that consider all relevant reflection effects to produce accurate simulations.

7.3.3 A complete two-pass method

A valid solution of Equation 7.1 can be obtained in the presence of both diffuse and specular reflectors, using a two-pass approach where the view-independent pass is extended to simulate specular-to-diffuse transfers [184, 165]. The notion of form factor is extended to represent the proportion of the energy leaving a given patch and reaching another patch after experiencing any number of specular reflections.

Formal justification of the two-pass approach

We begin by reexamining the global illumination equation (Equation 7.1). Assuming the BRDF can be separated into a diffuse component ρ_{bd}^D and a specular component ρ_{bd}^S such that

$$\rho_{bd} = \rho_{bd}^D + \rho_{bd}^S ,$$

the integral operator of Section 2.2.2 that describes the effect of reflection on a radiance distribution becomes

$$\mathcal{R} = \mathcal{R}^D + \mathcal{R}^S ,$$

where

$$(\mathcal{R}^D L)(x, \theta_0, \phi_0) = \int_\Omega \rho_{bd}^D(\theta_0, \phi_0, \theta, \phi) L(x, \theta, \phi) \cos\theta d\omega$$

and

$$(\mathcal{R}^S L)(x, \theta_0, \phi_0) = \int_\Omega \rho_{bd}^S(\theta_0, \phi_0, \theta, \phi) L(x, \theta, \phi) \cos\theta d\omega .$$

Let us now define the diffuse radiance distribution L_D by

$$L = L_D + \mathcal{R}^S L . \tag{7.10}$$

That is, L_D is obtained by subtracting from the total radiance distribution the specularly reflected light on the surfaces. This is consistent with the bidirectional paradigm where illumination information is recorded on diffuse surfaces. Equation 7.10 is essentially equivalent to Equation 7.1 with a "source term" of L_D. Thus we know from Section 2.2.2 that a solution to this type of equation can be formally expressed as a Neumann series:

$$L = \left[I - \mathcal{R}^S\right]^{-1} L_D \tag{7.11}$$

$$= \sum_{n=0}^{\infty} (\mathcal{R}^S)^n L_D . \tag{7.12}$$

Introducing a *global specular reflection operator*,

$$\mathcal{R}^{S^*} = \sum_{n=0}^{\infty} (\mathcal{R}^S)^n ,$$

we find a relationship between total radiance and its diffuse component:

$$L = \mathcal{R}^{S^*} L_D . \qquad \textbf{(7.13)}$$

The effect of the various reflection operators is illustrated in Figure 7.8. Operator $\mathcal{R}^D$ creates the distribution of radiance reflected once off diffuse surfaces, while $\mathcal{R}^S$ models one bounce off specular surfaces. $\mathcal{R}^{S^*}$ produces the distribution of radiance obtained by letting radiance experience any number of specular reflections.

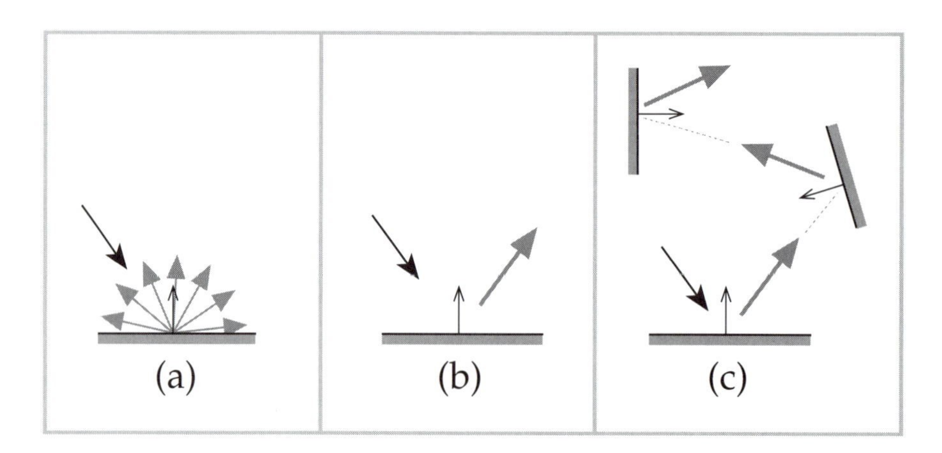

FIGURE 7.8 Effect of operators (a) $\mathcal{R}^D$ (b) $\mathcal{R}^S$ (c) $\mathcal{R}^{S^*}$.

Equation 7.13 shows that if the diffuse distribution L_D is computed, a view-dependent pass can produce a complete picture by restoring the specular reflections that immediately precede the eye along the light's path. Therefore a two-pass computational algorithm comes to mind, with a first stage devoted to obtaining the diffuse distribution L_D and a second stage that computes the visible specular effects.

Computing the diffuse distribution

According to the definition of L_D in Equation 7.1,

$$L_D = L_e + \mathcal{R}^D L .$$

Using Equation 7.13 we have

$$L_D = L_e + \mathcal{R}^D \mathcal{R}^{S^*} L_D. \tag{7.14}$$

Equation 7.14 is exactly equivalent to the general global illumination equation 7.1, with the only modification being the use of a combined reflection operator $\mathcal{R}^D \mathcal{R}^{S^*}$. This operator models any number of specular reflections, followed by *one* diffuse reflection, or LS^*D path segments.[3]

Using the same discretization technique that led to the diffuse radiosity equation, it is possible to compute the diffuse radiance distribution L_D, although *extended form factors* are required. These allow any number of specular bounces to take place between two diffuse reflections. The only change to the basic radiosity algorithm is the computation of these extended form factors.

Computing extended form factors

Just as the form factor was defined in terms of energy transfers in Section 3.1.4, it is possible to give a physical definition of the *extended form factor*. This definition assumes that there is one radiosity value at each patch, or in other words that constant elements are used to discretize the illumination equation:

> F_{ij}^{ext} is the proportion of the total power leaving patch P_i that reaches patch P_j after undergoing any number of specular reflections along the way.

Figure 7.9 describes the transfer of energy from a selected surface using extended form factors. The only practical algorithms available for computing extended form factors are restricted to a superposition of ideal diffuse and ideal specular behaviors, and even then only a limited number of specular reflections (sometimes just one) can be taken into account. Several algorithms are available, each based on one of the form factor computation techniques presented in Sections 3.3.3 and 5.1.3.

A simple yet very effective means of computing extended form factors is the *image method* [143]. With the additional assumption that all ideal specular reflectors are planar surfaces, the image method treats each specular patch as a window into a virtual, mirrored world. An image of the scene is constructed by reflecting all objects across the plane of the reflecting patch, and is merged with the actual scene to compute the form factors. As shown in the top half of Figure 7.10, this idea can be used in concert with the hemi-cube: all surfaces are first reflected across the specular patch to create their virtual images, and then projected back onto the hemi-cube's item buffers [184]. The bottom part of the same figure shows that when the ray casting method of Section 5.1.3 is used, only the current emitter need be reflected across the specular surface. In that case, and in contrast to the hemi-cube method,

[3]Note that the order of the terms in the regular expression is reversed relative to the order of the reflection operators. This is a consequence of the fact that regular expressions are parsed left-to-right while linear operators are applied right-to-left.

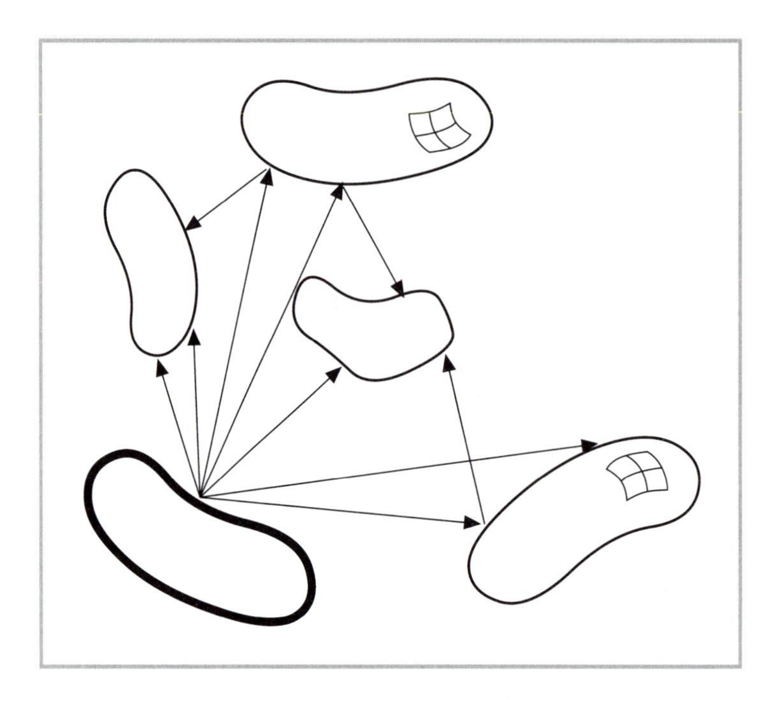

FIGURE 7.9 Schematic representation of radiosity exchanges using extended form factors.

the complexity of the environment is not increased: the number of patches to process does not change. This allows multiple specular reflections to be simulated, simply by reflecting the light source successively across several specular surfaces [164]. Using either method, care must be taken that the form factor assigned to virtual patches is weighted by the appropriate specular reflectance coefficient.

Another option is to use ray tracing to compute the specular reflections that take place between diffuse surfaces. The advantages of this approach are that curved surfaces can then be taken into account, and that recursive ray tracing allows the simulation of multiple specular reflections or refractions. However, the choice of the directions in which rays are to be sent is a difficult problem. When nonplanar specular reflectors are present, there is no simple way to predict what rays lead from one surface to another after reflecting on the specular object. Thus ray directions must be chosen a priori. Rays can either be distributed on the surface of a hemisphere surrounding a patch [110] or generated by adaptively subdividing a single projection plane [165]. In either case there is no guarantee that all objects will receive an adequate form factor. Thus the most reliable computation technique for extended form factors is the ray casting variation of the image method. Recursive ray tracing should be used only when the simulation of curved reflectors is required.

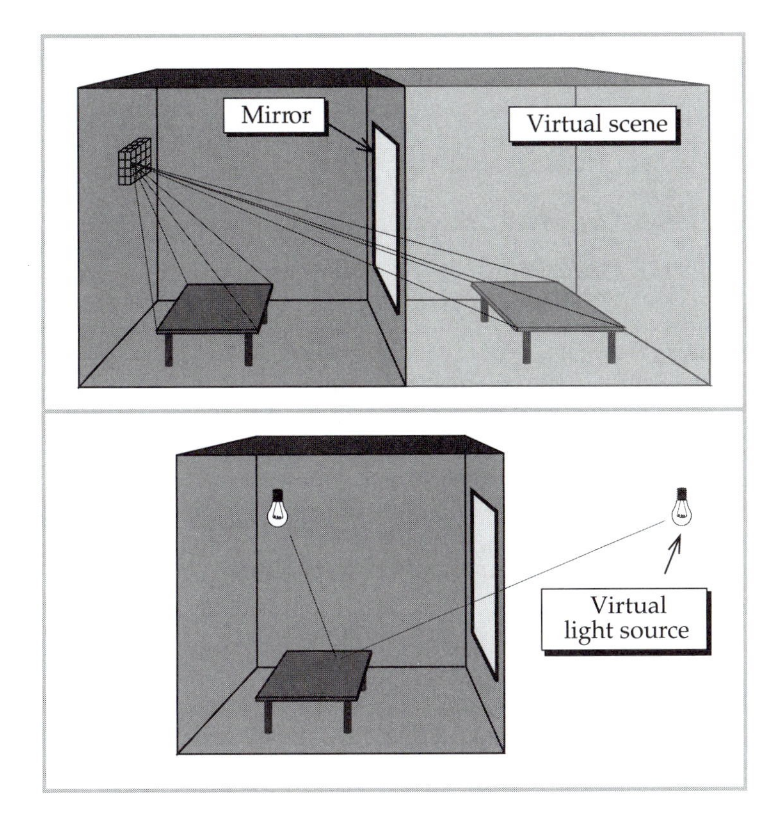

FIGURE 7.10 Computation of the extended form factors with the image method. Using the hemi-cube (top); using ray casting (bottom).

View-dependent pass

All the above methods generate extended form factors, which can either be used to assemble a matrix and solve for radiosities, or in a progressive refinement method. The radiosity values obtained do incorporate some effects due to specular transfers, but the solution is still completely view-independent. Once a viewpoint is chosen, a second pass is needed to incorporate view-dependent effects. The second pass can take various forms: classical ray tracing, distributed ray tracing, or a z-buffer based algorithm [184]. The last two are capable of rendering non-ideal specular reflections. However, it should be noted that only ideal specular reflectors are considered in the first pass; thus for a fully consistent simulation, ideal specular reflection should be considered in the second pass.

The image method, discussed above, can also be used for rendering planar mirrors, when the scene is displayed as a set of polygons [165]. Using a hardware z-buffer, images from virtual viewpoints can be computed and composited with the main image to obtain interactive frame rates. Thus animated walkthroughs can be generated for scenes that include specular surfaces. Of course this only works for reflectors that are both ideal specular and planar.

7.4 Radiosity with directional radiance distributions

In theory, the two-pass strategy presented above allows the computation of a complete solution of the global illumination equation. However, the effect of the global specular reflection operator $\mathcal{R}^{S^*}$ can only be computed for a small number of ideal specular reflections. Thus in practice the two-pass method using extended form factors can successfully simulate only a combination of ideal specular and ideal diffuse reflectors.

Most real materials cannot be closely approximated by such a combination; they also exhibit a directional diffuse character. Recall from the definition in Section 2.1.4 that directional diffuse denotes a component of the BRDF that has a smooth dependence on reflected direction. It is the term responsible for glossy surface highlights as well as gradual changes in appearance as a surface is viewed from a varying direction. In contrast, ideal specular reflection results in a mirrorlike appearance that is only realistic for very smooth surfaces. Thus whenever a physically accurate simulation is required, the directional diffuse behavior must be taken into account. Consider for example the application of computer graphics to exterior lighting design and driving simulation: the appearance of the road surface is a key ingredient, since highlights created by the reflection of the sun or other luminaires such as headlights can distract a driver. Yet these effects cannot be properly rendered using only ideal diffuse and ideal specular reflection [120]. The simulation of interreflection effects is also required for urban scenes or tunnel lighting.

The discrete directional radiosity method of Section 7.2 can use any type of BRDF, but is subject to severe discretization artifacts and is not currently tractable. This section shows how to overcome these difficulties, by separating the discretization of the surfaces of the scene and the representation of the directional radiance distribution at each point. The two-pass strategy is used to efficiently incorporate ideal specular reflection. However, unlike two-pass methods previously discussed, non-ideal effects are included in the first pass of the simulation.

7.4.1 Separation of ideal specular and directional diffuse reflection

The motivation of the two-pass approach given in Section 7.3.3 remains valid for non-ideal reflectors, since no assumption was made on the properties of the "diffuse" and "specular" components identified in the reflectance. One research avenue has focused on incorporating the directional diffuse component of the BRDF into the "specular" reflection operators, but with limited success because of the complexity of the resulting extended form factors [152].

The approach we describe here is to model directional diffuse reflection in the "diffuse" reflection operator. A central issue in this framework becomes that of representing the directional variation of radiance. Recall that one major cause of the precision problems encountered by the directional radiosity method of Section 7.2 is that the basis functions used were simple tensor products of "box" functions. This meant that the discretization of the space of directions had to be the same at all points (the same global cube was used for all patches). Since the complexity of the radiance distributions can vary from surface to surface depending on the BRDF of the underlying material, a more flexible representation should be used instead.

Study of a physical model of light reflection (such as the one in reference [78]) shows that the directional diffuse component of the BRDF has a smooth directional variation, as opposed to the discontinuities produced by the ideal specular term. Provided ideal specular reflection is treated separately, we can expect to find a compact representation that records the directional radiance distribution to within a given accuracy for a given surface [105].

These observations lead to a general radiosity algorithm for the simulation of arbitrary reflectances as described here. Following the two-pass strategy already mentioned, ideal specular reflectors are treated separately. Directional radiance information, representing the light reflected according to the directional diffuse component of the BRDF, is computed in the first pass. Since it is smooth it can be recorded on each surface using a minimal amount of storage. In essence this algorithm replaces the scalar radiosity value used in standard radiosity by a directional distribution. Since it is otherwise equivalent to standard radiosity, the concept can be incorporated into either progressive refinement or incremental systems.

During the first pass, the radiance reflected by a surface according to its ideal specular reflectance is not stored along with the directional diffuse radiance because of its very sharp—or even discontinuous—character. Instead it is propagated on the fly to other surfaces, as explained in Section 7.3.3.

The second pass of the algorithm uses a simple ray tracer to compute the specularly reflected radiance on visible surfaces, and otherwise simply extracts radiance values from the stored directional distributions. The specific issues raised by the computation of radiance distributions are discussed in the following sections.

7.4.2 Computing with radiance distributions

The representation of directional distributions using a simple discretization of the space of directions such as the global cube results in severe aliasing problems [152, 19]. Although a discrete representation is necessary for storing distributions in a digital memory, it is not required that the representation be discontinuous. In this section, radiance distributions are treated as a whole, without mention of their actual representation. Actual means for representing the distributions will be discussed in the next section.

If one examines the process of accumulating reflected radiance contributions from different emitters in the progressive radiosity approach, two important remarks can be made.

First, the range of possible radiance distributions reflected at a given point is completely determined by the local BRDF. Recall from Section 2.1.4 that the directional distribution of reflected radiance for a given incident ray is obtained by multiplying the BRDF by the incident flux density. This operation is illustrated in Figure 7.11 for an isotropic surface. Light is coming from an incident direction characterized by polar angle θ. The BRDF of the surface is multiplied by the incident flux density and aligned with the incident direction according to the azimuth angle ϕ.

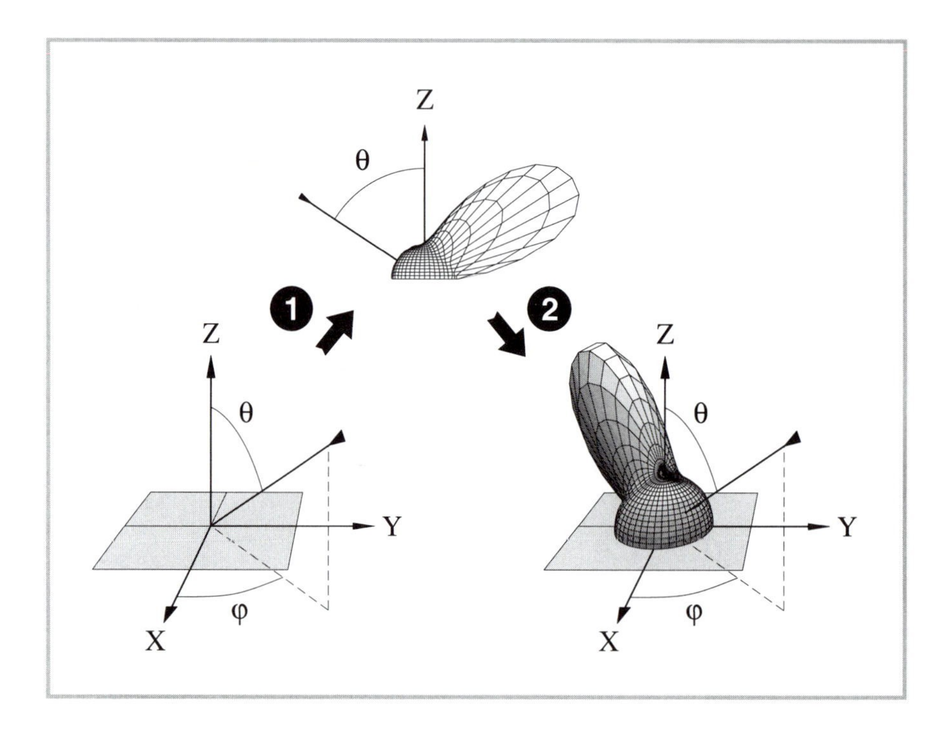

FIGURE 7.11 Use of the BRDF to determine the reflected radiance distribution.

Next, radiance distributions must be added together as different emitters in the scene distribute their energy. This corresponds to the operation of accumulating radiosity on the surfaces in the traditional progressive refinement algorithm. The summation of radiance distributions is shown in Figure 7.12. As the solution progresses, increasingly accurate representations of the directional radiance distribution on all the surfaces are obtained.

A practical algorithm can be derived from these observations. At each iteration of a progressive refinement algorithm, an emitting patch distributes its energy to other surfaces. Form factors are computed and weighted by the emitter's radiance distribution, to ensure that the energy is sent in the proper directions. Each receiver updates its local radiance distribution according to its BRDF, as explained above. Color Plates 27 and 28 show two

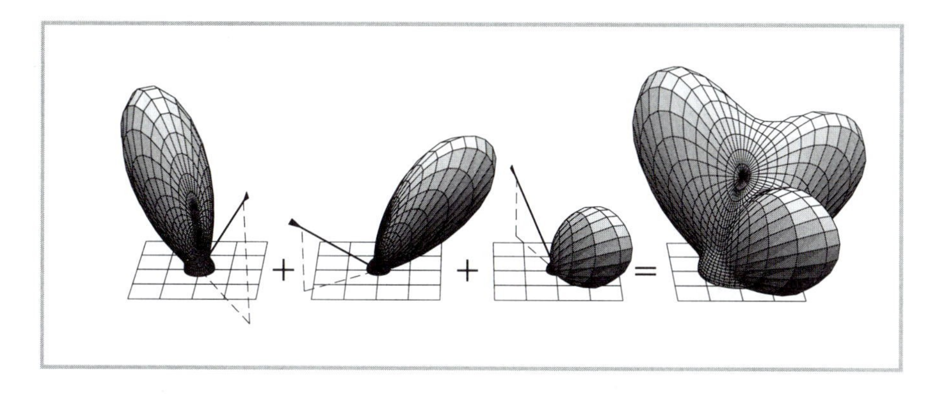

FIGURE 7.12 Addition of directional radiance distributions.

images of the same scene, computed for different viewpoints. In these images the radiosity solution generated directional radiance distributions for all nondiffuse surfaces.

7.4.3 Representation of directional distributions

The algorithm outlined above handles directional radiance distributions. In order to be able to operate on these distributions, they must be represented in a suitable form. Some of the possible options are considered below.

Recall that radiance is a function of both the position on the surfaces and the direction of propagation. Thus the distributions considered here are obtained by holding the position constant in the radiance function and considering it a function of direction only. This view of the problem amounts to decoupling the mesh used on the surfaces of the objects and the discretization of the space of directions.

Surfaces are meshed "as usual," and all the meshing techniques from Chapter 5 can be used, such as adaptive refinement in regions of high gradient. For each surface element, a local representation of the radiance distribution is maintained, depending on the local reflection characteristics. This two-step representation of radiance functions is in contrast to the simple scheme used in Section 7.2, and allows in particular an adaptation of the representation to the actual complexity of the radiance distributions.

Note that the operation of discretizing the space of directions to represent radiance distributions is not simpler than meshing a set of surfaces. In fact the most general radiance distribution includes discontinuities (due to ideal specular reflection) that would require the equivalent of discontinuity meshing (see Section 5.3.3). Fortunately the use of a two-pass method eliminates the need to treat discontinuities.

The global cubes of Section 7.2.2 provide a very simple mesh of the space of directions, but one that remains the same at all surface locations. Since the complexity of the illumination varies with location, a local representation is preferable. Also, the global cubes are built with "box" basis functions that are ill suited to the smooth radiance distributions. One alternative would be to use a piecewise polynomial (spline) representation, with a control mesh that can vary with location, to accommodate the local complexity of illumination. However, the addition, rotation, and scaling operations that must be performed repeatedly with these distributions are not easily implemented.

Representation using spherical harmonics

A slightly different approach consists of applying harmonic analysis techniques to the radiance distributions. This results in a compact representation because the smooth directional diffuse character of the BRDF translates into distributions dominated by low frequencies.

Since radiance distributions are functions of direction, spectral analysis is best done using *spherical harmonics*. Spherical harmonics are mathematical functions that form an orthogonal basis of the set of distributions on the unit sphere [43]. This infinite collection of basis functions is typically denoted by $Y_{l,m}(\theta, \phi)$ where $0 \leq l < \infty$ and $-l \leq m \leq l$. In direct analogy with a Fourier series in one dimension, any square-integrable function, $f(\theta, \phi)$, can be represented by an infinite series of the form

$$f(\theta, \phi) = \sum_{l=0}^{\infty} \sum_{m=-l}^{l} C_{l,m} \, Y_{l,m}(\theta, \phi), \tag{7.15}$$

where the coefficients are given by

$$C_{l,m} = \int_0^{2\pi} \int_0^{\pi} f(\theta, \phi) \, Y_{l,m}(\theta, \phi) \, d\omega \,. \tag{7.16}$$

A simplified representation of the first few spherical harmonic functions is shown in Figure 7.13.

Spherical harmonics share two other attributes with Fourier series: high-order terms represent the high-frequency components of the distribution, and a finite approximation to a function can be obtained by considering only a finite number of terms in its series. Thus a radiance distribution can be approximated as a vector of N coefficients. The choice of N depends upon the characteristics of the underlying BRDF and the desired accuracy of the approximation. Ideal diffuse surfaces require only one coefficient, and in general the more directional the BRDF, the more coefficients are required to account for the higher frequencies in the shape. Figure 7.14 shows a number of possible approximations of a reflectance function, obtained by considering a varying number of terms in the expansion. Although polygons are used to produce a shaded image, all the functions shown are in fact continuous in all derivatives.

Note that the spherical harmonics basis functions are not local, in the sense that they take non-zero values nearly everywhere on the sphere. This is in contrast to the previously mentioned finite-element basis functions that are non-zero only over a small number of elements. The use of non-local basis functions is usually avoided in finite-element applications because they tend to produce denser matrices, but in this particular

FIGURE 7.13 Simplified polar plot of some spherical harmonics basis functions. The absolute value of the function is plotted as the distance to the origin for directions in the upper hemisphere only. Darker lobes indicate negative values.

case the "form factor" is computed only once for a given surface location, and used for all directional functions.

The actual decomposition of a function involves a great deal of computation, as shown by the double integral in Equation 7.16. Fortunately, in the case of reflectance functions, this computation need only be done once per material [20]. In the case of isotropic BRDFs, the dependence on the polar angle of incidence θ_0 can be accounted for by representing each spherical harmonic coefficient as a function of θ_0 [164]. For general BRDFs, each spherical harmonic coefficient can itself be expressed as a vector of coefficients, by performing a second decomposition relative to the direction of incidence [199].

Regardless of the details of implementation, the representation using spherical harmonics has several advantages: the approximation is always continuous, and can be made more accurate simply by including more terms. Furthermore, once an approximation has been selected for the BRDF, the addition of radiance distributions on a surface, corresponding to the influence of different emitters, does not require any increase in storage space since the corresponding spherical harmonics coefficients are simply added. The quality of the

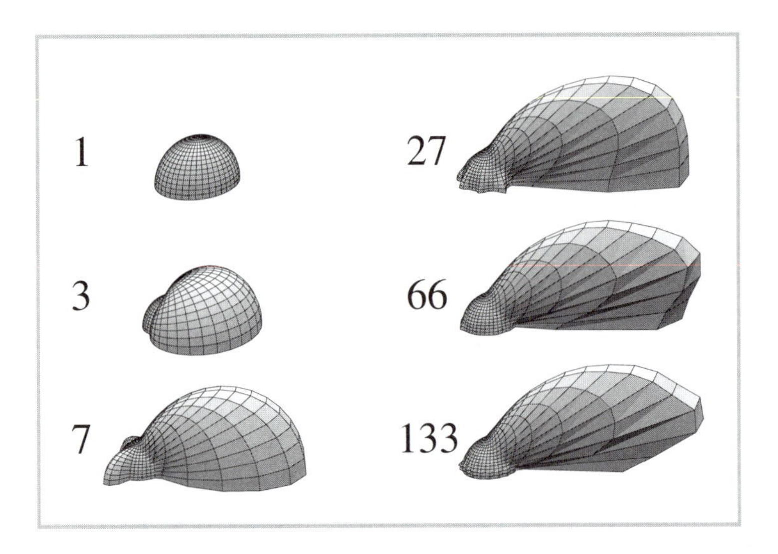

FIGURE 7.14 Effect of the number of coefficients on the accuracy of the spherical harmonics representation.

approximation is thus maintained with a fixed number of terms in the expansion. Finally, scaling, rotating, and adding are all accomplished very easily with this representation, as shown in Section A.2.3 in the Appendix.

7.5 Global illumination with participating media

In addition to the restriction to diffuse reflectors, the conventional radiosity method is built on another assumption: light is only allowed to interact with surfaces of objects; the air plays no role in the energy exchanges. Light travels along straight lines between surfaces and no attenuation takes place. This is evidenced for example by the conservation of radiance along the line of sight mentioned in Section 2.1.2.

This absence of interaction with the medium is what permits the transformation of the directional integral in the global illumination equation into an integral over the surfaces of the objects.

However, in order to be physically accurate the medium in which the objects are placed must be allowed to participate in radiative transfers. Common examples include fog, haze, smoke, and dust. The presence of a participating medium can have a number of effects on the distribution of light. Radiance can be reduced by absorption or scattering. Radiance is enhanced by emission or scattering from other directions. Thus scattering can account for either a decrease or an increase of radiance. The terms *out-scattering* and *in-scattering* are used to describe the scattering of light away from a given direction, or into a given direction, respectively, as shown in Figure 7.15.

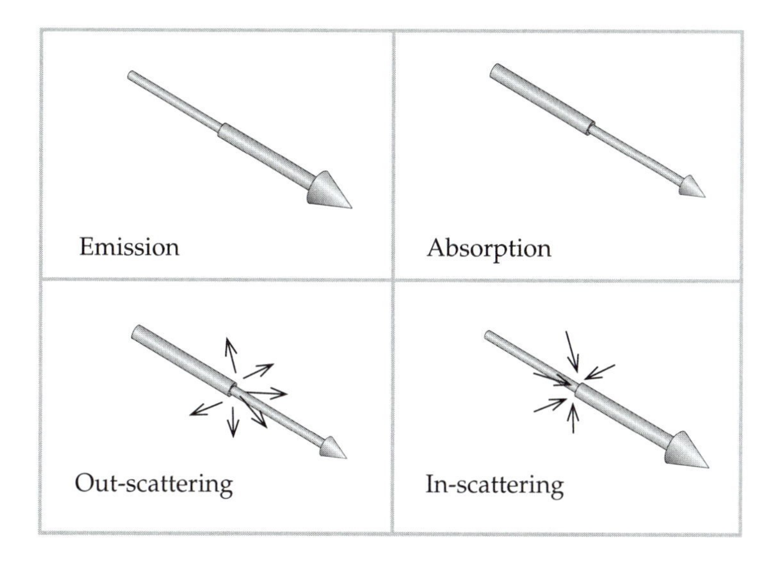

FIGURE 7.15 Processes contributing to the variation of radiance along a path at a particular differential volume element (after Rushmeier [140]).

The perceptible effect of participating media on the propagation of visible light is usually limited to absorption, such as atmospheric effects, and scattering by water droplets, as in clouds, or small particles, as in smoke. Several algorithms are available to include some of the effects of light scattering in synthetic images [111, 125]. For heat transfer applications, however, all phenomena must be accounted for, including blackbody thermal emission within the medium. In this section a general method for the simulation of these effects is outlined.

7.5.1 A general transfer equation

In the presence of a participating medium, light can interact with matter at any point in space, and it no longer suffices to describe the distribution of radiance on the surfaces of opaque objects. Instead radiance must be defined at all points in space, and a new governing equation is used to express the energy balance. Since the variation of radiance at a given point depends on the local properties of the medium, the general transfer equation involves derivatives of the radiance function and becomes an integro-differential equation.

The properties of the participating medium are expressed using the two scalar functions κ_a (called the *absorption coefficient*), measuring the fraction by which radiance is reduced per unit length due to absorption, and κ_s (the *scattering coefficient*), measuring the fraction by which radiance is reduced per unit length due to out-scattering. Both quantities have dimensions of inverse length.

The general transfer equation expresses the rate of change in radiance along a path as

$$\frac{dL}{ds} = -\kappa_t L + \kappa_a L_e + \kappa_s \int_{\Omega} L_i(\Theta) f(\Theta) d\omega \,, \tag{7.17}$$

where s is the path variable (a measure of the distance traveled along the path since the origin), and Ω denotes here the entire sphere of directions [96]. The various terms of this equation correspond to the following physical phenomena:

- $-\kappa_t L$ represents the attenuation of radiance due to absorption or out-scattering. κ_t is called the *extinction coefficient* and is defined as

$$\kappa_t = \kappa_a + \kappa_s$$

- $\kappa_a L_e$ represents the increase in radiance due to emission by the medium. L_e is the emitted radiance, and the presence of κ_a is a consequence of reciprocity principles from thermodynamics [160].
- The integral term represents the increase in radiance due to in-scattering, that is, the effect of light coming from all directions and scattered into the direction of interest. $f(\Theta)$ is the *phase function*, describing the directional probability distribution for scattering from direction Θ into the direction of the path.

Transmittance

Consider a pencil of light traveling from a surface into a participating medium. Only a fraction of the light leaving the surface will pass through the medium without being absorbed and scattered, and this fraction (called the *transmittance*) can be computed by considering the extinction term alone in Equation 7.17:

$$\frac{dL}{ds} = -\kappa_t L \,. \tag{7.18}$$

This can be integrated to yield the radiance at a distance s into the medium

$$L(s) = L(0) e^{-\int_0^s \kappa_t(u) du} \,. \tag{7.19}$$

Therefore the transmittance of the medium along the path is given by

$$\tau(s) = e^{-\int_0^s \kappa_t(u) du} \,. \tag{7.20}$$

Solution without scattering

Scattering within the medium is what makes Equation 7.17 so difficult to solve, since it involves a directional integral at each point in space. The simplified problem of a medium with no scattering is much easier to solve and yet can be used to represent a range of interesting physical conditions.

In that case the extinction coefficient κ_t is equal to κ_a, and Equation 7.17 reduces to

$$\frac{dL}{ds} = -\kappa_a L + \kappa_a L_e , \tag{7.21}$$

for which the solution is

$$L(s) = L(0)\tau(s) + \int_0^s L_e(u)\tau(s-u)\kappa_a(u)du . \tag{7.22}$$

Equation 7.22 can be used as the basis of a simple ray tracing algorithm, since the radiance leaving the medium in the direction of the eye is obtained by a simple one-dimensional integral. However, since scattering is ignored in this case, this method does not qualify as a "global illumination" simulation technique.

This derivation also provides a justification for the simple fog models commonly found in rendering packages (and in special-purpose hardware accelerators) and for volume rendering algorithms [47]. The effect of homogeneous haze can be modeled by using constant values for κ_a and L_e in Equation 7.22, which then reduces to

$$L(s) = L(0)e^{-\kappa_a s} + L_e\left(1 - e^{-\kappa_a s}\right) . \tag{7.23}$$

L_e represents an emission term which can be thought of as *ambient* light, or the product of multiple scattering inside the medium. Equation 7.23 shows that as an object becomes more and more distant in the presence of a hazy medium, its contributed radiance decreases exponentially while the contribution of the haze's radiance increases.

Formal solution using two passes

Let us consider again the general case of a scattering medium. One difficulty in the formulation of the problem is that radiance is both *produced* locally in the medium as a result of emission and in-scattering, and *transmitted* through it. Thus it is no longer a local quantity.

A formal solution of the general transfer equation is obtained by introducing a new quantity to describe the local production of light, and expressing the relationship between radiance and this quantity. Equation 7.17 can be rewritten as

$$\frac{dL}{ds} = -\kappa_t L + \kappa_t J , \tag{7.24}$$

where the *source radiance* J is defined by

$$J(s) = (1 - R(s))\, L_e + R(s) \int_\Omega L_i(\Theta) f(\Theta) d\omega . \tag{7.25}$$

This quantity accounts for both emission and in-scattering at s. $R(s)$ is the *scattering albedo* of the medium, defined by

$$R(s) = \frac{\kappa_s}{\kappa_t}.$$

Similar to the case of non-scattering media just discussed, a formal solution of Equation 7.24 is

$$L(s) = L(0)\tau(s) + \int_0^s J(u)\tau(s-u)\kappa_t(u)du\,. \quad \textbf{(7.26)}$$

This treatment is very similar to the separation in two passes made for nondiffuse reflectors in Section 7.3.3, where a simplified quantity L_D was introduced to represent the radiance diffusely reflected *locally*. This suggests that if the source radiance J can be computed in a first pass, the final radiance can be obtained using a ray tracing pass based on Equation 7.26.

In the next section a solution technique is outlined that allows the source radiance to be computed using a modified radiosity algorithm.

7.5.2 The zonal method for isotropically scattering media

The issue of computing the source radiance J is not any simpler than the general transfer problem. In particular it is very difficult to solve in the general case of an anisotropic scattering medium with arbitrary phase functions. However, it is currently possible to extend the radiosity paradigm to solve for J in the simplified case of an isotropically scattering medium; that is, a medium with a constant phase function such as

$$f_{\text{isotropic}} \equiv \frac{1}{4\pi}.$$

Energy balance equation

A method called the *zonal method* breaks up the volume containing the participating medium into discrete elements, in addition to the usual surface patches. Radiosities are defined both for surfaces (with $B_i = \pi L_i$) and volumes (with $B_k = \pi J_k$). Note that the source radiance J does not depend on direction since the method assumes that the medium has isotropic scattering and emission.

Energy balance equations are set up relating all the surface and volume radiosities, by introducing geometric *exchange factors* that extend the notion of form factor [86]. Since both surfaces and volumes have radiosities, three types of geometric factors are used: surface-to-surface $(\overline{S_i S_j})$, surface-to-volume $(\overline{S_j V_k})$, and volume-to-volume $(\overline{V_k V_m})$. The zonal equations are the following.

For surfaces:

$$B_i A_i = E_i A_i + \rho_i \left(\sum_{\text{surfaces } j} \overline{S_i S_j} B_j + \sum_{\text{volumes } k} \overline{V_k S_i} B_k \right) . \tag{7.27}$$

For volumes:

$$4\kappa_t(k) B_k V_k = 4\kappa_a(k) E_k V_k + R_k \left(\sum_{\text{surfaces } j} \overline{S_j V_k} B_j + \sum_{\text{volumes } m} \overline{V_m V_k} B_m \right) . \tag{7.28}$$

Here R_k is the albedo of the kth volume element, and V_k is its volume. These exchange factors are similar in meaning to the traditional form factor and obey the following reciprocity relations:

$$\overline{S_i S_j} = \overline{S_j S_i}, \qquad \overline{V_k S_j} = \overline{S_j V_k}, \qquad \overline{V_k V_m} = \overline{V_m V_k} .$$

Computing the exchange factors

The surface-to-surface factor $\overline{S_i S_j}$ has nearly the same expression as the usual form factor, with the addition of a transmittance term:

$$\overline{S_i S_j} = \int_{x \in P_i} \int_{y \in P_j} \frac{\cos\theta \cos\theta'}{\pi r^2} \tau(r) V(x, y) dx dy . \tag{7.29}$$

The surface-to-volume and volume-to-volume factors are given by the following expressions:

$$\overline{V_k S_j} = \int_{x \in V_k} \int_{y \in P_j} \frac{\cos\theta \kappa_t(k)}{\pi r^2} \tau(r) V(x, y) dx dy \tag{7.30}$$

$$\overline{V_k V_m} = \int_{x \in V_k} \int_{y \in V_m} \frac{\kappa_t(m) \kappa_t(k)}{\pi r^2} \tau(r) V(x, y) dx dy . \tag{7.31}$$

The notation used in these equations is explained in Figure 7.16. Note that in Equation 7.30, dx represents a volume element while dy represents a surface element. In Equation 7.31 they both represent a volume element.

Most of the form factor computation techniques presented previously can be adapted to compute these factors. For example a hemi-cube can be used [142]. All that is needed is a way to project the volume elements onto the hemi-cube faces. For volume-to-volume factors a global cube is used since all directions are equally important. For each cell of these cubes, the transmittance $\tau(r)$ must be computed. This is easily done for homogeneous media since it only depends on the distance traveled in the medium. Ray casting methods such as the one presented in Section 5.1.3 could just as well be adapted to compute the extra attenuation factors.

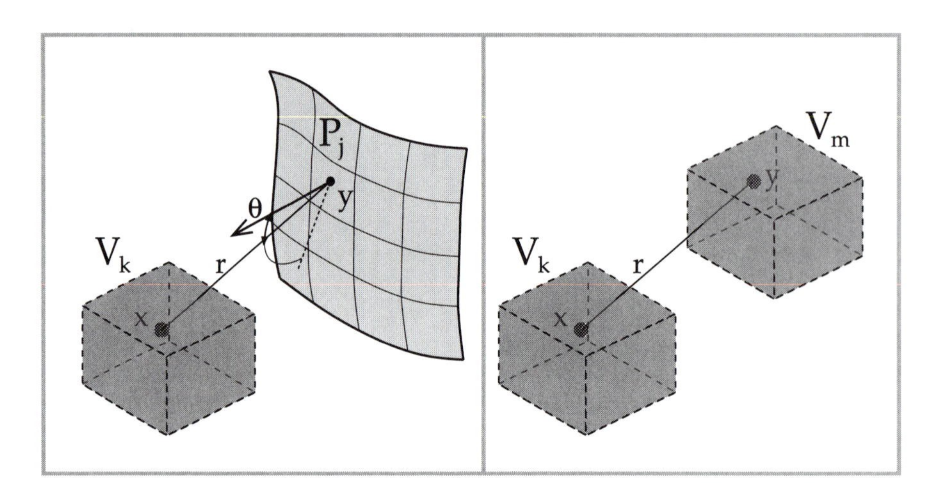

FIGURE 7.16 Geometry for the computation of exchange factors: (a) surface-to-volume factors. (b) volume-to-volume factors.

Complete solution

As mentioned above, the zonal method is inherently a two-pass method: the distribution of (isotropic) source radiance is computed first by solving Equations 7.27 and 7.28. This step can either be done by computing the full matrix of exchange factors, or by a progressive refinement strategy. The final radiance values are computed by a ray tracing pass that reconstructs the accumulated radiance along the line of sight. This reconstruction typically involves an interpolation stage between neighboring volume elements, to avoid a blocky appearance in the computed pictures.

An example image is presented in Color Plate 30. Notice how light entering the scene through a window is scattered by the participating medium and illuminates the entire room.

❐ ❐ ❐

The techniques presented in this chapter greatly extend the applicability of the radiosity algorithm. In particular, the ability to simulate more realistic reflectance behaviors is crucial to many application fields. For applications requiring a quantitatively accurate simulation of radiant energy, the general two-pass method of Section 7.4 offers a practical, although expensive, algorithm. Simpler techniques, such as the combination of a diffuse radiosity calculation and a view-dependent shading pass, can be used to produce images of high visual quality, at the cost of physical accuracy.

In the presence of nondiffuse reflectors, the notion of importance introduced in Section 4.5 is particularly useful, and current research efforts focus on the definition of importance-driven algorithms for nondiffuse materials. A continuous adjoint equation can be written to express the propagation of importance in the general case [31]. Since importance is also propagated according to the reflectance of the surfaces, directional reflectors greatly restrict the number of significant surfaces, for which a high accuracy is required. In fact, the inclusion of importance criteria is a promising avenue for making the three-point hierarchical radiosity algorithm mentioned at the beginning of Section 7.2 tractable, by drastically reducing the number of relevant point triples [11].

CHAPTER 8

Monte Carlo techniques for global illumination

The various techniques presented in the previous chapters for solving the global illumination problem were *deterministic* techniques. As demonstrated in other domains, *probabilistic* simulation techniques can be introduced that provide greater flexibility and easier extensibility to more general environments. Although this is usually done at the expense of precise solutions, this approach is also very appealing because of its simplicity.

These probabilistic techniques, which rely on random processes, are usually called Monte Carlo techniques. In the context of global illumination, these random processes appear in two different ways:

- by following light along a "random walk" between light sources and receivers, which can be thought of as shooting energy, similar to the progressive radiosity method described in Section 4.1;
- by using stochastic approximation techniques for evaluating the integral operator in the global illumination equation (Equation 2.30). This strategy amounts to gathering energy.

In the first case, the Monte Carlo technique is a simulation of a random process related to the underlying physical process. In the second case, randomness is introduced as a tool for solving a deterministic problem with an analytical formulation (integral equation).

The progressive radiosity method, presented in Chapter 4, can be physically interpreted as an energy-shooting strategy. Light from bright sources and other bright surfaces is progressively shot to all other surfaces in the environment. This can be readily generalized to a nondeterministic scheme. *Particles* (or *packets of light energy*, or *photon bundles*) are emitted from the light sources in different directions, chosen at random, and are tracked individually. When they collide with objects in the environment, they either lose their energy completely or experience reflection and/or refraction, thus changing their direction of propagation. Introducing randomness at each of these steps proves to be useful: it produces samples whose behavior is usually a good estimate of the global phenomenon. Standard Monte Carlo methods can be used to simulate this *particle model* and obtain an estimate of the global illumination. The reflected/refracted/emitted particle flux given by the number of particles per unit time is a measure of the illumination of points in the environment. This technique, called *particle tracing*, will be described in Section 8.2 (an example is developed in reference [128]).

Monte Carlo techniques are also widely used for estimating integrals. This approach is close in spirit to physical experimentation: statistical experiments are carried out and numerical results obtained from these experiments. For this reason, these techniques have also been coined "methods of statistical trials." When the integral part of the global illumination equation is approximated in such a way, a new formulation is obtained. It can also be interpreted as "tracing paths" along random walks which go from the receivers to the sources. These points are covered in Section 8.3.

Before explaining these two main uses of Monte Carlo approaches for the simulation of global illumination simulation, some useful probabilistic notations and results are given in Section 8.1.

8.1 Some probabilistic techniques

Some standard probabilistic notions are reviewed briefly here. The bibliography includes more detailed presentations of the basic probability techniques [55] and of Monte Carlo methods [97, 159].

8.1.1 Sampling a random variable

A *random variable* x is defined by its *probability density function* f over its definition space, region Ω. This function is non-negative ($f(x) \geq 0$ for all x in Ω) and has unit total "mass": if y ranges over some region Ω, and dy is the measure on the probability space, then

$$\int_{y \in \Omega} f(y) dy = 1 .$$

The probability that x will take a value in some subregion Ω' of Ω is given by

$$\Pr(x \in \Omega') = \int_{y \in \Omega'} f(y) dy .$$

The *expected value* of x is defined by

$$E(x) = \int_{y \in \Omega} y f(y) dy . \quad \textbf{(8.1)}$$

The expected value of the sum of two random variables is, by linearity of integration, the sum of the expected values of the two variables.

The statistical trials performed during Monte Carlo estimates give a good approximation of the underlying probability distribution. This is a consequence of a fundamental result, called the *law of large numbers*. It states that, if the random variables x_i are independent and identically distributed (that is, with the same probability distribution), then

$$\Pr\left(E(x) = \lim_{n \to \infty} \frac{1}{n} \sum_{i=1}^{n} x_i \right) = 1 . \quad \textbf{(8.2)}$$

In other words, the mean of the measured samples approaches the expected value of the random variable x, as n goes to infinity. The larger the number of samples, the better the agreement of the estimator with the actual value.

8.1.2 Random number generation

The integration techniques, as well as other Monte Carlo techniques described below, rely on an effective way to generate random numbers with a given distribution.

A random variable x is uniformly distributed over [0, 1] if, for all a and b in [0, 1],

$$\Pr(a < x < b) = b - a . \quad \textbf{(8.3)}$$

Let us suppose that we can draw a set of n random numbers $(\xi_i)_{1 \le n}$ uniformly distributed over the interval [0, 1]. We now show how to use these numbers in order to draw n numbers $(\eta_i)_{1 \le i \le n}$ according to some density function f defined over the interval $[a, b]$. The key to the problem is the introduction of the probability distribution function, or cumulative distribution function, F, defined by

$$F(x) = \int_{a}^{x} f(y) dy . \quad \textbf{(8.4)}$$

The distribution function $F(x)$ is the cumulative probability that a number is drawn between a and x. It is a monotonically increasing function, such that $F(a) = 0$ and $F(b) = 1$, as shown in Figure 8.1.

If ξ is uniformly distributed over the interval [0, 1], then $\eta = F^{-1}(\xi)$ is such that

$$\begin{aligned} \Pr(\alpha < \eta < \beta) &= \Pr(F(\alpha) < \xi < F(\beta)) \\ &= F(\beta) - F(\alpha) = \int_{\alpha}^{\beta} f(y) dy . \end{aligned}$$

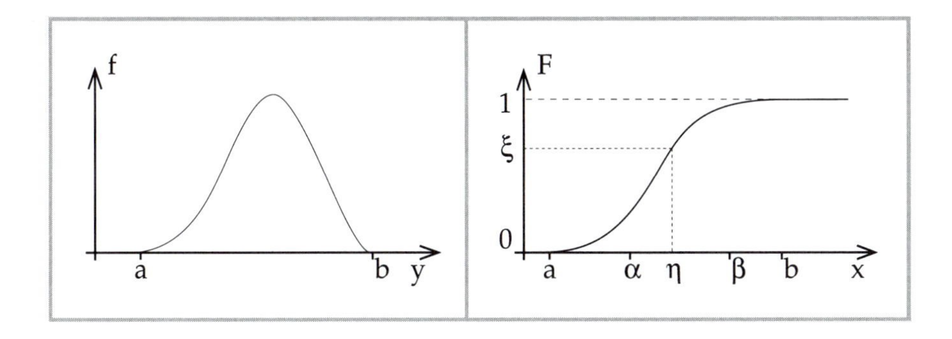

FIGURE 8.1 A probability density function and its associated cumulative distribution function.

As a consequence, if the $(\xi_i)_{1 \leq n}$ are uniformly distributed over the interval [0, 1], then the η_i

$$\eta_i = F^{-1}(\xi_i)$$

are distributed over $[a, b]$ according to the density function f.

This method generalizes to higher dimensions by introducing multidimensional distribution functions. For example, in two dimensions, if f is defined on $[a, b] \times [c, d]$, we consider

$$F(x, y) = \int_c^y \int_a^x f(u, v) du dv .$$

We first choose an x_i according to the distribution $F(x, d)$, considered as a distribution in the first variable only, and then choose y_i according to $F(x_i, y)/F(x_i, d)$. Note that when f can be written as a product of functions of a single variable as $f(x, y) = g(x)h(y)$, then the one-dimensional technique can be used independently on each dimension.

Sampling distributions

Another way to look at these random number generation schemes is to consider them as sampling techniques from the underlying probability distributions. As an example, consider, in two dimensions, the problem of sampling the direction of emission for a perfectly diffuse emitter. If the samples are drawn so as to distribute the emitted energy uniformly, the density function for θ in the range 0 to $\pi/2$ is $\sin 2\theta$; thus the associated cumulative distribution function is $\sin^2 \theta$. As $\sin^2 \theta = \xi$ implies $\theta = \sin^{-1} \sqrt{\xi}$, a "good" sample for angle θ is the inverse sine of the square root of a uniform random number in the range [0, 1].

Rejection sampling

Another technique, called *rejection sampling*, applies to any distribution function, but it should only be used when no direct formula is available, because it is computationally expensive. If f is bounded on the interval (a, b), rejection sampling first generates a pair of uniform random numbers (ξ_1, ξ_2) in $[0, 1]^2$. If $\xi_2 \cdot \sup f(x) < f[a + \xi_1(b - a)]$, then $a + \xi_1(b - a)$ is chosen as a random sample from the distribution f. Otherwise, the random pair is rejected and a new one is tested. As shown in Figure 8.2, when the point $(a + \xi_1(b - a),\ \xi_2 \sup f(x))$ is located above the representative curve of distribution function f, the random pair (ξ_1, ξ_2) is rejected (point A); otherwise $a + \xi_1(b - a)$ is chosen as a random sample from the distribution f.

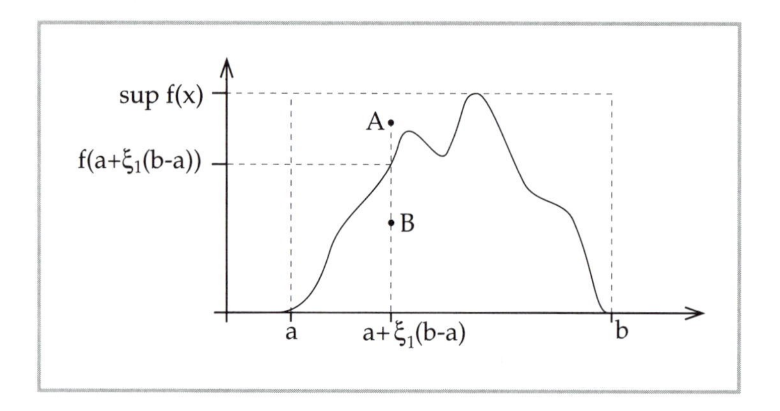

FIGURE 8.2 Rejection sampling.

8.2 Photon transport simulation

Photon transport can be simulated through the implementation of Monte Carlo techniques. Here we discuss the methods of application.

8.2.1 General principles

The main idea behind the Monte Carlo methods related to photon transport simulation is to use probability concepts to model stochastic physical events such as the emission, reflection, and absorption of light.

Such an approach has been widely used for computing radiative transfers in enclosures with both participating and nonparticipating media. One of the advantages of the method is the fact that the treatment of nondiffuse surfaces or polarization is conceptually no more difficult than that for diffuse surfaces and unpolarized radiation. Moreover, complex geometries are easily included in the scene models.

The paths of individual photon bundles are tracked beginning with emission at some location and ending with absorption at some other location. Random numbers are generated and compared with appropriate probability functions in order to determine the path of a photon bundle: which direction it should go, whether it should be reflected when it encounters a surface, and so on.

One could track such photon bundles until they hit the virtual film plane or until they are absorbed. In order to keep the computations feasible, some simplifications must be made. An important one is to assign a few discrete values of energy to the photon bundles.

The flux of photon bundles can be estimated by carrying out a time-independent simulation of the behavior of a sufficiently large sample of particles and keeping track of their paths of transport.

Monte Carlo simulations have been widely used in disciplines such as neutron transport [106] or heat transfer [18]. In the context of global illumination simulation, the process is called particle tracing.

8.2.2 Particle tracing

The algorithm

We suppose here that the environment does not contain participating media and that all objects are opaque and described by their geometry and the optical properties of their surfaces, such as directional emission distributions, emission spectra, and bidirectional reflectance distribution functions.

The algorithm consists of repeatedly tracking particles by following them along several steps repeated for many particles, as shown in Figure 8.3.

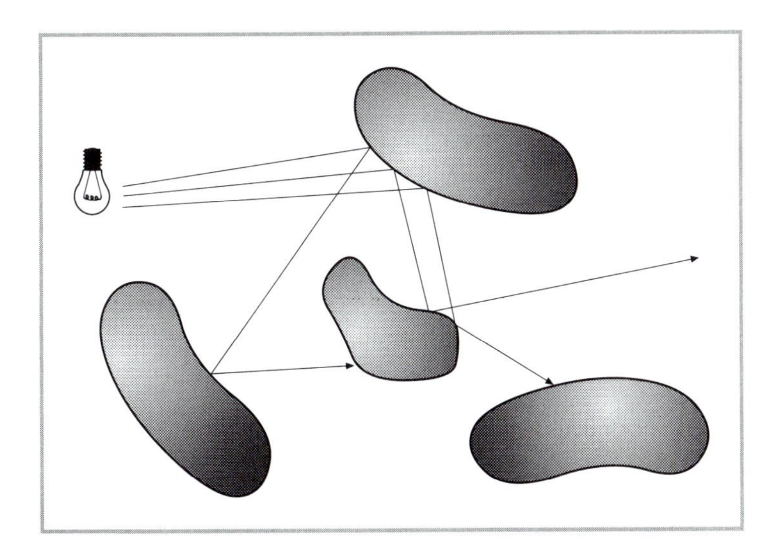

FIGURE 8.3 Particle tracing.

For each particle, the following steps are carried out.

1 Choose

- **a** the wavelength of the particle by sampling the *emission spectrum*,
- **b** the location of the particle on the emitter surface by sampling the *positional emission power distribution*,
- **c** the direction of propagation of the particle by sampling the *directional power distribution*.

2 Update the outgoing particle flux at the emitter surface.

3 Repeat the following steps until the particle is absorbed.

- **a** Find the first object hit by the particle.
- **b** Decide on the type of interaction—absorption or reflection—by testing a random number against some threshold reflection probability ρ (ρ is the directional-hemispherical reflectance at the surface, defined in Section 2.1.4).
- **c** If the particle is reflected:
  - **i** assign a reflected direction to the particle by sampling the BRDF,
  - **ii** update the outgoing particle flux on the reflecting surface according to the BRDF.

Step 3 (a), finding the nearest surface hit by a particle, is done by computing ray-surface intersections. This topic is studied extensively in computer graphics, for example, in the context of ray tracing [67]. The other steps of the algorithm are either updates of flux densities or sampling steps. These will now be described in more detail.

Computing flux densities

If we assume that there is no change in the emissive behavior for a light source over a period of time, then an equilibrium is established by the rate at which particles leave each surface of the environment. This rate determines the radiance of the objects.

Particle tracing techniques produce particle fluxes that are approximations of the actual light flux. An a priori discretization of the environment is performed by defining a mesh structure for each receiver surface, and illumination values are computed for each of these discrete regions/patches.

If the flux is assumed to be uniform over each patch, a simple count of the number of particles is sufficient. In contrast with its role in radiosity methods, the mesh structure plays no role in the actual simulation process that is carried out on the surfaces. It is used only for counting. But the choice of the mesh is still important, as it has a strong impact on the quality of the representation of the illumination gradients in the final rendered images.

To record the outgoing flux at each patch, a count is kept of all particles that are emitted or reflected. This count is an estimator of the equilibrium particle flux density on that patch. The number of particles leaving each patch is multiplied by the source power. The result is then divided by the product of the total number of particles and the area of the patch. This yields the computed value for the flux density.

For rendering the final image, techniques such as bilinear interpolation can be used, as explained in Section 3.2.3.

Sampling light sources

Particles are emitted in different directions from different positions on the surfaces of the light sources. Each particle originates from a light source. The assignment of an emitter surface to a particle is achieved by a random choice such that the probability of a particle being associated with a powerful light source is larger than the probability of a particle being associated with a less powerful light source.

With Monte Carlo simulation techniques, as opposed to radiosity techniques, it is easy to incorporate complex emitter surface shapes. If the emitter's power is uniform over the surface of the emitter, the particle density must be constant across the emitter's area. If the assumption does not hold, the emitter can be divided into smaller emitters with that property. Therefore one must find a good sampling strategy for the position of points on the surface.

A sampling stragegy can be found using a biparametric representation of the surface, if such a representation is available. As shown in Figure 8.4, a point is represented by two parameters u and v, and the surface is partitioned into infinitesimal strips. In order to enforce constant particle density, parameter u is a uniform random number between 0 and 1 and v is chosen as follows. The ratio between the area of an infinitesimal strip and the area of the surface gives the probability of a particle coming out of the strip. By computing the associated cumulative distribution function, as explained in Section 8.1.2, we get an expression for the random value of the other parameter v in terms of a uniform random number [128].

Spectral distribution

The distribution of wavelengths among the outgoing particles from a surface determines the color of the surface (see Section 2.1.2).

Given the spectral density function or emission spectrum of a source, rejection sampling, as described in Section 8.1.2, can be used to decide on the wavelength of a particle emitted at random. This method has to be used here because of the general form of

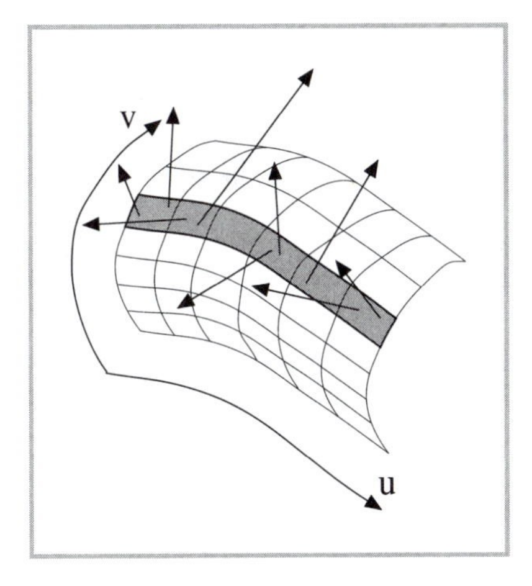

FIGURE 8.4 Sampling a light source.

the spectrum. An alternative way is to let several particles of different wavelengths follow the same path.

Direction sampling

Complex directional radiance distributions can be easily supported by Monte Carlo methods. It is generally assumed that the emission around a point has a circular symmetry, that is, it is independent of the azimuth angle ϕ (this angle was defined in Figure 2.3). The radiance distribution is usually specified as a function of the polar angle θ by means of a goniometric diagram (see the Appendix, Section A.1.5). Rejection sampling is then used to sample θ; whereas ϕ can be sampled as $2\pi\xi$, where ξ is a uniform random number in [0, 1].

For diffuse emitters, it is not difficult, using the example given in section 8.1.2, to prove that the random direction assigned to the particle is given by $(\sin^{-1}\sqrt{\xi_1}, 2\pi\xi_2)$, where ξ_1 and ξ_2 are uniform random numbers in [0, 1].

When dealing with reflection, the BRDF is used to choose the direction of reflection for a particle. For complex distribution functions, rejection sampling is used, whereas in some cases (such as Phong's reflection model, for example) closed fomulas can be obtained.

Type of collision

Deciding between reflection or absorption is performed by choosing a random number ρ uniformly between 0 and 1 and testing its value against the directional-hemispherical reflectance ρ_{dh} that was described in Section 2.1.4. If ρ is greater than ρ_{dh}, the particle is absorbed, otherwise it is reflected.

Russian roulette

Rather than probabilistically terminating the path followed by the particle according to the value of ρ, we can use this value to adjust a numerical "weight" associated with the particle. A particle path can then be stopped at a point where the weight falls below some threshold. This idea is similar to the one used in ray tracing when the depth of the ray tree is controlled adaptively.

Unfortunately, truncation introduces a systematic bias that may become significant when applied to a large number of paths. A simple technique, known as *Russian roulette*, can be used to eliminate this bias [9]. According to this technique, once the weight of a particle has fallen below a predefined threshold, the particle is either absorbed with probability p or survives (with probability $1 - p$), but then its weight is increased and multiplied by $1/(1 - p)$. If w is the weight of the particle before playing Russian roulette, and W its subsequent weight, the expected value of W, denoted by $E(W)$, is given by

$$\begin{aligned} E(W) &= \text{Pr(absorption)} * 0 + \text{Pr(survival)} * \frac{w}{1-p} \\ &= p * 0 + (1-p) * \frac{w}{1-p} \\ &= w, \end{aligned}$$

which is the original weight of the particle. Therefore, on average, the particle has the appropriate weight. The majority of insignificant particles can thus be ignored by artificially inflating the contributions of those that survive. The technique results in a slight increase in the variance, but this is compensated by the fact that more samples can be considered for the same overall cost. Eliminating the bias guarantees convergence to the correct result.

In general, care must be taken to avoid unnecessary bias when departing from naïve Monte Carlo techniques in an attempt to improve statistical efficiency.

8.2.3 Conclusion

Particle tracing techniques are simple to implement, and one of their main advantages is their high degree of generality. As already mentioned, complex object shapes, general reflectance functions, and so on, can be easily incorporated in the simulations. Moreover, generalizations to include participating media are also possible [128].

However, this simplicity is somewhat misleading. As mentioned by P. Shirley, in [157]: "One appeal of using Monte Carlo methods is that they are easy to correctly design and use. However, it is not so easy to design a *good* Monte Carlo method, where the computation can be completed to the desired accuracy relatively quickly. Here both cleverness and some analytic skills are required."

The accuracy of the results is closely related to the number of particles whose paths are traced. As soon as this number becomes large, efficiency becomes a concern, and some ad hoc techniques have to be implemented in order to keep computation times manageable.

Path tracing is similar in spirit to the progressive radiosity techniques, in that both use an energy-shooting strategy, and both result in images that are refined as the simulation proceeds. The approach of traditional radiosity described in Section 3.2.1, energy gathering, also has a stochastic counterpart. It will be presented as a random walk solution of the radiosity integral equation, in Section 8.3.3.

8.3 Monte Carlo integration and the illumination equation

In addition to the simulation of particle transport, Monte Carlo methods are also used in a different class of computational methods: to compute integrals using probabilistic techniques. We will now review these techniques and show how they can be used to solve the integral equations involved in lighting simulation.

8.3.1 Estimating integrals

The law of large numbers, given in Section 8.1.1, is the starting point for deriving ways of estimating integrals using random experiments. Let us suppose we want to obtain an estimation of $\int_{y\in\Omega} h(y)dy$. We write h as a product:

$$h = gf\,,$$

where the function f is arbitrary (its choice will be discussed later on).

If x is a random variable with probability distribution f (in the following we will denote this fact as $x \sim f$), we can approximate the expected value of $g(x)$ by a sum:

$$E(g(x)) = \int_{y\in\Omega} g(y)f(y)dy \approx \frac{1}{n}\sum_{i=1}^{n} g(x_i)\,.$$

Since $h = gf$, we obtain the following estimate for $\int_{y\in\Omega} h(y)dy$:

$$\int_{y\in\Omega} h(y)dy \approx \frac{1}{n}\sum_{i=1}^{n} \frac{h(x_i)}{f(x_i)}\,. \tag{8.5}$$

The reliability of the estimate can be measured by considering higher-order moments of the distributions involved.

Variance is the first of such high-order moments. For a random variable x, its variance $v(x)$ is the expected value of the square of the difference between x and $E(x)$:

$$v(x) = E([x - E(x)]^2) = E(x^2) - [E(x)]^2\,. \tag{8.6}$$

Variance (or its square root, called *standard deviation*) can be used to measure the reliability of the estimate of $\int_{y\in\Omega} h(y)dy$ given by Equation 8.5. The term $h(x_i)/f(x_i)$ is called a *primary estimator*; whereas

$$\frac{1}{n}\sum_{i=1}^{n} \frac{h(x_i)}{f(x_i)}\,, \tag{8.7}$$

the average of many primary estimators, is called a *secondary estimator*. Both estimates are good, but the secondary estimator is preferred because its variance is lower, which shows that its value is more likely to be close to the true one. As the samples are drawn independently, the variance of the estimate takes the simple form:

$$v\left(\frac{1}{n}\sum_{i=1}^{n} \frac{h(x_i)}{f(x_i)}\right) = \frac{1}{n} v\left(\frac{h}{f}\right)\,. \tag{8.8}$$

We are now in a position to discuss the quality of the estimate we get. First, it is clear from Equation 8.8 that we get better estimates as the number of samples, n, increases. One of the potential problems can be observed in Equation 8.8: the error behaves as the standard deviation, which, as the square root of the variance, is proportional to $1/\sqrt{n}$. In order to halve the error the number of samples must be quadrupled.

Variance reduction

As controlling the accuracy of the computations is one of the main difficulties in using Monte Carlo methods, it is useful to know techniques for reducing the variance.

Equation 8.8 shows that in order to improve the estimate, one should choose f such that the variance of the density h/f is as small as possible. Making a fair choice for f is called *importance sampling*: if f is large where h is large, there will be more samples in important regions.

Another well-known method, called *stratified sampling*, is to partition the domain of integration Ω, into several domains Ω_i, and to compute the integral over Ω as the sum of integrals over Ω_i. Usually only one sample is chosen in each Ω_i (with density f_i). This method gives the following value for the variance of the estimate:

$$v\left(\sum_{i=1}^{n}\frac{h(x_i)}{f_i(x_i)}\right)=\sum_{i=1}^{n}v\left(\frac{h(x_i)}{f_i(x_i)}\right).$$

Stratified sampling is often far superior to importance sampling, but there are some functions for which stratification carries no benefit. An example is a white noise function, where the variance is constant for all regions, no matter how small.

Multidimensional integration

One of the main advantages of Monte Carlo methods is their generality. The same principle for estimating a single integral can be used for multidimensional integrals. The only difficulty comes from the fact that the sample values have to be drawn in a multidimensional space according to a distribution function that is a function of several variables in a d-dimensional domain.

For simple examples where the domain is a square or a disk, for example, the selection of the sample is easy. As a more complex example, let us look at the evaluation of the form factor between patches P_i and P_j. The form factor was defined in Equation 3.19 by the integral

$$F_{ij}=\frac{1}{A_i}\int_{x\in P_i}\int_{y\in P_j}\frac{\cos\theta\cos\theta'}{\pi r^2}V(x,y)dxdy\,, \tag{8.9}$$

where A_i is the area of patch P_i, and $V(x,y)$ is the visibility function between x and y.

Here, the sampling space is $P_i \times P_j$. A random sample in this four-dimensional space is a pair of uniformly distributed random points from each surface patch (see Figure 8.5). The probability density is the constant $\frac{1}{A_iA_j}$. If we use one sample, we get the estimate

$$F_{ij}\approx A_j\frac{\cos\theta\cos\theta'}{\pi r^2}V(x,y)\,, \tag{8.10}$$

which can be improved by using more samples. The visibility term $V(x, y)$ is evaluated by shooting a ray between x and y. The method is valid whenever we know how to choose random points in a region.

As mentioned in Section 5.2, finite-element formulations of radiosity provide general techniques for computing approximate solutions of integral equations such as the diffuse illumination equation. These formulations introduce multiple integrals that must be computed with good accuracy. For example, as explained in Section 5.2.3, with the Galerkin method, the equivalent of the form factor is the quantity

$$\hat{F}_{ij} = \int_{x \in S} N_i(x)dx \int_{y \in S} \kappa(x, y) N_j(y)dy . \quad \textbf{(8.11)}$$

The presence of shape functions N_i and N_j inside the integrals makes this factor more difficult to compute than the standard form factor. Statistical estimates of the integral can be obtained by computing the kernel and shape functions for random pairs of points on two elements and using Monte Carlo techniques. These methods are general enough to solve complex cases, and their accuracy can be controlled.

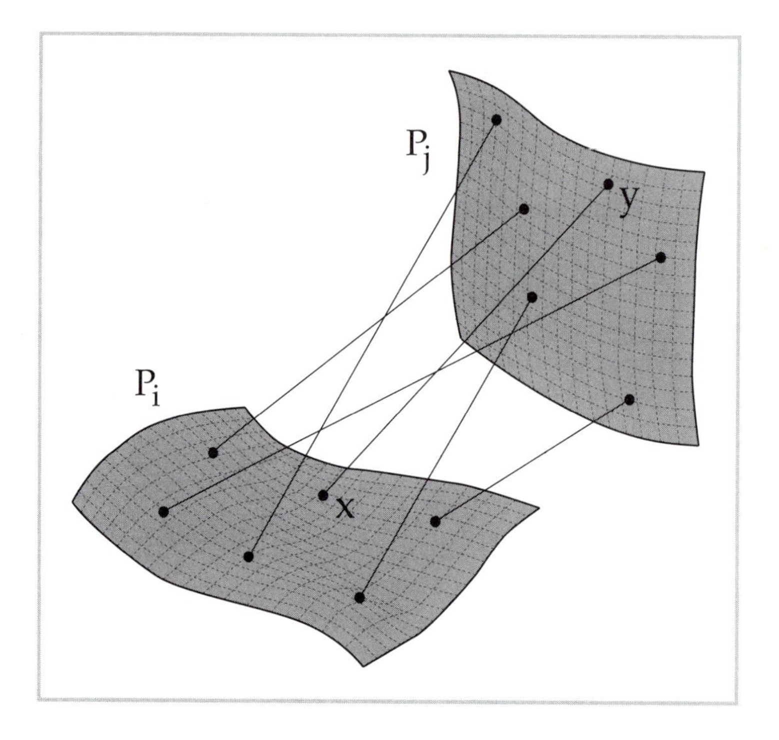

FIGURE 8.5 Form factor estimation using random samples.

8.3.2 Monte Carlo solution to the illumination equation

We know from Section 2.2 that the global illumination equation can be written as

$$L = L_e + \int_{\Omega} \rho L_i \cos\theta d\omega .$$

Using Monte Carlo techniques for computing integrals explained in Section 8.3.1, we could estimate the integral part of the illumination equation by simply averaging the radiance from a number of sampled directions from the incoming sphere. However, this approach is not feasible, since along a given direction, only the contribution due to emission is known; the contribution due to reflection should be computed by a similar integration around the first point hit by a ray in that direction.

The hemispherical contribution due to emitters can be separated from the contribution due to reflectors, each one being evaluated using different sampling techniques [41, 40]. The source term is estimated by sampling the light source surfaces. The interreflection term is estimated by sampling the surface BRDF. Radiance, emitted or reflected, from a sampled direction, is computed by tracing a ray in that direction, finding the first hit, and computing the appropriate radiance at that point.

This technique, called *distribution ray tracing*, results in an accurate solution to the global illumination equation. But the computation time can be prohibitive, as the number of rays that need to be shot is very large. In order to increase the efficiency of distribution ray tracing, several methods have been devised such as the use of a cache mechanism [192].

8.3.3 Random walk solution to the illumination equation

The illumination equation, of the form

$$L(x) = L_e(x) + \int_{x' \in S} \kappa(x, x') L(x') dx' ,$$

can be formally solved by repeatedly substituting L in the integral. This gives an expression of L as the sum of a series:

$$\begin{aligned} L(x) = {} & L_e(x) + \int_{x' \in S} \kappa(x, x') L_e(x') dx' \\ & + \int_{(x', x'') \in S^2} \kappa(x, x') \kappa(x', x'') L_e(x'') dx' dx'' \\ & + \int_{(x', x'', x''') \in S^3} \kappa(x, x') \kappa(x', x'') \kappa(x'', x''') L_e(x''') dx' dx'' dx''' \\ & + \dots \end{aligned} \tag{8.12}$$

This expression is similar to the Neumann series introduced in Section 2.2. A Monte Carlo solution to the integral equation is then computed by evaluating each of the integrals that appear in Equation 8.12 through Monte Carlo estimation.

A primary estimator for the first integral in the series is

$$\frac{\kappa(x, x')L_e(x')}{f_1(x')} : x' \sim f_1 ,$$

where x' is drawn at random according to the probability distribution f_1, and f_1 is chosen in order to get a good estimate. As mentioned in Section 8.3.1, importance sampling and stratified sampling are two tools that can be used to obtain such good estimates.

In a similar way, a primary estimator for the second integral is

$$\frac{\kappa(x, x')\kappa(x', x'')L_e(x'')}{f_2(x', x'')} : (x', x'') \sim f_2 .$$

As for the third integral, we get

$$\frac{\kappa(x, x')\kappa(x', x'')\kappa(x'', x''')L_e(x''')}{f_3(x', x'', x''')} : (x', x'', x''') \sim f_3 .$$

These expressions are approximated, as mentioned in Section 8.3.1, by the values of the functions at sample points. Although different sampling strategies could be used for the various integrals estimates, an easy way (which introduces no bias because of the linearity of the expected value) is to use sample points $x^1, x^2, \ldots, x^n$. The estimator for the sum of the first n terms in Equation 8.12 is

$$\begin{aligned}
L(x) = L_e(x) &+ \frac{\kappa(x, x^1)L_e(x^1)}{f_1(x^1)} \\
&+ \frac{\kappa(x, x^1)\kappa(x^1, x^2)L_e(x^2)}{f_2(x^1, x^2)} \\
&+ \frac{\kappa(x, x^1)\kappa(x^1, x^2)\kappa(x^2, x^3)L_e(x^3)}{f_3(x^1, x^2, x^3)} \\
&\vdots \\
&+ \frac{\kappa(x, x^1)\ldots\kappa(x^{n-1}, x^n)L_e(x^n)}{f_n(x^1, \ldots, x^n)} .
\end{aligned}$$

This can be seen as an estimate of $L(x)$ as a sum of a finite number of terms. It also can be seen in the following manner:

- x_1 is obtained by sampling directions around x using the BRDF at point x, and computing x_1 as the first hit in that direction;

- x_2 is obtained by sampling directions around x_1 using the BRDF at point x_1, and computing x_2 as the first hit in that direction;

  ...

- x_n is obtained by sampling directions around x_{n-1} using the BRDF at point x_{n-1}, and computing x_{n-1} as the first hit in that direction.

This computation can be interpreted as gathering radiance values along the random path shown in Figure 8.6 with reflections at points $x_1, x_2, \ldots, x_n$.

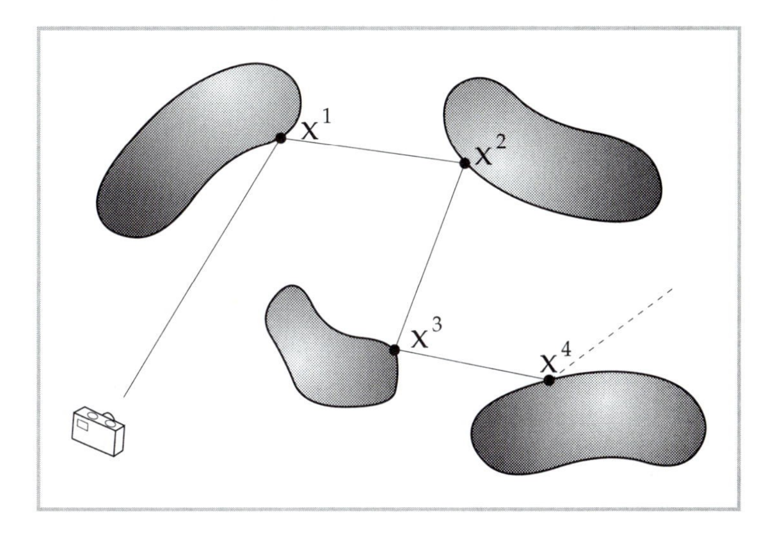

FIGURE 8.6 Gathering radiance values along a random path.

Importance sampling and stratification can be combined in the following way in order to reduce the variance in the simulation [100]. Both techniques are applied to the problem of sampling a new direction at each step of the random process. Through stratification, the integrals of direct and indirect illuminance are estimated independently. If many of the surfaces of the environment are far from ideal reflectors, the intensity of indirect illumination will be significantly less than direct illumination. Identifying the strata corresponding to first and subsequent generations of light paths can be accomplished using the geometry of the light sources. The stratified sampling technique will then always sample the lights, will sample independently the rest of the hemisphere, and then will combine the two parts after weighting them appropriately. This last renormalization is necessary to avoid introducing bias in the results. The role of importance sampling is to distort the probability densities of the direction chosen in order to emphasize those of high incidence illuminance. These important directions with respect to the point considered are sampled more frequently. They can be found by using some a priori information about the solution. For example, an earlier coarse illumination pass can be used to determine where important objects are located.

The application of this technique to the global illumination equation of Section 2.2 has been called *path tracing* [95]. Although pure path tracing is not in general a very efficient technique, careful use of variance reduction techniques, such as hierarchical and non-uniform sampling, can make it practical for some global illumination simulations.

8.4 Radiosity-based vs. Monte Carlo techniques for global illumination

Although radiosity-based and Monte Carlo techniques can each be pushed to their limits in order to simulate a wide variety of global illumination effects, it appears that better results, both in terms of efficiency and accuracy, can be obtained by combining different techniques for different parts of the simulation.

An attempt to get the best of the two different "worlds" has already been presented in Section 7.3: several hybrid/multipass methods retain most of the advantages of the radiosity and ray tracing techniques. This process can be carried further, leading to extended multipass methods. A typical one [26] consists of a series of passes. The rendering process begins with a progressive refinement radiosity pass with extended form factors that are computed using ray tracing. This pass provides a good approximation of the overall illumination. A refinement pass follows that performs a Monte Carlo path tracing from the eye and the lights to create shadows and caustics. This path tracing is directed *only* at surfaces considered bright enough to create such high frequency details. A subsequent pass continues to refine the image using Monte Carlo path tracing for accurate low frequency illumination effects such as color bleeding. This pass makes use of the results from the radiosity pass for high-order reflections. It is performed pixel by pixel, thus eliminating the radiosity meshing artifacts from the final image.

Several points should be stressed about this multipass method: light path classification, light source reclassification, and Monte Carlo integration.

The light path classification is a refinement of previous classifications [81]. As mentioned in Section 7.3.1, since each reflection mode along the light's path from the light (L) to the eye (E) can be characterized as diffuse (D) or specular (S), any path can be expressed as a string generated by the regular expression $L(D \mid S)^* E$. Ideal diffuse radiosity simulates $LD^* E$ paths, while traditional ray tracing simulates $LDS^* E$ or $LS^* E$ paths. A more precise decomposition cuts the paths in parts, where specific rendering techniques give better results in terms of efficiency and/or precision by exploiting the properties of the reflections in the shorter path considered. Two important decompositions are shown in Figure 8.7.

Direct illumination paths going from sources to the eye via one D followed by zero or more S's (top of Figure 8.7) are followed using Monte Carlo path tracing (MCPT). Paths containing at least two D's are called radiosity paths and are followed using a combination

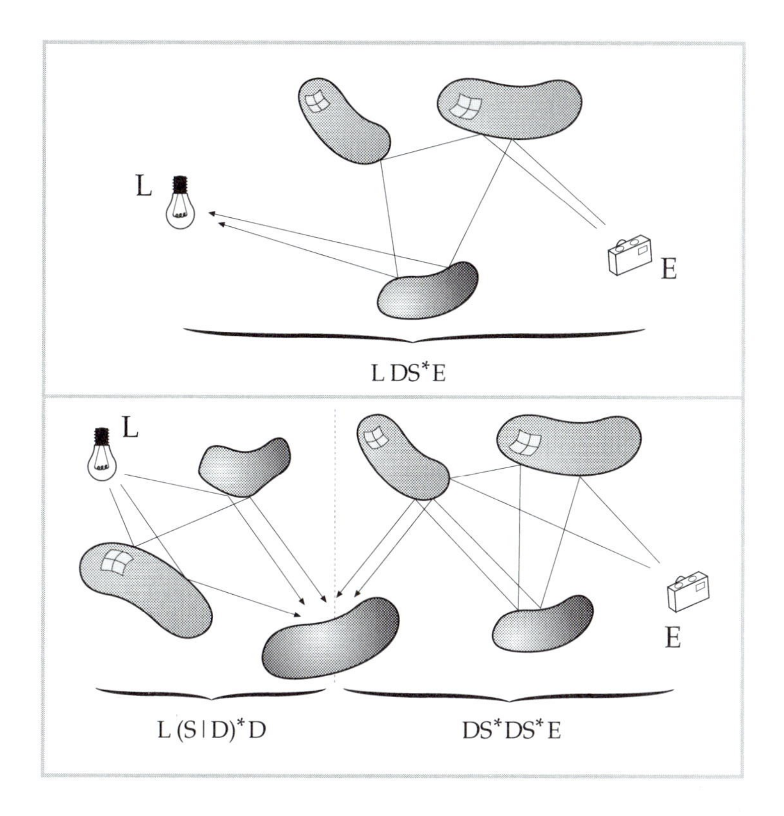

FIGURE 8.7 Direct illumination paths (top) and radiosity paths (bottom). (After Chen et al. [26].)

of the progressive refinement radiosity technique (PRR), with ray tracing for extended form factors, and MCPT. The part of the path from the eye to the second D is followed using MCPT. Arrows in Figure 8.7 indicate the direction of the paths followed during the passes of the simulation.

This distinction is very useful. Lighting in regions that are directly or indirectly visible *and* receive light directly from light sources is computed using Monte Carlo methods. Radiosity techniques would produce noticeable meshing artifacts in these regions where radiosity gradients can be high. On the other hand, where these gradients tend to be small, radiosity computations give an efficient way to compute subtle lighting effects.

In order to encompass any combination of S and D on a path between the source and the eye, *caustic paths* and *highlight paths* must also be considered. As shown in Figure 8.8, caustic paths are followed by light-ray tracing (LRT), which traces light from sources for caustic map generation. Highlight paths (LS^*E) are used for direct rendering of light sources, rendering of light sources through specular reflection, and production of highlights.

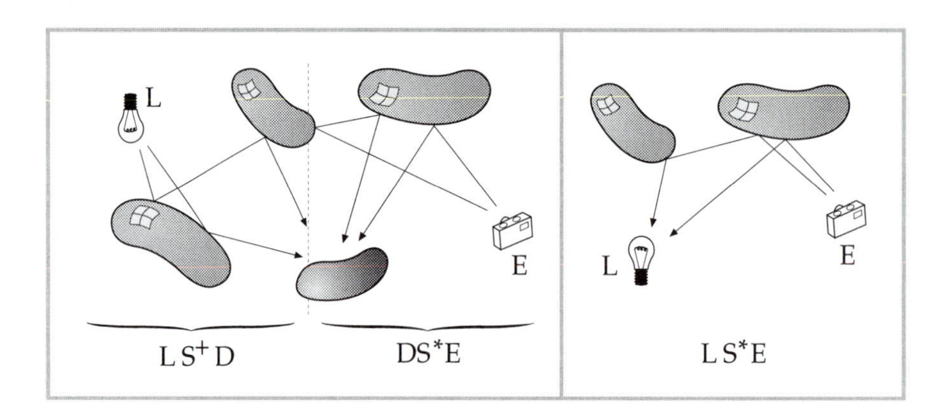

FIGURE 8.8 Caustic paths (left) and highlight paths (right). (After Chen et al. [26].)

The radiosity of light sources is usually substantially greater than the radiosity of other surfaces. Consequently, it would be beneficial to devote more work to the computation of the radiances from light sources. Several techniques have been devised to take advantage of this remark [26, 102, 158, 189], by treating light sources separately. Surfaces are considered as light sources if their radiosity is large enough. This is often called *light source reclassification*.

Color Plates 39 to 43 illustrate the steps of the multipass method. Plate 39 shows both the direct illumination from the light sources and the interreflections between other surfaces. Plates 41, 42, and 43 show the results of the PRR, MCPT, and LRT steps of the multipass method. Altogether, they compose the image shown in Plate 40.

Monte Carlo integration with a radiosity preprocess eliminates radiosity discretization effects from the final image, while avoiding the cost of pure path tracing. The surface discretization used in the radiosity solution does not appear in the final image, reducing the work required in meshing. Moreover, it makes the Monte Carlo computations more efficient: using the PRR solution reduces the length of the paths considered in Monte Carlo path tracing since paths end at diffuse surfaces, and the knowledge gained from the PRR phase can be used to reduce the variance of the trials, reducing the number of trials for a particular level of accuracy. A similar strategy to reduce path length and variance uses cached radiance values for higher-order interreflections [193].

❒ ❒ ❒

This chapter showed that Monte Carlo techniques can be successfully applied to the simulation of global illumination. Because they are based on simple concepts, they provide versatile tools that can be applied to a great variety of situations.

In particular, the use of stochastic estimates for the computation of integrals offers a general means of computing form factors. The most generic form factor integral, involving non-constant basis functions, can be computed in this way with little additional work. Moreover, the principles of statistical sampling can be used to estimate multidimensional integrals. Monte Carlo techniques are thus easily applied to higher dimensional problems, where several parameters are treated as random variables.

This wide applicability makes Monte Carlo methods very appealing. However, in order to obtain reliable simulations with controlled accuracy, specific techniques described in this chapter must be used. The design of a Monte Carlo algorithm that is both reliable and efficient requires some effort and good skills.

Each of the various global illumination techniques, such as ray tracing, radiosity, and Monte Carlo path tracing, has definite advantages. The combination of these techniques into multipass algorithms results in a powerful method that provides the user with "the best of both worlds." Another example of a fruitful cooperation between techniques is the use of radiosity results to guide Monte Carlo methods towards "accurate" importance sampling.

APPENDIX A

A practical guide for radiosity and global illumination

Computational techniques for global illumination have reached a level of maturity that opens new avenues in an ever-increasing number of industrial and scientific fields that rely on simulation tools to test the soundness of different solutions. In many cases substantial benefits are obtained from the use of an accurate global illumination method.

Despite this increasing popularity, the development of a complete simulation system remains a challenging task, as it requires careful treatment of all steps of the computation. There is no reason to embark on an expensive global illumination calculation if the results cannot be trusted because of a single coarse approximation in the pipeline. If accuracy is essential, all components of the simulation system must be designed with that goal in mind.

The purpose of this appendix is to identify some of the key issues faced in the development of an accurate simulation tool. Potential sources of error are discussed and a reexamination of the various algorithms is presented, this time with an emphasis on practical constraints.

A.1 Basic requirements

A first group of problems arise because of the constraints exerted on the simulation process by its environment. These include the input and output requirements, and the expectations of the user. Input and output issues include consideration of geometric or physical models, initial mesh generation for radiosity, use of measured data in the simulation, as well as the correct treatment of color and viewing conditions. User requirements such as interactive steering of the simulation must also be taken into account.

A.1.1 Geometry input and meshing

For image synthesis applications, lighting simulation is only one component of "image realism," albeit an important one. Another major component is the realism of the model of the scene. In fact, striking results can be obtained using a simple rendering scheme and a very detailed model, whereas the use of a sophisticated rendering technique with a simple model will tend to produce "unrealistic" images. For this reason any practical simulation tool for global illumination should be prepared to deal with complex scene geometries. Yet the importance of the model is often overlooked. The question most often asked when a radiosity picture is presented is: "How long did it take to compute?" However, for most images, rendering time is only a fraction of the time needed to model the scene.

Complex models are typically produced using special-purpose modeling or CAD software packages, which have no knowledge of the specific needs of global illumination algorithms. For architectural and lighting design applications, models of the architectural space are created using specialized CAD systems, and for other radiant exchange simulations the objects are often obtained from mechanical CAD descriptions.

A major requirement for the simulation tool is therefore the ability to import data from a variety of input formats, including CAD data. While this may seem a rather trivial point, it has a significant impact on many implementation choices. Most CAD programs support a number of output formats, the de facto standard being AutoCAD's DXF format. Reading geometrical information from such a format is not a difficult task in itself, but choices must be made regarding the use of imported geometry.

For instance, radiosity algorithms place additional constraints on the scene geometry. The most important radiosity requirement is that of *meshing*, or creating a set of surface patches to be used in the simulation. As shown in Chapter 5, the accuracy of a radiosity simulation is largely controlled by the quality of the underlying mesh. While it is fairly easy to generate a mesh on a surface, it is much harder to generate one that will produce good results for radiosity.

Complex models cannot be meshed "by hand" for practical applications. Instead, an automatic meshing module must be used that takes as input a geometrical description of the scene. The issues faced in mesh generation using geometry from a CAD program are well described in reference [13]. Inconsistencies may exist in the model that prevent an accurate simulation. For example several surfaces can exist at the same spatial location, and single surfaces may exist in the model that are not physically realizable (such as a one-sided wall with no thickness). As shown in Section 5.3.2 such situations tend to produce distracting artifacts in the solution. Clearly it is not sufficient to blindly chop the surfaces into a set of polygons. Other options are reviewed below.

Using a built-in mesher

In many CAD systems a meshing module is offered, typically as an option for structural analysis using stress/strain equations. Therefore one way to obtain a mesh for radiosity is to use the included mesher. A major benefit of this approach is that there is no need to write the corresponding code. Unfortunately this solution usually offers little control over the meshing algorithms, and makes it difficult to achieve adaptive subdivision of the mesh based on the radiosity solution. Still, some packages offer direct access to the meshing engine from a program, allowing tighter coupling between the simulation and the meshing module.

Since such meshing modules typically generate a set of independent polygons, the radiosity reconstruction process may be very crude, as no neighboring information is provided. The exception is when a topological data structure is created. Topological data structures will be explained in the next section. Built-in meshers produce output that is ill suited for hierarchical radiosity algorithms. These prefer as input a set of large polygons, to be subdivided hierarchically as part of the simulation process.

Using a custom mesher

If a built-in mesher lacks a topological structure, it will be difficult to perform a satisfactory reconstruction, thus, distracting image artifacts will result. In this case consider creating a meshing module tailored to the specific needs of the image synthesis algorithms used. This solution is appealing since it allows complete control over the subdivision process and can be smoothly integrated with the other data structures in the program (which are discussed in the next section). If hierarchical radiosity or discontinuity meshing is to be used, the subdivision process is tightly coupled to the radiosity computation and must be designed accordingly.

Do not underestimate the cost of designing and implementing a high-quality meshing module; it can easily account for the majority of the entire development effort.

Even when using a custom mesher the geometry imported from CAD programs must still be processed before submitting it to the radiosity algorithm, as indicated in Section 5.3.2. For instance, a concave polygon with holes is often exported from CAD systems as a set of disjoint convex elements. These coplanar elements should be grouped into the original polygon before radiosity meshing takes place. Surface normals must also be oriented in a consistent manner for all points on a given surface. This typically requires some user intervention, which should not be repeated unnecessarily. Thus the radiosity module should be able to reexport complete CAD data files with corrected normals to allow later modifications to take place without imposing a complete correction step each time a radiosity solution is desired.

Since the quality of a radiosity solution is highly dependent on the adequacy of the mesh, it is very hard to design a meshing module that will handle all possible cases correctly. A lot can be accomplished by keeping in mind the requirements of radiosity when modeling the geometry. For instance, to avoid shadow leaks, objects should not interpenetrate. In cases where the simulation is performed by radiosity-aware users, a simple, semi-interactive mesh-cleaning tool can save a lot of effort by shortening the trial-and-error loop. Unfortunately this kind of tuning cannot be relied upon if a simulation system is to be used by nonspecialists who do not have a precise idea of its inner workings.

Using no mesh at all

In some cases, and especially when the input data is not physically consistent, it may be better to do away with the mesh completely and resort to Monte Carlo path tracing. This means taking advantage of the fact that Monte Carlo simulation only uses scene geometry and does not require that topological data structures be superimposed. Also, since no screen-space or object-space reconstruction is performed, the corresponding artifacts are avoided. This simplicity comes at the cost of a view-dependent calculation. The public domain program, Radiance [191],[1] is a good example of a professional-quality simulation system that does not use any explicit mesh.

A.1.2 Data structures for radiosity

Since radiosity algorithms store illumination information in a view-independent manner, specific data structures are needed to associate radiometric data with the geometry of the scene. Furthermore, it is important that this information be accessible both for geometrical and topological queries. For example, the calculation of form factors requires visibility testing that is performed using the scene geometry, while reconstruction procedures require access to neighboring patches on the same surface—a request of a topological nature. Some of the possible choices are discussed in this section.

Polygonal representation

Traditional radiosity tessellates all objects in the scene, resulting in a polygonal mesh. However, recent developments allow the direct inclusion of curved elements in the mesh. One reason for using polygons is that they are a common denominator: any geometric primitive can be transformed into them. In addition, polygons are easy to use for final rendering, and can often be displayed at interactive rates on graphics-oriented computers.

The disadvantage of polygons is that when curved surfaces are present in the scene, very fine tessellation is sometimes needed to obtain a pleasing geometrical representation, thus adding unnecessary complexity to the illumination calculation.

Alternatives, such as "radiosity textures" [81] or surface sampling [183], dissociate the geometrical and illumination information. Geometrical information is left in its original form as a parameterized surface, and the illumination information is stored in a structure that operates directly in parameter space. The advantage of this situation is that the subdivision of the illumination structure is only driven by illumination considerations. All that is needed is a two-way mapping between parameter space and 3D space.

---

[1] To get a copy of Radiance, you may access the anonymous ftp account on `hobbes.lbl.gov` (128.3.12.38) or send a 60+ Mbyte 1/4-inch tape cartridge with return envelope to: Greg Ward, Lawrence Berkeley Laboratory, 1 Cyclotron Rd., 90-3111, Berkeley, CA 94720, USA.

Note however that geometry and illumination are not as independent as one may wish, since geometry can influence the illumination calculation. For instance, many subdivision decisions are made on the basis of geometrical information such as local curvature. Sampling density is also usually estimated in 3D space rather than in parameter space. Finally, polygon-free structures cannot be used for some primitives, such as implicit surfaces, for which no simple parametrization is available.

Space partitioning

Ray casting is now used almost universally in radiosity algorithms to determine visibility between two points. Since visibility computations typically account for most of the simulation time, particular attention should be paid to the efficiency of the ray casting engine.

Many efficient acceleration techniques are available to speed up ray casting, none of which has been proven superior to the others in all cases. Several implementations are available in the public domain[2] and can provide a good starting point for the development of a ray casting engine. In all cases it is well worth the effort to implement a good space partitioning scheme such as a hierarchy of bounding volumes or an octree. These techniques are not detailed here since they are covered extensively in the abundant ray tracing literature [67].

The Binary Space Partitioning (BSP) tree is another possibility to organize the geometrical data, especially in the case of polygonal scenes [176, 21]. In a BSP tree the supporting planes of the polygons are used to recursively split space into smaller regions. The advantage of this particular structure appears for example when discontinuity meshing is used, since critical surfaces can be handled in the same manner as regular objects [107]. The drawbacks of the BSP tree are that its structure is very dependent on the geometry of the objects, and that it only works with polygonal objects.

Besides these general-purpose acceleration techniques for ray tracing, other optimizations are possible because of the particular nature of radiosity computations using ray casting: a number of visibility queries have to be answered between different points on the same two patches. This is the case, for instance, when estimating a form factor for hierarchical radiosity methods, or when computing a radiosity kernel element between two shape functions using Monte Carlo quadrature, or when computing form factors from a number of vertices on a patch to a source patch. In all these cases, important savings can be realized by efficiently computing a list of potential occluders for the particular pair of patches being considered.

One possibility is to construct a *shaft*, or polygonal volume surrounding both patches and enclosing all the space between them, and cull away all portions of the scene that are known not to intersect the shaft [73]. Figure A.1 shows a shaft constructed from two surfaces. Note that a new shaft must be constructed for each pair of patches considered

[2] Good places to start looking for public domain ray tracers are the following ftp sites: `wuarchive.wustl.edu` (128.252.135.4) and `princeton.edu` (128.112.128.1) in the U.S., `nic.funet.fi` (128.214.6.100) and `ftp.informatik.uni-oldenburg.de` (134.106.1.9) in Europe, and `gondwana.ecr.mu.oz.au` (128.250.70.62) in Australia.

during the calculation. Alternatively, for static scenes, a *visibility graph* can be constructed once as a preprocess, and used later to establish visibility relationships between patches. A static processing algorithm whereby the scene is subdivided using a BSP tree has been described in reference [173]. Visibility relationships are incrementally computed during initialization between all leaves of the BSP tree. During processing, pairs of polygons can be classified as either fully visible, fully invisible, or partially visible to each other by consulting the tree. Acceleration techniques for visibility determination are crucial to the development of efficient radiosity implementations, and the reader is encouraged to consult the references for a more precise description.

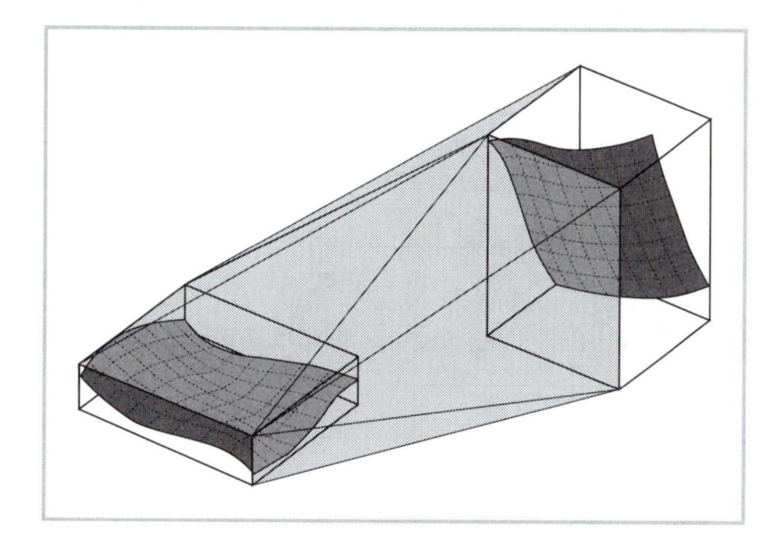

FIGURE A.1 Construction of a shaft to speed up visibility tests between two surfaces.

Connectivity information

Many operations in a radiosity algorithm rely on the availability of neighboring information: when performing adaptive subdivision, for example, it is important to have access to a patch's neighbors to avoid creating the T-vertices that were described in Section 5.3.1. Connectivity information is also needed for reconstruction schemes that guarantee continuity between patches.

Maintaining topological information also helps to avoid recomputation, for example when a vertex is shared by multiple coplanar patches and form factors are computed using ray casting. In this case the vertex-to-patch form factor should be computed only once.

Topological data structures also enable access to both patches and their vertices. These are used together at various stages of the algorithm. Vertices are used when computing form factors, as well as for radiosity interpolation for display. Patches are needed when computing area averages and distributing sample points for form factor computation.

Many topological data structures have been derived in the context of solid modeling and have been adapted to the radiosity algorithm [198]. One example, widely used in computer graphics, is the *winged-edge* data structure, in which the basic unit of information is a directed edge connecting two vertices, as shown in Figure A.2.

In addition to the pointers to its endpoints, an edge structure also holds pointers to the two adjacent faces, as well as four adjacent edges: two for each endpoint, representing the first edge encountered in the clockwise direction, and the first edge encountered in the counter clockwise direction.

With this information it is fairly easy to obtain a list of all edges adjacent to a given edge at a given vertex. In addition, a linked list of vertices or edges is often maintained to allow easy access to all objects in the scene. Redundant information is sometimes also stored, such as pointers, that allows more direct access to answers of frequent queries. Typical queries include

- What vertices are adjacent to vertex V? (for radiosity reconstruction and gradient computation),
- What vertices are on the border of face F? (for radiosity averaging),
- What faces are adjacent to vertex V? (for surface normal calculation).

Choosing the optimal topological data structure is difficult because the trade-off between the memory cost of storing redundant pointers and the performance improvement gained with faster response to queries is difficult to evaluate.

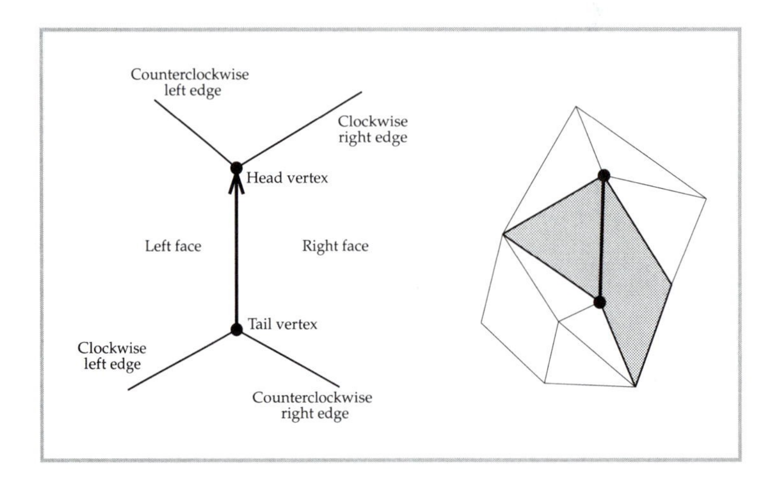

FIGURE A.2 Winged-edge data structure. An edge record contains pointers to all elements shown at the left, while the vertex and face records simply point to any of the adjacent edges. On the right-hand side the elements pointed to by an edge record in a sample mesh have been highlighted.

Winged-edge structures are created and maintained using manipulation routines based on "Euler operators." These are described in detail in reference [66]. While the implementation of these low-level operators requires great care because of the numerous pointers to handle, the resulting modular code is more robust and easier to maintain.

Hierarchy

The hierarchical formulation of radiosity is one of the most important advances towards making the method practical. Both the reduction in complexity and the possibility of adjusting the computational effort according to the desired precision are valuable features that should be integrated in a modern simulation tool.

To this end a hierarchical structure must be maintained that can either be a quadtree with pointers to the appropriate elements of the underlying topological structure, or a custom structure built on top of a winged-edge model. The quadtree structure is particularly easy to implement, and can easily be maintained in parameter space if curved surfaces are used. However, it may be difficult to use with arbitrarily shaped patches because of its fixed quaternary subdivision scheme. Custom hierarchical structures can be derived from a topological mesh by storing a linked list of all subpatches at each level of the hierarchy.

A.1.3 Accurate treatment of color

The sensation of color is a very important aspect of our visual experience, thus brightness variations alone do not suffice to characterize an image. For realistic image synthesis it is crucial to be able to faithfully represent the color of various objects, including some subtle effects such as color bleeding. The balance of colors plays a key role in creating the atmosphere of a scene, and color variations must be accurately reproduced to allow any aesthetic judgement. In particular, applications such as architectural or lighting design often require the simulation of complex illumination conditions involving different types of light sources with different colors. Examples include the combination of overhead fluorescent lighting and incandescent light, or a mixture of artificial light and daylight. In such cases, very precise handling and reproduction of color is needed. Among the literature on color science, the monograph by Wyszecki and Stiles [201] provides a good starting point for the interested reader. Some of the specific issues encountered in computer graphics are discussed in a book by Hall [74].

Color is not a relevant phenomenon outside the domain of visible light. Thus the material presented in this section is particular to the domain of realistic image synthesis.

Color reproduction

The physical basis for color is the variation of light intensity with wavelength. The color of a given radiation is completely specified by its spectral distribution, that is, the relative strength of the radiation at all visible wavelengths. An example of a *spectrum* representing the variation of spectral radiance as a function of wavelength was shown in Figure 2.5.

Fortunately, it is not necessary to completely specify the spectrum at all wavelengths to characterize the color perceived by a human observer. Several different spectra can in fact create the same impression of color, a phenomenon called *metamerism*. Studies in human vision show that in practice color can be represented in a three-dimensional space, because of the existence of three different types of color-sensitive receptor cells on the retina. A number of such three-dimensional spaces can be defined, by choosing three basis functions across the spectrum. Integrating a spectrum against these functions yields three scalar coordinates. Metamers of a given color are spectra that share the same three coordinates.

Metamerism is the rationale behind color CRT[3] technology, where the color sensation is created by mixing light from three different phospor types. In theory it is possible to reproduce any color sensation using three basis functions as represented by the monitor's red, green, and blue phospors. However, this would require negative scaling in some cases, and cannot be realized in practice. Thus only a limited range of colors can be reproduced on a CRT display.[4]

The CIE (Commission Internationale de l'Eclairage) standardized a set of three basis functions and the associated color space, known as CIE *XYZ* space. The corresponding basis functions $x(\lambda)$, $y(\lambda)$, and $z(\lambda)$ are plotted in Figure A.3.

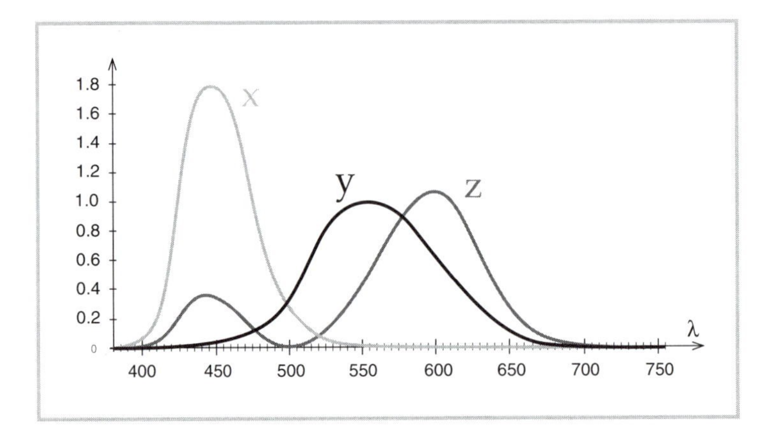

FIGURE A.3 CIE 1931 x, y, and z basis functions.

The *XYZ* color coordinates of a spectrum $L(\lambda)$ are determined by integrating it over the visible domain, weighted by the three basis functions:

$$X = \int L(\lambda)x(\lambda)d\lambda \quad \textbf{(A.1)}$$

[3]Cathode ray tube: refers to the vacuum tube used in television sets. This paragraph also applies to more recent technologies such as color LCD screens.

[4]This should be familiar to anybody who has tried to display a bright saturated yellow on a computer screen.

$$Y = \int L(\lambda)y(\lambda)d\lambda \quad \text{(A.2)}$$

$$Z = \int L(\lambda)z(\lambda)d\lambda\,. \quad \text{(A.3)}$$

The CIE basis functions were chosen to meet the following criteria. First, they all integrate to one over the visible spectrum. Therefore a "flat" spectrum for white light has coordinates $(1, 1, 1)$. Furthermore, all physically realizable colors lie in the first octant of *XYZ* space, thus no negative coordinates can exist. Finally one of the functions (y) is proportional to the luminous efficiency function that was introduced in Section 2.1.3. This means that the Y coordinate of a radiance spectrum is proportional to its luminance. Tabulated data for the CIE basis functions are available from several sources [201, 88, 74].

All points on a ray emanating from the origin in *XYZ* space represent variations of the same color, with different luminances. Thus it is possible to select two independent *chromaticity coordinates* by choosing a representative on each such line, for instance in the $X + Y + Z = 1$ plane. A spectrum's chromaticity is then represented by (x, y), with

$$x = \frac{X}{X + Y + Z} \quad \text{(A.4)}$$

$$y = \frac{Y}{X + Y + Z}\,. \quad \text{(A.5)}$$

To reproduce a color on a given CRT monitor, the chromaticities of the monitor phosphors must be known, as well as the monitor's "white point" [74]. These coordinates form a transformation matrix that can be inverted to yield the appropriate *RGB* coordinates from CIE *XYZ* coordinates. *RGB* coordinates specify the scaling factor for each of the primary colors associated with the monitor's phosphors. Note that the transformation is different for each monitor since phosphor chromaticities and white points vary from one model to the next. If the exact phosphor chromaticities are not known, the transformation associated with a reference monitor can be used. For example the conversion between CIE *XYZ* space and the *RGB* space for a standard NTSC[5] monitor is performed using the two inverse matrices:

$$\begin{bmatrix} X \\ Y \\ Z \end{bmatrix} = \begin{bmatrix} 0.67 & 0.21 & 0.14 \\ 0.33 & 0.71 & 0.08 \\ 0.00 & 0.08 & 0.78 \end{bmatrix} \begin{bmatrix} R \\ G \\ B \end{bmatrix} \quad \text{(A.6)}$$

$$\begin{bmatrix} R \\ G \\ B \end{bmatrix} = \begin{bmatrix} 1.730 & -0.482 & -0.261 \\ -0.814 & 1.652 & -0.023 \\ 0.083 & -0.169 & 1.284 \end{bmatrix} \begin{bmatrix} X \\ Y \\ Z \end{bmatrix} \quad \text{(A.7)}$$

This introduction to colorimetry shows that it is possible to display color information relatively accurately, provided the chromaticity information for the output device is known. Phosphor chromaticities vary slightly between different monitors, and local calibration

[5] National Television Systems Committee: the set of standard definitions for color television in the United States.

is necessary to ensure accurate reproduction. Having established a means for accurately displaying chromaticity, we now turn to the issues pertaining to the actual computation of radiance spectra.

Computing with color

The algorithms presented in this book are expressed for a monochromatic radiation, that is, light composed of a single wavelength. In order to capture color information, the computation must be carried out for all wavelengths across the spectrum of visible light. The treatment of color in radiosity is usually done through the use of a number of wavelength channels, with a set of surface radiosities for each channel. Different exitances and reflectivities are defined for each channel in the radiosity equation according to the spectral characteristics of the light sources and reflectors. Note however that the form factors, being purely geometric quantities, are computed only once no matter how many channels are being considered.

Following an established tradition in computer graphics, most radiosity implementations use three wavelength channels and map these channels directly to the three primary colors needed for CRT display, in effect performing the calculation in the monitor's *RGB* space. This practice is somewhat reasonable considering that most modeling systems do not operate with real spectral data but instead let users select colors directly on the screen using *RGB* coordinates.

However, it should be noted that the use of this perceptually based three-dimensional color model for color computation is not adequate. In particular, since each basis function covers a wide range of wavelengths, light at one wavelength actually influences other wavelengths as well. Furthermore, the computation is tied to a particular output device.

The CIE *XYZ* color space is preferred to the *RGB* space because it is device-independent, and particularly because the *Y* coordinate represents luminance. This means that it can be used to perform various computations such as luminance gradients for adaptive subdivision. However, in *XYZ* space the problem of "wavelength crosstalk" remains present.

Whenever accurate results are desired in terms of colorimetry, all computation should be carried out in the wavelength domain, before performing any integration against perceptual basis functions. Only after the results are obtained in the spectral domain is the final transformation to *XYZ* or the monitor's *RGB* actually made.

Typical reflectance spectra are continuous functions of wavelength across the visible spectrum. A wavelength sampling strategy can be based on the observation that such spectra can be approximated by low-order polynomials. Then, all spectral computation is performed at appropriate quadrature points chosen in the visible spectrum. A complete spectrum is reconstructed when needed by fitting a polynomial through the computed values. A small perceptual study determined that only four samples are sufficient to represent accurately all the reflectance spectra from a Macbeth ColorChecker chart [116]. Using wavelengths of 456.4, 490.9, 557.7, and 631.4 nm, the following transformation is used to obtain CIE chromaticity coordinates:

$$\begin{bmatrix} X \\ Y \\ Z \end{bmatrix} = \begin{bmatrix} 0.1986 & -0.0569 & 0.4934 & 0.4228 \\ -0.0034 & 0.1856 & 0.6770 & 0.1998 \\ 0.9632 & 0.0931 & 0.0806 & -0.0791 \end{bmatrix} \begin{bmatrix} L_{456.4} \\ L_{490.9} \\ L_{557.7} \\ L_{631.4} \end{bmatrix}. \quad \text{(A.8)}$$

This method is based on a perceptual assessment of the quality of color rendering, and provides a set of point samples that minimize the perceived error for smooth spectra. Thus it can be very inaccurate when rapid changes or even discontinuities exist in the spectra. *Line spectra*, in which a lot of power is concentrated in a narrow wavelength band, are common for artificial light fixtures with discharge lamps and require a more precise method. An example of a discontinuous spectrum is shown later in Figure A.4b.

Another sampling approach consists of subdividing the visible spectrum into a set of continuous domains and obtaining average spectral values for each domain using a box filter. A separate computation is carried out for each domain, and the final spectrum is obtained using the same box filters for reconstruction. This technique can be parametrized by the number of samples and is easily applicable to any wavelength domain. Its application to the visible domain has produced good results with nine wavelengths bands, whose boundaries were determined by trial and error [74]. This scheme can be applied to more general basis functions, but the selection of appropriate basis functions remains a difficult issue [131].

When artificial lights with line spectra are present, it may be better to represent separately the continuous portion of the spectrum and the spectral lines generated by the light sources. Although this method must be tuned to the light sources in a scene, it will guarantee that the power concentrated in these lines is not spread across a larger portion of the spectrum. The method becomes cumbersome when multiple luminaires with different spectral characteristics are present. We discuss spectral information for light sources in the next section.

Where to stop?

From the previous discussion it is apparent that two ingredients are needed for proper handling of color issues. The first is that all calculation be performed on accurate representations of the relevant spectra, either using a sufficient number of samples or carefully chosen samples. The second requirement is that the problem of color reproduction be addressed during rendering and display.

Although conceptually simple, the transformation from spectral information to *XYZ* space and display *RGB* space adds to the complexity of the global illumination simulator. It also introduces new issues such as the choice of a storage format for simulation results. It makes sense to avoid expressing spectral quantities in a form that depends on the specifics of a monitor, therefore *RGB* seems a bad choice. *XYZ* offers the advantage of device-independence, making it possible to display a consistent image on various displays.

When measured data for light source spectra or reflectances is not available, it is a waste to devote any effort to precise color treatment. If all color information is specified on a particular monitor, then it makes sense to use this monitor's *RGB* space for all computations.

Paradoxically, it may appear that the image looks worse after applying a proper reproduction procedure. This happens when displaying an image of a scene lit using incandescent light, where a distinct reddish tint becomes immediately noticeable. The problem is that our visual system constantly adjusts its color balance to help us perceive the natural color of objects independently of the illumination conditions. This "automatic recalibration" effect reduces the need for absolute color treatment to cases in which distinct sources of illumination with different spectral characteristics coexist in the environment.

An extensive treatment of color should deal with cases where the computed spectrum cannot be reproduced on a given monitor. A "best" replacement must be found within the given gamut [168]. Finally color issues should be addressed together with the problems of perceived brightness and optimal use of a monitor's limited dynamic range, which are discussed below.

A.1.4 General light sources and radiosity

In the derivation of the radiosity equation in Chapter 3, an assumption was made that light sources were emitting light *diffusely*. This assumption is convenient in that it allows us to treat light sources as regular patches, distinguished only by non-zero exitances. However it is questionable from the point of view of realism, since real light sources are almost never diffuse. Furthermore, some light sources are difficult to represent in the form of actual light-emitting objects. This is the case for sunlight, since light is scattered from the sky. Fortunately, nondiffuse and special light sources can be included in a radiosity simulator, even when only ideal diffuse reflectors are treated.

Reflected light typically represents only a small component of the total luminous flux leaving a light source, and this second-order effect can be safely neglected by considering that light sources do not reflect light at all. Therefore their influence on the environment is completely prescribed by their emissive characteristics. In contrast to nondiffuse reflectors, for which the reflected radiance distribution depends on the distribution of incoming energy, light sources possess a fixed radiance distribution. Thus they can be represented in the radiosity algorithm as a special class of objects that emit but do not receive light.

Most image synthesis algorithms offer a variety of light source models, often with no physical basis. These include for example point light sources and parallel light sources. Despite their lack of physical realism, such sources can be included in a radiosity simulator, for compatibility with other rendering systems. One difficulty is that these special light sources are not represented as surface patches, and thus may require a reformulation of the radiosity equations in which they are involved. For instance, point light sources and parallel light sources have no physical area, and are best described in terms of total emitted power. Alternatively, a fictitious unit area can be attributed to these lights for convenience, so that their power and exitance can be used interchangeably.

Modified form factors are computed to and from the light sources to account for the inconstant distribution of light. Note that since light sources do not reflect light we are not interested in computing the energy they receive, but only the energy they distribute. Starting with the definition of the form factor given in Section 3.1.4, a more general formulation can be obtained for the form factor from a light source (patch P_i) to a patch P_j:

$$F_{ij} = \frac{1}{A_i} \int_{x \in P_i} \int_{y \in P_j} S(\theta) \frac{\cos\theta'}{r^2} V(x, y) dy dx \,. \quad \textbf{(A.9)}$$

In Equation A.9, the directional characteristics of the light source are represented by a distribution function, $S(\theta)$, that describes the relative power distribution per unit solid angle [46]. This function is normalized such that

$$\int_{\Omega} S(\theta) d\omega = 1 \,,$$

and in the ideal diffuse case it reduces to

$$S(\theta) = \frac{\cos\theta}{\pi} \,.$$

Note that for point or parallel light sources no integration over P_i is performed, and the $1/A_i$ factor is removed. The following light source types are commonly offered for image synthesis applications.

- **Parallel light source**: This is used to model sunlight and can be thought of as an infinitely large light source at an infinite distance.
- **Spotlight**: This is a point light source with non-uniform exitance. One possible choice for distribution functions is

  $$S(\theta) = \frac{\cos^n\theta}{n+1}$$

  where θ is the angle with a reference direction [98]. Another possibility is to extract a distribution function from luminaire data, as explained in the next section.
- **Isotropic light source**: This is a point light source that radiates uniformly in all directions, with a distribution function of $S(\theta) = \frac{1}{4\pi}$.

A.1.5 Using measured radiometric data

For all applications that require accurate quantitative prediction, measured data must be used as input to the simulation. Here we discuss some of the possible sources of information for common illumination parameters.

Light sources

Two major types of information must be known for light sources, namely their spectral and directional characteristics. This information is made available by most manufacturers in machine-readable form, using a standard format defined by the Illumination Engineering Society [89].

Directional information is specified using a *goniometric diagram.* This plots the candlepower distribution as a function of angle from the principal direction. This plot is sometimes given for a prescribed total luminous power of 1000 lumens, in which case the effective total luminous power must also be given to allow proper scaling. Unless the luminaire has cylindrical symmetry, goniometric diagrams are given for multiple planes. Candlepower values for directions in other planes must be interpolated from the supplied data. For better results, elliptic interpolation can be used to obtain a smooth distribution [104]. Candlepower is expressed in candelas, defined as lumens per unit solid angle. Thus a luminance value for a given direction is obtained by dividing the candlepower value by the projected area of the light source for that direction. An example of a goniometric diagram is shown in Figure A.4a. From this plot we can compute the luminance for a light source area of 0.1 m $\times$ 0.2 m, in the direction 45° from normal, as $I = 35$ cd/(0.1 m $\times$ 0.2 m $\times$ cos 45°) $= 2475$ cd/m^2. As mentioned in the previous section, a relative power distribution function $S(\theta)$ can be computed by scaling the candlepower distribution function by the reciprocal of its integral over the entire sphere of directions.

Spectral information is given in the form of a relative spectral power distibution, $D(\lambda)$, a dimensionless quantity. Figure A.4b shows an example of such a spectral distribution.

Radiometric information such as spectral radiance can be obtained in the following manner. The relative spectral distribution of radiance is the same as the one specified. Let us denote by c the coefficient of proportionality:

$$L^{\lambda}(\lambda) = cD(\lambda)\,.$$

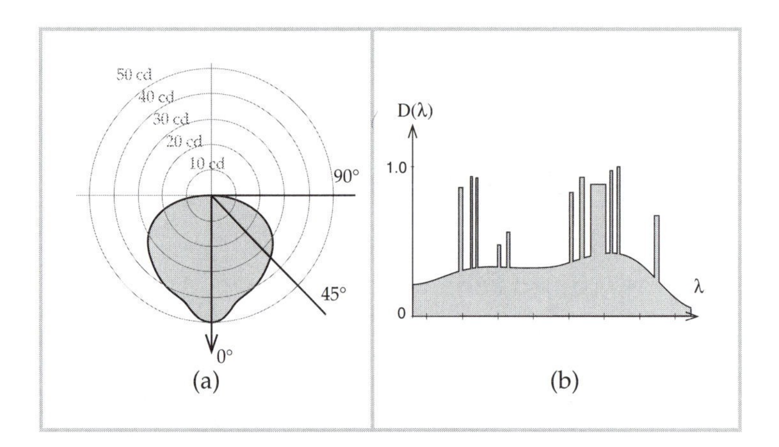

FIGURE A.4 Fictitious manufacturer data for a light source: (a) goniometric candlepower diagram; (b) relative spectral power distribution (adapted from Rushmeier [139]).

Then the light source luminance in the direction of interest, L, obtained from the goniometric diagram, can be recomputed as the integral of spectral radiance weighted by the luminous efficiency function $V(\lambda)$ that was defined in Section 2.1.3:

$$L = \int_{380nm}^{770nm} c D(\lambda) V(\lambda) d\lambda \,. \tag{A.10}$$

Using this formula, c can be computed, and spectral radiance is deduced from spectral luminous power:

$$L^{\lambda}(\lambda) = \frac{L}{\int_{380nm}^{770nm} D(\lambda) V(\lambda) d\lambda} D(\lambda) \,. \tag{A.11}$$

Skylight

Skylight may be taken into account by defining a special light source with non-uniform radiance. The irradiance resulting from skylight illumination must then be computed at each surface or vertex by integrating the skylight radiance distribution over the visible portions of the hemisphere [124].

Normalized distributions for sky luminance under a variety of conditions have been adopted by the CIE [34]. For an overcast sky, sky luminance is related to the zenithal luminance L_z by

$$L(\theta) = L_z \frac{1 + 2\cos\theta}{3} \,. \tag{A.12}$$

The zenithal radiance in turn depends on the height of the sun. In this equation, θ represents the angle between the zenith and the direction of interest. This simple luminance distribution corresponds to a uniform and thick cloud cover.

For a clear sky the following formula gives the sky luminance:

$$L(\theta, \gamma) = L_z \frac{(0.91 + 10e^{-3\gamma} + 0.45\cos^2\gamma)(1 - e^{-0.32\sec\theta})}{(0.91 + 10e^{-3\theta_0} + 0.45\cos^2\theta_0)(1 - e^{-0.32})} \,, \tag{A.13}$$

where γ is the angle between the direction of the sun and the direction of interest, and θ_0 is the angle between the zenith and the sun direction. This model is expensive to compute and yet does not account for all possible skylighting effects. Note that the spectral distribution of skylight is not predicted by these models. A more detailed discussion of several aspects of skylight illumination is available in references [101, 171].

Reflectances

As for light sources, reflectance data consists of both spectral and directional information. Spectral data is relatively easy to measure using an *integrating sphere* coupled to a spectrophotometer. The data for some pure materials can also be found in many handbooks [179, 144, 53].

Directional information is much more difficult to obtain, partly because of the expensive gonioreflectometers needed to fully characterize BRDFs. Furthermore, measurements produce massive amounts of data in the case of anisotropic reflectors, and a compact representation such as the one introduced in Section 7.4.3 is required to efficiently store and process this information.

Current research efforts include the design of low-cost reflectometers, together with the development of parametric models that reduce the amount of information to be passed along to the simulator [188]. One of the goals of this research is to assemble a library of reflectance data for public use. Research is also being conducted in providing the means to perform on-site measurements of materials, a necessary condition for accurate architectural simulation and site planning [186].

Consistency of measurements

Since physical light sources are defined with quantities based on precise units, it is very important to ensure that all these quantities are consistent. In particular, the distances and sizes in the geometric description of the scene should all be expressed in consistent physical units such as meters. This requirement is too often overlooked, especially when different CAD data files are combined to build a model. The typical result of an incorrect scale in the geometry of the scene is a very dark or very bright image. Consider for example illuminating with a standard lighting fixture a room the size of a football field.

A.1.6 Dynamic-range issues

Displaying an image in a realistic fashion is not an easy task because of the severe limitations of both printing technologies and CRT monitors, whose dynamic range is not sufficient to represent real-world scenes. For example the range of possible luminances in the physical world is 10^{-6} to 10^{4} cd/m^2, while luminances from a monitor are typically between 1 and 100 cd/m^2. This section discusses what transformations should be applied to the computed radiosities in order to produce an effective image on a display with limited dynamic range.

Characteristics of monitors

A first group of problems are due to the specific technology of CRT monitors. The displayed intensity is controlled by the electron gun voltage, which is itself generated from a digital pixel value by a digital-to-analog converter. The relationship between pixel value $n \in [0..1]$ and phosphor luminance L_{ph} is highly nonlinear, and is usually approximated by a power law

$$L_{ph} = L_{ph}^{max} n^{\gamma} , \tag{A.14}$$

where the exponent γ varies slightly from one monitor to the next (usually $\gamma \approx 2.4 \pm 0.2$). Some display devices provide built-in "gamma-correction," in the form of a lookup table used to map user pixel values to CRT gun voltages using a power law of the form

$$n = \left(n_{user}\right)^{\frac{1}{\gamma}} .$$

This in effect compensates for the nonlinearity of the monitor. If such a correction is not built in the display device, it should be explicitly computed and applied by the user.

The range of luminances that a monitor can produce depends not only on phosphor luminances, but also on the surrounding lighting conditions at viewing time. The lowest luminance will be that reflected on the screen from the environment. If we denote by L_{min} this minimum luminance level (which can be thought of as ambient lighting), then the *display luminance* leaving the surface of the screen is

$$L_d = L_{ph} + L_{min} , \qquad \textbf{(A.15)}$$

and is always contained between L_{min} and $L_{max} = L_{ph}^{max} + L_{min}$.

In many cases the level of ambient light around monitors is quite significant compared to the maximum phosphor luminance, resulting in a limited contrast ($L_{max}/L_{min} \approx 35$). The key to successful image display is to make optimal use of this restricted range of luminance, thus producing an impression that is subjectively similar to what a real observer would experience if subjected to the computed luminances.

Adaptation levels

Fortunately, it is possible to fool the human eye into believing that the image on a CRT screen represents a scene with much higher or lower luminance values than what is actually displayed. This is due to the fact that our visual system is not sensitive to absolute luminance levels, but instead to relative contrast within a limited range around some mean level determined by the *adaptation level* of the viewer. In other words the eye adjusts to the distribution of luminance, allowing us to see quite clearly even in dim environments. Adaptation may require some time though, as evidenced by the uncomfortable experience of driving into or out of a tunnel in bright sunlight. Adaptation means that it is possible to reproduce a given subjective impression by controlling the distribution of displayed luminance around the viewer's adaptation level.

Since no precise definition is available, the adaptation level is usually simply represented by a luminance value: for instance the *display adaptation level* for viewing a CRT monitor could be taken to be some fraction of the maximum phosphor luminance. Values proposed in the literature range from $L_{d,a} = 0.5L_{ph}^{max}$ [190] to $L_{d,a} = L_{ph}^{max}$ [181]. The maximum phosphor luminance level must be measured using a luminance meter, a typical value being 85 cd/m^2.

The *world adaptation level* for the computed image can be estimated by using a global average of all computed pixel luminances. Because of the wide range of luminances that can coexist in a scene, a logarithmic average gives the best results [181]. The world adaptation level is found from the following equation:

$$\log_{10}(L_{w,a}) = E\left[\log_{10}(L_w)\right] + 0.84 .$$

In this equation $E[X]$ denotes the statistical mean across the image. Instead of using a global average across the entire image, it may be appropriate to use a spatial map of local adaptation levels. This is a topic of ongoing research [30].

Transforming radiance values

Once the world and display adaptation levels are known, a transformation must be defined that will map world luminances to display luminances in a manner that preserves a high perceptual fidelity.

The simplest such transformation from world luminance to display luminance is a linear mapping. This simple mapping is appealing because it maintains luminance ratios, also known as *contrast* [190]. Experimental studies show that the minimum discernible difference in luminance is related to the adaptation level by a simple formula. The luminance scaling factor can be chosen such that this luminance difference in the real world corresponds to the luminance difference in viewing conditions. This means that details that would not be perceived under the real conditions are not visible. Thus the viewer's "resolving power" is the same, both in the real world and the displayed world. Based on experimental work relating resolving power and adaptation levels, the scaling factor can be defined as [35, 190]:

$$s = \left[\frac{1.219 + L_{d,a}^{0.4}}{1.219 + L_{w,a}^{0.4}}\right]^{2.5} . \tag{A.16}$$

The display luminance is then defined by

$$L_d = s \cdot L_w . \tag{A.17}$$

A more sophisticated transformation from world luminance to display luminance, based on other experimental studies relating brightness perception to luminance levels, results in the following nonlinear mapping [181]:

$$L_d = (L_w)^{\frac{\alpha_w}{\alpha_d}} \, 10^{\left(\frac{\beta_w - \beta_d}{\alpha_d}\right)} , \tag{A.18}$$

where α and β are computed from the world and display adaptation levels:

$$\alpha = 0.4 \log_{10} L_a + 2.92 , \tag{A.19}$$

$$\beta = -0.4(\log_{10} L_a)^2 - 2.584 \log_{10} L_a + 2.0208 . \tag{A.20}$$

This nonlinear scaling has the effect that darker scenes tend to lose contrast while bright scenes appear with very high contrast, the average luminance being roughly equivalent in all cases. This appropriately models the response of the human visual system.

Color Plate 45 demonstrates this property on a test scene. All images represent the same environment, which consists of ideal diffuse surfaces illuminated by a single extended light source with adjustable power. The image in the lower-left corner is displayed using the common linear scaling strategy, whereby the maximum pixel value is attributed to the brightest nonemitting surface. Since the radiosity algorithm is linear with respect to the exitance of the light source, this simplistic scaling strategy produces identical images for all possible light source settings. The other images correspond to five different emitter strengths, each increasing by a factor of 100, and are displayed with the nonlinear mapping of Equation A.18. Note how the use of appropriate adaptation levels and nonlinear scaling conveys a sense of the overall brightness of each scene.

In summary, a transformation from world luminance to display luminance must be performed to achieve a perceptually accurate display. Equation A.17 or Equation A.18 can be used for this purpose. Pixel values are then computed from the display luminance using equations A.14 and A.15. Equation A.15 must be inverted to express the desired pixel value as a function of phosphor luminance, and should be replaced by a linear equation if built-in gamma-correction is used. The necessary inputs for this transformation are the maximum phosphor luminance L_{ph}^{max} and the ambient luminance for the viewing conditions L_{min}. Both these quantities can be measured using a luminance meter.

Color and luminance

The preceding discussion of dynamic-range mapping in terms of luminance, restricted us to a grayscale image. A luminance channel can easily be obtained for a computed image, since it is proportional to the Y coordinate in the CIE XYZ space. A possible algorithm to generate images would then be to

1. convert the radiance values to XYZ space;
2. perform the dynamic-range mapping on the Y (luminance) channel;
3. transform the (x, y) chromaticity of the radiance spectrum to RGB values for each pixel;
4. scale the RGB values by the computed luminance factor.

Such a treatment of color attempts to preserve chromaticities while adjusting luminances; however, it is inappropriate since *color adaptation* also takes place in our visual system. This subject has received little attention in computer graphics and is a current area of research.

Antialiasing

A particularly noticeable problem with high dynamic-range images appears when antialiasing is performed on the world radiance or luminance values. For instance when a luminaire is visible, with a luminance that is orders of magnitude greater than that of other objects, a pixel partially covering the light source will receive a very large luminance.

After mapping luminances to display values, this pixel is likely to be set to the maximum value, as will all the pixels completely covered by the light source. Thus the antialiasing procedure will be defeated and the outline of the luminaire will appear jagged.

A simple solution to this problem consists of performing all antialiasing operations after the luminance-to-pixel transformation. Note that this requires some knowledge of the viewing conditions, thus defeating display-independence. In many cases it is preferable to store the result of the simulation in a floating-point format to represent the high dynamic range of luminances [187]. In that case antialiasing must be performed according to an approximate viewing setup.

A.1.7 Application to animation

Most applications of computer graphics involve movement and animation. Therefore a natural question is whether global illumination methods are adequate for dynamic environments.

As mentioned in Section 3.2 the radiosity solution is independent of viewing conditions. On the other hand, the solution is very sensitive to a modification of the scene's geometry. Therefore radiosity methods appear well suited only for a very restricted sort of animation, namely *viewpoint animation*, where the only time-dependent quantities are the viewing parameters. Fortunately, in architectural applications it is common for the model to remain fixed while the user explores the space.

The incremental algorithm of Section 6.2 can be used for interactive proofing of various illumination or design configurations, but it is not appropriate when a conventional animation sequence is sought. This is because of the differences in adaptive meshing and solution convergence for different frames; visually distracting inconsistencies would become readily noticeable.

Monte Carlo simulation is likely to provide better continuity between frames of an animation because the error is in the form of noise, which is much less distracting than coherent illumination defects. However, the cost of performing a full Monte Carlo simulation for each frame is equally likely to be prohibitive. Some efficiency can be gained by exploiting temporal coherence. This requires consideration of a four-dimensional representation of objects [65].

A.1.8 Interaction

The nature of the global illumination phenomena is complex, and the resulting simulation methods are all expensive in terms of computer resources. On the other hand many of the proposed applications require interaction, and thus a very short feedback loop. The dual nature of the radiosity simulation as a powerful numerical simulation tool and an interactive design tool can give rise to two very distinct implementations: a batch process for performing numerical computations, or an interactive application using special-purpose graphics capabilities.

As explained in Chapter 6, interactive walkthroughs are possible in a radiosity solution. Since it incurs almost no extra cost, this feature should always be exploited in a practical radiosity system, by making sure that the relevant information is easily accessible. The information needed is at minimum a set of polygons, with a number of radiosity values at each vertex. An *RGB* color can be derived from the spectral radiosities at each vertex, and then interpolated across the polygons.

Note that for diffuse scenes, shading calculation is neither necessary nor desirable in the viewing stage, since shadows and variations in illuminations are all expressed in the radiosity solution. Therefore a correct way to specify the color of the polygons is through the *ambient color* property available in most graphics languages.

However, highlights can be added to the scene at very little cost by taking advantage of the specular lighting model offered by most graphics hardware. Color Plate 26 shows an example of a scene rendered using a graphics accelerator with Phong shading. Highlights are useful in that they increase the visual richness of the scene and aid our three-dimensional perception. Note however that this remains an ad hoc technique that requires skillful manual placement of the associated point light sources. In any case, the resulting highlights do not have any physical meaning, and they detract from the accuracy of the radiosity solution.

A.2 Useful enhancements

The other implementation choices or recommendations reviewed here are suggested as important features of a radiosity computation system. They either improve the quality of the results by incorporating surface detail or improve the modularity and extensibility of the software by reflectance encapsulation.

A.2.1 Flexible computation of the form factors

Several form factor computation techniques allow a trade-off between performance and accuracy. It is very important to carry such choices all the way to the user, who is the only one in a position to decide what resources to allocate for a given simulation. Therefore the computation algorithm should be parametrized and cover a wide range of possibilities, from a "quick and dirty" approximation to a high-quality simulation.

The ray casting technique for the computation of form factors (Section 5.1.3) is a good example of such a parametrized method, where the number of sample points used on radiosity emitters can be varied at will. This method is being used in commercial products both because of this flexibility and because computing radiosity directly at polygon vertices simplifies the display process. Furthermore this algorithm allows for a fairly robust radiosity system.

This approach is not optimal, however, in that it treats all patches in a uniform manner, thereby potentially wasting computation resources. The notion of a hierarchy should always find its place in a modern radiosity implementation. This can mean a fairly simple modification of the code. All that is needed is to build a hierarchical data structure and to allow shooting to take place at various levels. A push/pull procedure must also be implemented to insure a correct distribution of energy, as explained in Section 4.4.3.

A.2.2 Surface detail: texture and bump mapping

As mentioned earlier, a key ingredient for realistic image synthesis, in addition to correct lighting, is the visual richness of the model. This can be increased by using a more detailed geometrical model of the objects in the scene, or through the inclusion of *surface detail* that does not contribute to the global solution. Typical examples of surface detail enrichment in image synthesis are texture mapping, which is the small-scale modulation of surface color, and bump mapping, which is the small-scale modulation of surface orientation. Both techniques are easily incorporated in a radiosity simulation package.

Texture mapping

As observed in the discussion of hierarchical methods (Section 4.4), the fine illumination details on a patch P_i have little importance as far as the illumination of other surfaces is concerned. Therefore when such detail is given by a texture map, an average reflectance ρ_i^{av}, computed from the texture map, can be used in the interreflection calculation. An average radiosity value is thus computed for the entire patch. For image rendering, the complete, detailed texture is used at each pixel to modulate the irradiance value H_i, which represents the incident flux density for patch i:

$$B_i(x) = E_i + \rho_i(x) H_i \,. \tag{A.21}$$

The irradiance value is itself obtained by noting that

$$H_i = \frac{B_i - E_i}{\rho_i^{av}} \,. \tag{A.22}$$

Texture mapping was used in Color Plates 7, 33, 34, and 35. Note that since a distinct color is used at each pixel, rendering must be done on a per-pixel basis. However, some recent graphics hardware products offer real-time texture mapping of polygons. Such systems can be used for interactive walkthrough animation. When texture mapping a polygon, color information from the texture is used together with the polygon color that is interpolated from the vertices. In order for the texture map to appear consistent with the scene illumination, it should be used to modulate the illumination computed during the radiosity process. Therefore the "color" specified at the vertices must be the irradiance value H_i from Equation A.22. Locations within the coordinate system local to the texture must be determined for all vertices.

Bump mapping

Bump mapping is the common name given to the operation of perturbing the normal of a surface according to a small-scale map, just like texture mapping perturbs its color.

Since the irradiance received at a surface depends heavily on its orientation, perturbing the orientation creates illumination variations that have a dramatic visual impact: the distinctive surface characteristics of various materials can be carried to the viewer in this way.

Since the shading calculation when using bump mapping depends on the perturbed normal, it must be evaluated at each pixel. This makes it more computationally demanding than texture mapping. Bump mapping is thus well suited to the Monte Carlo path tracing approach presented in Section 8.4. Every time the surface normal is used, such as when selecting a direction of reflection, the perturbation from the bump map is added to the original normal vector.

The inclusion of bump mapping in a radiosity simulator requires a small modification of the algorithm. Since radiosity is computed and stored on the surfaces, the range of variation of the surface normal across a given patch must be represented somehow. One possibility is to compute several radiosity values for each patch, each corresponding to different orientations of the surface normal. The radiosity corresponding to the average patch normal is used for interreflection calculations. At rendering time, when the perturbed normal is computed for a given pixel, radiosity values corresponding to the same normal are selected at each neighboring vertex (typically they are interpolated from the available radiosities). A normal interpolation step is then performed to yield the radiosity value for the current pixel [24].

A.2.3 Reflectance modeling

Data encapsulation

In many applications where precise results are sought, it is important to be able to simulate the most general class of reflectance behaviors. Use of encapsulated data types allows an easy extension of a radiosity simulator to more general reflectances. An ideal diffuse radiosity system can be built first and extended at a later stage to handle directional reflectors, provided the necessary interfaces are properly implemented.

This presentation is oriented towards the general two-pass method presented in Section 7.4. The key to extensibility is the design of appropriate data types to represent radiance distributions and general reflectances. General data types *reflectance* and *radiance distribution* can be defined, which map to scalar values in the ideal diffuse case, but map to more elaborate structures when needed. Care should be taken that all access and manipulation of radiometric quantities be done in a consistent way throughout the interface.

For this encapsulation to be effective, some operations in the radiosity algorithm must be expressed as operating on radiance distributions in order to apply in the context of directional reflectors. Although these operations reduce to scalar manipulations in the ideal diffuse case, they should be explicitly represented as radiometric computations, since they require some directional parameters that might not be otherwise available. Other operations, such as creation or deletion of reflectance or radiance variables, and file I/O routines, do not require special attention. There are two main operations requiring directional information:

- **Add incident contribution**: This operation updates the reflected radiance distribution in response to an incident energy flux. It requires knowledge of the incident direction relative to a local reference frame in order to allow proper evaluation of the BRDF. Note that it may be beneficial to maintain an irradiance value together with the radiance distribution: while in the ideal diffuse case radiosity and irradiance are simply proportional to each other, it will become difficult to compute irradiance when directional radiance distributions are represented. In the ideal diffuse case, all that is needed is a multiplication of the incident flux (obtained as the product of a form factor and a radiosity value) by the local diffuse reflectance.

- **Evaluate radiance**: This operation returns the radiance leaving a point in a given direction. In the ideal diffuse case this amounts to transforming the radiosity value into a radiance value (dividing by π), ignoring the direction altogether.

Note that the implementation of these operations must also consider the chosen spectral representation.

Representation using spherical harmonics

As mentioned in Chapter 7, one method for representing directional radiance distribution or BRDFs is to use a spherical harmonics expansion. Recall from Section 7.4.3 that there exists such an expansion for any square-integrable function defined on the sphere:

$$f(\theta, \phi) = \sum_{l=0}^{\infty} \sum_{m=-l}^{l} C_{l,m} \, Y_{l,m}(\theta, \phi) \,, \tag{A.23}$$

with coefficients given by

$$C_{l,m} = \int_0^{2\pi} \int_0^{\pi} f(\theta, \phi) \, Y_{l,m}(\theta, \phi) \, d\omega \,.$$

This section provides more details on how this representation can be created and manipulated. In real form, the normalized spherical harmonics are defined by

$$Y_{l,m}(\theta, \phi) = \begin{cases} N_{l,m} \, P_{l,m}(\cos\theta) \cos(m\phi) & \text{if } m > 0 \\ N_{l,0} \, P_{l,0}(\cos\theta)/\sqrt{2} & \text{if } m = 0 \\ N_{l,m} \, P_{l,|m|}(\cos\theta) \sin(|m|\phi) & \text{if } m < 0 \,, \end{cases} \tag{A.24}$$

where the normalizing constants, $N_{l,m}$, are given by

$$N_{l,m} = \sqrt{\frac{2l+1}{2\pi} \frac{(l-|m|)!}{(l+|m|)!}} \,, \tag{A.25}$$

and the $P_{l,m}(x)$ factors are *associated Legendre polynomials*. The latter can be evaluated with the recurrence relations

$$P_{l,m}(x) = \begin{cases} (1-2m)\sqrt{1-x^2}\,P_{m-1,m-1}(x) & \text{if } l = m \\ y\ x(2m+1)\,P_{m,m}(x) & \text{if } l = m+1 \\ x\left(\frac{2l-1}{l-m}\right)P_{l-1,m}(x) - \left(\frac{l+m-1}{l-m}\right)P_{l-2,m}(x) & \text{otherwise.} \end{cases} \quad \textbf{(A.26)}$$

The base case is $P_{0,0}(x) = 1$. Applying these in conjunction with recurrence relations for generating

$$\sin(\phi), \sin(2\phi), \ldots, \sin(m\phi) \quad \text{and} \quad \cos(\phi), \cos(2\phi), \ldots, \cos(m\phi)\,,$$

it is possible to evaluate spherical harmonic expansions using approximately ten floating-point operations per coefficient and no trigonometric function evaluations whatsoever [134].

BRDF approximation

The first step in the manipulation of directional radiance distributions consists of approximating the BRDF for each material using spherical harmonics. This amounts to selecting a finite number of terms in the expansion and representing the dependence of the BRDF on the outgoing direction using a truncated expansion. The dependence in the incident angle can be handled in a variety of ways. In the general case of anisotropic BRDFs, each coefficient can be represented by another spherical harmonic expansion relative to the incident direction [199]. For the simpler case of an isotropic BRDF, the incident azimuth angle plays no role since

$$\rho(\theta_0, \phi_0, \theta, \phi) = \rho(\theta_0, \phi_0 + \pi - \phi, \theta, 0)\,,$$

and a scalar function $B_{l,m}(\theta)$ is used for each spherical harmonic in the BRDF approximation to represent the variation of the associated coefficient over the entire range of incident angles:

$$\rho(\theta_0, \phi_0, \theta, 0)\cos\theta_0 \approx \sum_{l=0}^{N}\sum_{m=-l}^{l} B_{l,m}(\theta)\, Y_{l,m}(\theta_0, \phi_0). \quad \textbf{(A.27)}$$

The BRDF parameters are expressed here as angles with respect to a fixed local coordinate system. The vertical axis of this coordinate system corresponds to the surface normal at the point of interest, and the other axes are arbitrary. The $\cos\theta_0$ factor is included at this stage because it reduces evaluation time, since any time the BRDF is used it is immediately multiplied by $\cos\theta_0$. This scaling also tends to reduce ringing in the approximation because it insures that the approximated function smoothly goes to zero at grazing angles.

One method for representing the $B_{l,m}$ functions is to select a number of incident angles

$$\theta_j, \ j = 0, 1..q,$$

where

$$0 = \theta_0 \leq \theta_1 \leq \cdots \leq \theta_q = \pi/2.$$

At each of these angles the following coefficient are computed

$$b^j_{l,m} = \int_0^\pi \int_0^\pi \rho(\theta_0, \phi_0, \theta_j, 0) \ \cos\theta_0 \ \ Y_{l,m}(\theta_0, \phi_0) \ \sin\theta_0 \, d\theta_0 \, d\phi_0 , \qquad \textbf{(A.28)}$$

and the coefficients for other angles are obtained by interpolation using a one-dimensional cubic spline through the points $(\theta_0, b^0_{l,m})$, $(\theta_1, b^1_{l,m})$, ..., $(\theta_q, b^q_{l,m})$. Figure A.5 shows a few selected spline curves representing the variation of spherical harmonics coefficients over the range of incident angles.

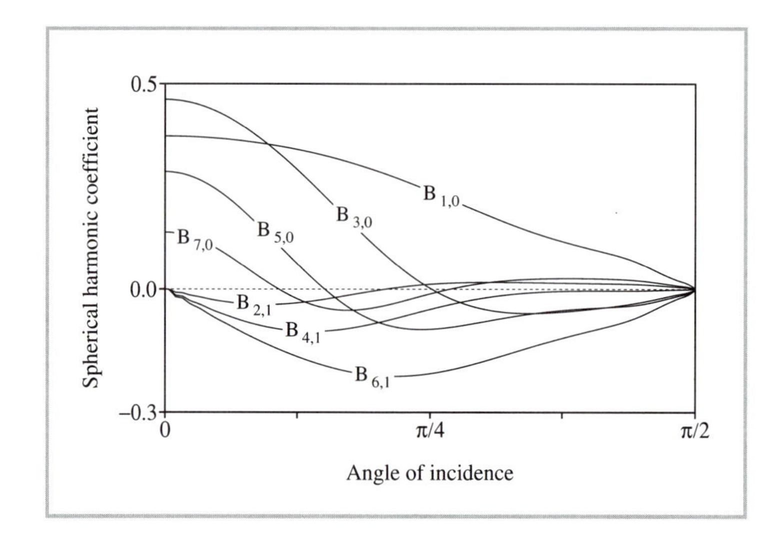

FIGURE A.5 Representation of the spherical harmonic coefficients using cubic splines.

The evaluation of Equation A.28 is expensive and must be carried out for a large number of (j, l, m) triplets. Fortunately this process is only done once for each BRDF, and the resulting spherical harmonic representation can be stored in a file for later use.

Note that the BRDF must be known in order to evaluate the integral in Equation A.28. If the BRDF is described with a set of measured values, an extra interpolation step is required to obtain a continuous function over the entire hemisphere.

For each distinct BRDF, q and a specific set of spherical harmonic coefficients must be selected to achieve the desired accuracy of approximation over all incident angles. The value of q affects the accuracy of the interpolation but does not otherwise influence the radiance distributions. In contrast, the number of coefficients used in the BRDF approximation directly determines the storage required for the radiance distributions. It is therefore important to keep this number reasonably small.

It may be practical to compute a large number of coefficients and store a precise description of the BRDF, and defer the selection of the number of coefficients to be used for computation until the actual simulation takes place. This allows the precision of the calculation to be adjusted depending on the resources available or the accuracy requirements for a particular run.

Finally, if the BRDF that we wish to approximate is only defined on the upper hemisphere, as with an opaque material, the function must be extended to the lower hemisphere before computing the approximation. This is done in such a way that the complete BRDF satisfies

$$\rho(\theta_0, \phi_0, \theta, 0) = -\rho(\pi - \theta_0, \phi_0, \theta, 0)\,. \tag{A.29}$$

This introduces a vertical symmetry that results in the elimination of all spherical harmonics for which $l + m$ is even. It also maintains C^1 continuity between the upper and lower hemispheres when the function is zero at the equator—a condition that is guaranteed if the $\cos\theta_0$ factor is included in the representation.

Operations on spherical harmonic coefficients

Within the framework of progressive radiosity, radiance distributions are computed incrementally by summing the directional distributions resulting from impinging shots. After accumulating the contributions from n sample points on other patches, the radiance distribution at vertex k on an isotropic surface is given by the following equation:

$$L_k(\theta_0, \phi_0) = \sum_{i=1}^{n} \Phi_i\, \rho_k(\theta_0, \phi_0, \theta_i, \phi_i)\,. \tag{A.30}$$

Here Φ_i is the incident flux density, or irradiance; θ_i is the polar angle of incidence; and ϕ_i is the azimuthal angle of incidence for the ith contribution.

We can interpret Equation A.30 as a sequence of four operations applied to the underlying BRDF ρ_k, for each contribution arriving at vertex k: retrieving the directional distribution for a given angle of incidence, scaling and rotating this distribution, and finally, adding it to the accumulated and unshot distributions stored at the vertex. Given a BRDF approximation of the form in Equation A.27 these operations are performed as follows:

1. For every radiance contribution we first evaluate the BRDF at the given angle of incidence, θ, by computing the spherical harmonic coefficients of the resulting directional distribution. This consists of evaluating an interpolating spline, $B_{l,m}$, for each coefficient.
2. Next, we scale the distribution by multiplying each of these coefficients by the incident flux density.
3. Assuming an isotropic BRDF, we rotate the distribution about the vertical axis, according to the incident azimuth angle, since

   $$\rho_k(\theta_0, \phi_0, \theta_i, \phi_i) = \rho_k(\theta_0, \phi_0 + \pi - \phi_i, \theta_i, 0)\,.$$

   This can be done by employing the following property of spherical harmonics that we present in real form:

   $$\begin{bmatrix} Y_{l,m}(\theta_0, \phi_0 + \alpha) \\ Y_{l,-m}(\theta_0, \phi_0 + \alpha) \end{bmatrix} = \begin{bmatrix} \cos(m\alpha) & -\sin(m\alpha) \\ \sin(m\alpha) & \cos(m\alpha) \end{bmatrix} \begin{bmatrix} Y_{l,m}(\theta_0, \phi_0) \\ Y_{l,-m}(\theta_0, \phi_0) \end{bmatrix}. \tag{A.31}$$

   This property follows from the definition of spherical harmonics given in Equation A.24. Rotation about this axis is therefore straightforward, and the usual symmetry of the BRDFs with respect to the incident plane[6] simplifies it even further. Because negatively subscripted spherical harmonics are odd functions with respect to ϕ_0, we are guaranteed that all such coefficients will vanish in the BRDF approximation. These coefficients reappear in the radiance distributions, however, because the symmetry is destroyed when the BRDFs undergo arbitrary rotations.
4. As the fourth and final step the resulting distribution is added to the current total by adding the corresponding coefficients.

It is apparent from these operations that summing scaled and rotated instances of a single representation introduces no additional coefficients once the symmetry has been broken. Therefore, *the storage required for a given radiance distribution does not grow as radiance is accumulated.* Furthermore, the radiance distributions retain the full accuracy of the original BRDF approximations.

To perform the shooting step, we must evaluate a radiance distribution in the directions of all vertices towards which energy is shot. This requires evaluating the $Y_{l,m}$ functions associated with the coefficients of the radiance distribution in each of these directions. These evaluations can be performed efficiently using the recurrence relations mentioned in Equation A.26.

---

[6] A common property that will be violated by anisotropic materials.

Bibliography

[1] Miguel P. N. Águas and Stefan Müller. Mesh redistribution in radiosity. In *Proceedings of Fourth Eurographics Workshop on Rendering*, pages 327–335. Eurographics, June 1993. Technical report EG 93 RW.

[2] John M. Airey, John R. Rohlf, and Frederick P. Brooks, Jr. Towards image realism with interactive update rates in complex virtual building environments. *Computer Graphics*, 24(2):41–50, March 1990.

[3] A. A. Appel. An efficient program for many-body simulation. *SIAM J. Sci. Stat. Computing*, 6(1):85–103, 1985.

[4] Arthur Appel. Some techniques for shading machine renderings of solids. *AFIPS 1968 Spring Joint Computer Conf.*, 32:37–45, 1968.

[5] James R. Arvo. Backward ray-tracing. In SIGGRAPH '86 course notes ("Developments in Ray Tracing"), August 1986. Also appeared in SIGGRAPH '89 course notes ("Radiosity"), August 1989.

[6] James R. Arvo, editor. *Graphics Gems II*. Academic Press, San Diego, 1991.

[7] James Arvo, Kenneth Torrance, and Brian Smits. A framework for the analysis of error in global illumination algorithms. In *Computer Graphics Proceedings, Annual Conference Series:* SIGGRAPH '94 (Orlando, FL). ACM SIGGRAPH, New York, July 1994.

[8] James Arvo. The irradiance jacobian for partially occluded polyhedral sources. In *Computer Graphics Proceedings, Annual Conference Series:* SIGGRAPH '94 (Orlando, FL). ACM SIGGRAPH, New York, July 1994.

[9] James Arvo and David Kirk. Particle transport and image synthesis. *Computer Graphics*, 24(3):63–66, August 1990.

[10] Larry Aupperle and Pat Hanrahan. A hierarchical illumination algorithm for surfaces with glossy reflection. In *Computer Graphics Proceedings, Annual Conference Series:* SIGGRAPH '93 (Anaheim, CA), pages 155–162.

[11] Larry Aupperle and Pat Hanrahan. Importance and discrete three point transport. In *Proceedings of Fourth Eurographics Workshop on Rendering*, pages 85–94. Eurographics, June 1993. Technical report EG 93 RW.

[12] Rui Manuel Bastos, António Augusto de Sousa, and Fernando Nunes Ferreira. Reconstruction of illumination functions using bicubic hermite interpolation. In *Proceedings of Fourth Eurographics Workshop on Rendering*, pages 317–326. Eurographics, June 1993. Technical report EG 93 RW.

[13] Daniel R. Baum, Stephen Mann, Kevin P. Smith, and James M. Winget. Making radiosity usable: Automatic preprocessing and meshing techniques for the generation of accurate radiosity solutions. *Computer Graphics*, 25(4):51–60, August 1991.

[14] Daniel R. Baum, Holly E. Rushmeier, and James M. Winget. Improving radiosity solutions through the use of analytically determined form-factors. *Computer Graphics*, 23(3):325–334, July 1989.

[15] Daniel R. Baum and James M. Winget. Real time radiosity through parallel processing and hardware acceleration. *Computer Graphics*, 24(2):67–75, March 1990.

[16] Larry Bergman, Henry Fuchs, Eric Grant, and Susan Spach. Image rendering by adaptive refinement. *Computer Graphics*, 20(4):29–38, August 1986.

[17] James F. Blinn. Models of light reflection for computer synthesized pictures. *Computer Graphics*, 11:192–198, August 1977.

[18] M. Quinn Brewster. *Thermal Radiative Transfer & Properties*. John Wiley & Sons, New York, 1992.

[19] Chris Buckalew and Donald Fussell. Illumination networks: Fast realistic rendering with general reflectance functions. *Computer Graphics*, 23(3):89–98, July 1989.

[20] Brian Cabral, Nelson L. Max, and Rebecca Springmayer. Bidirectional reflection functions from surface bump maps. *Computer Graphics*, 21(4):273–281, July 1987.

[21] A. T. Campbell III and Donald S. Fussell. Adaptive mesh generation for global diffuse illumination. *Computer Graphics*, 24(4):155–64, August 1990.

[22] Z. Cendes and S. Wong. c^1 quadratic interpolation over arbitrary point sets. *IEEE Computer Graphics and Applications*, 7(11), November 1987.

[23] Sudeb Chattopadhyay and Akira Fujimoto. Bi-directional ray tracing. In Tosiyasu Kunii, editor, *Computer Graphics International '87*, pages 335–343. Springer Verlag, Tokyo, 1987.

[24] Hong Chen and En-Hua Wu. An efficient radiosity solution for bump texture generation. *Computer Graphics*, 24(4):125–134, August 1990.

[25] Shenchang Eric Chen. Incremental radiosity: An extension of progressive radiosity to an interactive image synthesis system. *Computer Graphics*, 24(4):135–144, August 1990.

[26] Shenchang Eric Chen, Holly Rushmeier, Gavin Miller, and Douglass Turner. A progressive multi-pass method for global illumination. *Computer Graphics*, 25(4):165–174, July 1991.

[27] L. Paul Chew. Constrained Delaunay triangulations. *Algorithmica*, 4:97–108, 1989.

[28] L. Paul Chew. Guaranteed-quality triangular meshes. Technical report 89-983, Department of Computer Science, Cornell University, Ithaca, NY, April 1989.

[29] Norman Chin and Steven Feiner. Near real-time shadow generation using bsp trees. *Computer Graphics*, 23(3):99–106, July 1989.

[30] K. Chiu, M. Herf, P. Shirley, S. Swamy, C. Wang, and K. Zimmerman. Spatially nonuniform scaling functions for high contrast images. In *Proceedings Graphics Interface '93*, pages 245–253. Morgan Kaufmann, San Francisco, 1993.

[31] Per H. Christensen, David H. Salesin, and Tony D. DeRose. A continuous adjoint formulation for radiance transport. In *Proceedings of Fourth Eurographics Workshop on Rendering*, pages 95–104. Eurographics, June 1993. Technical report EG 93 RW.

[32] Per Christensen, Eric Stollnitz, David Salesin, and Tony DeRose. Wavelet radiance. In *Proceedings of Fifth Eurographics Workshop on Rendering* (Darmstadt, Germany), June 1994.

[33] C. G. Christou, B. G. Cumming, A. J. Parker, and A. P. Zisserman. Development of a radiosity-based image synthesis system to investigate vision. In SIGGRAPH '93 course notes (#22, "Making Radiosity Practical"), August 1993.

[34] CIE. Standardization of luminance distribution of clear skies. Publication TC 4.2, 1973.

[35] CIE. An analytic model for describing the influence of lighting parameters upon visual performance. Volume 1: Technical foundations. CIE 19/2.1, Technical Committee 3.1, 1981.

[36] Michael F. Cohen, Shenchang Eric Chen, John R. Wallace, and Donald P. Greenberg. A progressive refinement approach to fast radiosity image generation. *Computer Graphics*, 22(4):75–84, August 1988.

[37] Michael F. Cohen and Donald P. Greenberg. The hemi-cube: A radiosity solution for complex environments. *Computer Graphics*, 19(3):31–40, July 1985.

[38] Michael F. Cohen, Donald P. Greenberg, David S. Immel, and Philip J. Brock. An efficient radiosity approach for realistic image synthesis. *IEEE Computer Graphics and Applications*, 6(3):25–35, March 1986.

[39] Michael F. Cohen and John R. Wallace. *Radiosity and Realistic Image Synthesis*. Academic Press, Boston, 1993.

[40] Robert L. Cook. Stochastic sampling in computer graphics. *ACM Transactions on Graphics*, 5(1):51–72, January 1986.

[41] Robert L. Cook, Thomas Porter, and Loren Carpenter. Distributed ray tracing. *Computer Graphics*, 18:137–147, July 1984.

[42] Robert L. Cook and Kenneth E. Torrance. A reflectance model for computer graphics. *ACM Transactions on Graphics*, 1:7–24, 1982.

[43] R. Courant and D. Hilbert. *Methods of Mathematical Physics*. Interscience Publishers, Inc., New York, 1953.

[44] Franklin C. Crow. Summed-area tables for texture mapping. *Computer Graphics*, 18:207–212, July 1984.

[45] P. M. Dew, T. R. Heywood, and R. A. Earnshaw, editors. *Parallel Processing for Computer Vision and Display*. Addison-Wesley, Reading, MA, 1989.

[46] Julie O'Brien Dorsey, François Sillion, and Donald P. Greenberg. Design and simulation of opera lighting and projection effects. *Computer Graphics*, 25(4):41–50, August 1991.

[47] Robert A. Drebin, Loren Carpenter, and Pat Hanrahan. Volume rendering. *Computer Graphics*, 22(4):65–74, August 1988.

[48] George Drettakis. *Structured Sampling and Reconstruction of Illumination for Image Synthesis*. Ph.D. thesis, Department of Computer Science, University of Toronto, January 1994. CSRI technical report 293 (ftp site ftp.csri.toronto.edu:csri-technical-reports/293).

[49] George Drettakis and Eugene Fiume. Accurate and consistent reconstruction of illumination functions using structured sampling. *Computer Graphics Forum*, 12(3):273–284, September 1993.

[50] George Drettakis and Eugene Fiume. A fast shadow algorithm for area light sources using back projection. In *Computer Graphics Proceedings, Annual Conference Series:* SIGGRAPH '94 (Orlando, FL), ACM SIGGRAPH, New York, July 1994.

[51] George Drettakis. Simplifying the representation of radiance from multiple emitters. In *Proceedings of Fifth Eurographics Workshop on Rendering* (Darmstadt, Germany), June 1994.

[52] Steven M. Drucker and Peter Schröder. Fast radiosity using a data parallel architecture. In *Proceedings of the Third Eurographics Workshop on Rendering*, Bristol, UK, May 1992.

[53] Bruce H. Billings and Dwight E. Gray, editors. *American Institute of Physics Handbook*. McGraw-Hill, New York, 1972.

[54] Ernst R. G. Eckert and Robert M. Drake. *Heat and Mass Transfer*. McGraw-Hill, New York, 1959.

[55] W. Feller. *An Introduction to Probability Theory and Its Applications*. John Wiley & Sons, New York, 1957.

[56] James D. Foley, Andries van Dam, Steven K. Feiner, and John F. Hughes. *Computer Graphics, Principles and Practice,* 2nd ed. Addison-Wesley, Reading, MA, 1990.

[57] David Forsyth, Chien Yang, and Kim Teo. Efficient radiosity in dynamic environments. In *Proceedings of Fifth Eurographics Workshop on Rendering* (Darmstadt, Germany), June 1994.

[58] Akira Fujimoto, Takayuki Tanaka, and Kansei Iwata. Arts: Accelerated ray-tracing system. *IEEE Computer Graphics and Applications*, pages 16–26, April 1986.

[59] Thomas A. Funkhouser and Carlo H. Séquin. Adaptive display algorithm for interactive frame rates during visualization of complex virtual environments. In *Computer Graphics Proceedings, Annual Conference Series:* SIGGRAPH '93 (Anaheim, CA), pages 247–254. ACM SIGGRAPH, New York, August 1993.

[60] Thomas A. Funkhouser, Carlo H. Séquin, and Seth J. Teller. Management of large amounts of data in interactive building walkthroughs. In *Proceedings of the 1992 Symposium on Interactive 3D Graphics* (Cambridge, MA), pages 11–20. ACM, March 1992.

[61] Benjamin Gebhart. *Heat Transfer*. McGraw-Hill, New York, 1961.

[62] David W. George, François Sillion, and Donald P. Greenberg. Radiosity redistribution for dynamic environments. *IEEE Computer Graphics and Applications*, 10(4), July 1990.

[63] Reid Gershbein, Peter Schröder, and Pat Hanrahan. Textures and radiosity: controlling emission and reflection with texture maps. In *Computer Graphics Proceedings, Annual Conference Series:* SIGGRAPH '94 (Orlando, FL). ACM SIGGRAPH, New York, July 1994.

[64] Ziv Gigus and Jitendra Malik. Computing the aspect graph for line drawings of polyhedral objects. *IEEE Trans. on Pattern Analysis and Machine Intelligence*, 12(2):113–122, February 1990.

[65] Andrew Glassner. Spacetime ray tracing for animation. *IEEE Computer Graphics and Applications*, 8(2):60–70, March 1988.

[66] Andrew Glassner. Maintaining winged-edge models. In James Arvo, editor, *Graphics Gems II*. Academic Press, San Diego, 1991.

[67] Andrew S. Glassner, editor. *An Introduction to Ray Tracing*. Academic Press, San Diego, 1989.

[68] Cindy M. Goral, Kenneth E. Torrance, Donald P. Greenberg, and Bennett Battaile. Modeling the interaction of light between diffuse surfaces. *Computer Graphics*, 18(3):213–222, July 1984.

[69] Steven Gortler, Michael F. Cohen, and Philipp Slusallek. Radiosity and relaxation methods. Technical report TR 408–93, Princeton University, Princeton, NJ, 1993.

[70] Steven J. Gortler, Peter Schröder, Michael F. Cohen, and Pat Hanrahan. Wavelet radiosity. In *Computer Graphics Proceedings, Annual Conference Series:* SIGGRAPH '93 (Anaheim, CA), pages 221–230. ACM SIGGRAPH, New York, August 1993.

[71] Henri Gouraud. Continuous shading of curved surfaces. *IEEE Transactions on Computers*, 20(6):623–629, June 1971.

[72] L. Greengard. *The Rapid Evaluation of Potential Fields in Particle Systems*. MIT Press, Cambridge, MA, 1988.

[73] Eric A. Haines. Shaft culling for efficient ray-traced radiosity. In P. Brunet and F. W. Jansen, editors, *Photorealistic Rendering in Computer Graphics*, pages 122–138. Springer Verlag, New York, 1993.

[74] Roy Hall. *Illumination and Color in Computer Generated Imagery*. Springer Verlag, New York, 1989.

[75] J. M. Hammersley and D. C. Handscomb. *Monte Carlo Methods*. John Wiley & Sons, New York, 1964.

[76] Pat Hanrahan and David Saltzman. A rapid hierarchical radiosity algorithm for unoccluded environments. In C. Bouville and K. Bouatouch, editors, *Photorealism in Computer Graphics*. Springer Verlag, New York, Eurographics Seminars series, 1992.

[77] Pat Hanrahan, David Saltzman, and Larry Aupperle. A rapid hierarchical radiosity algorithm. *Computer Graphics*, 25(4):197–206, August 1991.

[78] XiaoDong He, Kenneth E. Torrance, François Sillion, and Donald P. Greenberg. A comprehensive physical model for light reflection. *Computer Graphics*, 25(4), August 1991.

[79] Paul Heckbert. Discontinuity meshing for radiosity. In *Proceedings of the Third Eurographics Workshop on Rendering* (Bristol, UK), pages 203–226, May 1992.

[80] Paul Heckbert. *Simulating Global Illumination Using Adaptive Meshing*. Ph.D. thesis, CS Division (EECS), University of California, Berkeley, June 1991.

[81] Paul S. Heckbert. Adaptive radiosity textures for bidirectional ray tracing. *Computer Graphics*, 24(4):145–154, August 1990.

[82] Nicolas Holzschuch, François Sillion, and George Drettakis. An efficient progressive refinment strategy for hiearchical radiosity. In *Proceedings of Fifth Eurographics Workshop on Rendering* (Darmstadt, Germany), June 1994.

[83] John E. Hopcroft and Jeffrey D. Ullman. *Introduction to Automata Theory, Languages, and Computation*. Addison-Wesley, Reading, MA, 1979.

[84] Robert W. Hornbeck. *Numerical Methods*. Quantum Publishers, New York, 1975.

[85] Hoyt C. Hottel. Radiant heat transmission. In W. H. McAdams, editor, *Heat Transmission*, 3rd ed. McGraw-Hill, New York, 1954.

[86] Hoyt C. Hottel and Adel F. Sarofim. *Radiative Transfer*. McGraw-Hill, New York, 1967.

[87] John R. Howell. *A Catalog of Radiation Configuration Factors*. McGraw-Hill, New York, 1982.

[88] Illumination Engineering Society. *IES Lighting Handbook*. IES, New York, reference edition, 1981.

[89] Illumination Engineering Society. IES standard file format for electronic transfer of photometric data and related information. Lighting measurement series LM-63, IES, New York, 1991.

[90] Illumination Engineering Society and American National Standards Institute. ANSI standard nomenclature and definitions for illuminating engineering. Technical report ANSI/IES RP-16-1986. IES, New York, approved by ANSI June 23, 1986.

[91] David S. Immel, Michael F. Cohen, and Donald P. Greenberg. A radiosity method for non-diffuse environments. *Computer Graphics*, 20(4):133–142, August 1986.

[92] Frederik W. Jansen and Alan Chalmers. Realism in real-time. In *Proceedings of Fourth Eurographics Workshop on Rendering*, pages 27–46. Eurographics, June 1993. Technical report EG 93 RW.

[93] G. R. Jones, C. G. Christou, B. G. Cumming, and A. J. Parker. Accurate rendering of curved shadows and interreflections. In *Proceedings of Fourth Eurographics Workshop on Rendering*, pages 337–347. Eurographics, June 1993. Technical report EG 93 RW.

[94] James T. Kajiya. Anisotropic reflection models. *Computer Graphics*, 19(3):143–150, July 1985.

[95] James T. Kajiya. The rendering equation. *Computer Graphics*, 20(4):143–150, August 1986.

[96] J. T. Kajiya and B. P. Von Herzen. Ray tracing volume densities. *Computer Graphics*, 18, July 1984.

[97] Malvin H. Kalos and Paula A. Whitlock. *Monte Carlo Methods*. John Wiley & Sons, New York, 1986.

[98] John Kawai, James Painter, and Michael Cohen. Radioptimization: Goal-based rendering. In *Computer Graphics Proceedings, Annual Conference Series:* SIGGRAPH '93 (Anaheim, CA), pages 147–156. ACM SIGGRAPH, New York, August 1993.

[99] David Kirk and James Arvo. Unbiased sampling techniques for image sampling. *Computer Graphics*, 25(4):153–156, July 1991.

[100] David Kirk and James Arvo. Unbiased variance reduction for global illumination. In P. Brunet and F. W. Jansen, editors, *Photorealistic Rendering in Computer Graphics*, pages 45–51. Springer Verlag, New York, 1993.

[101] R. Victor Klassen. Modeling the effect of the atmosphere on light. *ACM Transactions on Graphics*, 6(3):215–237, July 1987.

[102] A. Kok and F. Jansen. Source selection for the direct lighting calculation in global illumination. In P. Brunet and F. W. Jansen, editors, *Photorealistic Rendering in Computer Graphics*, pages 75–82. Springer Verlag, New York, 1993.

[103] Birgitta Lange. The simulation of radiant light transfer with stochastic ray-tracing. In P. Brunet and F. W. Jansen, editors, *Photorealistic Rendering in Computer Graphics*, pages 30–44. Springer Verlag, New York, 1993.

[104] Eric Languénou and Pierre Tellier. Including physical light sources and daylight in a global illumination model. In *Proceedings of the Third Eurographics Workshop on Rendering* (Bristol, UK), pages 217–225, May 1992.

[105] Bertrand Le Saec and Christophe Schlick. A progressive ray-tracing based radiosity with general reflectance functions. In C. Bouville and K. Bouatouch, editors, *Photorealism in Computer Graphics*. Springer Verlag, New York, EurographicSeminars series, 1992.

[106] E. E. Lewis and W. F. Miller, Jr. *Computational Methods of Neutron Transport*. John Wiley & Sons, New York, 1984.

[107] Dani Lischinski, Filippo Tampieri, and Donald P. Greenberg. Discontinuity meshing for accurate radiosity. *IEEE Computer Graphics and Applications*, 12(6):25–39, November 1992.

[108] Dani Lischinski, Filippo Tampieri, and Donald P. Greenberg. Combining hierarchical radiosity and discontinuity meshing. In *Computer Graphics Proceedings, Annual Conference Series:* SIGGRAPH '93 (Anaheim, CA), pages 199–208. ACM SIGGRAPH, New York, August 1993.

[109] Dani Lischinski, Brian Smits, and Donald P. Greenberg, Bounds and error estimates for radiosity, In *Computer Graphics Proceedings, Annual Conference Series:* SIGGRAPH '94 (Orlando, FL). ACM SIGGRAPH, New York, July 1994.

[110] Thomas J. V. Malley. A shading method for computer generated images. Master's thesis, University of Utah, Salt Lake City, June 1988.

[111] Nelson L. Max. Atmospheric illumination and shadows. *Computer Graphics*, 20:117–124, August 1986.

[112] Nelson L. Max. Light diffusion through clouds and haze. *Computer Vision, Graphics, and Image Processing*, 33, 1986.

[113] Nelson L. Max. Optimal hemicube sampling. In *Proceedings of Fourth Eurographics Workshop on Rendering*, pages 185–200. Eurographics, June 1993. Technical report EG 93 RW.

[114] Nelson L. Max and Michael J. Allison. Linear radiosity approximation using vertex-to-vertex form factors. In David Kirk, editor, *Graphics Gems III*, pages 318–323. Academic Press, San Diego, 1992.

[115] Gregory M. Maxwell, Michael J. Bailey, and Victor W. Goldschmidt. Calculations of the radiation configuration factor using ray casting. *Computer-aided Design*, 18(7):371–379, September 1986.

[116] Gary W. Meyer. Wavelength selection for synthetic image generation. *Computer Vision, Graphics, and Image Processing*, 41:57–79, 1988.

[117] Don Mitchell and Pat Hanrahan. Illumination from curved reflectors. *Computer Graphics*, 26(4):283–291, July 1992.

[118] Stefan Müller and Frank Schoffel. Fast radiosity repropagation for interactive virtual environments using a shadow-form-factor-list. In *Proceedings of Fifth Eurographics Workshop on Rendering* (Darmstadt, Germany), June 1994.

[119] M. J. Muuss. Workstations, networking, distributed graphics and parallel processing. In D. F. Rogers and R. A. Earnshaw, editors, *Computer Graphics Techniques, Theory and Practice*. Springer Verlag, New York, 1990.

[120] Eihachiro Nakamae, Kazufumi Kaneda, Takashi Okamoto, and Tomoyuki Nishita. A lighting model aiming at drive simulators. *Computer Graphics*, 24(4):395–404, August 1990.

[121] László Neumann and Attila Neumann. Radiosity and hybrid methods. *ACM Transactions on Graphics*, 1994. *In press*.

[122] F. E. Nicodemus, J. C. Richmond, J. J. Hsia, I. W. Ginsberg, and T. Limperis. Geometric considerations and nomenclature for reflectance. Technical report, National Bureau of Standards (USA), October 1977.

[123] T. Nishita and E. Nakamae. Continuous tone representation of three-dimensional objects taking account of shadows and interreflection. *Computer Graphics*, 19(3):23–30, July 1985.

[124] T. Nishita and E. Nakamae. Continuous tone representation of three-dimensional objects illuminated by skylight. *Computer Graphics*, 20(4):125–132, August 1986.

[125] Tomoyuki Nishita, Yasuhiro Miyawaki, and Eihachiro Nakamae. A shading model for atmospheric scattering considering luminous intensity distribution of light sources. *Computer Graphics*, 21(4):303–310, July 1987.

[126] Wilhelm Nusselt. Graphische bestimmung des winkelverhaltnisses bei der wärmestrahlung. *Zeitschrift des Vereines Deutscher Ingenieure*, 19(3):72–673, 1928.

[127] Derek Paddon and Alan Chalmers. Parallel processing for rendering. In *Proceedings of the Third Eurographics Workshop on Rendering* (Bristol, UK), May 1992.

[128] Sumant N. Pattanaik. *Computational Methods for Global Illumination and Visualization of Complex 3D Environments*. Ph.D. thesis, Birla Institute of Technology & Science, Pilani, India, February 1993.

[129] Sumant Pattanaik and Kadi Bouatouch. Haar wavelet: a solution to global illumination with general surface properties. In *Proceedings of Fifth Eurographics Workshop on Rendering* (Darmstadt, Germany), June 1994.

[130] Sumant N. Pattanaik and S. P. Mudur. Adjoint equations and random walks for illumination computation. *ACM Transactions on Graphics*, 1994.

[131] Mark S. Peercy. Linear color representations for full spectral rendering. In *Computer Graphics Proceedings, Annual Conference Series:* SIGGRAPH '93 (Anaheim, CA), pages 191–198. ACM SIGGRAPH, New York, August 1993.

[132] Bui Tuong Phong. Illumination for computer generated pictures. *Communications of the ACM*, 18(6):311–317, June 1975.

[133] Franco P. Preparata and Michael Ian Shamos. *Computational Geometry—An Introduction*. Springer Verlag, New York, 1985.

[134] William H. Press, Saul A. Teukolsky, William T. Vetterling, and Brian P. Flannery. *Numerical Recipes in C*, 2nd ed. Cambridge University Press, New York, 1992.

[135] Claude Puech, François Sillion, and Christophe Vedel. Improving interaction with radiosity-based lighting simulation programs. *Computer Graphics*, 24(2):51–57, March 1990.

[136] Rodney J. Recker, David W. George, and Donald P. Greenberg. Acceleration techniques for progressive refinement radiosity. *Computer Graphics*, 24(2):59–66, March 1990.

[137] Mark C. Reichert. A two-pass radiosity method driven by lights and viewer position. Master's thesis, Program of Computer Graphics, Cornell University, Ithaca, NY, January 1992.

[138] Frédéric Riesz and Béla Sz.-Nagy. *Leçons d'Analyse Fonctionnelle*. Académie des sciences de Hongrie, Budapest, 1952.

[139] Holly Rushmeier. Radiosity input/output. In SIGGRAPH '92 course notes (#11, "Radiosity"), August 1992.

[140] Holly Rushmeier. Solution methods for radiatively participating media. In SIGGRAPH '92 course notes (#18, "Global Illumination"), August 1992.

[141] Holly Rushmeier, Charles Patterson, and Aravindan Veerasamy. Geometric simplification for indirect illumination calculations. In *Proceedings Graphics Interface '93*. Morgan Kaufmann, San Francisco, 1993.

[142] Holly E. Rushmeier and Kenneth E. Torrance. The zonal method for calculating light intensities in the presence of a participating medium. *Computer Graphics*, 21(4):293–302, July 1987.

[143] Holly E. Rushmeier and Kenneth E. Torrance. Extending the radiosity method to include specularly reflecting and translucent materials. *ACM Transactions on Graphics*, 9(1):1–27, January 1990.

[144] A. Sala. *Radiant Properties of Materials*. Elsevier, Amsterdam, 1986.

[145] David Salesin, Dani Lischinski, and Tony DeRose. Reconstructing illumination functions with selected discontinuities. In *Proceedings of the Third Eurographics Workshop on Rendering* (Bristol, UK), pages 99–112, May 1992.

[146] Hanan Samet. *The Design and Analysis of Spatial Data Structures*. Addison-Wesley, Reading, MA, 1990.

[147] Chris Schoeneman, Julie Dorsey, Brian Smits, James Arvo, and Donald P. Greenberg. Painting with light. In *Computer Graphics Proceedings, Annual Conference Series:* SIGGRAPH '93 (Anaheim, CA), pages 143–146. ACM SIGGRAPH, New York, August 1993.

[148] Peter Schröder. Numerical integration for radiosity in the presence of singularities. In *Proceedings of Fourth Eurographics Workshop on Rendering*, pages 177–184. Eurographics, June 1993. Technical report EG 93 RW.

[149] Peter Schröder and Pat Hanrahan. Wavelet methods for radiance calculations. In *Proceedings of Fifth Eurographics Workshop on Rendering* (Darmstadt, Germany), June 1994.

[150] Peter Schröder, Steven J. Gortler, Michael F. Cohen, and Pat Hanrahan. Wavelet projections for radiosity. In *Proceedings of Fourth Eurographics Workshop on Rendering*, pages 105–114. Eurographics, June 1993. Technical report EG 93 RW.

[151] Peter Schröder and Pat Hanrahan. On the form factor between two polygons. In *Computer Graphics Proceedings, Annual Conference Series: SIGGRAPH '93 (Anaheim, CA)*, pages 163–164. ACM SIGGRAPH, New York, August 1993.

[152] Min-Zhi Shao, Qun-Sheng Peng, and You-Dong Liang. A new radiosity approach by procedural refinements for realistic image synthesis. *Computer Graphics*, 22(4):93–101, August 1988.

[153] Peter Shirley. A ray tracing method for illumination calculation in diffuse-specular scenes. In *Proceedings of Graphics Interface '90*, pages 205–212. Canadian Information Processing Society, Toronto, May 1990.

[154] Peter Shirley. Discrepancy as a quality measure for sampling distributions. *Eurographics '91*, pages 183–194, September 1991.

[155] Peter Shirley. *Physically Based Lighting Calculations for Computer Graphics*. Ph.D. thesis, University of Illinois at Urbana-Champaign, 1991.

[156] Peter Shirley. Time complexity of Monte Carlo radiosity. *Eurographics '91*, pages 459–466, September 1991.

[157] Peter Shirley. Monte Carlo simulation and integration. In SIGGRAPH '92 course notes (# 18, "Global Illumination"), August 1992.

[158] Peter Shirley and Changyaw Wang. Direct lighting by monte carlo integration. In P. Brunet and F. W. Jansen, editors, *Photorealistic Rendering in Computer Graphics*, pages 52–59. Springer Verlag, New York, 1993.

[159] Y. A. Shreider. *The Monte Carlo Method*. Pergamon Press, New York, 1966.

[160] Robert Siegel and John R. Howell. *Thermal Radiation Heat Transfer*, 3rd ed. Hemisphere Publishing, New York, 1992.

[161] François Sillion. Detection of shadow boundaries for adaptive meshing in radiosity. In James Arvo, editor, *Graphics Gems II*, pages 311–315. Academic Press, San Diego, 1991.

[162] François Sillion. Radiosity with changing input. In SIGGRAPH '93 course notes (#22, "Making Radiosity Practical"), August 1993.

[163] François Sillion. Clustering and volume scattering for hierarchical radiosity calculations. In *Proceedings of Fifth Eurographics Workshop on Rendering* (Darmstadt, Germany), June 1994.

[164] François Sillion, James Arvo, Stephen Westin, and Donald P. Greenberg. A global illumination solution for general reflectance distributions. *Computer Graphics*, 25(4):187–196, August 1991.

[165] François Sillion and Claude Puech. A general two-pass method integrating specular and diffuse reflection. *Computer Graphics*, 23(4), August 1989.

[166] Brian Smits, James Arvo, and Donald P. Greenberg. A clustering algorithm for radiosity in complex environments. In *Computer Graphics Proceedings, Annual Conference Series:* SIGGRAPH '94 (Orlando, FL). ACM SIGGRAPH, New York, July 1994.

[167] Brian E. Smits, James R. Arvo, and David H. Salesin. An importance-driven radiosity algorithm. *Computer Graphics*, 26(4):273–282, July 1992.

[168] Brian E. Smits and Gary W. Meyer. Newton's colors: Simulating interference phenomena in realistic image synthesis. In C. Bouville and K. Bouatouch, editors, *Photorealism in Computer Graphics*. Springer Verlag, New York, EurographicSeminars series, 1992.

[169] E. M. Sparrow and R. D. Cess. *Radiation Heat Transfer*. Hemisphere Publishing Corporation, Washington, D.C., 1978.

[170] Ephraim M. Sparrow. On the calculation of radiant interchange between surfaces. In Warren Ibele, editor, *Modern Developments in Heat Transfer*. Academic Press, New York, 1963.

[171] Atsushi Takagi, Hitoshi Takaoka, Tetsuya Oshima, and Yoshinori Ogata. Accurate rendering technique based on colorimetric conception. *Computer Graphics*, 24(4):263–272, August 1990.

[172] Seth J. Teller. Computing the antipenumbra of an area light. *Computer Graphics*, 26(4):139–148, July 1992.

[173] Seth J. Teller and Patrick M. Hanrahan. Global visibility algorithms for illumination computations. In *Computer Graphics Proceedings, Annual Conference Series:* SIGGRAPH '93 (Anaheim, CA), pages 239–246. ACM SIGGRAPH, New York, August 1993.

[174] Seth J. Teller and Carlo Séquin. Visibility preprocessing for interactive walkthroughs. *Computer Graphics*, 25(4):61–69, August 1991.

[175] Seth Teller, Celeste Fowler, Thomas Funkhouser, and Pat Hanrahan. Partitioning and ordering large radiosity computations. In *Computer Graphics Proceedings, Annual Conference Series:* SIGGRAPH '94 (Orlando, FL). ACM SIGGRAPH, New York, July 1994.

[176] William C. Thibault and Bruce F. Naylor. Set operations on polyhedra using binary space partitioning trees. *Computer Graphics*, 21(4):153–162, July 1987.

[177] K. E. Torrance and E. M. Sparrow. Off-specular peaks in the directional distribution of reflected thermal radiation. *Journal of Heat Transfer—Transactions of the ASME*, pages 223–230, May 1966.

[178] K. E. Torrance and E. M. Sparrow. Theory for off-specular reflection from roughened surfaces. *Journal of the Optical Society of America*, 57(9):1105–1114, September 1967.

[179] Y. S. Touloukian and D. P. DeWitt. *Thermophysical Properties of Matter*, volumes 7 and 8: Thermal Radiative Properties. IFI/Plenum, New York, 1972.

[180] Roy Troutman and Nelson L. Max. Radiosity algorithms using higher order finite element methods. In *Computer Graphics Proceedings, Annual Conference Series:* SIGGRAPH '93 (Anaheim, CA), pages 209–212. ACM SIGGRAPH, New York, August 1993.

[181] Jack Tumblin and Holly Rushmeier. Tone reproduction for realistic images. *IEEE Computer Graphics and Applications*, 13(6):42–48, November 1993.

[182] Richard S. Varga. *Matrix iterative analysis* (Chapter 3). Prentice-Hall, Englewood Cliffs, NJ, 1962.

[183] Christophe Vedel. Improved storage and reconstruction of light intensities on surfaces. In *Proceedings of the Third Eurographics Workshop on Rendering* (Bristol, UK), pages 113–121, May 1992.

[184] John R. Wallace, Michael F. Cohen, and Donald P. Greenberg. A two-pass solution to the rendering equation: A synthesis of ray-tracing and radiosity methods. *Computer Graphics*, 21(4):311–320, July 1987.

[185] John R. Wallace, Kells A. Elmquist, and Eric A. Haines. A ray tracing algorithm for progressive radiosity. *Computer Graphics*, 23(3):315–324, July 1989.

[186] Gregory J. Ward. Personal communication.

[187] Gregory J. Ward. Real pixels. In James Arvo, editor, *Graphics Gems II*. Academic Press, San Diego, 1991.

[188] Gregory J. Ward. Measuring and modeling anisotropic reflection. *Computer Graphics*, 26(4):265–272, July 1992.

[189] Gregory J. Ward. Adaptive shadow testing for ray tracing. In P. Brunet and F. W. Jansen, editors, *Photorealistic Rendering in Computer Graphics*, pages 11–20. Springer Verlag, New York, 1993.

[190] Gregory J. Ward. A contrast-based scalefactor for luminance display. In Paul S. Heckbert, editor, *Graphics Gems IV*. Academic Press, San Diego, 1994.

[191] Gregory J. Ward. The RADIANCE lighting simulation and rendering system. In *Computer Graphics Proceedings, Annual Conference Series:* SIGGRAPH '94 (Orlando, FL). ACM SIGGRAPH, New York, July, 1994.

[192] Gregory J. Ward and Paul S. Heckbert. Irradiance gradients. In *Proceedings of the Third Eurographics Workshop on Rendering* (Bristol, UK), May 1992.

[193] Gregory J. Ward, Francis M. Rubinstein, and Robert D. Clear. A ray tracing solution for diffuse interreflection. *Computer Graphics*, 22(4):85–92, August 1988.

[194] Colin Ware and Steven Osborne. Exploration and virtual camera control in virtual three dimensional environments. *Computer Graphics*, 24(2):175–183, March 1990.

[195] Alan Watt and Mark Watt. *Advanced Animation and Rendering Techniques*. ACM Press, New York, 1992.

[196] Mark Watt. Light-water interaction using backward beam tracing. *Computer Graphics*, 24(4):377–385, August 1990.

[197] Joseph H. Weaver. *Applications of Discrete and Continuous Fourier Analysis*. John Wiley & Sons, New York, 1983.

[198] Kevin Weiler. Edge-based data structures for solid modeling in curved-surface environments. *IEEE Computer Graphics and Applications*, 5(1):21–40, January 1985.

[199] Stephen H. Westin, James R. Arvo, and Kenneth E. Torrance. Predicting reflectance functions from complex surfaces. *Computer Graphics*, 26(4):255–264, July 1992.

[200] Turner Whitted. An improved illumination model for shaded display. *Communications of the ACM*, 23:343–349, 1980.

[201] Gunter Wyszecki and W. S. Stiles. *Color Science: Concepts and Methods, Quantitative Data and Formulae*, 2nd ed. John Wiley & Sons, New York, 1982.

[202] H. Xu, Q. Peng, and Y. Liang. Accelerated radiosity method for complex environments. *Eurographics '89*, pages 51–61, September 1989.

[203] Harold R. Zatz. Galerkin radiosity: A higher-order solution method for global illumination. In *Computer Graphics Proceedings, Annual Conference Series:* SIGGRAPH '93 (Anaheim, CA), pages 213–220. ACM SIGGRAPH, New York, August 1993.

[204] Yining Zhu, Quensheng Peng, and Youdong Liang. Peris: A programming environment for realistic image synthesis. *Computers and Graphics*, 12(3/4):299–307, 1988.

Index